Labor's Cold War

THE WORKING CLASS
IN AMERICAN HISTORY

Editorial Advisors
James R. Barrett
Alice Kessler-Harris
Nelson Lichtenstein
David Montgomery

*A list of books in the series appears
at the end of this book.*

Labor's Cold War

Local Politics in a Global Context

EDITED BY

SHELTON STROMQUIST

University of Illinois Press

URBANA AND CHICAGO

Library of Congress Cataloging-in-Publication Data
Labor's cold war : local politics in a global context /
edited by Shelton Stromquist.
p.   cm. — (The working class in American history)
Includes bibliographical references and index.
ISBN-13: 978-0-252-03222-6 (cloth : alk. paper)
ISBN-10: 0-252-03222-5 (cloth : alk. paper)
ISBN-13: 978-0-252-07469-1 (pbk. : alk. paper)
ISBN-10: 0-252-07469-6 (pbk. : alk. paper)
1. Labor unions—United States—Political activity—History—
20th century. 2. Anti-communist movements—United States—
History—20th century. 3. Cold War. 4. Labor unions and
communism—United States—History—20th century.
I. Stromquist, Shelton, 1943–
HD6510.L33   2008
322'.209730904—dc22   2007020854

Contents

Acknowledgments

Collections of essays are by their nature collective undertakings, a mode of operation rather unusual among historians, whose work commonly reflects the solitary nature of their research and writing. This collective undertaking grew out of a conference whose fruits warranted wider circulation. In spring 2000, the Center for Recent United States History (CRUSH)—itself a collaboration between the University of Iowa, the State Historical Society of Iowa, and the Herbert Hoover Presidential Library and National Park Service—convened a "scholars' seminar" to explore the latest research on labor and the Cold War. The effort was part of a year-long, university-wide reconsideration of the Cold War, its origins, social and political consequences, and longer-term impact on America's relations with the world community, organized by visiting scholar Robert Newman.

In the day-long seminar, based on a wide-ranging discussion of nearly a dozen pre-circulated papers, we discovered exciting connections that gave the papers a degree of thematic convergence—around labor and the local politics of the Cold War as it played out in union halls, community organizations, local and regional policy debates, and in the search for a viable progressive politics in an atmosphere of aggressive anticommunism. As a result of the stimulating conversation about these themes and the individual authors' subsequent revisions of their work, the present volume took shape. Although each essay stands on its own merits, each has also grown through the wider discussion of which it has become part.

None of this would have been realized without the contributions of many hands at each step of the way. Professors emeritus Ellis W. Hawley and Lawrence Gelfand laid the foundation for the Center for Recent United States

History's impressive record of scholarly public programming. Each of the Center's member institutions—the University of Iowa Department of History, the University Library and its Special Collections, the State Historical Society of Iowa, the Hoover Presidential Library, and the National Park Service—has contributed in myriad ways to sustaining the Center and reaching out to new and wider constituencies. Members of the Center's board, many of whom participated in this seminar, have guided the Center with a steady hand over many years. We wish to thank them—Bob McCown, John Schacht, Karen Mason, Nancy Baker, Marvin Bergmann, Mary Bennett, Tim Walch, Matt Schaeffer, Linda K. Kerber, Colin Gordon, the late Ken Cmiel, Allen Steinberg, and Bruce Fehn—for encouraging enterprises such as these. Mary Strottman, administrative assistant in the history department, provided vital logistical and budget support. John McKerley, graduate research assistant in the history department did things big and small that made the whole effort go more smoothly than it might have. Jay Semel and his colleagues at the University of Iowa's Obermann Center for Advanced Studies provided crucial supplemental funding and overall coordination of the yearlong public programming on the Cold War.

The professional staff at the University of Illinois Press has been unfailingly helpful at each step of the publication process. From acquisitions to book design and publication, Laurie Matheson, Angela Burton, and Cope Cumpston have handed this project off from one department to the next in ways that smoothed the process and have produced a book with which we can all be proud to be associated.

Each of the authors has benefited enormously from support of librarians and archivists at innumerable repositories charged with keeping and maintaining access to the rich collections without which such new research would be unimaginable. Each of us, as well, has a bevy of colleagues, friends, and mentors who have sustained us and given critical perspective on our work. As editor of the volume, my own list of advisers and colleagues is a long one, beyond recounting here. We have benefited from careful and constructively helpful readings of the manuscript by three anonymous reviewers. David Montgomery, whose impact on the field of labor history has been immeasurable, continues to be an inspiration for us all. The work of those who have blazed new trails in the study of labor and the Cold War has also given us guidance in these endeavors. They include Jim Barrett, Steve Rosswurm, Steve Meyer, Nelson Lichtenstein, Mike Honey, Ellen Schrecker, George Lipsitz, Ron Fillipelli, and Mark McCulloch.

Finally, I am grateful beyond measure for the love and support of my family, for their forbearance and for the convoy of love in the midst of grief that they have given so generously. This work, as with so much else, is for them: for Ann, partner in life and love; for Chris, Matt, Laura Brueck, and for dearest Elizabeth, whose loving and generous spirit we will carry with us always.

Introduction: Was All (Cold War) Politics Local?

SHELTON STROMQUIST

Legend has it that Tip O'Neill's father took him aside after his first political defeat and pointedly reminded him that "all politics is local. Don't forget it." It was a lesson he carried with him for the rest of his political life. From the perspective of a Massachusetts congressman representing the heavily Irish American precincts of North Cambridge, there can have been little doubt about the validity of the proposition.[1] But, it also represents an insight that historians might do well to take seriously as they assess the character and meaning of domestic Cold War politics in the United States. We have understandably been mesmerized by the international and national scope of the Cold War and its impact on so many facets of public life in the United States.[2] But, from that vantage point we have served up a history that understates the transformative impact of anticommunism within the *local* political cultures most directly relevant to the work and community lives of Americans. In the process we may also have underestimated the contested nature and diverse outcomes of those local struggles. Local studies may also help us understand the political continuities and sometimes strange bedfellows that created political space for ongoing progressive politics. These essays seek to contribute to a reorientation of Cold War historiography by recovering and reassessing the "local politics" of the Cold War.

The Cold War has been the subject of remarkably well-crafted national studies that focus on Cold War diplomacy and its anticommunist fallout in U.S. domestic politics.[3] We now recognize the pervasive influence of the phenomenon generically labeled "McCarthyism" and its penetration of diverse spheres of American life—from academia to Hollywood to the higher reaches of scientific research.[4] Amply documented in recent years has also been the splintering of the American labor movement under the fallout of the Taft-Hartley Act and the political pressures generated by competitive union raiding, the intervention of a highly mobilized Catholic Church, and the hectoring of the mainstream media.[5] The history of the Communist Party itself during this period has now been richly retold in memoirs of party activists and in histories that examine the political consequences of the party's shifting ideological lines in the pre- and postwar eras.[6]

But, despite this rich vein of historical writing on the Cold War and its domestic politics, we have only begun to see accounts that focus attention on the "local politics" of anticommunism.[7] In union halls and community political campaigns, the Cold War played out in ways that rewove the fabric of local political cultures whose patterns had been aligned in the Depression era. The Cold War, seen through the prism of local anticommunist politics, re-legitimated a conservative, aggressively pro-capitalist political culture that had been discredited by the Great Depression and the triumphs of the New Deal. It breathed life into a new, liberal anticommunism, fracturing local Popular Front alliances that undergirded labor's postwar power and the promise of a revived New Deal capable of guaranteeing a full employment economy and the social reconstruction of the cities.[8] Supported by allies in industrial unions and community coalitions, African American and Latino workers hoped to build on hard-won wartime employment gains to address the pressing social needs of their communities, but they found themselves in a rapidly changing political environment that proved less hospitable to their aspirations.[9] Women workers had carved out new social space in wartime workplaces and in their unions. They expected the contributions of their war work to elevate their status within the working class. But, from the outset, the Popular Front had been for them a mixed legacy, and its collapse under the Cold War political and cultural assault also had mixed consequences.[10]

In this new effort to understand the realm of local Cold War politics and its relationship to national developments, this volume joins another recent collection of local studies.[11] Together they offer a rich and variegated tapestry of locally focused studies on myriad topics. Each collection addresses some of the same issues—the varieties of anticommunism, the splintering of local CIO affiliates, raiding and jurisdictional competition, and the consequences of renewed polarization between white and nonwhite workers—but each also makes a somewhat different contribution to the new, local history of labor and anticommunism.[12] Our collection seeks to argue not just for the diversity of local experience but for the persistence of a progressive, pragmatic politics in the face of polarizing national and international pressures. Labor's struggles are situated in community contexts where outcomes were more ambiguous.

The global anticommunist context manifested in the occupation of Japan and Germany and in the outbreak of war on the Korean peninsula also had direct and profound consequences for the outcome of local struggles. The local stories we tell in this volume complicate rather than illustrate a bipolar national and international narrative. Local actors become historical agents of some significance beyond the boundaries of their own communities. In some sense, the national and international stories are driven by the conflicts that played out in local settings.

The seismic shifts in domestic political culture during the Cold War were, then, to a large extent, the cumulative product of innumerable local struggles that broke out in communities and local unions across the country. Almost by definition, any local struggle in isolation seems limited in scope and significance. But cumulatively they suggest a magnitude and depth of change in American public life the rich texture of which national studies fail to capture. By the early 1950s the optimism of the immediate postwar years over the prospects for restoring the domestic New Deal had been significantly eroded.[13] The counterpart and in some ways the root of bipolar antagonism on a national and global scale lay in the political polarization that infected the day-to-day lives of ordinary Americans in local communities. Latent and often long-standing antagonisms based on differences in race, religion, class, and political ideology took on new life as Cold War anticommunism colored local politics for a generation or more.

These essays, in varied ways, capture the local political contexts in which Cold War anticommunism took root.[14] Rosemary Feurer, for example, examines the delicate fabric of local progressive alliances in the St. Louis region as the labor-left fought for an expanded New Deal-style public sector in the face of conservative political mobilization.[15] David Lewis-Colman reconstructs the efforts of black rank-and-file autoworkers in Detroit to assert their claims to union leadership as Cold War politics colored virtually all internal union struggles.[16] Kenneth Burt shows how Los Angeles Latino political activist Edward Roybal fought off a conservative anticommunist challenge while at the same time constituting a new left-liberal coalition independent of direct Communist Party influence in order to pursue the Left's own fair employment agenda.[17] Left-led unionism in the Southwest, most notably the Union of Mine, Mill, and Smelter Workers became, as James Lorence demonstrates, an important vehicle for an indigenous Mexican American radicalism that battled the political constraints imposed by local anticommunist forces.[18] Lisa Kannenberg documents the pragmatic efforts of local UE leaders in Schenectady to maintain the integrity of a once powerful local union amidst the cross currents of anticommunist local politics.[19] Eric Fure-Slocum situates

Milwaukee's postwar fight over public housing in a Cold War context that pitted proponents of "labor's city" against conservative real estate interests, whose anti-public housing efforts gained political energy as new currents of anticommunist propaganda fractured the labor left.[20] Examining the Pacific Coast region, Robert Cherny describes a prewar anticommunist network that laid the foundation for the virulent postwar anticommunist campaigns that polarized politics in local communities.[21] Cumulatively these essays demonstrate that the local politics of anticommunism was contested, and its outcomes the result of strategic, pragmatic, yet principled political choices made by local actors in ways that national studies have failed to adequately document.

These essays provide us with a cast of intriguing characters, some of whom were Communist political activists of national significance, like Bill Sentner, Harry Bridges, and Clinton and Virginia Jencks. Others, such as Shelton Tappes, Juan Chacón, Edward Roybal, Tony Rios, and Leo Jandreau were independent, shrewdly pragmatic, and deeply committed leftists, who steered their unions and communities in progressive directions despite the conservative riptide they faced. Their stories, acted out in local settings, complicate the traditional "rise and fall" narrative of left-wing politics in the decade following the Second World War.

These local stories also connect in important ways to national and international developments. If Cold War anticommunism manifested itself locally and recast local political conflicts, it also had important global implications. As Seth Wigderson's essay reveals, economic policy debates stimulated by the Korean War had great local significance and provided an early test for the influence of the CIO's newly adopted anticommunism. The anticipated "wages of anticommunism," promised by the CIO leadership proved scant indeed.[22] Christopher Gerteis's essay demonstrates that Cold War labor politics turned out to be a cumbersome export as U.S. labor experts injected their own brand of liberal anticommunism into the turmoil of postwar Japanese industrial relations.[23] Purveyors of a new American style of industrial relations found that the model did not travel particularly well, or at least encountered *local* resistance of rather formidable proportions in many local, international contexts.

Complicating Anticommunism

A number of essays in this collection complicate the history of both the anticommunist movement and the Communist Party. Robert Cherny, like Ellen Schrecker, documents the antecedents of postwar anticommunist mobilization. By situating his account in the West Coast region, he helps to contextualize and localize the powerful forces that came to be directed at the militant unionism of the West Coast, most notably the longshoremen led by Harry Bridges. While anticommunist networks were well developed by the outbreak of World War II, in Cherny's view they were largely superseded after the hiatus of wartime alliances by more centralized anticommunist activity coordinated through the agency of the FBI. The real significance of the prewar *non-governmental* anticommunist networks may lie not in the information gathering and direct action they undertook but in the ways they shaped a conservative, *local* political climate less hospitable to Popular Front-style politics.

But these essays, and other studies, also suggest a much more diverse community of anticommunists than is often acknowledged. Liberals, disaffected former CP members, Social Democrats, Catholic trade unionists, and growth-oriented urban reformers played significant parts within a movement of diverse interests.[24] How these interests and the organizing they spawned overlapped and reinforced each other can best be seen through local studies. As David Lewis-Colman shows, some trade union liberals, like Walter Reuther and his allies in the UAW, crafted an alternative approach to civil rights grounded in their own fiercely anticommunist union caucus. Within Detroit UAW locals, they simultaneously challenged the independent black caucus and the Communist Party. In Milwaukee, as Eric Fure-Slocum demonstrates, liberal proponents of public housing, after a bitter fight tinged with anticommunism, accepted racially demarcated public housing linked to an aggressive business program of downtown investment. But these essays also identify key "in-between" activists who, in the face of growing anticommunist power in local unions and communities, developed an alternative, pragmatic left politics. Shelton Tappes, Tony Rios, Edward Roybal, and Leo Jandreau are representative of those who navigated at some personal and political cost the anticommunist political shoals of the postwar period to salvage a degree of progressive momentum in the decade that followed.[25]

While these essays do not primarily examine the role of the Communist Party in the World War II era, they do contribute to the general revaluation of the party that is underway. As Ellen Schrecker has noted, the Communist Party bears some responsibility for shaping the very repression that nearly destroyed it in the Cold War and that obliterated "the larger universe in which the party operated."[26] Robert Cherny has characterized Schrecker's approach to conceptualizing the CP's political role as "both-and"; that is, the Communist Party's political strategy must be understood as *both* progressive/reformist in orientation *and*, what Schrecker terms, "a revolutionary, Soviet-led conspiracy."[27] Revisionist studies of the CPUSA, emphasizing the party as an indigenous social movement capable of adapting to a culturally and racially diverse but often hostile political environment, have locked horns with the older, and now more recent, literature that emphasized Soviet domination and Stalinist manipulation of the American movement. This latter view has also been augmented by an outpouring of documents from the former Soviet Union's archives that purport to show the CPUSA as a mere puppet of the Comintern.[28] A growing body of critical studies of the CP, while not underestimating the brute force of the anticommunist crusade, nevertheless show pointedly the ways in which the party contributed to its own demise as the leader of a broad left coalition.[29] Critics have typically identified strategic and organizational errors of the CP as stemming from excessive secrecy, an authoritarian style, and democratic centralism that left many popular front supporters and some party members wary and mistrustful of the party cadre. More specifically, the party's failure to acknowledge the Stalinist purges of the 1930s and 1940s, its rigid adherence to the Soviet line on the Hitler-Stalin pact in 1939, and its revocation in 1941 undermined the party's credibility. Wartime super-patriotism led the CP at times to fail to support rank-and-file grievances or to promote the trade union socialization of new workers. The decision to support the Henry Wallace campaign in 1948 proved strategically disastrous, and in the context of growing repression the party functioned in an increasingly sectarian manner, dramatically eroding its base of support in the face of massive state-sponsored repression.[30] Local studies, including a number of essays in this volume, reveal the consequences of the CP's new postwar ideological rigidity. But they also highlight the capacity of many left-wingers, including members of the party, to adapt to an intensely polarized Cold War environment in ways that held together the remnants of a local progressive political presence.[31]

Roots of the Anticommunist Crusade

Much of the historical attention given to the domestic anticommunist movement has focused on the period 1948 through 1952. In such a narrative the passage of Taft-Hartley in 1947 provides a kind of opening act and the end of the Korean War a certain closure. This chronology tends to emphasize the centrality of Joe McCarthy, the HUAC hearings, and the purging of Communist-led unions from the CIO. As a *national* story it has some coherence. However, new research—some of it reflected in these essays—suggests deeper political roots and an earlier relevant chronology to the story. As Cherny shows, anticommunist networks, including the American Legion, local police "red squads," the National Guard and military intelligence, segments of the labor movement, and some local civic and business organizations were quite active in the 1930s. Their intelligence gathering and local political mobilization lay the groundwork for the crusades that would follow the war.[32]

The massive postwar strikes reflected labor's unprecedented strength and collective bargaining stature coming out of the war, but they also revealed the fragility of that strength. Lisa Kannenberg shows that the failure to achieve price controls through collective bargaining or the maintenance of the wartime Office of Price Administration (OPA) signified a turning tide. By the fall midterm elections in 1946 red-baiting of left-supported local and congressional candidates was already in full swing.[33] Certainly the bitter UAW strike at Allis Chalmers that began in April 1946 and lasted into early 1947 posted another early warning that local anticommunist mobilization backed by national union leaders would play a crucial part in taming an aggressive, left-led labor movement. Its impact on the coalition promoting public housing—what right-wing opponents termed "political housing"—in Milwaukee was profound.[34] Nonetheless, the promise of a rebuilt New Deal capable of sustaining a broad Popular Front politics in the postwar era did not die easily. As Rosemary Feurer demonstrates, the coalition galvanized by the UE and its leaders in the St. Louis region, including open Communist Bill Sentner, showed considerable capacity to mobilize broad union and community support on behalf of a proposed Missouri Valley Authority. The years 1944–45 witnessed an intensification of that campaign. But by late fall 1945 the effort to expand public power and regional planning had stirred conservative opposition that now described the coalition as "un-American" and evidence of "Totalitarianism on the March."[35]

Even overseas the campaign to thwart a resurgent labor left drew concerted liberal anticommunist intervention in the months immediately following World War II. As Christopher Gerteis and other historians of Japanese labor have shown, a cadre of anticommunist American labor specialists had begun the task of building "an American-styled, business friendly" labor movement in Japan by late 1945. The task, even in war-ravaged Japan, was not as simple as they initially envisioned, and parallel complications can be found in other parts of postwar Europe and in the decolonizing world.[36] Well before Joe McCarthy reared his head as a national figure, the anticommunist campaign had taken hold locally in the United States and around the world.[37]

Anticommunism and the Politics of Race

Some recent scholarship assessing the contributions of the Communist Party to building a strong labor movement has emphasized the party's role in organizing working people outside basic industry. Steve Rosswurm notes that many of the eleven left-led unions expelled from the CIO "organized working people who were largely peripheral both to basic industry and to the concerns of most trade union leaders." They "were peripheral because of the kind of workers they were—often people of color and/or women." On those grounds, among others, he argues, "historians have seriously misjudged the expelled unions."[38]

Without question the Communist Party played a critical role in broadening and diversifying the base of the organized working class. Through its efforts with the unemployed in major cities in the early 1930s and its organizing of agricultural and cannery workers in the West and Southwest and African Americans in key mass production industries, the Left changed the face of the organized American working class.[39]

The anticommunist crusade reversed this tide by contributing to the expulsion of some of the unions in which minority and female workers were most heavily represented. The collapse of "Operation Dixie" played a key role in this process.[40] However, as a number of local studies suggest, the story is more complicated. James Lorence shows that the Union of Mine, Mill, and Smelter Workers played a pivotal role in supporting the organization of Mexican American miners in the Southwest. But that organizing had its own indigenous roots, and its vitality survived the vicious red-baiting and expulsion of Mine-Mill from the CIO.[41] In Los Angeles, according to Kenneth Burt, Mexican American political activists had a more ambiguous relationship with the CP and the labor left. Initially regarded with some suspicion by the CP, the Latino Community Services Organization (CSO) built its strength despite concerted conservative opposition. With a significant foothold in the city council by the late 1940s, the CSO kept the CP at arm's length, even as it forged a broad coalition around fair employment issues.[42] And in Detroit, according to David Lewis-Colman, the battle against discrimination in the shop, the union hall, and the community attracted CP support for African American activists, like Shelton Tappes. But for Tappes, that struggle was primary; his association with the party secondary. Although red-baited by conservative and liberal anticommunist forces within the UAW, Tappes and some other black activists kept their distance from the party, believing, as he would eventually testify, that the CP "exploited" the "Negro issue."[43]

What Was Lost—An Alternative Politics in Postwar America

The anticommunist crusade succeeded in marginalizing the Communist Party as a presence in American public life, but more consequentially, it destroyed the Popular Front in, what Michael Denning has called, the "shake-down of 1947–48." He notes that "One part—the Communists and their 'fellow travelers'—was repressed and expelled from public culture. . . . An-other part—the social democrats that made up the purged CIO as well as the Cold War cultural fronts like the Congress for Cultural Freedom—was incorporated as a chastened junior partner in the postwar order."[44] Many of the essays in this collection suggest a less dichotomous story. At least in the immediate postwar years an alternative left politics seeking to revitalize the New Deal showed some promise of success. The campaign for a Missouri Valley Authority is suggestive of such revitalization. In the areas of public housing and urban renewal, Communists and social democrats put forward a vision of what the city might become that grew directly out of public hous-ing initiatives begun in the Depression. For some reformers, working at times in concert with the party, the city held an almost-utopian promise.[45] This politics suggested a radically different approach to urban development and planning. And for a time it challenged the race-based notions of public housing that would eventually triumph in most postwar cities. More broadly, the Left envisioned a vital and growing public sector, the use of national planning to produce greater job security, income equity, and the provision of national health insurance.[46] The failure of this alternative politics had important local as well as national ramifications, but it did not necessarily eclipse altogether the space for left politics. Difficult though that alternative path may have been, Edward Roybal in Los Angeles held together a coali-tion in the Mexican American community that continued the fight for fair employment and access to housing. In Schenectady, Leo Jandreau's decision to take the remnants of the UE into the IUE allowed him and his allies to preserve the local union's strength and fight another day. The "cry-in" of Tôhô actresses in a bitter film industry strike in postwar Tokyo signified defeat at the hands of American anticommunist labor policies but also the surging activism of women who would play a significant role in local Japanese labor struggles over the next decade.[47]

These local studies, then, tell a complicated story of the postwar anti-communist crusade and its consequences. The anticommunist movement was both more diverse and more deeply rooted than historians have often acknowledged. Its power in local community contexts grew in part from its long-term presence within a network of conservative local organizations that included veterans' organizations, business associations, the Catholic Church, conservative elements of AFL and CIO-affiliated unions, and determined segregationists and other right-wing activists. Aided by new liberal allies, a virulent local anticommunist politics in many cases erupted well before the campaign took coherent shape on the national stage. But, those *local* anticommunist campaigns were contested. They had to contend with remnants of a "Popular Front" independent of the CP and prepared to fight pragmatically for those elements of the Left's vision that could be salvaged—fair employment, open housing, anti-discrimination in the workplace (and the bowling alley), a genuine civil rights movement, and a public sector still capable of addressing the needs of working-class Americans. Such local struggles planted seeds for the growth of a new popular politics led by a reconstituted left that would blossom in the 1960s and beyond.[48]

Notes

1. Speaker Tip O'Neill with Gary Hymel, *All Politics Is Local: And other Rules of the Game* (New York: Random House, 1994), xv–xvi; John Aloysius Farrell, *Tip O'Neill and the Democratic Century* (Boston: Little, Brown, 2001), 30–31, 64–65.

2. We have a number of truly outstanding national studies of the Cold War and its domestic politics. Most recent is the impressive synthetic work of Ellen Schrecker, *Many Are the Crimes: McCarthyism in America* (Princeton, N.J.: Princeton University Press, 1998). Older, but also important are David Caute, *The Great Fear: The Anti-Communist Purge under Truman and Eisenhower* (New York: Simon and Schuster, 1978); David M. Oshinsky, *A Conspiracy So Immense: The World of Joe McCarthy* (New York: Free Press, 1983); and Richard Fried, *Nightmare in Red: The McCarthy Era in Perspective* (New York: Oxford University Press, 1990).

3. Important studies that deal with the international context of Cold War politics in the United States include the old but still useful David Caute, *The Great Fear;* Melvyn P. Leffler, *A Preponderance of Power: National Security, the Truman Administration, and the Cold War* (Stanford, Calif.: Stanford University Press, 1992); Richard M. Freeland, *The Truman Doctrine and the Origins of McCarthyism* (New York: Alfred A. Knopf, 1972); and Jeff Broadwater, *Eisenhower and the Anti-Communist Crusade* (Chapel Hill: University of North Carolina Press, 1992).

4. The literature on the anticommunist purges in Hollywood is substantial. See, for instance, Larry Ceplair and Steven Englund, *The Inquisition in Hollywood: Politics in the Film Community, 1930–1960* (Garden City, N.Y.: Anchor Press, 1980); Lary May, *Recasting America: Culture and Politics in the Age of Cold War* (Chicago: University of Chicago Press, 1989); and James J. Lorence, *The Suppression of "Salt of the Earth": How Hollywood, Big Labor, and Politicians Blacklisted a Movie in Cold War America* (Albuquerque: University of New Mexico Press, 1999). For the Cold War in academia, see Ellen Schrecker, *No Ivory Tower: McCarthyism and the Universities* (New York: Oxford, 1986); and Noam Chomsky et al., *The Cold War and the University: Toward an Intellectual History of the Postwar Years* (New York: New Press, 1997). For the Cold War's impact on scientific research, see, among other things, the outstanding study by Jessica Wang, *American Science in an Age of Anxiety: Scientists, Anticommunism, and the Cold War* (Chapel Hill: University of North Carolina Press, 1999).

5. Here too the proliferation of work in recent years has been significant. See especially

the essays in Steve Rosswurm, *The CIO's Left-Led Unions* (New Brunswick, N.J.: Rutgers University Press, 1992); Stephen Meyer, *"Stalin over Wisconsin": The Making and Unmaking of Militant Unionism, 1900–1950* (New Brunswick, N.J.: Rutgers University Press, 1992); Nelson Lichtenstein, *Walter Reuther: The Most Dangerous Man in Detroit* (New York: Basic Books, 1995; rpt. Urbana: University of Illinois Press, 1997); Joshua B. Freeman, *In Transit: The Transport Workers Union in New York City, 1933–1966* (New York: Oxford University Press, 1989); and Michael Honey, *Southern Labor and Black Civil Rights: Organizing Memphis Workers* (Urbana: University of Illinois Press, 1993). Older general works include Bert Cochran, *Labor and Communism: The Conflict that Shaped American Unions* (Princeton, N.J.: Princeton University Press, 1977); and Harvey A. Levenstein, *Communism, Anticommunism, and the CIO* (Westport, Conn.: Greenwood Press, 1981). Studies of three left-wing unions bear particular mention: Toni Gilpin, "Left by Themselves: A History of the United Farm Equipment and Metal Workers' Union, 1938–1955" (Ph.D. diss., Yale University, 1992); Rosemary Feurer, *Radical Unionism in the Midwest, 1900–1950* (Urbana: University of Illinois Press, 2006); and David M. Lewis-Colman, *Race against Liberalism: Black Workers and the UAW in Detroit* (Urbana: University of Illinois Press, 2008).

6. Particularly noteworthy studies of the CP are James R. Barrett, *William Z. Foster and the Tragedy of American Radicalism* (Urbana: University of Illinois Press, 1999); Maurice Isserman, *Which Side Were You On?: The American Communist Party during the Second World War* (Middletown, Conn.: Wesleyan University Press, 1982; rpt. Urbana: University of Illinois Press, 1993); Roger Keeran, *The Communist Party and the Auto Workers* (Bloomington: Indiana University Press, 1980); Joseph R. Starobin, *American Communism in Crisis, 1943–1957* (Cambridge, Mass.: Harvard University Press, 1972). Critical of much of the new scholarship on American Communism are Theodore Draper, "American Communism Revisited," *New York Review of Books*, May 30, 1985, 32–37; see also Harvey Klehr and John Earl Haynes, *The American Communist Movement: Storming Heaven Itself* (New York: Twayne, 1992). Representative of the useful memoirs of Communists are Al Richmond, *A Long View from the Left: Memoirs of an American Revolutionary* (Boston: Houghton Mifflin, 1973); and Dorothy Healey, *Dorothy Healey Remembers: A Life in the Communist Party* (New York: Oxford University Press, 1990).

7. Exceptions to this generalization include Philip Jenkins, *Cold War at Home: The Red Scare in Pennsylvania, 1945–1960* (Chapel Hill: University of North Carolina Press, 1999); Paul Lyons, *Philadelphia Communists, 1936–1956* (Temple University Press, 1982); Stephen Meyer, *"Stalin over Wisconsin"*; Rosemary Feurer, *Radical Unionism in the Midwest*; and *American Labor and the Cold War: Grassroots Politics and Postwar Political Culture*, Robert Cherny, William Issel, and Kieran Walsh Taylor, eds. (New Brunswick, N.J.: Rutgers University Press, 2004).

8. Some noteworthy studies examine the promise of social reconstruction in the immediate postwar years and the conflicts that undermined that promise. See, for instance, Eric Fure-Slocum, "The Challenge of the Working-Class City: Recasting Growth Politics and Liberalism in Milwaukee, 1937–1952" (Ph.D. diss., University of Iowa, 2001); Henry Kraus, *In the City was a Garden* (New York: Renaissance Press, 1951), Nelson Lichtenstein, "From Corporatism to Collective Bargaining: Organized Labor and the Eclipse of Social Democracy in the Postwar Era," in *The Rise and Fall of the New Deal Order, 1930–1980;*

Steve Fraser and Gary Gerstle, eds. (Princeton, N.J.: Princeton University Press, 1989); and Michael Denning, *The Cultural Front: The Laboring of American Culture in the Twentieth Century* (London: Verso, 1998), especially 463–72.

9. See, for instance, Michael Honey, *Southern Labor and Black Civil Rights: Organizing Memphis Workers;* Penny Von Eschen, *Race Against Empire: Black Americans and Anti-colonialism, 1937–1957* (Ithaca, N.Y.: Cornell University Press, 1996); Gerald Horne, *Black and Red: W. E. B. Du Bois and the Afro-American Response to the Cold War, 1944–1963* (Albany: State University of New York Press, 1986); Roger Horowitz, *Negro and White, Unite and Fight!: A Social History of Industrial Unionism in Meatpacking, 1930–90* (Urbana: University of Illinois Press, 1997); and David Lewis-Colman, "Black Working-Class Politics and Identity in Detroit, 1941–72" (Ph.D. diss., University of Iowa, 2001).

10. The gender politics of the Left and labor in the Popular Front period remains an understudied subject. For suggestive directions, see especially Kate Weigand, *Red Feminism: American Communism and the Making of Women's Liberation* (Baltimore: Johns Hopkins University Press, 2001), 1–14, 67–96, 139–58; Dennis Deslippe, *"Rights, Not Roses": Unions and the Rise of Working-Class Feminism, 1945–80* (Urbana: University of Illinois Press, 2000); Van Gosse, "'To Organize in Every Neighborhood, in Every Home': The Gender Politics of American Communists between the Wars," *Radical History Review* 50 (1991): 109–41; Dorothy Sue Cobble, *The Other Women's Movement: Workplace Justice and Social Rights in Modern America* (Princeton, N.J.: Princeton University Press, 2004), 19, 28–29; Elaine Tyler May, *Homeward Bound: American Families in the Cold War Era* (New York: Basic Books, 1988); and Vivian Gornick, *The Romance of American Communism* (New York: Basic Books, 1977).

11. Cherny et al., *American Labor and the Cold War.*

12. Ibid. See especially the essays by William Issel, David Palmer, Gerald Zahavi, Don Watson, Kenneth Burt, Randi Storch, and Michael Honey.

13. One of the very best studies of the changing political culture of postwar America is George Lipsitz, *Class and Culture in Postwar America: "a rainbow at midnight"* (New York: Praeger, 1981).

14. The essays were first presented at a "Scholars' Seminar" hosted by the Center for Recent United States History (CRUSH) at the University of Iowa in March 2000.

15. See Feurer's essay in this collection; see also her book, *Radical Unionism in the Midwest.*

16. See Lewis-Colman's essay in this collection; see also his longer study, "Black Working-Class Politics and Identity in Detroit."

17. See Burt's essay in this collection; see also his essay, "Latino Empowerment in Los Angeles: Postwar Dreams and Cold War Fears, 1948–1952," *Labor's Heritage* 8:1 (Summer 1996): 4–25.

18. See Lorence's essay in this collection; see also James J. Lorence, *The Suppression of "Salt of the Earth."*

19. See Kannenberg's essay in this collection, as well as her work, "The Product of GE's Progress: Labor, Management, and Community Relations in Schenectady, New York, 1930–60" (Ph.D. diss., Rutgers University, 1999).

20. See Fure-Slocum's essay in this collection; see also Fure-Slocum, "Challenge of the Working-Class City."

21. See Cherny's essay in this collection; see also his work on Harry Bridges, "Constructing a Radical Identity: History, Memory, and the Seafaring Stories of Harry Bridges," *Pacific Historical Review* 70:4 (2001): 571–99.

22. See Wigderson's essay in this collection; see also his work, "The UAW in the 1950s" (Ph.D. diss., Wayne State University, 1989).

23. See Gerteis's essay in this collection; see also his longer work, "Japanese Women, Their Unions, and the Security Treaty Struggle, 1945–60" (Ph.D. diss., University of Iowa, 2001). For Latin America, see Christopher Welch, "Searching for Allies: The United States and Latin American Labor, 1945–51" (Ph.D. diss., American University, 1998).

24. A revisionist literature of significant proportions has reevaluated the role of the Catholic Church and its labor-activist priests in postwar anticommunist politics. See, for instance, William Issel, "'A Stern Struggle': Catholic Activism and San Francisco Labor, 1934–58," in Cherny et al., *American Labor and the Cold War*, 154–76; Joshua Freeman and Steve Rosswurm, "The Education of an Anti-Communist: Father John F. Cronin and the Baltimore Labor Movement," *Labor History* 33 (Spring 1992): 217–47; and Dennis Deslippe, "'A Revolution of Its Own': The Social Doctrine of the Association of Catholic Trade Unionists in Detroit, 1939–50," *Records of the American Catholic Historical Society of Philadelphia* 102 (Winter 1991): 19–36. Useful on both the Catholic and liberal strains of anticommunism is Richard Gid Powers, *Not without Honor: The History of American Anticommunism* (New York: Free Press, 1995), 191–212.

25. See essays in this volume by Cherny, Lewis-Colman, Burt, Fure-Slocum, and Kannenberg. See also David Palmer's similar story of Lou Kaplan, a self-described "anarchist with a program," in Palmer, "'An Anarchist with a Program': East Coast Shipyard Workers, the Labor Left, and the Origins of Cold War Unionism," in Cherny et al., *American Labor and the Cold War*, 85–117.

26. Ellen Schrecker, *Many Are the Crimes*, 41.

27. Robert Cherny, "Review of Ellen Schrecker, *Many Are the Crimes*," H-Net Book Review, published by H-Labor@h-net.msu.edu (May 1999). See also Schrecker, *Many Are the Crimes*, 4–5.

28. The historiographical debates over the nature of American Communism are both longstanding and have been periodically reinvigorated by new revisionist currents and new sources. An older literature, critical of the CP, grounded in the work of Theodore Draper, *The Roots of American Communism* (New York: Viking Press, 1957) and *American Communism and Soviet Russia* (New York: Viking Press, 1960), has been augmented by the abundant writings of Harvey Klehr, *The Heyday of American Communism: The Depression Decade* (New York: Basic Books, 1984); and John Earl Haynes, *Communism and Anti-Communism in the United States: An Annotated Guide to Historical Writing* (New York: Garland Press, 1987). Since the opening of the archives of the former Soviet Union, Klehr and Haynes have jointly authored a whole series of books that emphasize Soviet domination of the CPUSA: *The American Communist Movement: Storming Heaven Itself*; with Fridrikh Irorevich Firsov, *The Secret World of American Communism* (New Haven, Conn.: Yale University Press, 1995); with Kryill M. Anderson, *The Soviet World of American Communism* (New Haven, Conn.: Yale University Press, 1998); *Venona: Decoding Soviet Espionage in America* (New Haven, Conn.: Yale University Press, 1999); and Haynes, *Red Scare or Red Menace? American Communism and Anti-Communism in the Cold War Era* (Chicago: Ivan R. Dee, 1996).

The work of revisionists emphasizing the CPUSA as a bona fide American social movement with significant roots in an indigenous left and considerable influence during certain
periods—most notably the depression and World War II eras—is abundant. Particular
mention might be made of works dealing with the role of the party in African American communities: Mark Naison, *Communists in Harlem during the Depression* (Urbana:
University of Illinois Press, 1983), Robin D. G. Kelley, *Hammer and Hoe: Alabama Communists during the Great Depression* (Chapel Hill: University of North Carolina Press,
1990); Michael Honey, *Southern Labor and Black Civil Rights: Organizing Memphis Workers* (Urbana: University of Illinois Press, 1993); and Mark Solomon, *The Cry Was Unity:
Communists and African Americans, 1917–1936* (Jackson: University of Mississippi Press,
1998). Other revisionist work has been more general or biographical in focus: Schrecker,
of course; Maurice Isserman, *Which Side Are You On? The American Communist Party
during the Second World War;* Fraser Ottanelli, *The Communist Party of the United States:
From Depression to World War II* (New Brunswick, N.J.: Rutgers University Press, 1991);
James R. Barrett and Rob Ruck, *Steve Nelson: American Radical* (Pittsburgh: University
of Pittsburgh Press, 1981); Barrett, *William Z. Foster;* Vivian Gornick, *The Romance of
American Communism;* Al Richmond, *Long View from the Left;* Dorothy Healey; *Dorothy
Healey Remembers: A Life in the American Communist Party;* and Bryan Palmer, *James P.
Cannon and the Origins of the American Revolutionary Left, 1890–1928* (Urbana: University
of Illinois Press, 2007).

29. Continuing historiographical debates are lively and reflect an ongoing search for
common interpretive ground in what remains a highly polarized literature. See, for instance, the at-times acrimonious debate between Theodore Draper and many revisionist
historians in response to his articles "American Communism Revisited" and "Popular
Front Revisited," in the *New York Review of Books* 32 (May 9, May 30, Aug. 15, Sept. 26,
1985); and more recently, John Earl Haynes, "The Cold War Debate Continues: A Tradi-
tionalist View of Historical Writing on Domestic Communism and Anti-Communism,"
Journal of Cold War Studies 2:1 (2000): 76–115; John Earl Haynes and Harvey Klehr, "The
Historiography of American Communism: An Unsettled Field," *Labour History Review*
68:51 (Apr. 2003): 61–78; and Bryan Palmer, "Rethinking the Historiography of United
States Communism," *American Communist History* 2:2 (2003): 139–214, including com-
ments by Dubofsky, Barrett, Haynes, and McIlroy, and his response, "Communist History:
Seeing It Whole. A Reply to Critics."

30. See, in particular, the insightful comments of Schrecker in Rosswurm, *CIO's Left-Led
Unions,* 15–26; Steve Rosswurm, "Introduction," *CIO's Left-Led Unions,* 8–11; and James
Barrett, *William Z. Foster,* 226–28, 250–51. For the role of the state in postwar repression
of Communists and Communist sympathizers, see Robert Cherny's essay in this volume
and Ellen Schrecker, *Many Are the Crimes,* especially chaps. 3, 6, and 7.

31. See especially the essays of Burt, Kannenberg, and Lewis-Colman in this volume.
More local studies would no doubt reveal more such instances, but see, for example,
the role of Don Harris as a UPWA, then FE, and ultimately UAW militant, in Shelton
Stromquist, *Solidarity and Survival: An Oral History of Iowa Labor in the Twentieth Cen-
tury* (Iowa City: University of Iowa Press, 1995), 173–75, and extensive interviews with
Harris in the Iowa Labor History Oral Project (ILHOP), State Historical Society of Iowa.
See also, Matt Mettler, "A Crossroads in Labor Militancy: The Rise and Fall of the Quad
Cities FE-UE, 1949–55" (paper, Midwest Labor Historians Conference, Apr. 2005), for a

discussion of the pragmatic choices made by FE militants in the Moline, Illinois, John Deere locals about whether to affiliate with the IAM or the UAW in the aftermath of the CIO expulsions.

32. See Cherny's essay in this volume.

33. See Kannenberg's essay in this volume. For the significance of the most important of the large postwar strikes and the battle over price controls, see Lichtenstein, *Most Dangerous Man*, 220–47.

34. See Eric Fure-Slocum, in this collection, and Steve Meyer, *"Stalin over Wisconsin,"* 157–212.

35. See Rosemary Feurer's essay in this volume.

36. See Christopher Gerteis's essay in this volume. See also Joe B. Moore, *Japanese Workers and the Struggle for Power, 1945–47* (Madison: University of Wisconsin Press, 1983). In a parallel fashion, AFL and CIO representatives worked in different ways to rebuild anticommunist unions in Europe. See, for instance, the work of AFL representative Joe Keenan in Germany and the CIO's man in Greece, Clint Golden, discussed in Denis Macshane, *International Labour and the Origins of the Cold War* (Oxford: Oxford University Press, 1992), 90–94, 129–33.

37. For other international contexts, see Christopher Welch, "Searching for Allies: The United States and Latin American Labor, 1945–51" (paper, CRUSH seminar on "Labor's Cold War," Mar. 2000); Cliff Welch, "Labor Internationalism: U.S. Involvement in Brazilian Unions, 1945–65," *Latin American Research Review* 30:2 (1995): 61–89; Victor Silverman, *Imagining Internationalism in American and British Labor, 1939–49* (Urbana: University of Illinois Press, 2000); Ronald Filippelli, *American Labor and Postwar Italy, 1943–1953: A Study in Postwar Politics* (Stanford, Calif.: Stanford University Press, 1989); Carolyn Eisenberg, "Working-Class Politics and the Cold War: American Intervention in the German Labor Movement, 1945–49," *Diplomatic History* 7:4 (1983): 283–306; and Gigi Peterson, "'A Dangerous Demagogue': Containing the Influence of the Mexican Labor-Left and Its United States Allies," in Cherny et al., *American Labor and the Cold War*, 245–76.

38. Steve Rosswurm, *CIO's Left-Led Unions*, 5–6.

39. The key role played by the Communist Party in organizing black workers and battling discrimination within CIO unions is well documented in recent scholarship. See especially Robin D. G. Kelley, *Hammer and Hoe*; Mark Naison, *Communists in Harlem*; and Robert Rogers Korstad, *Civil Rights Unionism: Tobacco Workers and the Struggle for Democracy in the Mid-Twentieth-Century South* (Chapel Hill: University of North Carolina Press, 2003). Kelley and Korstad emphasize the agency of black workers within a broad "Popular Front" energized by Communist organizers committed to interracial unionism. See also Paul C. Young, "Race, Class, and Radicalism in Chicago, 1914–1936" (Ph.D. diss., University of Iowa, 2001); and David Lewis-Colman, "Black Working-Class Politics and Identity in Detroit, 1941–1972." For the Southwest, see Benny J. Andres Jr., "Power and Control in Imperial Valley, California: Nature, Agribusiness, Labor, and Race Relations, 1900–1940" (Ph.D. diss., University of New Mexico, 2003).

40. See Michael Honey, *Southern Labor and Black Civil Rights*; George Lipsitz, *Class and Culture*; Michael K. Honey, "Operation Dixie, the Red Scare, and the Defeat of Southern Labor Organizing," in Cherny et al., *American Labor and the Cold War*, 216–44; and Korstad, *Civil Rights Unionism*, 290–92, 298–300.

41. See Lorence's essay in this collection.

42. See Burt's essay in this collection.

43. See Lewis-Colman's essay in this collection. See also Randi Storch on the impact of the CP's shifting line on race on proponents of labor interracialism, "The United Packinghouse Workers of America, Civil Rights, and the Communist Party in Chicago," in Cherny et al., *American Labor and the Cold War,* 72–84.

44. Denning, *Cultural Front,* 464.

45. See Fure-Slocum's essay in this collection. A classic account of the cooperative efforts of public housing residents to save "their" homes in the face of red-baiting and concerted opposition of conservative business and government officials is Henry Kraus, *In the City Was a Garden* (New York: Renaissance Press, 1951). See also Heather Thompson, *Whose Detroit? Politics, Labor, and Race in a Modern American City* (Ithaca, N.Y.: Cornell University Press, 2001).

46. See Wigderson's essay in this collection on the CIO's interest in national planning at the end of World War II. For the fight over national health insurance, see Colin Gordon, "Why No National Health Insurance in the U.S.?: The Limits of Social Provision in War and Peace, 1941–1948," *Journal of Policy History* 9:3 (1997): 277–310, and his *Dead on Arrival: The Politics of Health Care in Twentieth-Century America* (Princeton, N.J.: Princeton University Press, 2003).

47. See Gerteis's essay in this collection. For another case of the persistence of a progressive legacy, see Margaret Miller, "Negotiating Cold War Politics: The Washington Pension Union and the Labor Left in the 1940s and 1950s," in Cherny et al., *American Labor and the Cold War,* 205–15.

48. For a very helpful discussion of the legacies the "old left" bequeathed to the "new left," see Maurice Isserman, *If I Had a Hammer . . . : The Death of the Old Left and the Birth of the New Left* (New York: Basic Books, 1987).

1. Anticommunist Networks and Labor: The Pacific Coast in the 1930s

ROBERT W. CHERNY

Recent historians have found the origins in the 1920s and 1930s of several varieties of anticommunism.[1] Ellen Schrecker, for example, describes the emergence, by the late 1930s, of anticommunist networks consisting of the American Legion, HUAC, the FBI, some union leaders, and groups from the Left. During the 1930s, several such loose anticommunist networks were to be found in the three Pacific Coast states. Though they involved a number of governmental and non-governmental groups, the FBI was not obviously or centrally involved until at least 1940.

On the Pacific Coast, many anticommunist activities in the late 1930s revolved around Harry Bridges. Bridges first attracted attention as a leader in the 1934 Pacific Coast longshore and maritime strikes and the San Francisco general strike. Almost immediately, allegations arose that he was a member of the CP and hence subject to deportation to his native Australia. Bridges became president of his local and then of the Pacific Coast District of the International Longshoremen's Association. In 1937, he led the Pacific Coast District into the Congress of Industrial Organizations as the International Longshoremen's and Warehousemen's Union (ILWU) and became both its first president and CIO western regional director. Bridges's growing fame as a militant, left-wing labor leader quickly brought demands that he be deported. Four hearings or trials followed, between 1939 and 1955, two of which were appealed to the U.S. Supreme Court. These extended legal actions generated a mountain of records that reveal a great deal about Pacific Coast anticommunist networks. There were also anticommunist efforts directed against other unions and other individuals, of course. Given the large volume of evidence generated by the Bridges cases, however, this essay will focus on the anticommunist activities that centered on Bridges and the ILWU.[2]

For the Pacific Coast in the 1930s, there were many anticommunist groups and individuals. Some worked together, others held apart. Some competed, and some denigrated the others. Insofar as they left a record of their reasons for opposing Communism, they nearly all indicated that they considered Communism to be un-American. Beyond that, they varied in their purposes, methods of operation, and relations to the state. The most prominent anticommunist groups were the American Legion, police red squads, the National Guard and Military Intelligence, business leaders and organizations, and organized labor (both AFL and CIO). Others, including some officials of the Immigration and Naturalization Service (INS), non-CP leftists, and the Catholic Church, were involved at less prominent levels. Some people fit into more than one category, and some don't fit comfortably into any category. Nor did these individuals and organizations form anything like a smoothly functioning machine. On the contrary, individuals and organizations sometimes distrusted and even undercut each other, not necessarily because of suspicions of disloyalty (though that surfaced occasionally) but typically through personal disputes and jealousies. The FBI was not obviously involved until the eve of World War II, when it stepped up its surveillance of the CP and, at the same time, moved to limit the anticommunist activities of other groups.

This survey of anticommunism on the Pacific Coast begins with the most visible and vocal of the anticommunist groups, the American Legion and local police red squads. It then looks at the other groups and concludes with the FBI.

The American Legion

The American Legion was launched in May 1919, and it grew rapidly in the Pacific Coast states, especially California. By October 1919, the Legion claimed thirty thousand members in California, and more than forty-six thousand by August 1920. From its first statewide meeting in October 1919, the Legion took a strong stand against radicals, and it quickly acquired a reputation for being anti-union.[3] In 1934, Homer Chaillaux, the California state commander, offered the governor "adequate force" to end the longshore and waterfront strikes. Soon after, Chaillaux moved to the national organization, where he became the director of the National Americanism Commission.[4]

Chaillaux quickly called for all state Legion organizations to report on "radical activities."[5] The California Department of the American Legion was already doing that. By 1935, Harper "Moke" Knowles had emerged as the central figure in the Legion's anticommunist efforts in California. Owner of a small, family business in San Francisco, he served as chairman of the anti-radical division of the state American Legion, called first the Subversive Activities Committee and later the Radical Research Committee. Formed in 1934 to collect and analyze information on radicals, the committee counted among its members a number of law-enforcement officers. Knowles's counterpart in the Oregon department of the Legion was William D. Browne, a member of the Portland Police Department's red squad, but neither the Oregon nor the Washington Legion seems to have mounted efforts comparable to that in California.[6] In Oregon, Browne seems to have been the only member of the committee.[7] In Washington, the Legion's Division of Subversive Activities Investigations had branch offices around the state, but most surveillance seemed to be of labor organizations.[8]

Knowles described the major task of his committee as collecting and distributing information on radicalism, radical groups, and individual radicals—all those considered potentially subversive. In 1936, he also claimed for his organization a central place among anticommunist efforts on the Pacific Coast: "We have a very close working arrangement with the Army, Navy, State Bureau of Criminal Identification and investigation, police departments, sheriffs [sic] offices, state peace officers' association, immigration inspectors, private detective agencies, manufacturers, labor and industrial associations, farmers's [sic] protective association, Chambers of Commerce, civic, fraternal and other veterans' groups. . . . We work in co-operation with the U.S. Secret Service, Department of Justice, Post Office inspectors, WPA and other relief organizations. . . . Special Agents of public utilities such as the telephone, telegraph, railroad and steamship companies are usually found helpful. . . . We have a few undercover agents who are members of the subversive groups and they report regularly in writing to us."[9] Knowles's activities brought a commendation from Chaillaux for "your success in co-ordinating the activities of your Commission with those of various groups in California which seek to expose the Communist activities which have been detrimental to coast payrolls."[10]

In 1939, Knowles bragged that his committee's card file covered thousands of people. Asked about the purpose of these records, Knowles replied that they existed "so that various facts might be available for the committee . . . for Congressional groups . . . or law enforcement officers, or anybody else." Knowles claimed that the committee had received "records on individuals and criminal records" from police departments in San Francisco, Los Angeles, Portland, and San Diego, along with the California Bureau of Criminal

Identification and Investigation and "a great many sheriffs and police officers" in "all the major cities." The relationship was reciprocal, for the committee provided information from its files to police departments when asked. Law enforcement agencies assisted the Legion in other ways; for example, C. S. Morrill, head of the California Division of Criminal Identification and Investigation, ordered a driver's license issued under an assumed name at Knowles's request. The Legion committee also received reports from informants inside unions and radical groups, who, Knowles estimated, numbered a hundred or so, and from a private detective agency.[11]

Knowles supplied information to military and naval intelligence and to the INS, but, he stressed, the committee's relationship with those federal agencies was "one way. . . . We would offer it rather than receive it." Knowles denied that he or his committee had ever received financial assistance from employers but also acknowledged that "we have exchanged information with a number of employer organizations," including the Industrial Association and the Associated Farmers, and also with the Better America Federation (for all of which, see below), the U.S. Chamber of Commerce (which had its own subversive activities committee), and unions that he declined to identify.[12] The INS files on Bridges also establish that Knowles actively lobbied government officials for action against those he accused of being Communists.[13]

Stanley Doyle, nicknamed Larry and also known as Pat Morton, C. E. Burke, Rex, and Big Boy, worked closely with Knowles and was perhaps the most active of all those seeking to deport Bridges in the late 1930s. Charles Martin, governor of Oregon, commissioned Doyle as an Oregon special agent, apparently in 1935.[14] Elected in 1934, Martin brought to the Oregon governorship his experience as a career Army officer. Though elected as a Democrat and a New Deal supporter, Martin quickly turned to the Right. Doyle was just one of the special agents Martin commissioned to combat Communism—Gary Murrell, Martin's biographer, claims that "Martin built one of the most nefarious spy networks then existing in the country with the possible exception of California."[15]

Doyle, an Irish lawyer with a melodramatic flair and an anti-Semitic streak that matched that of Governor Martin,[16] served as a special prosecutor in the trial of Dirk De Jonge, who was prosecuted under Oregon's criminal syndicalism law in 1934–35 on the charge that he was a member of the Communist Party and had assisted in the conduct of a meeting held under the auspices of the CP.[17] In 1935, Doyle acted as defense attorney for a group of vigilantes, including Legionnaires, who were on trial for tarring and feathering leftists in Sonoma County, California. Though he seems to have been a loner, in California Doyle worked most closely and most consistently with

Knowles. Doyle was very active in the American Legion, sometimes sent correspondence on the letterhead of Knowles's committee, and had headed the Legion's Societe des 40 Hommes et 8 Chevaux (often called the 40 et 8), described by one historian of the Legion as "a secret society" of "the most active Legionnaires."[18] Presenting himself as an Oregon special agent, Doyle ranged up and down the entire Pacific Coast, devoting most of his efforts to finding proof that Bridges was a CP member. Doyle sent his reports to Wallace "Buck" Wharton, executive secretary to Governor Martin.[19]

Gerard Reilly, Solicitor for the Department of Labor, was sent to the West Coast by Secretary of Labor Frances Perkins in 1937 to evaluate evidence that the Portland INS office had submitted as the basis for deportation charges against Bridges. Reilly assessed Governor Martin as "out to make political capital of the case," and as "a charming and colorful figure, but frankly fascistic in his conversation." Reilly also reported that Captain J. J. Keegan of the Portland Police Department considered Doyle to be "a racketeer and blackmailer" and concluded that Doyle "might be quite capable of framing witnesses."[20] By 1939, Doyle had left the West Coast and claimed to be living in Minnesota and practicing law there and in Chicago.[21]

Red Squads

The American Legion's anti-radical committees maintained close relations with police red squads, especially those in Portland and Los Angeles. Frank Donner, in *Protectors of Privilege: Red Squads and Police Repression in Urban America,* treats the emergence and growth of red squads in several cities during the 1920s and 1930s, including the one in Los Angeles, led by Captain William F. "Red" Hynes—whose nickname came from his hair color, not his politics. A labor spy before joining the LAPD in 1922, Hynes became head of the red squad in 1927. "More than any other single individual," Donner claims, "Hynes was influential in shaping the agenda of the modern red squad and in exploiting the career opportunities as its chief." An appearance before the Fish Committee in 1930 catapulted him into the nation's headlines and led other cities to seek his advice in setting up their own red squads. Under Hynes's aggressive leadership, the LA red squad savagely assaulted virtually any leftist meeting or demonstration and meted out much the same to union picket lines. Hynes worked closely with Harper Knowles in San Francisco.[22] In the late 1930s, the La Follette Committee hearings revealed Hynes's close ties to the LA Chamber of Commerce and to its Merchants and Manufacturers Association—the M&M—the group that created and at times brutally maintained LA's reputation as the city of the open shop. Donner summarizes

Hynes's career as "a close linkage of repression and corruption." After LA
elected a reform mayor in 1938, and following the La Follette Committee
revelations, LAPD involvement in labor matters largely ended and its red
squad was either dissolved or severely reduced.[23]

In comparison with the brutal efficiency of the LA red squad, its Portland
counterpart sometimes more closely resembled the Keystone Kops. In 1938,
the Oregon chapter of the National Lawyers Guild issued a fifty-three-page
report on the Portland red squad, revealing that the two officers most closely
associated with the squad were Walter Odale, who began his anti-radical
police activities in 1922 with forays against the IWW, and William D. Browne,
an American Legion activist and head of the Oregon Legion's counterpart
to Knowles's committee. Browne had served in the Division of Criminal
Intelligence in the U.S. Army during World War I. Odale was too old for
military service during World War I, but the Lawyers Guild reported that
he had worked in the intelligence service of the Spruce Corporation during
the war—a time when the Northwest buzzed with rumors of IWW plots to
cripple the war effort through lumber strikes. Odale was a captain in the
Oregon National Guard before World War I, and, like Doyle, held a special
agent's commission from Governor Martin.

In addition to Odale, Browne, and a few other police officers, the Lawyers
Guild counted as a member of the Portland red squad George Stroup, an
American Legion activist who preceded Browne as head of the committee
on subversive activities. Odale acknowledged that the Portland red squad
"cooperated with . . . the Legion in matters pertaining to subversive activities,"
but insisted nothing was improper in the relationship. The Lawyers Guild
found that Stroup shared an office with Odale and had access to the police
files there, and that American Legion posts across Oregon had raised more
than $11,000 (equivalent to more than $160,000 in 2007) for anticommunist
activities. Like Knowles's operation in San Francisco, the Portland red squad
and its American Legion counterpart employed undercover operatives and
compiled an extensive file on alleged radicals, ranging over much of Oregon
and sometimes as far afield as Los Angeles. Like its LA counterpart, the
Portland red squad's offices were separate from the regular police department—first in the American Legion's headquarters and later in the Railway
Exchange Building, with the rent, according to the Lawyers Guild, from
"private contributions."[24]

Keegan, the police captain responsible for the Portland red squad, gave
his full backing to Odale and the squad, as did the mayor of Portland and,
apparently, Governor Martin. The Portland Chief of Police, Harry M. Niles,
directed his officers to cooperate with Knowles. In 1937, after a series of ar-

ticles in the Portland *Oregonian* about the red squad's work, it was moved into the regular Portland police headquarters and apparently put under closer supervision by Keegan. When Gerard Reilly was in Portland that year, he interviewed Keegan and concluded that his "ability is very latent."[25]

National Guard and Military Intelligence

Just as there were close connections between the American Legion's subversive activities committees and police red squads, so too were there individuals in both of those groups with connections to the National Guard or the Army's Military Intelligence Division (MID). In Oregon and California, the National Guard was significantly involved in anticommunism, but the full extent of MID involvement is difficult to determine.[26] Some individuals were prominent in both the Legion and the National Guard. In other instances, individuals who came out of MID devoted their retirement to anticommunist activities. In at least one instance, the National Guard paid an informant to infiltrate the CP.

One retired MID officer stands out for the significance of his work in army intelligence while on active duty and for the extent of his work in anticommunist activities while in retirement. Ralph H. Van Deman has been called the "Father of U.S. Military Intelligence." A graduate of Harvard and medical school, he began an Army career in 1891 and first worked in MID in 1897. In 1899, he was assigned to the Philippines, where, in 1901, he helped to establish military intelligence. In 1904, he became a member of the first class to attend the Army War College. Eventually, at his urging, the Army gave intelligence operations increased emphasis and put Van Deman in charge. During World War I, he included in the charge of military intelligence "the manifold domestic problems arising from the fact of our mixed population." With the imprisonment of Tom Mooney in 1916 and the development of a left-led movement to secure his release, Van Deman's military intelligence undertook surveillance of those efforts, reporting on rallies and campaign materials. These efforts produced War Plan White, a contingency plan for a war at home, against Americans who opposed the war or who might seek to overthrow the government as the Bolsheviks had done in Russia. According to Joan Jensen, in her study *Army Intelligence in America,* MID looked upon the American Legion as "an unarmed volunteer intelligence auxiliary." In October 1921, the War Department replaced War Plan White with Emergency Plan White, a peacetime contingency plan that did not include surveillance of civilians. Nonetheless, some MID officers continued their relation with the Legion, and the MID also developed informal relations with the Bureau of Investigation, whose director, J. Edgar Hoover, became a reserve officer in MID in 1922.[27]

MID surveillance of civilians was significantly reduced during the 1920s. Van Deman had promoted a plan to create an MID reserve, but the army was not interested. Something similar was carried out through the quarter-master reserve corps, but was limited largely to army officers assigned to college Reserve Officer Training Corps units. MID efforts expanded, however, in the early 1930s, under Chief of Staff Douglas MacArthur. Such surveil-lance eventually extended to Communists, Socialists, pacifists, strike leaders, and Civilian Conservation Corps camps (which were run by the army). In 1934, General Malin Craig, commander of the Ninth Corps, which had its headquarters at the Presidio of San Francisco, reported his unit's extensive surveillance activities during the 1934 maritime strikes.[28] One San Francisco longshoreman, an opponent of Bridges, reported that he went to MID at the San Francisco Presidio to discuss alleged Communist activity in his union and that the MID referred him to Knowles and the American Legion.[29] There are also a few copies of Military Intelligence reports on union matters in the files of the War Department at the National Archives, most of them from 1940.[30]

Van Deman, however, lost his position as head of MID in 1918, apparently because Secretary of War Newton Baker felt his surveillance of civilians had gone too far. During the 1920s, Van Deman served briefly as a National Guard instructor in Berkeley and was stationed at posts in California and Washington. Upon retiring in 1929, he settled in San Diego and devoted much of his time to assembling information on radicals, a task that he continued until his death in 1952. His biographer describes these efforts: "Working with the knowledge and cooperation of the War Department, Navy, and Federal Bureau of Investigation, he developed a voluminous library of Communist literature, a photo gallery, newspaper clippings, and information reports. He provided information to various federal agencies and local police depart-ments."[31]

Van Deman's collection included reports from the San Diego and LA police departments, the Imperial County sheriff's department, Harper Knowles and the American Legion, the Associated Farmers, the Industrial Association, the Better America Federation, the Ninth Corps military intelligence, the commandant's office for the 11th Naval District (San Diego), and various undercover operatives. By 1936, the Ninth Corps intelligence officer was sending so much material to Van Deman that a special rubber stamp was made to facilitate those operations. After Van Deman's death, part of his vast collection was transferred to the Senate Internal Security Subcommittee and later to the National Archives. The INS, FBI, and CIA used those files as late as the 1960s.[32]

Another former MID officer active in West Coast anticommunist efforts was Henry R. Sanborn, a Reserve Lieutenant Colonel in Army Intelligence. He published the *American Citizen,* an anticommunist tabloid distributed widely throughout northern California. The scattered surviving copies of this paper carry stories about the dangers of Communist subversion and blame Communists for a long list of labor disputes in California. Most issues included short biographies, complete with photographs, of one or a few CP members, set up like police mug shots.[33] In 1937 Sanborn worked closely with Keegan to develop affidavits against Bridges.[34]

In addition to these surveillance efforts by MID and former MID officers, the California National Guard conducted surveillance activities. The key figure was David Prescott Barrows, who received a Ph.D. in anthropology from the University of Chicago in 1898, taught at the San Diego state normal school, served as an educational administrator in the Philippines, then became a professor and, soon after, an administrator at the University of California. During World War I, he volunteered, became an officer, and served with MID in the Philippines and the AEF in Siberia. In 1919, he became president of the University of California but resigned in 1922 to become chairman of the Political Science Department. He was the first president of the California American Legion and an officer of the National Guard.[35]

Both a UC professor and a major general in the National Guard during the 1930s, Barrows explained that he had set the "'G-2' Section of my staff [to] securing and compiling data on seditious organizations in California," including college student organizations. He also maintained working relations with Colonel Sanborn.[36] Appointed to command the National Guard troops that took control of the San Francisco waterfront in 1934, he later claimed that the troops under his command in 1934 had prevented "your Communist leadership, your Communist general staff" from overthrowing the government of San Francisco. He also worried over similar dangers facing the state and prepared "a careful study . . . of the localities in the state where considerable numbers of laborers are congregated and where we know that Communist propaganda has started and where violence will probably arise."[37] He also urged the substantial expansion of the state National Guard, but with careful investigation of any new recruits.[38] In 1939, he appeared as a witness against Harry Bridges, testifying as an expert on Marxism.[39]

The Oregon National Guard also undertook surveillance of the CP. Laurence Milner, a major in the Oregon National Guard, spent the years 1933–37 as a paid undercover operative within the CP in Oregon. During those four

years, he produced some 1,400 reports for the Oregon Adjutant General—
roughly one per day. When Dirk De Jonge was tried in 1934–35 for violating
Oregon's criminal syndicalism act, Milner was a defense witness and perjured
himself in order to maintain his cover within the Left. At Bridges's INS hearing in 1939, Milner testified that he had acted under National Guard orders
when he had served as chauffeur for Bridges, other left-wing union officials,
their lawyers, and leaders of the CP.[40]

The involvement in anticommunist activities by the Oregon and California
National Guard and by retired MID officers, and the involvement by MID
itself in surveillance, introduces an element into the account of West Coast
anticommunist networks that has not been developed by recent historians
of anticommunism.

Business and Civic Leaders

Several business or civic organizations and a few individual business leaders
surface repeatedly in the sources of information on Pacific Coast anticommunist networks. Among the most prominent were the Industrial Association
of San Francisco, the Associated Farmers, and the Better America Federation.
The first two received extensive attention from the La Follette Committee
during its hearings in California.

In 1921, the San Francisco Chamber of Commerce served as midwife to the
birth of the Industrial Association of San Francisco. The Industrial Association described itself as committed to "the public interest" and "the welfare of
the city." Their magazine, *American Plan,* proclaimed that unions no longer
served any useful purpose except as social clubs, and maintained that wage
levels and working conditions should follow from recommendations of "impartial wage boards" consisting of representatives of labor, employers, and
the public, all appointed by the Industrial Association, acting on behalf of the
public. From the early 1920s until the mid-1930s, the Industrial Association
closely governed labor relations in the San Francisco construction industry
and involved itself elsewhere as well.[41] In 1934, the longshore and maritime
strikes reached their bloody denouement on July 3 and 5 when the Industrial
Association took control of the employers' side of the strike and began to
move cargo using strikebreakers protected by police.

During the decade and a half when the Industrial Association dominated
San Francisco's labor relations, it never wanted for funds. Each of the eight
hundred members paid annual dues of twelve dollars, but the major source
of Industrial Association funds came in special assessments. The first came
in 1921, a million dollars (nearly ten million in 2007 dollars) raised to combat

a building trades strike. A third of the total came from only thirty firms, including banks, railroads, other public utility companies, and oil companies.[42] Five such assessments between 1921 and 1934 raised about five million for the Industrial Association. The La Follette Committee secured the association's income records for 1936. That year, banks provided 17 percent of the total, followed by public utilities (especially railroads) with 15 percent, oil companies with 11 percent, and various interlocking Hawaiian interests (most with their mainland headquarters in San Francisco) with 9 percent.[43]

The Industrial Association had its own undercover operation, concentrated at first in the building trades, where the major objective was to discourage union organizing on job sites. Under the leadership of Samuel Johnson, a former commander of the Hawaiian National Guard and a veteran of the AEF's Siberian operation of 1919, these undercover operations employed a staff of detectives and informants within unions. In the 1930s, this undercover operation was extended to Communist organizations and efforts to organize farmworkers throughout the state.[44] After the La Follette Committee hearings, however, and in the face of a permanently changed structure for labor relations, the Industrial Association was dissolved and its assets turned over to the new San Francisco Employers' Council, an organization that assisted employers in collective bargaining.[45]

Carey McWilliams, in the mid-1930s, labeled the Associated Farmers of California as "Farm Fascism."[46] Since then, several historians have also described the Associated Farmers, and few have been more generous than McWilliams. The Associated Farmers was formed in March 1934, in response to organizing and strikes by the CP's Cannery and Agricultural Workers Industrial Union (CAWIU). Of the $28,305 ($426,000 in 2007 dollars) in income that the La Follette Committee identified for the Associated Farmers in 1934, 36 percent (the largest single contribution) came from the Industrial Association; for 1935, the Industrial Association provided about a fifth of a total of nearly $25,000. Other major contributors included the same companies that supported the Industrial Association—banks, railroads, utilities, and Hawaiian interests.[47] For a few months in 1938, Harper Knowles added to his Legion duties those of secretary for the Associated Farmers.[48]

The Associated Farmers launched a statewide anticommunist propaganda campaign, developed files of information on union organizers, sought to deny relief or welfare funds to striking farmworkers, tried to secure anti-picketing laws (modeled after those of Los Angeles and San Francisco) in agricultural counties, and sought indictments of CAWIU leaders under criminal syndicalism laws. Seventeen CAWIU leaders, most of them CP members or leaders, were brought to trial early in 1935. The Associated Farmers paid generously to assist the prosecution, including nearly $3,000 in "salary" for Captain Hynes of the LA red squad. Eight of the defendants were convicted and sent to prison. After the CAWIU was dissolved the next year, the Associated Farmers kept a close vigil against other efforts to unionize farmworkers, helped to mobilize vigilantes (including American Legion members) against strikers in 1935, set loose a reign of terror (orchestrated by Sanborn) in the Salinas area in 1936 aimed at an AFL effort to organize packing-shed workers, and immediately took the offensive against the United Cannery, Agricultural, Packing, and Allied Workers of America (UCAPAWA) when it sent organizers into California's fields in 1937. The La Follette Committee, in 1937, charged the organization with "flagrant and violent infringement of civil liberties."[49]

The Better America Federation of Los Angeles appears frequently as a participant in anticommunist activities. Beyond an article by Edwin Layton in 1961, however, historians have paid little attention to this organization, and Layton was limited by his sources and dealt largely with the period before 1930.[50] The Margaret Ann Kerr Papers at the Hoover Institution, Stanford University, provide significant additional information. Founded in 1917 as the Commercial Federation of California and led by Harry M. Haldeman (grandfather of Nixon's chief of staff), the organization initially defined itself as a lobbying organization for California businesses. In 1920, this organization changed itself into the Better America Federation and redefined its purpose as "stimulating and assisting loyal American citizens to constructive action along political and educational lines" and "combating subversive elements inimical to free enterprise and the ideals of our country." Most early officers came from medium-sized California businesses, and several reports listed Harry Chandler of the Los Angeles *Times* as co-founder with Haldeman. Haldeman left under a cloud in the late 1920s, though his son, Harry F. Haldeman, became a director in the 1930s. The central figure in the BAF through most of its existence seems to have been Margaret Kerr, who was hired in 1920 and held the title Secretary and General Manager until the dissolution of the BAF in 1963. Kerr was actively involved with the Friday Morning Club, the Native Daughters of the Golden West, the American Sentinels, and American Women Inc., served as an officer of the LA Chamber of Commerce, worked closely with the American Legion, and claimed to have made the initial survey in 1929 that prompted the creation of the Fish Committee. On several occasions, she worked for months at a time for congressional committees, including the House Judiciary Committee in 1935 and HUAC in 1942.[51]

Surviving records reveal little about BAF finances in the 1930s. Layton notes that Southern California Edison contributed $3,000 annually during the 1920s. The Kerr Papers include a list of subscribers for 1951 comprising more than a hundred companies (some from outside California), thirteen individuals, the University of Southern California, and the State of California. A quarter of the receipts in 1951 came from the oil industry, and a fifth from aviation companies.[52]

By the 1930s, the BAF had an enormous collection of material—by 1950, they claimed "over 100 steel files." In the early 1930s, Van Deman began to use the BAF as a repository for his vast collection, and the BAF retained possession of those materials until 1963, when the BAF was dissolved. Among the Kerr papers are blank CP membership books, photostatic copies of internal CP membership documents, a few transcriptions of CP meetings, and lists of CP members, mostly from southern California, complete in most cases with party dues book numbers—suggesting that the BAF had extensive access to CP records in southern California. In the late 1930s, the BAF maintained working relations with the Portland INS office, the LA police department (whose chief wrote a letter to assist BAF fundraising), Knowles, and Van Deman, sometimes providing materials to the Portland INS that it could not obtain elsewhere.[53]

Some business figures seem to have participated in anticommunist efforts as individuals, outside of any identifiable institutional framework. Doyle, in 1937, claimed that A. C. Mattei was providing funds for both Sanborn and Keegan.[54] In an affidavit in 1950, James Stewart (alias John Ferguson) stated that Mattei had paid him some $5,000 ($68,000 in 2007 dollars) to cooperate with the INS and Portland Police.[55] A. C. "Bert" Mattei, president of Honolulu Consolidated Oil, was a pillar of the San Francisco business community and a friend and political confidante of both California Governor Frank Merriam and former president Herbert Hoover.[56] His company, Honolulu Consolidated Oil, was a part of the interlocking Hawaiian interests, including Matson Navigation, that centered on the families of the Big Five factoring companies. Like all companies with operations in with Hawaii, Mattei's business necessarily required ocean shipping.

Though Mattei may have provided funds for the Portland Police investigation of Bridges, Doyle indicated that his funding and that of Knowles did not come from Mattei. Doyle also claimed not to receive a salary from the state of Oregon, but he nonetheless supported both himself and, as he put it, "a lot of hungry witness [sic] scattered from Seattle to Los Angeles."[57] Reilly found that "Doyle was said at one time to have worked for an employers' association," and learned from Robert Wohlforth, executive secretary of the La Follette Committee, that "Sanborn, Doyle, Harper Knowles and [others] . . . are really undercover agents of the Industrial Association of San Francisco and the

Committee has evidence of their being on its payroll."[58] Unfortunately, the California files of the La Follette Committee in the National Archives contain only newspaper clippings. Both Harper Knowles and Stanley Doyle seem to have had working relationships with several companies. Doyle claimed that Pacific Bell provided equipment to tap telephones, and that NBC once provided false identification at his request.[59]

Organized Labor

In San Francisco, some influential leaders of AFL unions had long been wary of both radicals and longshoremen. Michael Casey, president of the San Francisco Teamsters, Local 85, and Paul Scharrenberg, prominent in both the Sailors Union of the Pacific and the state federation, came from unions that worked closely with longshoremen. If longshoremen were to close down the docks, Scharrenberg's Sailors and Casey's Teamsters could not work. If waterfront employers tried to break a strike, Sailors and Teamsters faced a dilemma—either support the strikers and endanger their own relations with employers, or ignore the strikers and destroy labor solidarity. Scharrenberg condemned longshore strikes in 1916 and 1919 as the work of "an active and organized radical minority" that he blamed for destroying the longshore union.[60] In the early 1920s, Scharrenberg's union, the Sailors' Union of the Pacific, tried to purge its own ranks of radicals, especially members of the IWW.[61] Casey expressed repeated concern about radicals and the damage they could do.[62] Shortly before the 1934 longshore strike, Casey complained that "most all the officers of the Longshoremen are radicals of the worst type" and predicted trouble for his local: "We will be in a tough spot, with our membership driving in on the docks, where nigger strikebreakers will be unloading and loading ships."[63] Eventually Casey became somewhat reconciled to Bridges's leadership, and there is no evidence that he participated in efforts to deport Bridges or in other anticommunist activities, though he did cooperate with the Industrial Association's efforts to end the 1934 longshore strike through federal intervention.[64]

Portland Teamsters' officials took pride that they had transferred union funds to the Portland red squad to fight Communism.[65] Jack W. Estabrook, secretary of the Portland Warehousemen's Union, a Teamsters local, specified: "I have given Captain Keegan money for the purpose of investigating un-American activities. . . . Harry Bridges was the man that was mentioned practically all the time." Estabrook made clear that he was simply the "messenger boy" for Al Rosser, head of the Portland Teamsters Joint Council, which sent weekly payments to the city's red squad over several months.

According to Estabrook: "They had been telling us right along that they were investigating Bridges and other people that were trying to get into our organization, and also there was a lot of talk about that time of some fellow that was supposed to be hired by the Communist Party, the way I understood it, to kill [Dave] Beck [Teamster leader in Seattle] and Rosser and myself and a few more of the fellows up north." At Keegan's request, the Teamsters also gave money to Doyle, helped to secure a job for one witness against Bridges, and gave money to another witness against Bridges.

Estabrook had no qualms about providing such assistance, so long as it was all properly documented for the union's records: "As far as I am concerned, in my organization, we are willing at all times, have been and always will be, to contribute money to any fund; and we are proud to do it and happy to do it, to investigate anybody that doesn't agree with our government." Estabrook's patriotic anticommunism coincided with protecting his union's jurisdiction over warehouse workers, a jurisdiction claimed by the ILWU: "If I thought there was an organization, such as the Communists or anyone else, trying to get into my organization . . . or if I thought another union was trying to take men and women away from us . . . I wouldn't stop at anything."[66]

The 1934 coast-wide maritime strike brought the revival of West Coast seafaring unions and a near-complete rout of their old leaders, including Scharrenberg. The new head of the SUP was Harry Lundeberg, a seafarer born in Norway and influenced by syndicalism and the Industrial Workers of the World (IWW). Chairman of the SUP strike committee in Seattle in 1934, Lundeberg emerged with a reputation for militancy and a wide following among northwestern seamen. In 1935, he won election as the SUP's secretary-treasurer—the executive officer. Fearing Lundeberg, leaders of the moribund International Seamen's Union (ISU) rescinded the SUP charter and the SUP became independent. Relations between the SUP and Bridges's Longshoremen soured over jurisdictional claims, the SUP's propensity for "quickie" job-actions (spontaneous localized strikes), and the handling of cargo from ships declared "unfair." Lundeberg also became highly critical of Communist attempts to influence the maritime unions. Lundeberg was initially attracted to the CIO, and John L. Lewis considered the SUP a likely CIO recruit, but when Lewis chartered the National Maritime Union and the ILWU, Lundeberg backed away, fearing Communist influence in the NMU and ILWU and fearing too that, if the SUP joined the CIO, it would lose its autonomy in the much larger NMU. In October 1938, the AFL chartered the Seafarers' International Union (SIU), with the SUP as its core and Lundeberg as its president.

At one point during the struggle between Bridges and Lundeberg, when both men's unions were part of the Maritime Federation of the Pacific (an am-bitious effort to create a central body for all Pacific Coast maritime unions), the *Voice of the Federation,* the newspaper of the federation, became a major object of struggle. In 1936, Barney Mayes became editor, and his appointment brought an outcry from the CP and its supporters, for Mayes, it turned out, was a Trotskyist, and he was soon pushed aside. Ralph Chaplin, a Wobbly famed as the author of "Solidarity Forever," became editor for a brief time in 1937. When he allied himself with the SUP and Lundeberg, he was also quickly forced out by the Bridges faction.[67] Later, Chaplin cooperated with the INS in its efforts to deport Bridges.[68] In 1937, anti-CP forces within the Maritime Federation formed the Progressive Union Committee, bringing together Trotskyists, old-time Wobblies, a few former CP members, and "pure and simple" AFL unionists, all under the leadership of Lundeberg.[69]

Lundeberg earned a reputation as an outspoken anticommunist who never backed away from a fight. SIU organizers included SUP veterans, conserva-tive former ISU members, left-wing anticommunists (including Trotskyists and Wobblies), and a few unsavory waterfront characters. An organized Trotskyist (Socialist Workers Party) faction developed within the SUP but never gained real power.[70] Lundeberg's anticommunism soon carried him to the Republican party rather than to the Left. The SUP newspaper, *West Coast Sailors,* which Lundeberg edited, was blunt and hard-hitting, unmerci-fully lambasting employers and labor opponents. Those not sharing his own staunch anticommunism received Lundeberg's special vitriol and were often labeled "commies."[71]

In 1937, Gerard Reilly, investigating the evidence against Bridges, reported to Secretary of Labor Frances Perkins that Aaron Sapiro had offered, on behalf of Lundeberg, to assist the prosecution of Bridges.[72] (Lundeberg, however, claimed in 1939, "I never was and never intend to become involved in the Bridges deportation mess—nor to my knowledge do any of the people I work with in the union field.")[73] An Oakland native and a lawyer, Sapiro became prominent for his legal work on behalf of agricultural marketing coopera-tives, and he gained national headlines by his lawsuit against Henry Ford over Ford's anti-Semitism. However, he had also been disbarred in both New York and Illinois for unprofessional behavior, and had been tried with Al Capone (and acquitted) on extortion charges in Chicago.[74] In 1937, Sapiro was counsel for the Sailors' Union of the Pacific. Reilly reported that Sapiro was acting on Lundeberg's directions, "although he said that Lundberg [sic] did not want to be brought into the case, as he feared that any deportation against Bridges may be regarded as working class prosecution, and hence a boomerang, unless Bridges was first discredited in the public mind." Reilly also suggested that "Sapiro's best source of information is Norma Perry." Perry was Lundeberg's secretary and had formerly been both Bridges's secretary and an active CP member.[75]

Other officials of the California state federation and of the AFL also worked with anticommunist groups to block organizing efforts by left-leaning unions. Paul Scharrenberg, secretary of the state federation in the early 1930s, and Edward Vandeleur, his successor, were especially prominent in these efforts. Ivan Cox had served as secretary of the San Francisco longshore local in the early 1930s and lost his office when the Bridges faction accused him of malfeasance. In 1938, he specified that he had been given a job by Vandeleur after he signed an elaborate deposition prepared by Doyle that sketched a fantastic Communist plot involving Bridges, CP leaders, Hollywood celebrities, and many others.[76] James Stewart claimed that he received $1,000 from Vandeleur, which the Portland Police used to finance the wiring of Bridges's hotel room in 1937.[77] Scharrenberg, in 1934, assured the Associated Farmers that the AFL had no interest in organizing farmworkers and promised to help to combat the radicals who wanted to do so. Vandeleur gave similar assurances in 1936, and discharged a militant, but not Communist, organizer whom the employers especially disliked. In 1937, facing an organizing drive by the newly chartered, and very red, UCAPAWA, Vandeleur fashioned a master contract by which the employers gave exclusive representation rights for shed and cannery workers to the state federation (and later the Teamsters).[78] Paul Eliel of the Industrial Association testified before the La Follette Committee that some union members, mostly "old-time unionists" or "disgruntled fellows," had volunteered information to the Industrial Association.[79]

Though most AFL leaders had long been anticommunist, the CIO was a different story. Clarence Hathaway, in Moscow in September 1936, reporting to the Anglo-American secretariat of the Comintern on behalf of the Political Bureau of the CPUSA, explained that members of the Political Bureau had discussed labor matters with John L. Lewis and Sidney Hillman, and that "they have shown a readiness to consult with us and make known their policy." In response to CP requests, Lewis had reinstated Communists and militants who had been expelled, and he hired between forty and fifty Communists as CIO organizers. "They have brought our people in everywhere," Hathaway concluded.[80] In April 1937, Earl Browder, in Moscow, assured the Anglo-American secretariat, "With the CIO and its leadership we have the closest cooperative relations."[81] Soon after, in 1937, Lewis chartered the Pacific Coast longshoremen as the ILWU and appointed Harry Bridges as western regional director. In August 1937, "T. Ryan" (Eugene Dennis) reported that "for the first time in the history of our Party we are beginning to establish our

34 ROBERT W. CHERNY

'legal citizenship' in the labor movement on a wide scale."[82] And in December 1938, Roy Hudson told the National Committee that "the other progressive forces who constitute the CIO . . . more and more accept us as part of the CIO and labor movement, and . . . are willing to collaborate with us."[83] The CP seemed almost to feel that they had a pledge that the CIO would not discriminate against party members. But, within the CIO, anticommunists moved to reduce the influence of Communists soon after the American CP leaders made their optimistic reports in Moscow.

As various CIO unions and organizing committees put down roots on the West Coast, disputes began to develop around the role of CP members. In July 1938, William Dalrymple, Field Director for the Steel Workers Organizing Committee (SWOC) in California, wrote to Philip Murray to recommend that the charters be lifted from SWOC lodges in San Francisco and Oakland. "I charge here and now," Dalrymple seethed, "that party membership means more than does the UNION to these DESTRUCTIVE ELEMENTS. . . . I dont [sic] want anything that Russia has."[84] Dalrymple followed up a few days later with a letter to Lewis describing a CP member in Oakland as "determined to either ruin or rule the SWOC, in the State of California."[85] Later that month, Herman Stuyvelaar, secretary of the San Francisco CIO Council, criticized SWOC, and Dalrymple fumed: "I have swallowed all of this rot coming from a bunch of destructionists who put party above organization, and I am not going to stand for it."[86]

In early August 1938, the *San Francisco Examiner* published an "exclusive" on "a move to crush Communist party influences that have developed within the CIO on the Pacific Coast." According to the *Examiner,* the revolt was being organized by leaders of "five militant CIO unions in southern California"—the United Rubber Workers, United Automobile Workers, International Ladies Garments Workers, United Shoe Workers, and SWOC. The *Los Angeles Examiner,* the next day, added that efforts were underway to oust Bridges as regional director. On August 8, the five southern California union leaders, claiming to represent one-fifth of all CIO members on the West Coast, announced they were withdrawing from local and state Industrial Union Councils (IUCs) and blasted Bridges for running a "Communist dictatorship" and controlling IUCs through "paper locals." Bridges publicly dismissed them as "a few conspiring officials," and Lewis sent John Brophy to quash the rebellion as the national presidents of the Shoe Workers and Rubber Workers repudiated the actions of their locals.[87] In the meantime, Paul Scharrenberg wrote to William Green that "we have quietly, but I think effectively encouraged the revolt among C.I.O. unions in Southern California."[88]

CIO officials in Oregon and Washington conducted a mini-purge in the period from 1939 to 1941. In September 1939, Richard Francis, president of the Washington State Industrial Union Council and secretary-treasurer of United Mine Workers (UMWA) District 10, reported to John L. Lewis that the state IUC meeting was "in constant turmoil and disruption by the factions of the International Longshoremen's and Warehousemen's Union, various delegates of City Industrial Union Councils, and a faction led by Harold J. Pritchett, President of the International Woodworkers of America." These groups, Francis charged, "are not out to build the CIO organized labor movement in this State but to further the interests of the Communist Party."[89]

With the Molotov-Ribbentrop Pact in mid-1939, the CP and its supporters within the CIO unions demanded American neutrality. During 1940, they also condemned Roosevelt as a warmonger and pulled out all stops first to deny him renomination and then to deny him endorsement by CIO affiliates. The April 6, 1940, edition of *People's World* (the CP's West Coast newspaper) was a special entitled "The Yanks Are Not Coming," and it was dedicated entirely to keeping the United States out of the "Imperialist War." In California and elsewhere, CP vitriol extended to liberal Democrats who continued to support Roosevelt.[90] Bridges followed the lead of both John L. Lewis and the CP to strongly oppose the reelection of Franklin D. Roosevelt and to condemn "the attempted betrayals and sellouts of the New Deal."[91]

By late 1939, shortly after the Molotov-Ribbentrop Pact and the invasion of Poland, a small purge was underway within the CIO. In October 1939, Lewis reduced Bridges's authority as CIO Regional Director by limiting his territory to California and adding separate directors for Oregon and Washington. Lewis made clear, according to the *New York Times*, that the purpose was to reduce Communist influence, but said nothing specific about Bridges.[92] The two new West Coast regional directors, however, were Francis, in Washington, and Dalrymple, in Oregon—both of whom, Lewis knew, were strongly anticommunist.

Hugh Lovin has provided a good treatment of some aspects of the CIO purge of the Left in the Pacific Northwest in 1939–41, but he completed his study before some important CIO internal correspondence became available to researchers. With regard to the International Woodworkers of America (IWA), Lovin describes how Lewis persuaded the IWA's two factions, one on the Left, led by the international president, Harold Pritchett, and the other including outspoken anticommunists, to accept an agreement that included the appointment of Adolph Germer as IWA Director of Organization. Known as an effective organizer and an anti-CP leftist, Germer, as Lovin notes, "insisted upon total control over all organizers assigned to IWA organizational work and, upon gaining unobstructed command, required the organizers to abandon their 'side interests' such as Yanks-Are-Not-Coming committees." The IWA's Left tried to abrogate the agreement and replace Germer in late 1940, but Lewis's successor, Philip Murray first investigated, then insisted that the agreement be maintained and respected. In October 1941, after the Left within the IWA did an abrupt about-face on the issue of American neutrality following Germany's invasion of the Soviet Union, the opposition took control at the IWA national convention and voted in an anti-CP slate of officers.[93]

In March 1940, Francis reported that local unions in Washington were considering withdrawing from Communist-dominated local IUCs and that he was doing his best to keep them in. At the same time, he urged "that we cannot much longer delay cleaning house of these subversive elements."[94] By August 1940, Francis was moving toward a showdown over so-called paper locals—those that claimed a large membership, paid per caps only on a few, and sought exemptions to vote the full membership they claimed. Claiming that paper locals gave the CP an edge in the state IUC, Francis vowed "to clean up this Communist racket."[95] When he lacked the votes, he precipitated a crisis by dismissing the entire council as illegally constituted.[96] In preparation for a subsequent meeting in March 1941, Francis used UMWA funds to assist some locals "who are in favor of the correct CIO program and not that of the Communist Party" to have all their delegates present.[97] At the meeting, left-wing delegates bolted rather than vote on an anticommunist resolution. The anticommunist resolution then carried and the meeting elected state IUC officers who, according to CIO National Representative H. C. Fremming, "are all known to be 'white'"—that is, anticommunist.[98]

Dalrymple had been conducting similar operations in Oregon. In August 1940, he issued a broadside to all CIO local unions in Oregon denouncing the CP for interfering in the CIO. "The CIO is NOT a Communist Party," he proclaimed, "It is a labor organization—AN AMERICAN LABOR ORGA-NIZATION—and we are here and now serving notice on the officers and members of the Communist Party that they must refrain from interfering with our affairs."[99] His effort garnered support from a number of CIO locals across the state.[100]

Francis's and Dalrymple's efforts seem to have inspired other CIO unions in the Northwest. During the summer of 1940, the Seattle Newspaper Guild voted out the CP sympathizers in its leadership and passed an anticommunist resolution. A few other northwestern CIO locals took similar actions.[101] In October 1940, Ken Hunter, SWOC organizer in San Francisco, wrote to Allen Haywood that "Mr. Bridges would be better able to serve himself and unionism if he were replaced as CIO Director in California." Hunter continued, "As matters now stand the CIO in California is identified as a synonym for Mr. Bridges." Fred H. Hart, another SWOC representative, seconded Hunter's request, noting that, "with Mr. Bridges removed, we will move ahead faster and will be able to live up to the principal [sic] of our beloved organization much better."[102]

Dalrymple's work in Oregon brought a strong response by California CIO leaders, notably Louis Goldblatt of the ILWU and state IUC. Dalrymple responded by characterizing Goldblatt's statement as "slimy, scurrilous, lying."[103] When Bridges joined in the criticism, Dalrymple announced that he no longer had any interest in defending Bridges (then raising funds to fight deportation)—that he was "not going to carry the torch for anybody or any set of red card members."[104] By February 1942, Bridges and his followers wanted to purge both Dalrymple and Francis,[105] but any further purges seem to have been set aside for the duration of the war.

Attacks on Roosevelt by the CP or CP sympathizers brought rebukes even within the ILWU. When Bridges spoke out against Roosevelt at his own San Francisco local, he received both applause and boos,[106] and one reporter described Bridges's attack on Roosevelt as "away out of line with the overwhelmingly pro-Roosevelt sentiment among his men."[107] In the last membership meeting of the San Francisco local before the election, after a sequence of motions, amendments, and a substitute, the members voted to endorse Roosevelt.[108] The Seattle ILWU local went much further, and demanded that Bridges resign as ILWU president.[109] Not even Harry Bridges could persuade rank-and-file longshoremen to oppose Roosevelt.

The influence of the Molotov-Ribbentrop Pact in sharpening anticommunism within West Coast CIO unions and the purge within the CIO in the Northwest have not yet found their historian. Most historians have looked only at the CIO purge of the Cold War period, and have not recognized that the acceptance of the CP within the CIO was always tenuous at best, dependent upon particular circumstances in particular unions. Almost from the beginning, some West Coast CIO leaders chafed at the role of CP members or sympathizers in their organizations and councils, and the events of 1939–40 seem to have focused that anticommunism in particular ways.

Conclusions and Implications

Most of the highly visible anticommunist groups, notably the American Legion and the business and civic groups, justified their opposition to Communism through patriotism, but often added that they blamed Communists for the disruption of business through strikes and other union activities. Such groups typically looked to the state—local, state, and federal—to take a leading role against the Reds, both through the government's police powers and through legal actions, especially criminal syndicalism prosecutions and deportations, but even vagrancy if no other charge were convenient. Many of these groups focused on creating elaborate files on alleged radicals, and they often planted or recruited undercover informants—ranging from private detectives to disgruntled union members to high-ranking members of the CP itself—to provide reports for their voluminous files. Those files, in turn, were used in a number of arenas, from the INS to HUAC, to urge legal action against individuals. Some of these groups also operated outside the bounds of legitimate state authority to organize vigilante groups to terrorize strikers and radicals.

Most AFL union leaders, some CIO leaders, and most non-CP leftists also opposed Communism, but most of them took a different attitude toward the role of the state. Unionists, like nearly all other anticommunists, typically spoke a language of patriotism but also expressed concerns about the role of Communists within unions. Anticommunist labor leaders typically charged that CP members had divided loyalties, and that their loyalty to the CP was greater than their loyalty to their union. They described CP members as disrupting unions, and as exhibiting a "rule or ruin" attitude. Most AFL and many CIO leaders responded similarly, by working within their organizations to drive CP members from elected offices and to remove individual CP members from appointed offices. Occasionally they urged national officers to intervene with locals that they considered hopeless of redeeming themselves. In these efforts, they often added to their patriotic language a set of arguments justifying their position as being in defense of "one-hundred percent unionism," a variation on the old "pure and simple unionism" that had little place for resolutions on world peace or racial justice—Lundeberg sometimes referred to the Left as "the resolutionists." Non-CP leftists—socialists, Trotskyists, old Wobblies—sometimes found themselves in marriages of convenience with conservative unionists. Though some anticommunist union leaders and some non-CP leftists provided assistance to governmental anticommunist efforts, including legal prosecutions, more seem to have looked upon the struggle as one within their unions.

The FBI is curiously absent from most sources of information on West Coast anticommunist activities in the 1930s. In the mid-1920s, Attorney General Harlan F. Stone had ordered Hoover to stop routine surveillance of radicals unless there were indications of a violation of the law. Thereafter, the FBI surveillance of radical groups seems to have been minimal on the

West Coast.[110] In the case of Harry Bridges, the FBI did not open a file on him until ordered to do so by the attorney general in 1940.[111] The FBI began to develop close surveillance of the motion picture industry only in 1942.[112] Nor is there much indication prior to World War II of other direct or extensive FBI involvement in other anti-CP efforts on the Pacific Coast. The San Francisco field office opened a file on the CP only in 1936, and the San Diego and Seattle field offices did not do so until 1941. Only in Portland and Los Angeles did the FBI field offices have files on the CP before the mid-1930s. In all the West Coast field offices, there seems to have been relatively little anticommunist activity until 1941, when all five began more actively and systematically to collect information on the CP and all five initiated new files on the CP.[113]

All of this preceded World War II and the Cold War. Maurice Isserman has suggested that World War II brought a lull in some anti-CP efforts, and there is evidence for that in the Pacific Coast states. Bridges was welcomed into tripartite (labor, industry, government) groups to increase wartime productivity on the docks even as the federal government simultaneously tried to deport him. The American Legion gave up its research program and limited its anticommunism to resolutions and lobbying. The Los Angeles and Portland red squads disappeared from sight after the late 1930s. The Industrial Association was gone by 1940, and, indeed, by 1950 shipping company executives were testifying on behalf of Bridges as he underwent yet another deportation trial. Neither the BAF nor the Associated Farmers seems to have played as prominent a role in opposing the CP and organized labor after World War II as they had before.

Several of these changes derive from initiatives undertaken by the FBI. In 1936, Hoover persuaded President Roosevelt that a civilian agency—the FBI—was better suited for surveillance of civilian radicals than was MID. Continuing MID efforts, however, brought further presidential involvement and, in 1940, MID, the Office of Naval Intelligence, and the FBI divided up areas of responsibility in such a way as to give the FBI responsibility for all counterintelligence within the United States and to relieve the army and navy of that responsibility except for their own internal operations. This Delimitation Agreement brought an offer from the American Legion to work, henceforth, with the FBI. By 1940, Van Deman had also developed an official relationship with the FBI.[114]

Also in 1940, Hoover initiated three FBI outreach programs, one aimed at the American Legion. The Legion had been highly supportive of the Dies Committee from its inception, but Hoover was generally critical of that committee's tactics and accomplishments. He developed the FBI–American Legion Contact Program in order both to put an end to the Legion's independent anti-subversion programs and to wean the Legion away from the Dies Committee (and probably the MID), and he was largely successful in ending the Legion's programs. Though internal FBI evaluations constantly questioned the value of the American Legion contact program for national security, such issues were secondary to the program's political success. One internal FBI memorandum in 1952 explained that the purpose of the program was "to prevent that organization [the American Legion] from conducting investigations in the security field." The program was continued because otherwise "the legion might again attempt to embark on its [own] investigative activities."[115] Hoover developed a similar outreach program to local police departments, a program called the FBI Law Enforcement Officers Mobilization Plan for National Defense.[116] Whether or not this program was intended to produce the decline of local red squads, the two events coincide in time. Finally, in 1940, the INS was moved from the Labor Department to the Justice Department, and FBI agents began to replace INS inspectors in at least some cases involving aliens—most obviously Harry Bridges.

Thus, the FBI's efforts to limit activities by the American Legion, MID, and local red squads were accompanied by an increase in activities by the FBI itself. By World War II, the scattered, sometimes competing, sometimes amateurish anticommunist efforts of the American Legion, red squads, the National Guard, MID, and INS during the 1930s had all largely given way to the programs of the FBI—which were typically more centralized, better funded, and often more professional.

Notes

1. Michael J. Heale, *American Anti-Communism: Combating the Enemy Within, 1830–1970* (Baltimore: Johns Hopkins University Press, 1990); Richard Gid Powers, *Not Without Honor: The History of American Anticommunism* (New York: Free Press, 1995); Ellen Schrecker, *Many Are the Crimes: McCarthyism in America* (Boston: Little, Brown and Company, 1998).

2. For an overview of Bridges's career, see Charles P. Larrowe, *Harry Bridges: The Rise and Fall of Radical Labor in the U.S.* (New York: Lawrence Hill and Co., 1972); for his various trials, see Stanley I. Kutler, chapter 5 of *The American Inquisition: Justice and Injustice in the Cold War* (New York: Hill and Wang, 1982). Bridges always denied that he had ever been a member of the Communist Party. However, materials in the papers of the Communist Party of the United States (fond 515) and the papers of the Anglo-American Secretariat (fond 495), Russian State Archive of Social and Political History (hereinafter RGASPI), indicate that Bridges was elected to the Central Committee of the CPUSA in 1936 and suggest that he may have held party leadership at the district level in the mid-1930s. Those materials also suggest, however, that Bridges did not consider himself bound

by decisions in party meetings. A full discussion appears in my paper, "Harry Bridges and the Communist Party: New Evidence, Old Questions; Old Evidence, New Questions" (Organization of American Historians annual meeting, 1998).

3. *San Francisco Examiner,* Oct. 7, 10, Nov. 13, 1919; Fred W. Smith, comp., *History: American Legion, Department of California, 1919–1928* (Paso Robles, Calif.: Fred J. Smith and Sons, 1928), 8, 11, 48.

4. William Pencak, *For God & Country: The American Legion, 1919–1941* (Boston: Northeastern University Press, 1989), 223–24.

5. Ibid., 238.

6. Knowles to Robert M. Thurston, May 12, 1936, Document 454, and Knowles to Cecile S. Hambleton, Apr. 5, 1938, Document 208, Harry Bridges Case Files, Norman Leonard Papers, Labor Archives and Research Center, San Francisco State University, hereafter Leonard Papers. (Some of Knowles's committee's files found their way into the hands of Bridges's attorneys through the assistance of a pro-union janitor in the Veterans' Building, where the committee had its office; see Harry Bridges Case Files, Norman Leonard Papers, Labor Archives and Research Center, San Francisco State University.) Regarding Knowles, see also Official Report of Proceedings before the Immigration and Naturalization Service of the Department of Labor, Docket no. 55973/217, *In the Matter of Harry Bridges—Deportation Hearing,* vol. 19: 3133–3311. Other records involving Knowles and his committee were given to the Meiklejohn Library by an anonymous donor, and subsequently transferred to the Labor Archives and Research Center, San Francisco State University, where they are catalogued as the Surveillance Papers.

7. Oregon Chapter, National Lawyers Guild, *Report of the Civil Liberties Committee* (1938, no other information on publication), 6.

8. Pencak, *For God & Country,* 231.

9. Knowles to Thurston, May 12, 1936, Document 454, Leonard Papers.

10. H. L. Chaillaux to Knowles, Apr. 20, 1936, Document 11, Leonard Papers.

11. Knowles testimony, Bridges Deportation Hearing, 1939, vol. 19: 3133–3311. There is no way of evaluating Knowles's claims; my requests to secure access to national American Legion records in Indianapolis were denied, and there are only a few files that remain in the San Francisco American Legion office, none of which permit an evaluation of Knowles's description of his committee's operations.

12. Knowles testimony, Bridges Deportation Hearing, 1939, vol. 19, 3133–3311. See also, Hynes to Frank G. Martin, May 1, 1936, Document 2031, Knowles to C. S. Morrill, Aug. 1, 1936, Document 18; Morrill to Knowles, Aug. 6, 1936, Document 18a; H. M. Niles to Knowles, July 15, 1937, Document 38a; William D. Browne to Knowles, July 25, 1938, Document 58, all in Leonard Papers.

13. See, e.g., Knowles to D. W. MacCormack, Apr. 15, 1936, copy in box 6, Van Deman Collection, Records of the U.S. Senate Internal Security Subcommittee of the Senate Judiciary Committee, 1951–75, RG 46, National Archives.

14. The file on Doyle's commission is missing from the Oregon State Archives. See the file on Special Agents' Commissions, carton 39, Governor Record Group, RGG4, Accession 57-98/1, file D-G, Oregon State Archives. Correspondence there suggests that the file may have been sent to the La Follette Committee, but the National Archives files for that committee's work in California includes only newspaper clippings.

15. Gary Murrell, *Iron Pants: Oregon's Anti-New Deal Governor, Charles Henry Martin* (Pullman: Washington State University Press, 2000), 148–49, 172.

16. Murrell, 156, 171.

17. The case was appealed to the U.S. Supreme Court, which reversed De Jonge's conviction; see *De Jonge v. State of Oregon*, 299 U.S. 353 (1937).

18. Knowles testimony, Bridges deportation hearing, vol. 19–20, 3175–e to 3474. For the 40 et 8, see Pencak, *For God & Country*, 96. The California Department, in a history published in the late 1920s, called the 40 et 8 the Legion's "fun organization" and "the playground" of the Legion, but also acknowledged that "the 40 et 8er, as an individual, is singled out for the work he has done for the Legion"; see Smith, *History*, 63, 68.

19. For Doyle, see Knowles testimony, Bridges deportation hearing, vol. 19–20, 3175–e to 3474; and series 1, box 3, Surveillance Papers, Labor Archives. For indication that Doyle worked without pay, see Doyle to Wallace Wharton, executive secretary to the governor, Jan. 24, 1938, in ibid., folder 5. There is no mention of Doyle anywhere in the Wallace Wharton files in the Oregon State Archives; see RGG4, 55-6, Carton 1. For an example of a letter from Doyle on the letterhead of the Radical Research Committee of the California American Legion, see Doyle to Joseph M. Carson, July 17, 1937, file c-6405274, pt. 1, box 6, Harry Bridges INS file, National Archives Pacific Region, San Bruno, California.

20. Gerard Reilly to the Secretary, Oct. 13, 1937, folder "Reilly, Gerard D., Oct. 1–Oct. 13, 1937," box 38, Frances Perkins Papers, Columbia University.

21. Doyle testimony, Bridges Deportation Hearing, 1939, vol. 44, 7622–73, and vol. 45, 7674–7724; see also the account of the conviction of Doyle for battery in Oct. 1939, in San Francisco *American Civil Liberties Union News*, Oct. 1939, 1.

22. Hynes to Frank G. Martin, May 1, 1936, Document 2031, Leonard Papers.

23. Frank Donner, *Protectors of Privilege: Red Squads and Police Repression in Urban America* (Berkeley: University of California Press, 1990), 59–63, 250.

24. Lawyers Guild, *Report*, esp. 5–10, 44–46. There are no files from the red squad in the Portland Archives and Records Center, though there is a file of the mimeographed "Weekly Report of Communist Activities" prepared by it. Ralph O'Hara, the director of the Portland Police Museum, told me on August 17, 1989, that the red squad had never had a separate official existence, that it had initially had an office in American Legion headquarters before its office in the Railway Exchange Building, that the Legion may have paid its office rent, and that any records were probably either in the possession of the Legion or were taken by Odale when he retired.

25. Lawyers Guild, *Report*, esp. 49–50; H. M. Niles to Knowles, July 15, 1937, Document 38a; William D. Browne to Knowles, July 25, 1938, Document 58, Leonard Papers; Gerard Reilly to the Secretary, Oct. 13, 1937, folder "Reilly, Gerard D., Oct. 1–Oct. 13, 1937," box 38, Frances Perkins Papers, Columbia University.

26. The National Archives has a card file index to MID surveillance reports on radical activities in the San Francisco Bay Area. Though the index is extensive, the actual files to which it refers were removed from the National Archives by the army in the early 1950s and never returned. Efforts to locate them have been unsuccessful. Until and unless the army returns the files that it removed from the National Archives, we may not know the full extent of MID surveillance efforts.

27. Joan M. Jensen, *Army Intelligence in America, 1775–1980* (New Haven, Conn.: Yale

University Press, 1991), 178, 194, 197–200; Roy Talbert Jr., *Negative Intelligence: The Army and the American Left, 1917–1941* (Jackson: University Press of Mississippi, 1991), 6–27, 234; Marc B. Powe, "A Sketch of a Man and His Times," in *The Final Memoranda: Major General Ralph H. Van Deman, USA Ret., 1865–1952, Father of U.S. Military Intelligence,* ed. Ralph E. Weber (Wilmington, Del.: Scholarly Resources, Inc., 1988), ix–xii, esp. ix–xii.

28. Jensen, *Army Intelligence in America,* 202–4.

29. Statement of Ivan Francis Cox, made on the 31st Day of August 1938, in Room 612, 216 Pine Street, in the Presence of Richard Gladstein and Ernest Besig, Document 2023, Harry Bridges Case Files, in Leonard Papers.

30. Major John H. Wilson to AC of S, G-2, War Department, Washington, D.C., July 6, 1940, MID 101-4-1607/2; Major John S. Griffith to Western District Supervisor, July 31, 1940, MID 183-2-223/87; Major G. R. Carpenter to Asst. Chief of Staff, G-2, War Department, Washington, D.C., Sept. 9, 1940, MID 10110-2666/293 (part 16); all in RG 165, Records of the War Department, General and Special Staffs, National Archives.

31. Jensen, *Army Intelligence in America,* 171, 205; Talbert, *Negative Intelligence,* 234; Powe, "A Sketch of a Man and His Times," xix, xxii.

32. Talbert, *Negative Intelligence,* 234, 249; Van Deman Collection, Records of the U.S. Senate Internal Security Subcommittee of the Senate Judiciary Committee, 1951–75, RG 46, National Archives. As of 1971, the part not given to the Senate Internal Security Subcommittee was kept at the San Diego Title Trust and Insurance Company, under the control of an officer of the California National Guard's intelligence unit.

33. Affidavit of Henry R. Sanborn, *California v. Arthur James Kent,* Doc. 2110, Harry Bridges Case Files, Leonard Papers. Sanborn's paper, *American Citizen,* was published at San Rafael between 1935 and 1937; copies can be found at the University of California, Berkeley, and at Stanford University.

34. Carbon copy of letter from Doyle, Oct. 17, 1937, series 1, box 3, folder 5, Surveillance Papers.

35. Gray Brechin, *Imperial San Francisco: Urban Power, Earthly Ruin* (Berkeley: University of California Press, 1999), 300–302; Smith, *History,* 11.

36. Barrows to Provost Deutsch, Aug. 1, 1934, marked confidential, Barrows to Sanborn, Dec. 22, 1936, David Prescott Barrows Collection, Bancroft Library.

37. Barrows to General Seth E. Howard, Adjutant General of the California National Guard, July 12, 1934 (one of two letters to Howard on that date), box 6, Barrows Collection.

38. Ibid.

39. Barrows testimony, Bridges deportation hearing, 1939, vol. 42, 7329–7540.

40. Milner testimony, Bridges deportation hearing, 1939, vol. 2, 152–342, vol. 3, 343–404.

41. William Issel and Robert W. Cherny, *San Francisco, 1865–1932: Politics, Power, and Urban Development* (Berkeley: University of California Press, 1986), 96–98; Eric Levy, "The 1926 San Francisco Carpenters' Strike" (master's thesis, San Francisco State University, 1986).

42. Issel and Cherny, *San Francisco,* 95–98; U.S. Congress, Senate, Committee on Education and Labor, *Hearings,* 76th Congress, 3d Session (hereinafter, La Follette Committee hearings, 76th Congress), part 60: 22111–43.

43. Information on donations to the Citizens' Committee of 1921 comes from the "Industrial Association" file, carton 10, Labor Council Records; for later financial information, see La Follette Committee hearings, 76th Congress, part 60: 22125–35. The Industrial Association destroyed most of its records in anticipation of a subpoena from the La Follette Committee; see La Follette Committee hearings, 76th Congress, part 60: 21957–62, 22138–40.

44. La Follette Committee hearings, part 60, 76th Congress, 21967–68.

45. San Francisco *Labor Relations*, Sept. 1938, 1–4.

46. Carey McWilliams, *Factories in the Field* (1936, 1939; Santa Barbara: Peregrine Publishers, Inc., 1971), chap. 14. See also the contrasting view in Stephen Schwartz, *From West to East: California and the Making of the American Mind* (New York: Free Press, 1998), 309–10.

47. U.S. Congress, Senate, 77th Congress, 2d Session, *Report of the Committee on Education and Labor*, part 4, 692–94; Cletus E. Daniel, *Bitter Harvest: A History of California Farmworkers, 1870–1941* (Ithaca, N.Y.: Cornell University Press, 1981), 251–52.

48. Knowles testimony, Bridges deportation hearing, 1939, 3219.

49. This summary is based largely on U.S. Congress, Senate, 77th Congress, 2d Session, *Report of the Committee on Education and Labor*, part 4, 694–95; and U.S. Congress, Senate, 78th Congress, 1st Session, *Report of the Committee on Education and Labor*, part 5, 737–66; Daniel, *Bitter Harvest*, 252–57, 278–81; Dick Meister and Anne Loftis, *A Long Time Coming: The Struggle to Unionize America's Farm Workers* (New York: Macmillan, 1977), 35–36, 42–43, 46, 77–79; Kevin Starr, *Endangered Dreams: The Great Depression in California* (New York: Oxford University Press, 1996), 82, 162–94. For the events in Salinas, see also the contrasting view in Schwartz, *From West to East*, 272–73.

50. Edwin Layton, "The Better America Federation: A Case Study of Superpatriotism," *Pacific Historical Review* 30 (1961): 137–48. Layton's major source was the collection of BAF publications collected by John R. Haynes, and Layton's treatment ends in the late 1920s. For brief treatments by others, see Carey McWilliams, *Southern California Country: An Island on the Land* (New York: Duell, Sloan and Pearce, 1946), 291; Jules Tygiel, *The Great Los Angeles Swindle: Oil, Stocks, and Scandal during the Roaring Twenties* (New York: Oxford University Press, 1994), 183–84; Starr, *Endangered Dreams*, 155–56. The BAF's *Confidential Bulletin* described itself as "a bi-weekly digest of subversive activities," but copies are rare; the only listing in World Cat is for the State Historical Society of Wisconsin. I have not examined those holdings, nor located others.

51. Margaret Ann Kerr Papers, Hoover Institution on War, Peace, and Revolution, Stanford University, boxes 1 and 2, esp. the photostat of her registration form for the American Legion's Counter-Subversion Area Conference, 1949, box 2; Layton, "Better America Federation," 146.

52. Layton, "Better America Federation," 139; "Subscribers 1951," Kerr Papers, box 1.

53. Kerr Papers, boxes 1 and 2; John R. Heldring to Van Deman, May 27, 1938; V. W. Tomlinson to Margaret A. Kerr, May 27, 1938; V. W. Tomlinson to R. P. Bonham, May 27, 1938; Kerr to Heldring, May 24, 1938; all in file 1600-499908, pt. 1, Los Angeles, California, box 9, Harry Bridges INS file, National Archives Pacific Region, San Bruno, California; Kerr to Thomas B. Shoemaker, Oct. 19, 1939, file C-6405274, pt. 2, box 6, Bridges INS file.

54. Carbon copy of report from Doyle, Nov. 24, 1937, folder 5, box 3, series 1, Surveillance Papers.

55. Affidavit of James Stewart [James Ferguson], June 6, 1950, Bancroft Library, University of California, Berkeley; an abridged version was printed in the San Francisco *Dispatcher,* July 21, 1950, 4–7. Elinor Kahn Kamath told me of her trip to Britain to secure the affidavit in an interview on Apr. 8, 1987.

56. For Mattei's ties to Hoover, see, e.g., Hoover to Mattei, Sept. 27, 1936, and Mattei to "Chief," Sept. 30, 1936, folder 3315 (2), box 431, Herbert Hoover Papers, Post-Presidential Individual, Herbert Hoover Presidential Library; for his ties to Merriam, see Mattei to Merriam, Feb. 27, 1934, and Merriam to Mattei, Mar. 6, 1934, boxes 18, 47, Frank F. Merriam Papers, Bancroft Library.

57. Carbon copy of report from Doyle, Sept. 26, 1937; carbon copy of letter from Doyle, Oct. 17, 1937, folder 5, box 3, series 1, both in Surveillance Papers.

58. Reilly to Houghteling, Oct. 6, 1937, folder "Reilly, Gerard D., Oct. 1–Oct. 13, 1937," box 38, Perkins Papers, Columbia. See also Reilly to the Secretary, Oct. 13, 1937, ibid., and Reilly to the Secretary, Dec. 20, 1938, folder "Reilly, Gerard D., Dec. 6–20, 1938," box 38, Perkins Papers, Columbia.

59. Copy of Stanley M. Doyle to John P. Boyd, Oct. 21, 1949, attached to Stanley M. Doyle to Westbrook Pegler, Oct. 21, 1949, folder Unions, Longshoremen, box 91, Westbrook Pegler Papers, Herbert Hoover Presidential Library.

60. Paul Scharrenberg, "The San Francisco Longshore," Longshoremen file, carton 2, Scharrenberg Correspondence, Bancroft Library.

61. Hyman Weintraub, *Andrew Furuseth: Emancipator of Seamen* (Berkeley: University of California Press, 1959), 160–63; Paul S. Taylor, *The Sailors' Union of the Pacific* (New York: Ronald Press Company, 1923), 142–46; Stephen Schwartz, *Brotherhood of the Sea: A History of the Sailors' Union of the Pacific, 1885–1985* (New Brunswick: Transaction Books for the Sailors' Union of the Pacific, 1986), 59; San Francisco *Labor Clarion,* Sept. 16, 1912, 3, 6; Nov. 11, 1921, 14; Dec. 16, 1921, 16; Mar. 3, 1922, 6.

62. See, e.g., Casey to Daniel J. Tobin, May 15, 1916, folder 5, box 13, series 1; Casey to Hughes, Sept. 27, 1919, folder 2, box 14, series 1; Casey to Hughes, telegram, Oct. 2, 1919, folder 2, box 14, series 1, International Brotherhood of Teamsters Papers, State Historical Society of Wisconsin. John O'Connell, closely associated with Casey in the leadership of Local 85 and secretary of the Labor Council, considered the 1919 longshore strike to have been precipitated by "irresponsibles," "radicals," and "adventurers," who made "arbitrary and unreasonable" demands"; see "Transforming a Company Union," *American Federationist* 37 (1930): 61.

63. Casey to D. J. Tobin, Mar. 27, 1934, folder 6, box 16, series 1, Teamsters Papers, State Historical Society of Wisconsin. Tobin reproduced that portion of Casey's letter and sent it to Louis Howe, Roosevelt's chief secretary, commending Casey's analysis to the White House, and Howe forwarded it to Secretary of Labor Frances Perkins; Howe to Perkins, Apr. 7, with Tobin to Howe, Apr. 2, attachment, filed under White House Correspondence for Mar. and Apr., 1934, box 105, General Records of the Department of Labor, Office of the Secretary, Secretary Frances Perkins, General Subject Files, 1933–41, RG 174, National Archives, Washington (hereinafter, Perkins Papers, National Archives).

64. Paul Eliel, *The Waterfront and General Strikes, San Francisco, 1934* (San Francisco: Hooper Printing Company, 1934), 86–87.

65. Stewart affidavit, Bancroft Library; in an interview on July 27, 1987, Dave Beck denied that any Teamsters funds of which he was aware had been used for such a purpose. There

is nothing in the correspondence between bay area Teamsters officials and the national office related to this; see International Brotherhood of Teamsters Papers, State Historical Society of Wisconsin. Nor is there anything in the correspondence of William Green; see American Federation of Labor Papers, State Historical Society of Wisconsin.

66. Estabrook testimony, Bridges deportation hearing, 1939, vol. 42, 7441–7549. Doyle also referred to "certain demands made by the Portland Police on officials of the Brotherhood of Teamsters"; Doyle to Wharton, Oct. 1, 1937, Surveillance Papers. Stewart also claimed that he received $500 from Al Rosser, head of the Teamsters in Portland; Stewart affidavit, Bancroft Library.

67. The struggle over the *Voice of the Federation* has been described by Bruce Nelson, *Workers on the Waterfront: Seamen, Longshoremen, and Unionism in the 1930s* (Urbana: University of Illinois Press, 1988), 217; Ottilie Markholt, *Maritime Solidarity: Pacific Coast Unionism, 1929–1938* (Tacoma: Pacific Coast Maritime History Committee, 1998), 303–7, 350–51; and Schwartz, *From West to East*, 267, 277.

68. INS Report of Investigation, Apr. 2, 1954, file 0901/12228 [Chicago, Ill., 1935–55], box 10, Harry Bridges INS files.

69. Markholt, *Maritime Solidarity*, 325.

70. Richard Kirk, "A Letter to American Trotskyists," pamphlet, reprinted form *Revolutionary Age*, vol. 3, no. 4. Kirk notes that, within the SUP, the Trotskyists' "fanatical anti-Stalinism sounded more like *anticommunism*, and had distinctly reactionary connotations" (22). Kirk also notes that "most of the Syndicalists, with whom we were allied and whom we supported uncritically, were racists, including Lundeberg" (26–27).

71. For Lundeberg, see my entry on him in the *American National Biography*; Stephen Schwartz, *Brotherhood of the Sea: A History of the Sailors' Union of the Pacific, 1885–1985* (New Brunswick: Transaction Books for the Sailors' Union of the Pacific, 1986), chap. 8; Frank J. Taylor, "Roughneck Boss of the Sailors' Union," *Saturday Evening Post* (Apr. 18, 1953); Curtis Fields Jr., "A Labor Boss Signs On—and Off," *Washington Post* (Sept. 7, 1947); and *New York Times*, Jan. 29, 1957; *San Francisco Chronicle*, Jan. 29, 1957. For Lundeberg's attacks on "commies," see nearly any issue of *West Coast Sailors* in the late 1940s or early 1950s.

72. Reilly to the Secretary, Oct. 13, 1937, folder "Reilly, Gerard D., Oct. 1–13, 1937," box 38, Perkins Papers, Columbia.

73. *West Coast Sailors*, July 13, 1939.

74. "Sapiro, Aaron," in *San Francisco Chronicle* clipping file; *San Francisco Chronicle*, May 8, 1937.

75. Reilly to the Secretary, Oct. 13, 1937, folder "Reilly, Gerard D., Oct. 1–13, 1937," box 38, Perkins Papers, Columbia. For the CP version of Norma Perry's move from Bridges to Lundeberg, see Estolv Ethan Ward, *The Gentle Dynamiter: A Biography of Tom Mooney* (Palo Alto, Calif.: Ramparts Press, 1983), 235–37.

76. Statement of Ivan Francis Cox, Made on the 31st day of Aug. 1938, in Room 612, 216 Pine Street, in the Presence of Richard Gladstein and Ernest Besig, Document 2023, Harry Bridges Case Files, Leonard Papers.

77. Stewart affidavit, Bancroft Library.

78. Daniel, *Bitter Harvest*, 273–81.

79. La Follette Committee hearings, part 60, 76th Congress, 21968.

80. Meeting of the Secretariat of Comrade Marty, Sept. 15, 1936, marked Confidential, file 16, delo 14, fond 495, Papers of the Anglo-American Secretariat, RGASPI. The Anglo-American Secretariat was the intermediary body between Communist Parties in English-speaking countries and the executive committee of the Comintern.

81. Transcript of meeting of the Anglo-American Secretariat on the American Question, Apr. 4, 1937 (participants: Browder, Foster, Ford, Trachtenberg), marked confidential, delo 521, opis 20, fond 495, RGASPI.

82. MEMORANDUM ON THE JUNE PLENUM OF THE CPUSA AND SOME ASPECTS OF THE LATEST POLITICAL DEVELOPMENTS IN AMERICA AND THE WORK OF THE COMMUNIST PARTY, marked confidential, with handwritten notations "T. Ryan" and "Aug. 9-1937," delo 515, opis 20, fond 495, RGASPI.

83. Minutes, plenary session of the CPUSA National Committee, Dec. 3–5, 1938, delo 94: opis 14, fond 495, RGASPI.

84. William Dalrymple to Phillip Murray, July 3, 1938, part 1, series 1, reel 13, CIO Files of John L. Lewis (microfilm).

85. Dalrymple to John L. Lewis, July 7, 1938, part 1, series 1, reel 13, Lewis CIO Files.

86. Dalrymple to Van Bittner, July 25, 1938, part 1, series 1, reel 13, Lewis CIO Files.

87. *San Francisco Examiner*, Aug. 4, 1938, 1; Los Angeles *Examiner*, Aug. 5, 1938, 11; Los Angeles *Examiner*, Aug. 8, 1938, 1; *San Francisco Chronicle*, Aug. 9, 1938; Los Angeles *Examiner*, Aug. 13, 1938, 5.

88. Scharrenberg to Green, Aug. 19, 1938, folder 1, box 34, series 11C, AFL Papers, State Historical Society of Wisconsin.

89. Richard Francis to John L. Lewis, Sept. 10, 1939, part 2, reel 14, Lewis CIO Files.

90. See, e.g., San Francisco *People's World*, Apr. 6, 1940; Apr. 11, 1940, 1; Apr. 15, 1940, 1; Apr. 17, 1940, 2; Apr. 19, 1940, 1; Apr. 23, 1940, 4; Apr. 24, 1940, 3; Apr. 29, 1940, 1; May 2, 1940, 2; May 9, 1940, 1.

91. See, e.g., *Longshoremen's Bulletin C.I.O.* [ILWU Local 1-10], no. 52, Sept. 24, 1940.

92. *New York Times,* Oct. 17, 1939.

93. Hugh T. Lovin, "The CIO and That 'Damnable Bickering' in the Pacific Northwest 1937–1941," *Pacific Historian* 23 (1979): 66–79, esp. 72.

94. Francis to Kathryn Lewis, Mar. 22, 1940, part 2, reel 14, Lewis CIO Files.

95. Francis to Lewis, Aug. 21, 1940, part 2, reel 14, Lewis CIO Files.

96. A. E. Harding to Lewis, Sept. 26, 1940, part 2, reel 14, Lewis CIO Files

97. Francis to Lewis, Feb. 8, 1941, part 2, reel 14, Lewis CIO Files.

98. Robert C. Cummings, "J. C. Lewis Defends Action of Convention," *Seattle Post-Intelligencer,* Mar. 4, 1941; H. C. Fremming to John L. Lewis, Mar. 4, 1941, part 2, reel 14, Lewis CIO Files.

99. Dalrymple to officers and members of all affiliated CIO local unions in the state of Oregon, Aug. 22, 1940, part 2, reel 13, Lewis CIO Files.

100. Dalrymple to Allan Haywood, Oct. 10, 1940, with attachment, A. L. Gregg to Dalrymple, Sept. 7, 1940, part 2, reel 13, Lewis CIO Files.

101. *Business Week,* Oct. 12, 1940, 47–48.

102. Ken Hunter to Allen S. Haywood, Fred J. Hart to Haywood, both Oct. 11, 1940, part 1, series 2, reel 22, Lewis CIO Files.

103. Dalrymple to Goldblatt, Apr. 26, 1941, part 2, reel 13, Lewis CIO Files.

104. Dalrymple to Philip Murray, Apr. 26, 1941, part 2, reel 13, Lewis CIO Files.

105. Dalrymple to Haywood, Feb. 27, 1942, part 2, reel 13, Lewis CIO Files.

106. *Longshoremen's Bulletin C.I.O.* [ILWU Local 1-10], no. 52, Sept. 24, 1940.

107. *San Francisco Chronicle,* Jan. 25, 1940; Bridges to Rosco Craycraft, Aug. 17, 1940, Bridges correspondence, ILWU library; John Brophy Oral History, Columbia University, 853–54; unidentified clipping, dateline Nov. 1, 1940 (AP), file: Harry Bridges, Material about, 1939–43, ILWU History Collection, ILWU Library; *San Francisco Chronicle,* Nov. 5, 1940; *Business Week,* Nov. 16, 1940, 34.

108. *Longshoremen's Bulletin C.I.O.* [ILWU Local 1-10], no. 2, Oct. 29, 1940.

109. *San Francisco Chronicle,* Nov. 5, 1940.

110. Jensen, *Army Surveillance in America,* 200.

111. John Edgar Hoover, Memorandum for the Immigration and Naturalization Service, Aug. 27, 1940, file C-6405274-D [2/2], box 2, Harry Bridges INS file, National Archives Pacific Region, San Bruno, California.

112. J. Edgar Hoover to Special Agent in Charge, Los Angeles, Calif., Sept. 6, 1942, vol. 1, FBI file number 100-138754,Communist Infiltration—Motion Picture Industry (COMPIC).

113. One of the FBI's staff for Freedom of Information and Privacy Act requests provided me with this information during a telephone call on Aug. 23, 2000; the San Francisco field office accumulated 102 volumes (each volume equivalent to about two hundred pages) on the CP between 1936 and 1959, and volume 1 covers 1936–40; the Los Angeles field office developed 112 volumes during 1921–59, with volume 1 covering 1921–25 and volume 2 covering 1925–41; the Seattle field office had 101 volumes for 1941–59, and volume 1 begins in 1941; and, in the Portland field office (for which I did not get the total number of volumes), volume 1 covers 1924–41.

114. Jensen, *Army Surveillance in America,* 211, 213–14, 264; Talbert, *Negative Intelligence,* 234, 256–59. A subsequent Delimitation Agreement in early 1942 put further limits on the army and navy and extended the exclusive jurisdiction of the FBI.

115. For an overview of the three new programs in 1940, see Richard Gid Powers, *Secrecy and Power: The Life of J. Edgar Hoover* (New York: Free Press, 1987), 256; for Hoover's attitude toward Dies, see 231, 281. For more information on the American Legion's involvement in the program, see Pencak, *For God and Country,* 312–14. For internal FBI memoranda evaluating the program and outlining its political purposes, see A. H. Belmont to D. M. Ladd, Oct. 2, 1952; and Belmont to Ladd, July 31, 1950; both in FBI American Legion Contact Information [microfilm edition of the FBI file] (Wilmington, Del.: Scholarly Resources, 1984).

116. Powers, *Secrecy and Power,* 256.

2. Labor's Community-Based Campaigns for Economic and Environmental Planning, and Cold War Politics: The UE's St. Louis District, 1941–48

ROSEMARY FEURER

Too long our American forests, rivers, minerals have been
exploited for private profit. Too long our soils have been neglected
and abused. . . . Our life becomes constantly more urban and more
mechanical. . . . The speed-up has spread throughout our entire
civilization and is no longer to be found only in our industrial
plants. . . . [We must choose] long-range goals with care. It means
we must be very much on guard against taking over into our social
planning the same standards of value which created our difficulties.
In the field of resource development and conservation, it means
an emphasis on the so-called renewable or living resources;
forests, soil, waters, wildlife, recreation, and scenery. In regional
planning, it means the dispersion of industries and cities and
the encouragement of our smaller communities. This is not to
disparage our engineering works . . . But it is to say that men do
not live by consumers' goods alone.[1]

—CIO Committee on Regional Development and Conservation

This prescient declaration comes from a late 1940s CIO pamphlet in support of a campaign for the Missouri Valley Authority, a long-forgotten program for economic, environmental, and social planning in the postwar era.
The campaign developed from the Left labor activists in District Eight of
the United Electrical Workers (UE), who coalesced with farmers and other
community-based organizations to present a visionary idea for economic
planning. These activists put forward a vision of the future that represented
a prefigurative environmentalism that derived from the practice of grassroots
community-labor coalitions. Left activists had been a critical part of the vi-

sion and practice of community-based mobilizations that developed from the 1930s, but Cold War politics vanquished the impetus for the campaign and program. This campaign expresses what was lost in the transition to Cold War labor politics.

District Eight's campaign reflected a deepening understanding of the need for community-based efforts that challenged management's right to direct the economy. The CIO movement had raised hopes among left labor activists that workers would be a force for change not only on the shop floor but also in the larger society. Bill Sentner, the District's president and an open Communist Party member, sought to direct workers toward these broad goals. Sentner developed a community-based focus to organizing that derived from his politics, his experiences in the early 1930s in the unemployed movement, and his dealings with the periphery of the electrical industry.[2] Despite the constraints of the wartime "politics of sacrifice" that diminished the potential for class politics, District Eight sought to expand a role for workers in determining the shape of the political economy in the war and postwar period.[3]

The Wartime Political Economy and District Eight's Community-Based Planning

By 1941, defense mobilization had been converted into what one scholar calls "a branch of corporate America."[4] Large corporate interests guided defense production, resulting in a private planning system and concentration of defense contracts. Two-thirds of all wartime defense contracts were awarded to one hundred of the largest corporations. Major employers such as General Electric and Westinghouse were given "cost-plus profit" contracts. Those corporations reaped the most benefits of huge modern government-built plants and could subcontract to whomever they wished. In the metal industries, the Defense Plant Corporation "underwrote virtually the entire machine tool production in the country."[5]

In exchange for labor's cooperation in the war effort, national CIO leaders sought an equal rather than subordinate role for labor in defense mobilization. They proposed the Industry Council Plan (ICP), commonly referred to as the Murray Plan, after its titular author, Phillip Murray, the new CIO president. The Murray Plan called for organizing Industry Councils, composed of representatives of government, labor, and management to plan production. These councils would coordinate the nation's wartime production needs and labor supply, have the power to allocate natural resources without corporate interference, to distribute orders for production, and to direct manpower in a rational and humane way. They would ensure that human issues such as labor supply, unemployment levels, or housing availability were considered in allocating contracts, and that small business would receive a share of the contracts. Criticizing the slowness of conversion, Murray Plan advocates suggested that planning that included labor could be more efficient and cost-effective for the nation than corporate-dominated mobilization. Historian Nelson Lichtenstein argued that the Murray Plan was an attempt to "direct the collectivist tendencies of a publicly-financed war mobilization in more progressive, and pro-labor directions."[6] The most publicized attempt to implement a Murray Plan was Walter Reuther's "500 planes a day" proposal for the automobile industry. Reuther, director of the UAW's General Motors department, recommended a tripartite board that would direct the conversion of Detroit auto factories into airplane production. The plan was relentlessly opposed by the industry and rejected by the Roosevelt administration.[7]

Even as some CIO officials grew increasingly frustrated with their subordinate position in wartime agencies, they were unable or unwilling to mobilize workers in support of the Murray Plan. Divided in their position respecting war preparations, CIO officials did little more to promote the plan during 1940 and 1941 than make appeals to sympathetic liberals in higher government echelons, though the CIO's own representative in the government war mobilization apparatus, Sidney Hillman, refused to advocate the Murray Plan. Hillman also excluded the UE from the minimal efforts to gain leverage within the wartime agencies because the organization was "tinged with red" and did not endorse the war effort, influenced as it was by the CP's foreign policy agenda. Yet even after the UE "squared itself" with the CIO officialdom by endorsing the war effort, it still remained ostracized from the inner circles that were planning the CIO's approach to gaining leverage in government.[8]

Yet it is not accurate to conclude, as has a leading scholar of the CIO, that the "Murray Plan and the analogous proposals by Reuther for the auto industry in particular, represented the only serious attempt to institutionalize labor participation and some meaningful measure of control over the operation of the economy."[9] The Left in UE District Eight used the Murray Plan as a platform, but developed a different approach to promote labor's inclusion in wartime planning. Sentner viewed mobilization for the war as an opportunity that might allow U.S. labor to be directed in the more politicized direction of the British Labor Party.[10] He hoped that wartime exigencies that disrupted the existing political economy of the cities might provide an opportunity for unions to help define labor market conditions and production issues.

Corporate control of planning, along with restrictions on production of consumer goods, threatened not only to entrench corporate control and con- centration, but devastate communities that won no major defense contracts as well.[11] As war orders rose among the largest companies in the United States, civilian production was curtailed in consumer products sectors. Workers in District Eight's region, employed mostly by small manufacturers, were especially threatened by the pending curtailment of production by summer of 1941. This was especially the case in Evansville, Indiana, where District Eight was conducting an organizing drive.[12]

When layoffs began in mid-August 1941, Evansville's UE organizer James Payne, originally from St. Louis's Johnston-Tinfoil Plant (and who had joined the Communist Party), led a core group of union supporters in a campaign they called "Prevent Evansville from Becoming a Ghost Town."[13] District Eight asked union and civic and business leaders to request the establish- ment of a federal program that would "be administered through joint and bona fide union-management-government cooperation" at the local level. It would ensure that before reductions in the production of consumer goods were instituted, government must give enough primary war contracts and subcontracts to "take up the slack" of unemployment caused in cities such as Evansville. It also proposed that laid-off workers would get "first claim on jobs with other companies in the community," while excessive overtime would be eliminated until unemployment was reduced.[14]

The UE organizing committee got Evansville's Mayor Dress to convene a midwestern meeting of community labor and industry representatives to help save Evansville's jobs in the refrigeration industry. Evansville UE workers collected thousands of petitions supporting the idea. They found enthusiastic response both from workers and merchants and reported this to congressional representatives.[15]

Mayor Dress organized a huge Midwest conference on priorities in Chi- cago, composed of "city officials, labor leaders, managers of industry and other civic leaders." Fifteen hundred delegates representing labor, manage- ment, and civic leaders from hundreds of cities in eleven midwestern states came together, beginning September 12.[16] Only eighty labor delegates were there, and fifty-four of them were from thirty different UE plants. The others were mainly UAW workers from Indiana, Michigan, Illinois, and Wisconsin. But as Sentner reported, it soon was apparent that others were "depending on the labor people to help steer the meeting" and "give it tone and direction." The major AFL representative at the conference was Al Couch of Iowa, an ally of the UE during the Maytag strike of 1938. James Carey presented the working program drawn up by the UE. "With the practical proof of labor's ability vividly before them," Sentner later told a District Eight gathering, "the delegates freely accorded to labor its right to participate."[17]

The results of the conference were an impressive demonstration for what Sentner called District Eight's "grassroots" approach to gaining a voice for labor in the wartime economy. The conference program endorsed "equal participation of management and labor in determining a proper and adequate retraining program and allocation of primary and sub-contracts." It endorsed the aim of keeping maximum local employment and urged "all possible steps be taken to avoid serious dislocations in non-defense industries."[18] Sentner was one of two labor representatives on a committee of seven elected to draw up a more comprehensive program of action and steer the program. That committee then elected Sentner to serve as one of the two Washington representatives of the Chicago "confab," as it came to be known. Sentner soon found himself with an office in OPM, a position of equality with the industry representative. District representative Robert Logsdon remarked that the industry representative was "considerably in awe of Sentner."[19]

This certainly must have been a satisfying rejoinder to Sidney Hillman's exclusion of the UE and the Left. Moreover, Sentner later told District delegates to an unemployment conference that "while the top echelon in Washington had impugned the Murray Plan as unworkable, derided it as socialistic, or simply dismissed it without consideration, the Chicago conference participants seemed to have no problem in gaining [the support of] small business and those left outside the contract allocations crowd." Certainly, as Sentner recognized, this was in part because small business was using labor to "suck up to FDR" to get war contracts. Nevertheless, labor's role opened avenues for inclusion in the community and the national planning, a goal consistent with curtailing business control of the economy and the labor market.[20]

By early October, District Eight leaders were convinced that the Evansville campaign could be a model for the CIO. Already UE organizers were using it "with great and promising results" in Newton, Iowa, and in Dayton, Ohio. In Mansfield, Ohio, Dick Niebur, an organizer originally from the Maytag (Newton, Iowa) plant, organized a priorities conference that, as Sentner put it, "secured his niche in the Holy Trinity of Mansfield Patron Saints for having come to the assistance of their city in its darkest hours."[21]

As a result of the Chicago conference and "the hell we've raised in Evansville and Iowa," Evansville and Newton were named as "test towns" for "an experiment for community-based solving of unemployment and dislocations caused by [war] priorities." These Priorities Unemployment Areas attempted to coordinate the transition from consumer goods production to defense contracts on the community level. Sentner's proposals for "worker training on the job" were eventually incorporated into the experiment.[22] Under these plans, companies kept workers employed and provided training to upgrade workers' skills in the transition to war work, in part through the use of unemployment insurance funds.[23]

Sentner asserted that community-based campaigns for the Murray Plan were "the solution to the national question of labor unity and its results on National Defense efforts."[24] He proposed calling regional conferences of organizers to develop strategies on unemployment. In testimony before the Tolan Committee hearings on defense priorities, Sentner called for the organization of community-based labor-industry-government councils.[25] Logsdon argued that Evansville, Newton, and Dayton showed they could be the means "to a nationwide dealing with the problems."[26]

But prospects of using the UE's model in the CIO grew dimmer over the fall of 1941. Besides hostility from Hillman, even the strongest Murray Plan supporters in the top echelons of the CIO seemed to have given up. Lyle Dowling of the UE national office wrote glumly to Sentner in late October that it seemed that there would only be a pro-forma push for the plan. James Carey, secretary of the CIO, and Allen Haywood, organizational director of the CIO, "made it clear" that a CIO conference on the priorities issue "would not be permitted to take any action" to push for the plan: Carey and Haywood, "the great little Murray-Plan boys" were "losing interest in the CIO industry council plan. They now represent it as a desirable, but utopian thing." Besides, Dowling concluded, "so far as being a labor organization with the old punch, the CIO is losing it."[27]

Pearl Harbor also dealt a serious blow to the potential for District Eight's strategy. The sudden expansion of wartime contracts and subcontracting after Pearl Harbor alleviated some of the dire predictions of decline of smaller industrial cities. Already by January of 1942, Sentner reported that Evansville's Mayor Dress wanted "to junk the Emergency Conference." Workers' interest diminished because of a flush job market. Sentner retained an office in the new War Production Board operated by Donald Nelson, and this helped the UE in gaining a few appointments to government posts, since Hillman, who "still has us on the s . . . list," refused appointments to wartime boards over which he had control.[28] Sentner continued to complain of the "dullards" appointed to government agencies by Hillman and others in the CIO, people he felt were "used as a barrier against labor's full participation directly in every branch of the WPB." Yet contesting this would mean "taking on" the top CIO apparatus, which could be disastrous.[29]

Throughout the war "bottlenecks" from uncoordinated or self-interested resource allocation resulted in layoffs and uncertainty that slowed UE organizing drives. For instance, in September 1942, just as the St. Louis Small

Arms Plant's employment levels rose past twenty thousand, three thousand workers were laid off because the War Production Board decided to divert more copper to "other munitions channels." Sentner telegrammed Nelson that the bottlenecks were due to the WPB's control by business: "If there isn't copper enough to operate this huge plant at 100% of capacity then the empty buildings and thousands of laid off workers are monuments to the dead wood, the misfits and those who think in terms of competitive business habits and business as usual who have been infesting the ranks of the so-called dollar-a-year-men."[30]

Such rhetorical flourishes underscored the absence of a concerted CIO campaign to assert its power in wartime. With no CIO program for implementing the Murray Plan and in the context of the no-strike pledge, District Eight's left leadership searched for ways to keep alive the challenge to management power and to uphold their pledge to maintain shop floor rights for workers. In late 1941, Sentner wrote bitterly: "I personally believe that the forces around Roosevelt and to some degree Roosevelt himself, are consciously going into the direction of the French ruling class who embraced Fascism rather than turn France over to the people of France."[31]

The CIO's inability to more aggressively shape the national context of labor relations caused District Eight's left to reconsider its role strategically. The need for political education of their membership worried Logsdon, who noted workers who recognized the great gulf that separated their interests from management on the shop floor needed to be better educated about the political context that meant so much for labor's ability to make gains. The easing of red-baiting and the steady dues receipts raised the possibility that the Left could influence the CIO on a local and national scale. But the job of politicizing workers could only be undertaken after organizing them, and that was the main task that the District undertook in 1942–43.[32]

During the war period, District Eight leaders articulated a critique of the wartime political economy and its portents for the postwar economy, a critique that increasingly made racial and gender issues more central to its organizational identity and agenda. Logsdon and Sentner suggested that the "failure by industry to make full use of women and Negroes in the war effort" was an indication of not only the ineptitude, but also of the undemocratic spirit that guided mobilization. They called for plans to "integrate women and Negroes into plants for employment—don't squeeze them into certain jobs."[33]

Postwar Community-Based Planning

As the war wound down, tension over layoffs and the shape of the postwar economy and labor market were foremost in workers' minds. District Eight's wartime workers, especially those at the St. Louis Small Arms Plant, expe-rienced a continual threat of layoffs after 1943. Logsdon complained that wartime planning that excluded labor's concerns over maldistribution of war contracts, failed to consider available manpower, and was unwilling to make full use of women and African Americans in the war effort signified not only a bad approach for the war, but held troubling implications for the postwar world.[34]

After 1943, District Eight representatives continually sought to raise other possibilities for the postwar economy and to place workers' concerns at the center of discussions of postwar issues. They succeeded in getting St. Louis Mayor Kaufman to establish a city-based postwar planning committee to include representatives of the CIO and AFL, suggesting that this kind of committee was the "first step in a nationwide application of the principles of community cooperation" for a new postwar world. They organized CIO shop steward councils to discuss the postwar economy as a base for future mobilization.[35] In 1944, the District hosted five "Community Leadership for Reconversion and Postwar Employment" conferences on postwar planning, held in Moline, Illinois, Mt. Carmel, Illinois, Newton, Iowa, Evansville, In-diana, and St. Louis, Missouri. Worker representatives were elected on the basis of two men and two women from each factory department, with an emphasis on "activating the rank and file" to mobilize for the issue. District leaders invited government, church, civic organizations, women's and civil rights groups to the conferences. In addition, they tried to garner business support for (or at least diffuse their opposition to) postwar planning.[36]

At these conferences, Sentner suggested that a postwar world of "unem-ployment and chaos, human misery and despair can and will be avoided" only by community-based planning that was part of national planning of postwar conversion and full employment. Sentner called for planning for an economy that would create more interesting jobs and suggested the need for reduction of working hours to thirty per week after the war.[37] It would be a life guided not by consumerism but "more time for study, development of family life, more time for recreation, physical development of American men and women." He noted that labor must "fight a much tougher fight than [ever] before—fight to join with industry and whoever else, engineers, chemists, physicians, economists, etc. of this country for [the] benefits of [an] expand-ing economy on [the] basis of [the] increased efficiency and productivity of this country." Sentner continued to emphasize that labor needed to propose a world where work could be more interesting and skilled, and where women and blacks were not forced back to service and low-paying jobs.[38]

The conference indicated little support from business for an expansion of labor rights. In a preview of future battle lines, George Smith of the St. Louis Chamber of Commerce interrupted the discussion at one point to remind workers that the point of the "free enterprise system" was to make a profit, not to create jobs. Frank Meehan, representative of the putatively liberal business group, the Committee for Economic Development (CED), noted that the CED's definition of "full employment" did not mean everyone should be entitled to a job: "We believe in a free enterprise system and probably some men and women want to retire, some are working now will want to retire, especially women."[39]

William McClelland, president of Union Electric, St. Louis's leading utility, expressed similar views in an August 1944 CED report. He argued against the need for the CIO-backed national legislation that would have set up an overall planning authority for the postwar era. He saw "no need to legislate" to meet future postwar needs. Sentner, charging that the CED "considers St. Louis in a vacuum" instead of "in relation to the state and nation as a whole," sent a letter protesting these views: "The CED does not appear to be concerned that working mothers and wives of wounded veterans and young women will want to be assured jobs in the postwar period. Nor do they stop to consider the special problem involved in advancing democratic opportunities for Negroes to retain their newfound jobs. Negro citizens will not willingly leave their industrial jobs where they are earning seventy cents to a dollar an hour, to take menial jobs and domestic service at 40 and 50 cents." Sentner called instead for support for nurseries to aid working women in the postwar.[40]

The District proposed specific alternatives that would build connections between workers' concern for jobs and their broader concerns about the postwar world. By mid-1944 District Eight became involved in a campaign to concretely promote postwar planning on a community and regional basis. The campaign for a Missouri Valley Authority (MVA), which sought to establish an agency empowered to plan for and develop the nine-state area along the Missouri River Valley, arose in the midst of the dramatic flood of 1944 and in the context of the debate about postwar labor concerns.

The Missouri Valley Authority Campaign

The concept of an MVA owed much to the popularity of the Tennessee Valley Authority (TVA). By the end of World War II, the TVA enjoyed growing public support, not only because it brought electrical power to the Tennessee Valley and solved navigation problems, but also, according to David Lilienthal, head of the TVA, because it was an example of "Democracy on the

March," the title of his acclaimed 1944 book. Lilienthal promoted the idea of the TVA as a decentralized regional planning approach involving the people who lived in the valley. Later TVA developments and subsequent analyses raised questions about the legitimacy of Lilienthal's claims. Nevertheless, in the 1930s and 1940s, the "TVA idea" continued to be associated with the popular notion of democratically exercised power.[41]

Bills to establish other river-based authorities were submitted throughout the 1930s. In 1937 President Roosevelt, in a message to Congress, endorsed the establishment of seven other authorities. The National Resources Planning Board (NRPB) researched and advocated additional authorities. Such proposals lacked grassroots support, however, and as the New Deal's political fortunes began to deteriorate after 1938, the prospects for the NRPB's proposals eroded. In 1943, as war mobilization eclipsed New Deal planning, Congress dismantled the NRPB. Despite the TVA's popularity, prospects for other planning authorities seemed dismal indeed.[42]

Then, in the spring and summer of 1943 and 1944, record flood waters came sweeping relentlessly through the lands bordering the lower Missouri River, especially from Sioux City down to the confluence with the Mississippi twelve miles above St. Louis. The annual run off of melting snow in the Upper Valley states of Montana and North and South Dakota, combined with record rains in 1944, caused damage totaling more than $110 million dollars. From Kansas City to St. Louis, levees built by towns and farmers' districts succumbed to the muddy waters that brought sand and farmland dirt from as far away as Montana. The flood inundated farmland and forced the evacuation of St. Charles, Missouri, leaving thousands homeless. In St. Louis, the flood contributed to the rising Mississippi crest, as Coast Guardsmen, engineers, and civilians struggled to hold the St. Louis levee intact with thousands of sandbags.[43]

The devastation provided an opening for the Army Corps of Engineers (ACE) to expand its role in Missouri River development. The ACE drew much of its support from private interests that supported improved navigation, and its main concern was deepening the Missouri River channel. Congress gave it a mandate for flood control in the 1930s.[44] Seizing the opportunity provided by the floods to expand its control over the Missouri River, ACE representative Colonel Lewis Pick, "a shrewd, ambitious bureaucrat-soldier," submitted to Congress a brief, hastily drawn twelve-page proposal requesting $661 million dollars for flood control, promising an end to floods through a series of dams and reservoirs on the Missouri and its tributaries, municipal and agricultural levees, and irrigation projects for dry Upper Valley states such as Montana and North and South Dakota. Historian Donald Worster concludes that the plan "proposed the complete dismantling of the natural river." ACE submitted separate legislation to deepen the lower Missouri's river channel from six feet to nine feet. Because deepening the channel would require the release of additional waters from the Upper Valley, especially in dry spells, to sustain it, the ACE's twin proposals made its claims to balance flood control, navigation interests, and Upper Valley irrigation interests dubious. Nevertheless, the U.S. House flood control committee passed the Pick Plan in March 1944.

The Bureau of Reclamation (BR), an agency created in 1902 and supported by irrigation interests in the Upper Valley, opposed the Pick Plan, as it threatened control over irrigation in the Upper Missouri Valley. Charging that the ACE was using the flood control plan to mask its navigation interests, the BR proposed its own "Sloan" plan, which promised to protect irrigation on the Upper Missouri Valley, incorporating some of the flood control features of the Pick Plan but also seeking to construct eight to nine new reservoirs in the Upper Valley in order to furnish irrigation to dry land and hydroelectric power to rural residents at an estimated cost of $1.3 billion. Sloan's plan excluded navigation provisions, thereby defining the major conflict over water use between the two agencies, and between the upper and lower river interests. "One agency wanted to spread the river over fields," concludes Donald Worster, "while the other insisted on letting it flow in deep steady currents in order to float commercial traffic."[45]

As the Pick Plan rolled its way toward congressional approval, the *St. Louis Post Dispatch,* in a widely disseminated editorial, called for a campaign for the creation of a Missouri Valley Authority in order to implement a unified plan for flood control and Missouri River development. An MVA, the *Post-Dispatch* argued, would replace the patchwork approach and bureaucratic haggling between the federal agencies (and the private interests that backed these agencies) over river issues. The *St. Louis Star-Times* also quickly backed the idea and called for a "genuine grassroots movement" up and down the valley for an MVA.[46]

District Eight's leadership and the shop delegate conferences endorsed a campaign for the MVA as a way to promote postwar planning for full employment, as well as to place labor at the center of the "public interest" in the postwar period. The District Executive Board committed one staff research job, arguing that an MVA would mean local and regional planning for "control, in the public interest, of the flow of waters and the erosion of land."[47]

District Eight's campaign began by outlining its comprehensive plan for the river in a pamphlet, *One River, One Plan.* In keeping with the District's stress on postwar planning for jobs, the pamphlet predicted that five hundred thousand jobs would be created within five years from projects such as dam building, irrigation, electrification, soil conservation, and reforestation. In many respects the pamphlet agreed with the dominant view expressed by the ACE about control of the natural river for development or economic growth purposes. It stressed that electrification of rural areas (only 30 percent of all farms in the Missouri River basin had been electrified) through cheap public power would create a new market for electrical products in the region. Irrigation would become available to small farms, thus opening up opportunities that had mainly benefited agribusiness previously. Through postwar planning for the Missouri River Valley basin, "its abundant resources ought to make for significant peace-time expansion." The pamphlet also stressed that public involvement in utilization of water resources would bring overdue consideration of the "devastating effect of exploitation." Moreover, inclusion of soil and water conservation as well as reforestation were aspects left out of the Pick and Sloan plans.[48]

District Eight used *One River, One Plan* to launch a community-based grassroots campaign for the MVA, a campaign it sought to keep out of the hands of the technocrats who had dominated the NRPB. The District sought to promote a structure that would create "one broad committee that can pull in as many farm, labor, industry and civic people" in order to increase the effectiveness of the campaign, as well as to establish that the set-up would necessitate continued "mass action of the citizens in the Valley," even after the bill passed.[49]

District Eight staff soon found the "right" liberal engineer to help them formulate the bill. Walter Packard had been director of the New Deal's Resettlement Administration in five southwest states. Donald Worster has written that Packard represented a "community"-oriented type of New Dealer, committed to planning and a "cooperative commonwealth" in the United States. Packard was one of the most vocal critics of agribusiness interests and private power within the Reclamation Bureau, where he had worked on the Central Valley Project, an irrigation and power project in central California. His charge that the Central Valley Project had helped to entrench large growers had earned him the rage of western corporate and agricultural interests. He wrote to Sentner, "Our experience with the Central Valley Project in California amply demonstrates the need for vigilance in protecting the rights of labor and the consumer, both in the setting of policy and in administration." He warned: "It is not enough to secure an authority. It is equally important to see that the authority represents sound public policy. This can be accomplished only by a determined drive by labor, farmers, consumers and liberal elements, generally. These groups should be brought together in a concerted campaign in the public interest."[50]

The response to *One River, One Plan* was encouraging, "exceed[ing] UE's wildest dreams," both among its own members and workers in other unions, including the rival AFL unions. The issue "caught on like no pork chops issue ever did," Sentner recounted, not only because of workers' concerns for postwar security but "also because there's hardly a union man or woman [in the District] that isn't tied either through family or tradition to the rural areas and the woes they've suffered through Old Man River." Indeed, many electrical workers and especially many defense workers had only recently migrated from the rural areas of Missouri and maintained ties to their rural past. James Davis, an autoworker and secretary of the Missouri CIO, who quickly embraced the MVA proposal, was "raised within three-quarters of a mile of the Missouri River." He lamented that he had "seen the place I was raised on covered with about a foot of sand that probably came from Montana."

Thus it was not only the promise of jobs that attracted workers and unions to the proposal. After all, the Army Engineers' plan also promised development and jobs. In Iowa, AFL leaders had forged cordial relations with CIO unions, ties that eluded the rival federations in other states. These AFL leaders helped District Eight representatives gain the cooperation of building trades unions for the proposal. The Army Engineers had traditionally bid out contracts for their projects, often resulting in undercutting the union-established prevailing wage for construction work. The MVA, its supporters argued, would follow the TVA's practice of hiring workers directly and paying the union's prevailing wages.[51]

Farmers and farm groups also responded enthusiastically to the MVA campaign and took a central role in it. District Eight increased contact with farmers across the nine states, especially with two important farm organizations, the Missouri Farmers Association and the National Farmers Union.[52] These organizations bitterly opposed the Army Corps of Engineers, based on past experience. Writing to Sentner in summer 1944, Missouri Farmers Association leader H. E. Klinefelter condemned the Pick Plan as an "army engineers' scheme." He balked at a proposal for a nine-foot channel, charging the Corps had "all but ruined the Missouri River with their attempts to develop a six-foot channel," and urged reducing the army engineers' authority by establishing "some independent agency that hasn't any axes to grind."[53]

The *Missouri Farmer,* journal of the 86,000 member organization, endorsed the MVA "in the hope that by superseding the new flood control law with an MVA, at least SOME of these monumental dams might be replaced with extensive soil conservation measures which are quite as effective as dams—if not more so—in holding back floods." In the Upper Valley, according to a *St. Louis Star-Times* investigation, "many small farmers, dirt farmers, [and] small town merchants" were "skeptical toward grandiose plans for irrigation," such as those proposed by the Bureau of Reclamation, which had usually benefited large farmers only.[54] But the MVA pamphlet pledged that water resources would favor small farmers over agribusiness. In addition, the pledge of public power from water resources won over many farmers. The National Farmers Union (NFU), a grassroots organization headquartered in Denver, had proposed in 1942 that the "TVA be made a pilot operation for the nation." By late August, the NFU began its own campaign among its 250,000 members, using *One River, One Plan* as its tool. Glenn Talbott, president of the North Dakota Farmers Union and chair of the NFU's water resources conservation committee, wrote that the organization would "do everything in our power to secure this type of approach."[55]

The coalition with farmers affected the perspectives of the labor activists, especially regarding the farmers' stress on soil conservation over dams for flood control, a point that would eventually challenge prevailing notions of "taming the river." Naomi Ring, the District's MVA staff researcher, received a series of letters from farmers and soil conservationists stressing that an MVA should make soil conservation and erosion a central consideration. In August she wrote that *One River, One Plan* (for which she had apparently been the primary author) had been her first "encounter with river development . . . I have come to the conclusion that more stress should have been put on irrigation, soil conservation and the general well-being of the farmers."[56]

Within a short time, District Eight supporters of the MVA were seeking to integrate their farmer allies' concerns into their approach. Sentner wrote to another correspondent who worried about the navigation provisions of the MVA that "MVA would only undertake regional projects that are both feasible and benefit a maximum amount of the people in the valley; therefore, I am sure we will have no worry." Klinefelter wrote Sentner that regarding concerns about soil and flood control issues, "I do not believe we are very far apart on the subject."[57]

MVA supporters recognized that it would encounter stiff opposition from the BR and ACE, but were gratified to win support from the Rural Electrification Administration (REA), a governmental agency that had promoted public power projects and cheap electricity for rural regions in the New Deal Administration. The REA was defunded during the war and its staff had an obvious interest in promoting the MVA. Ring used Packard's contacts in the REA to secure staffers' support and advice. She reported to Sentner that after a meeting between herself, Packard, and REA, REA was willing to "go along" with the labor-farmer coalition that was developing out of the UE's efforts because of the respect they had for Packard, adding, "The fact that you and Packard are so 'close' gave them more confidence in the role labor will have to play in an MVA organization."[58]

MVA legislation, written by Packard, REA staff, and District Eight representatives, was submitted in August 1944 by Senator James Murray of Montana. Later, Missouri Representative John Cochran sponsored another version in the House.[59] Both allowed the authority two years to develop a plan that would "reconcile and harmonize" the requirements for flood control, navigation, reclamation, and power "to secure the maximum public benefit for the region and the nation." The plan would then be submitted for congressional approval. A board of three directors who "would utilize to the fullest possible extent the advice and assistance of the people of the region, including local and state governments," would govern the MVA. MVA directors were barred from having any financial interest in any potential development. The bill gave the MVA "broad powers to sell and distribute electric power and water and to fix rates" for sale to consumers, with a preference for sale to cooperatives. It barred dams not approved by the MVA. Evidence that environmental concerns were already gaining ground in conceptualizations of the MVA was apparent in a provision that gave the authority the power to "prevent pollution of the waters of the Missouri and its tributaries."[60] On September 22, Roosevelt sent a message to Congress strongly endorsing the bill and calling for more such proposals. Vice-Presidential candidate Truman also wholeheartedly endorsed the legislation.[61]

In the fall, the grassroots campaign began. UE delegates shepherded support for the bill through the Missouri CIO Convention, which endorsed it and voted to call a nine-state meeting of CIO unions to help organize for it. The Missouri CIO and UE representatives pushed the national CIO convention, held in November, to make the MVA part of their "People's Program of 1944."[62] Farmers groups increased their efforts. The Cooperative League, a two-million member association advocating cheap power, and the Consumers Cooperative Association also endorsed the measure.[63]

The momentum for an MVA was strong enough to prompt what James Patton of the National Farmers Union called a "shameless, loveless, shotgun marriage" between the Army Corp of Engineers and the Bureau of Reclamation. In early November the two agencies quickly collaborated on a new proposal comprising six pages, called Pick-Sloan, which combined the elements of the two plans into what the agencies claimed was a comprehensive Missouri Basin Plan. They divided up jurisdiction, with the BR having au-

thority over the Upper Valley and the Corps retaining control on all navigation and Lower Valley projects. As scholar Donald Spritzer has pointed out,
"The new plan said nothing about how the water would be proportioned
to meet conflicting needs," and while it called for hydroelectric power, the
program did not include public power projects. Finally, as the *Post-Dispatch*
later noted, Pick-Sloan also even violated the standards of the Bureau of Reclamation, however loosely they had been enforced, which stated that those
who benefited from irrigated water should pay for the costs. The program
even retroactively applied its provisions to money still owed by agribusiness
interests to the Reclamation Bureau. Pick-Sloan was nothing more than "a
subsidy for the privileged interests," wrote Walter Packard. There were no
provisions for soil conservation or other environmental measures.[64]

After much wrangling, and fearing that Pick-Sloan might be approved with
the anti-MVA provisions, MVA congressional allies worked out a compromise with Pick-Sloan backers, despite protests from grassroots supporters
in farm and labor groups. Senator Murray consented to postpone the push
for MVA legislation until the next Congress in return for the promise of
early hearings and the elimination of provisions from the Pick-Sloan Bill
that would prevent the ability of MVA to supersede it. Murray reasoned
that because only $400 million dollars had been appropriated (for the initial
phase of the Pick-Sloan project), the fight for an MVA was best postponed
until it had more momentum. The Pick-Sloan bill passed Congress in late
December 1944. FDR's statements that Pick-Sloan should not be considered
a substitute for the MVA, and that its provisions could indeed be integrated
with an MVA, buoyed MVA proponents.[65]

A new determination took hold among MVA advocates. In a representative
expression of that urgency, *The Missouri Farmer* issued a scathing editorial
with extensive detail of what Pick-Sloan would mean to Missouri farmers
and rural residents. The editorial charged that the twenty-six proposed Missouri dams were intended chiefly for a deeper channel as desired by Kansas
City interests, rather than for the ostensible purpose of flood control. The
commentary estimated that the dams would "ruin approximately 900,000
acres of Missouri's best farm land, and force some 20,000 families out of
their homes." The dams would "ruin" six counties and parts of five others.
The proposed Table Rock Dam in Taney County would flood "most of the
best land" in three counties. Parts of other counties "will be flooded while
lakes of water and mud will destroy . . . some of the world's finest springs
and beauty spots in Wayne, Reynolds, Shannon, Carter and Ripley counties." Chillicothe "will be located on a peninsula—an enormous lake will
almost cover up Livingston County and a corner of Linn county." A dam on

the Grand River meant that a fourth of Davies County "will be inundated," and dams on the Meramec River and Big River would "blight" Franklin and Jefferson counties. The editorial concluded that most people in the affected areas "appear not to comprehend what has been done to them," and that "the few" who understood Pick-Sloan "seem to believe that their Government 'will not do this thing to us' as one of them recently put it."[66]

Warning that without action on the part of the citizenry "It will be done!" the *Missouri Farmer* predicted "that when the people living in these condemned areas of Missouri learn the full import of the new flood control law they will never return any Missouri Congressman to office who voted for it!" Upper Missouri farmers also argued that navigation would dominate the purposes even under this "compromise" plan.[67]

The November 1944 elections, in which the UE and the CIO contributed a significant number of new voters and consequently influenced the outcome of the elections, seemed to confirm for the Left the merits of political mobilization with concrete issues such as the MVA. The St. Louis CIO-PAC, under the direction of UE staff, enrolled hundreds of supporters, who in turn registered sixty thousand new voters. In Evansville, Charles Wright, president of Evansville's Servel local, won a state representative seat. These advances helped to further Logsdon's suggestion about moving toward meaningful political activism.[68]

Assessing Sentner's role in the kind of varied activity that included the campaign for an MVA, the St. Louis office of the Federal Bureau of Investigation reported that Sentner "manifests . . . a belligerent aggressive offense on behalf of labor which is designed to take the part of labor in all its controversies in the St. Louis area. Subject strenuously endeavors to inject himself, as well as the U.E., into any social problem which touches the labor field. It is estimated that the local St. Louis papers carry news stories concerning him on an average of one story or more each week."[69] The FBI recognized the effectiveness of the Left in political mobilization.

In mid-December, Sentner outlined a plan for a grassroots campaign for the next legislative session. Noting that the campaign had unified various labor, farmer, and consumer groups, Sentner outlined plans for a "movement [that] should become the broadest movement developed since the days of the Populist[s]." Sentner emphasized that the "movement should be local in character but should be linked with the national program." Unions could "be the force that ties in these regional projects with the overall national program, thus prevent[ing] these projects from becoming a political football with regional trades in Congress, etc." District Eight representatives persuaded their national union office to allocate a staff member to work for the establishment of a St. Louis MVA committee, a nine-state committee, and a national committee to support the MVA.[70] UE emphasized to its farm organization friends that it preferred to get "community people to take the lead rather than one of the Congressmen," as some had suggested, in order to keep the campaign a grassroots drive.[71]

In January 1945, the St. Louis Committee was formally established, with engineer Raymond Tucker as chair and with representatives from labor, law, veterans groups, women's groups, and church groups. Chambers and Sentner worried that the committee was "weak on industry people," whom they thought were necessary to combat criticism of the MVA as socialistic.[72] With District Eight's guidance, the group established a speaker's bureau. Over the course of the next few months, the St. Louis Committee speakers went before groups such as the St. Louis Women's Chamber of Commerce, Liberal Voters League, St. Louis Branch of the NAACP, local posts of the Veterans of Foreign Wars, Missouri Federation of Women's Clubs, and many church groups. By spring 1945, the campaign was yielding "strong official backing from the Catholic Church." This campaign also helped to develop some support among business, especially from small businesses, using the argument that by electrifying farms in the Missouri Valley, industrial expansion would help many St. Louis businesses. Then, in April 1945, the St. Louis Committee scored a major victory when, in a referendum, the St. Louis Chamber of Commerce members voted to endorse the MVA.[73]

By early 1945, other city-based committees were being organized in the nine-state region, including one in Kansas City and another in St. Charles County. In February 1945, District Eight helped establish a national CIO committee for an MVA, which declared plans for "reaching every CIO member in the nine-state region on the importance of regionally administered MVA." In addition, other state CIO federations pledged to organize for an MVA and to disseminate educational materials and information on MVA through local unions to individual CIO members.[74] Further, the seeds planted in 1944 among AFL unions were beginning to develop into a real coalition. In Kansas City, the AFL "has taken hold and is circulating all the building trades unions in the nine states for support" and was starting to establish a nine-state building trades MVA committee. Both the AFL and the CIO held valley-wide conferences on the MVA to promote and organize for it. Finally, in spring 1945, a "Friends of the Missouri Valley" national committee was established. Sentner was among the endorsers, but stressed that the campaign should remain focused on the local mobilization.[75]

As the campaign progressed, and even as the issue of jobs and development remained a primary emphasis in the arguments for an MVA, proponents sought to differentiate their proposal from Pick-Sloan by arguing that only through the MVA would concerns for the environment be taken into account. A model speech for the speakers' bureau read: "We are in the process of closing a three-century long epoch of planless exploitation of the human, natural, and physical resources of North America. During these three centuries, it has been assumed that untrammeled individual initiative would somehow yield the greatest long-run social progress. Now we know the error of that assumption. The practices of the past compel the immediate formulation of regional and national plans. Not to do so now may lead to disaster not many years hence." Another CIO representative suggested that the "present practice regarding rivers is to work backwards. We spend millions of dollars to buy fertilizer to replace ruined soil. We spend millions of dollars to purify river water polluted by soil. But we refuse to spend money to eliminate the conditions which would lead to soil protection and a pure flow of water."[76]

The new MVA Bill, submitted in February 1945, put more emphasis on soil conservation and promised to "restore the declining water table, protect wild game; conserve water, soil, mineral and forest resources," and to ensure development through energy dispersion in the Upper Valley. It also added to the MVA's duties the "disposal of war and defense factories to encourage industrial and business expansion," in line with the growing hold of the idea of decentralization of power from Washington, D.C. Structurally, the proposed and revised legislation added an advisory committee to be composed of representatives of labor, farmer, business, and citizens' groups, reflecting proponents' attempts to enhance the viability of public input into decentralized, regional planning.[77]

By summer 1945, the coalition had expanded and affected opinion in the nine-state area. Over fifty organizations sponsored a "Missouri Conference on MVA," organized by the St. Louis group.[78] This meeting launched a Regional Committee for an MVA, headquartered in Omaha. Its first conference attracted hundreds of leaders of various groups, including farmers' groups, labor groups, women's groups, the NAACP, and the VFW, vowing to organize a petition drive for one million signatures to spur Congress to support an MVA.[79] A Gallup poll during the summer revealed that three out of every four people in the Missouri River areas favored an MVA.[80]

But the MVA's political fortunes in 1945 failed to match the expectations raised by such polls. Murray had expected the bill would be sent to the Agriculture Committee as he had requested and as had been the case with the TVA and similar legislation. But Vice President Truman, in the first of what many in the campaign would later view as a series of outrageous betrayals despite his vocal support, referred the bill to the Commerce Committee, chaired by a senator hostile to the MVA. Early in his political career Truman had been a close ally of the ACE and Kansas City navigation interests, and in fact "was a friend of Pick's."[81] The MVA bill faced an uphill battle as it steered slowly through two hostile subcommittees, one of which was chaired by John Overton, head of an organization formed to oppose the MVA.[82]

Behind these strong congressional opponents was a growing overlapping coalition opposing the MVA, totaling thirty organizations, which began to undertake a richly financed campaign to influence public opinion. The leader of the opposition was the National Association of Electric Companies (NAEC), formed in the summer of 1945 and composed of 170 private power companies. They placed full-page advertisements in newspapers across the nine-state region, financed a weekly radio program, and subsidized the publication of a book attacking the TVA. (A later investigation suggested that the NAEC had made kickback arrangements with their suppliers to finance anti-MVA propaganda in each state.)

Another powerful new organization, the Missouri Valley Development Association, worked with the power interests but also began to organize the many other groups that had a stake in keeping out an MVA. These included Upper Valley cattlemen (who opposed it because they feared loss of rangeland to irrigation), barge-line operators and river construction contractors (two of many groups with a financial stake in navigation), the Associated General Contractors (who opposed it because an MVA would hire workers directly instead of contracting out to private companies), the National Reclamation Association, an Upper Valley group composed of power companies, railroads, chambers of commerce, and corporate ranchers who sought to maintain their entrenched position with the BR.

The Mississippi Valley Development Association (MVDA), which represented navigation interests and was headed by St. Louisan Laclan Macleay, lined up the key testimony at the congressional hearings. The MVDA was especially successful in organizing governors and state legislatures and business groups to go on record against the MVA.[83] The MVDA set up an anti-MVA office in St. Louis, specifically to target the St. Louis Chamber of Commerce. By October, it was successful in keeping the Chamber of Commerce from moving on its favorable referendum vote to support the MVA. As commentators noted, that vote had been "a blow" to anti-MVA forces and had "hampered their campaign ever since. . . . When they attempt to brand MVA and its supporters as 'socialistic,' opponents lay themselves open to the retort, 'The St. Louis Chamber of Commerce voted to support MVA. Is that organization socialistic?'"[84]

Opponents were unified in their arguments against the MVA: it would establish a "super-government" and was a step toward "state socialism" and it was unnecessary in light of the Pick-Sloan plan. As Sentner later put it, "All of these organizations assailed MVA as 'un-American' and a 'threat to private enterprise.'" Anti-MVA pamphlets with titles such as "Totalitarianism on the March" suggested that sinister forces were involved in the MVA campaign. The MVDA called for an investigation of the pro-MVA campaign, accusing it of "un-American activities."[85]

Opponents also charged that most of the pro-MVA advocates at the congressional hearings were "unqualified" to testify on river problems. James Davis, now head of the CIO nine-state committee, chafed at this allegation. He retorted that he had "seen with his own eyes" the "mistakes made by army engineers," whose experts had "ruined the farm owned by his family in the Missouri bottomlands." Davis concluded: "My experience has been very practical, something I could see." Davis criticized Pick-Sloan for ignoring "any attempt to integrate soil conservation, erosion control, community development or cheap power," as called for by the citizenry. He also noted that Murray's bill at least provided a role for "the farmer, the business man, and labor," and it "reaches all walks of life."[86] Davis's remarks show that the campaign had ignited a challenge to the technocratic proclivities of the New Deal. The promotion of decentralized planning, and wide participation by citizens in planning, was the counterpoint to tendencies within liberalism derived from the Progressive Era. The mobilizations for the MVA had catalyzed alternative ways of thinking about the notion of "expertise."

By the fall, when it was clear that the MVA bill was being picked apart in committee hearings, Senator Murray asked that further hearings be postponed. Meanwhile, Sentner and other activists outlined the longer-term political fight that would have to be waged, state by state, around the issue. Sentner reflected cogently on the entrenched opposition, but he remained focused on the growth of the coalition that had come together over the issue. The campaign for the MVA, he noted, "has united progressive forces . . . as they have never been united before," had been the catalyst for the organization of citizens' groups in various cities, including St. Louis, and had united farm and labor groups in a way that no other issue had been able to do. District Eight officials were also impressed with the way that the Farmers' Union leadership had integrated women into the leadership of the organization, and were encouraging further exchange and coalitions, not only with them but with groups such as the Catholic Rural Life Congress. The "movement . . . is . . . a major political movement with all of the elements of populism which is so native to our section of the country" that could help to propel progressives to electoral positions.[87]

In the middle of the war, Sentner seemed sanguine about the Left's influence on this coalition and on the CIO agenda. The community-based approach to labor's involvement in planning, overridden in the early years of the
war by the Hillman forces, had come to the fore during the course of the war.
"We can be proud that the CIO has made our community action program its
own." James Matles, noting that District Eight's community campaigns had
helped the entire UE formulate their agenda, wrote to Sentner, "[I] feel that
the development of such a program on a national scale should put our outfit
out in the front not only as far as the labor movement is concerned but even
as far as the nation is concerned." In late 1945, Sentner boasted to District
shop stewards that the national UE was calling for advice for its showdown
with GE in the great 1945–46 strike. District Eight organizer Vic Pasche was
sent to that campaign, a signal that the UE was thinking seriously about how
to develop further its community-based campaigns.[88]

The Cold War and the liabilities of association with the CP quickly and
inexorably eroded the hope of a unified progressive movement. Anticommunism redefined civic life in the postwar era, and a fratricidal labor war
allowed capital to exert more power in the community and nation. While
the UE has always been noted as a key target of the right-wing coalition
that formed inside and outside the CIO, the significance of the role this
opposition played in killing full-fledged community-based campaigns has
not been adequately assessed. In District Eight, as I have detailed elsewhere,
the coalition against Sentner and the Left was a coalition of socialists, liberals, anticommunist Catholics, and Far-Right reactionaries, but in the end,
right-wing ideological presumptions defined the movement. The campaigns
against the district reinforced the notion that the programmatic agenda of
the Left in the UE was totalitarian, a mechanism for state control, the very
charge made by the anti-MVA forces. Only the power of the Cold War and
the powerful liabilities of the CP's association with the Soviet Union could
make such a charge stick for District Eight, which was among the most
democratic of the CIO union districts, with direct election of representatives.
It is notable that Harold Gibbons, another proponent of community-based
coalitions in St. Louis, was a key figure in the local anti-UE movement. He
devoted significant resources to eliminating the UE left, but in the end this
rendered him a lonely proponent of the community-based labor movement
in the St. Louis area.[89]

The MVA proposal continued to garner significant popular support in the
postwar era, at least through 1948, after another major flood brought attention to the issue. But Sentner's vision of a unified locally driven grassroots
campaign for the MVA was stymied by the factionalism and anticommunism

that gripped postwar-era labor politics. The National Farmers' Union, the other key grassroots organization, was also subject to red-baiting for its stance against U.S. foreign policy. The style of mobilization for an MVA under CIO leadership was far more hierarchical and ineffective. The leadership of the CIO centralized this campaign and sought to exclude Sentner from representation on the MVA committees, appointing lackluster bureaucrats to organize it. It is notable that St. Louis backers of the MVA were much more comfortable with Sentner's leadership role in this period than were the national CIO officials, at least until 1947, when Cold War politics made Sentner the target of red-baiting. In 1948, when the MVA reemerged as key potential legislation, District Eight was in the third year of an effort to beat back a national and local anticommunist campaign, in which union raiding absorbed all financial resources. The CIO resisted decentralization of the campaign, fearing left-led unions would be more actively involved, and enforced a "policy of excluding representatives from progressive CIO unions" from the MVA committees, a repeat of Hillman's strategy. By 1948, it was carefully policing the MVA support groups for any signs of unorthodox behavior. Learning that the head of a Montana committee for the MVA was supporting Henry Wallace's presidential campaign, the CIO ordered its affiliates to withdraw financial assistance for the state's MVA campaign.[90]

While publicly calling for planning, the CIO could not mount any solid campaign for it in the face of the rebounding postwar economy and the deepening Cold War. Pent-up consumer demand boosted the economy until late 1948, when a severe recession set in. With the onset of the Cold War and the hot war in Korea, defense spending surreptitiously crept in as a jobs program that both the CIO and conservatives could accept. It was a new kind of planning that replaced the grand visions articulated during the war.

In order to fully understand what was lost with the emergence of anticommunism in the Cold War era, we need to better understand the role of the Left in building a coherent vision and strategy for social transformation with unions as the base. In the ten years before District Eight's left-wing activists faced a campaign intended to eliminate their influence, they had developed a deep and abiding commitment to challenging the corporate political economy through concerted community mobilizations. They had developed a union cadre committed to their leadership who agreed with them on that score, if not with the CP more generally. District Eight's experiences should caution us against accepting the conclusion offered by Lizabeth Cohen that by the 1930s, there was "one national story to be told" about the labor movement and its relationship to the state and to capitalism. District Eight's story reinforces the work of historians and geographers who remind us that both labor and capital build power through the local spatial terrain—that both labor and capital build their power on "spatial fix"—"certain configurations of the landscape . . . in order for them to reproduce themselves . . . from day to day and from generation to generation." Jane Wills has remarked: "Workers' traditions are more than simply free-floating ideas. Ideas need to 'take place' in some material sense if they are to be reproduced and reinvented. . . . It is only by challenging the spatial despotism of capital through organization and struggle in particular places that workers can begin to reverse this decline." It was that difficult project that District Eight's Left sought to engage with the MVA and other projects, and which was cut short by anticommunism. One analyst has suggested that the "debate over valley authorities was one of the few wide-ranging explorations into the structure of the American economy," an "inquiry into large issues . . . of political economy."[91] For District Eight's Left, it was an attempt to engage in a type of prefigurative community-based mobilization and politics that drew on workers' own hopes for a better postwar world. Given the reemergence of a scholarship that views the CP unionists as simply an arm of a party that sought to service the needs of the Soviet Union, the local struggle for an MVA shows that the Left in UE District Eight had carried forward an aim of challenging capitalism without the baggage of totalitarian intent. Indeed, one could argue that by purging the Left, the legacy of community-based labor organizing was dealt a serious blow in the Midwest.

Notes

I reviewed the William Sentner papers before they were processed and organized. I have attempted to ascertain the final folder location for the material as ultimately processed. Sometimes that was not possible. In those cases, I have designated the citation as "unprocessed."

1. CIO committee on Regional Development and Conservation, folder 821, James Davis Papers, Collection 3666, Western Historical Manuscripts Collection, University of Missouri, Columbia (hereafter JDP).

2. For background on Sentner, the district, and the unemployed movement, see Rosemary Feurer, *Radical Unionism in the Midwest, 1900–1950* (Urbana: University of Illinois Press, 2006); and "Crossing the Boundaries between Community and Union: The Nutpickers Union in St. Louis, 1933–1934," in Staughton Lynd, ed., *We Are All Leaders: The Alternative Unionism of the Early 1930s* (Urbana: University of Illinois Press, 1996). See the entire collection for perspectives on the role of community-based labor protest in the early 1930s.

3. For an introduction to some of these issues, see Gary Gerstle, *Working-Class Americanism: The Politics of Labor in a Textile City, 1914–1960* (Cambridge: Cambridge University Press, 1989); Nelson Lichtenstein, *Labor's War at Home: The CIO in World War II*

(New York: Cambridge University Press, 1982); Mark Leff, "The Politics of Sacrifice on the American Home Front in World War II," *Journal of American History 77* (Mar. 1991): 1296–1318.

4. Steven Fraser, *Labor Will Rule: Sidney Hillman and the Rise of American Labor* (Ithaca, N.Y.: Cornell University Press, 1993), 482.

5. Gerald T. White, *Billions for Defense: Government Financing by the Defense Plant Corporation during World War II* (Tuscaloosa: University of Alabama Press, 1980), 48; Paul A. C. Koistinen, "The Hammer and the Sword: Labor, the Military, and Industrial Mobilization, 1920–1945," (Ph.D. diss., University of California, Berkeley, 1964), 664; see also Koistinen, *Arsenal of World War II: The Political Economy of American Warfare, 1940–1945* (Lawrence: University Press of Kansas, 2004).

6. Lichtenstein, *Labor's War at Home,* 41, 88–89.

7. Ibid., 41, 85; Nelson Lichtenstein, *The Most Dangerous Man in Detroit: Walter Reuther and the Fate of American Labor* (New York: Basic Books, 1995), 154–74; Fraser, *Labor Will Rule,* 473–84.

8. James Matles to John L. Lewis, July 22, 1940, "UE National Correspondence folder," unprocessed William Sentner Papers, Washington University Archives, St. Louis, Missouri (hereafter WSP). William Sentner to Russ Nixon, Jan. 14, 1942, D-8/71, United Electrical Workers Archives, University of Pittsburgh, Pittsburgh, Pennsylvania (hereafter UEA).

9. Fraser, *Labor Will Rule,* 474.

10. Lyle Dowling to William Sentner, Jan. 8, 1942, D-8/40, UEA.

11. Fraser, *Labor Will Rule,* 480.

12. James Payne to Julius Emspak, Aug. 12, 1941, and attachments, O/1081, UEA; Report of District President, District 8 Convention, Sept. 20–21, 1941, O/1322, UEA.

13. James Payne to Julius Emspak, Aug. 12, 1941, O/1081, UEA; James Payne to Julius Emspak, July 17, 1941, O/1080; William Sentner to James Matles, Aug. 6, 1941, D-8/67, UEA.

14. William Sentner to James Matles, Aug. 6, 1941, D-8/67, UEA; James Payne to Julius Emspak, Aug. 12, 1941, and attachments: resolution and petition, O/1081, UEA.

15. James Payne to James Matles, Aug. 18, 1941, O/1081, UEA. James Payne to James Matles, Aug. 25, 1941, and attached *Tavern Journal,* O/1081, UEA; unidentified newspaper clipping, "Union Heads to Air Problems of Job Lay-offs," Aug. 27, 1941, O/1082, UEA.

16. *Evansville Courier,* Sept. 2, 1941; *Chicago Daily Tribune* Sept. 13, 1941.

17. *UE News,* Sept. 20, 1941; William Sentner, Report on Midwest Emergency Conference on Unemployment Due to Priorities, O/1321, UEA; James Payne to James Matles, Sept. 10, 1041, O/1082, UEA.

18. William Sentner, Report on Midwest Emergency Conference on Unemployment Due to Priorities, O/1321, UEA.

19. William Sentner, Report on Midwest Emergency Conference; *UE News,* Sept. 20, 1941; Robert Logsdon to James Matles, Dec. 3, 1941, O/722, UEA; Donald B. Howard to William Sentner, Jan. 5, 1942, D-8/52, UEA.

20. William Sentner, Report on Midwest Emergency Conference; William Sentner, Memorandum on Chicago Midwest Emergency Conference, Sept. 12, 1941, O/1321, UEA.

21. William Sentner to James Matles Aug. 20, 1941, D-8/667, UEA; *UE News,* Oct. 25, 1941, Oct. 1, 1941.

22. Report of the District President, p. 4, District 8 Convention, Sept. 20–21, 1941, O/1322, UEA.

23. William Sentner to Joseph J. Weiner, Aug. 27, 1941, O/1320, UEA.

24. William Sentner to James Matles, Oct. 1, 1941, D-8/667, UEA.

25. William Sentner to Julius Emspak, Oct. 20, 1941, D-8/69, UEA; Statement by William Sentner to the House Committee Investigating National Defense Migration, St. Louis, Nov. 26, 1941, p. 7, unprocessed WSP.

26. "Defense Unemployment in the Industry," Robert Logsdon to James Matles, Dec. 3, 1941, O/722, UEA.

27. Dowling to Bill Sentner, Oct. 1941, "UE National Office Correspondence" folder, unprocessed WSP.

28. William Sentner to Russ Nixon, Jan. 14, 1942, D-8/71, UEA; William Sentner to Lyle Dowling, Oct. 13, 1941, D-8/69, UEA; William Sentner to Lyle Dowling, Apr. 20, 1942, D-8/75, UEA.

29. William Sentner to James Emspak, Feb. 16, 1943, D-8/81, UEA; Russ Nixon to James Emspak, Feb. 18, 1943, D-8/132, UEA.

30. *Globe Democrat,* Sept. 5, 1942.

31. William Sentner to Lyle Dowling, Nov. 26, 1941, O/1310, UEA.

32. Robert Logsdon to James Matles, Dec. 3, 1941, O/722, UEA.

33. Minutes, Regular Meeting of the Executive Board, p. 19, UE District 8, Jan. 30, 1943, D-8/5, UEA; *UE News,* Dec. 30, 1944, Aug. 12, 1944.

34. Robert Logsdon, Remarks to District 8 Semi-Annual Convention, Oct. 14, 1944, folder 5, box 5, series 1; William Sentner to Harry S. Truman, May 29, 1944, D-8/88, UEA.

35. *Local Review,* Feb. 5, 1943; *UE News,* Mar. 11, 1944, Apr. 14, 1944; Robert Logsdon to Julius Emspak, Mar. 20, 1944, D-8/125, UEA; William Sentner to James Emspak, Aug. 25, 1944, D-8/669, UEA.

36. William Sentner to James Matles, July 14, 1944; Russ Nixon to William Sentner, July 23, 1944, both in folder 3, box 1, series 6, WSP.

37. *Globe Democrat,* Sept. 7, 1942, in Morgue files, Mercantile Library, St. Louis; *Globe-Democrat,* July 12, 1942; District Executive Board Report, Jan 30, 1945; *St. Louis American,* Apr. 2, 1943.

38. "30 hour Week Predicted at Postwar Parley," undated *St. Louis Globe-Democrat* article in "War box," unprocessed WSP; *UE News,* Aug. 19, 1944.

39. "Civic leaders Urge Unity in Task of Providing Jobs after War," unidentified newspaper article, July 31, 1944, in War box, WSP.

40. William Sentner to William McClellan, Aug. 30, 1944, D/8-89, UEA.

41. Erwin C. Hargrove and Paul K. Conkin, eds., *TVA: Fifty Years of Grass-Roots Bureaucracy* (Urbana: University of Illinois Press, 1983); Walter L. Creese, *TVA's Public Planning: The Vision, the Reality* (Knoxville: University of Tennessee Press, 1990). The TVA perfectly reflected two tendencies that contested for the soul of liberalism in the 1930s and 1940s—the first espoused technocratic solutions to political problems and the other sought to democratize American life. Recent histories have questioned whether the TVA deserves the democratic merits attributed to it. The transfer of power to technocratic experts at the local level, with few mechanisms to include local residents in the planning process,

held grave consequences for local residents, many of whom were forcibly displaced by TVA projects. See William Bruce Wheeler and Michael J. McDonald, *TVA and the Tellico Dam, 1936–1979: A Bureaucratic Crisis in Post-Industrial America* (Knoxville: University of Tennessee Press, 1986); William U. Chandler, *The Myth of the TVA: Conservation and Development in the Tennessee Valley, 1933–1983* (Cambridge, Mass.: Harper and Row, 1984).

42. "Memo: Re: M. V. A.," folder 1, box 1, series 2, William WSP; Marion Clawson, *New Deal Planning: The National Resources Planning Board* (Baltimore: Johns Hopkins University Press, 1981).

43. *New York Times*, May 24, 1944; Henry Hart, *The Dark Missouri* (Madison: University of Wisconsin Press, 1957), 120.

44. *St. Louis Post-Dispatch*, July 17, 1951; John T. Farrell, *Heartland Engineers: A History* (Kansas City: Army Corps of Engineers, 1993).

45. Donald Worster, *Rivers of Empire: Water, Aridity, and the Growth of the American West* (New York: Pantheon, 1985), 268–69; Paul Scheele, "Resource Development Politics in the Missouri Basin: Federal Power, Navigation, and Reservoir Operation Policies, 1944–1968," (Ph.D. diss., University of Nebraska, 1969), 35, 41, 45, 49.

46. *Post-Dispatch*, May 14, 1944; *Star-Times*, May 29, 1944.

47. District Executive Board, "MVA Report," folder 17, box 2, series 2, WSP; NR press release, May 21, 1944, folder 2, box 1, series 2, WSP; Mark W. T. Harvey, "North Dakota, the Northern Plains, and the Missouri Valley Authority," *North Dakota History* 59:3 (1992): 28–39, credits the farm organizations for the revival of the MVA.

48. *One River, One Plan;* "Post War Planning and the Missouri River Valley Basin," July 13, 1944, folder 2, box 1, series 2, WSP; District Executive Board, "MVA Report," Aug. 1944; untitled fact sheet, folder 17, box 2, series 2, WSP.

49. Naomi Ring to Bill McMurphy, Sept. 26, 1944, folder 1, box 1, series 2; Wm. Mc-Murphy to Naomi Ring, Oct. 6, 1944, folder 1, box 1, series 2; see also, William Sentner to Jerry O'Connal, Sept. 26, 1944, all in WSP.

50. Worster, *Rivers of Empire*, 249–50; Walter E. Packard to William Sentner, July 29, 1944; Paul G. Pinsky to William Sentner, July 18, 1944; William Sentner to Walter Packard, July 22, 1944; Walter Packard resume, July 18, 1944, all in folder 2, box 1, series 2, WSP.

51. See letters "Correspondence, One River, One Plan" folder 3, box 1, series 2; William Sentner in *The Worker Magazine*, Oct. 8, 1944, folder 1, box 1, series 2, WSP; "Statement by James A. Davis before Congress," undated, folder 798, JDP.

52. "UE Role on M.V.A.," folder 1, box 1, series 2, WSP.

53. H. E. Klinefelter to William Sentner, July 21, 1944, folder 2, box 1, series 2, WSP.

54. *Star-Times*, Oct. 18, 1944.

55. *Post-Dispatch*, Sept. 11, 1944; "Patton Urges Farm Union to Stand Firm for MVA," unidentified newspaper article, Nov. 21, 1944, folder 4, box 1, series 2, WSP; Glenn Talbott to Naomi Ring, Aug. 31, 1944, folder 2, box 1, series 2, WSP.

56. Naomi Ring to Kenneth Simons, *Bismarck Tribune* (North Dakota), Aug. 31, 1944, folder 2, box 1, series 2, WSP.

57. Naomi Ring to Glenn Talbott, Sept. 5, 1944, reply to Talbott's letter of Aug. 31, 1944; William Sentner to A. M. Piper, Sept. 1, 1944; H. E. Klinefelter to Sentner, Aug. 10, 1944, all in folder 2, box 1, series 2, WSP.

58. Naomi Ring to William Sentner, Aug. 18, 1944, folder 2, box 1, series 2, WSP.

59. William Sentner to Frances Saylor, July 29, 1944, series 2, box 1, folder 2, WSP. In this letter, Sentner describes the drafting of the legislation. See also Frances Saylor to William Sentner, July 6, 1944, box 1, series 2, folder 2, WSP. Most other histories, including Donald E. Spritzer, in "One River, One Problem: James Murray and the Missouri Valley Authority," *Montana and the West: Essays in Honor of K. Ross Tool,* ed. Rex. C. Myers and Harry W. Fritz (Boulder: Pruett Publishing, 1984), 125, assert that the bill was written by Murray and his staff with the assistance of David Lilienthal. Murray, however, tended to underplay any role of organized labor in strategizing for the bill.

60. *Post-Dispatch,* Aug. 18, 1944.

61. *Star-Times,* Nov. 16, 1944.

62. "MVA Report," (Sept. 1944), folder 17, box 2, series 2, WSP; William Sentner to Glenn Talbott, Oct. 12, 1944; William Sentner, "Speech on the Missouri Valley Authority," folder 6, box 2, series 2, WSP.

63. *Post-Dispatch,* Oct. 14, 1944, Oct. 16, 1944; "Patton Urges Farm Union to Stand Firm"; Spritzer, "One River, One Problem," 127.

64. *Post-Dispatch,* Nov. 18, 1944; Spritzer, "One River, One Problem," 128; *Post-Dispatch,* Nov. 30, 1944; Walter Packard to Thomas Blaisdell, Dec. 6, 1944, folder 1, box 1, series 2, WSP. Michael Lawson, *Damned Indians: The Pick-Sloan Plan and the Missouri River Sioux, 1944–1980* (Norman: University of Oklahoma Press, 1982), recounts the devastation to Native Americans.

65. Spritzer, "One River, One Problem," 158; Walter Packard to James Patton, Dec. 6, 1944; Nov. 21, 1944, folder 4, box 1, series 2, WSP. *Post-Dispatch,* Nov. 29, 1944; Douglas S. Smith, "Missouri Valley Authority: The Death of Regional Planning" (master's thesis, University of Missouri, 1991), 112; *Star-Times,* Nov. 16, 1944; *Post-Dispatch,* Nov. 29, 1944, Nov. 15, 1944.

66. *Missouri Farmer,* Dec. 1944.

67. Ibid.

68. "Political Action" files, unprocessed WSP; *UE News,* June 17, 1944, Nov. 15, 1944.

69. FBI-HQ, 100-18332–38, box 5, series 4, WSP.

70. Bill (Sentner) to Bill (Chambers), Dec. 12, 1944, folder 17, box 2, series 2, WSP; "MVA Report," (Aug. 1944), folder 17, box 2, series 2, WSP.

71. "Program for the Development of the Campaign," attached to William Sentner to Bill Chambers, Dec. 12, 1944, folder 17, box 2, series 2; William Chambers to H. E. Klinefelter, Dec. 27, 1944, folder 1, box 1, series 2, WSP.

72. William Chambers to Clifford McEvoy, Dec. 21, 1944, folder 1, box 1, series 2, WSP; William Sentner to Glenn Talbott, folder 2, box 1, series 2, WSP; St. Louis Committee for an MVA, "Statement of Principles," Jan. 10, 1945, folder 794, JDP; *Post-Dispatch,* Jan. 21, 1945; William Chambers, "Memorandum" to Bill Sentner and Jack Becker, Jan. 18, 1945, folder 17, box 2, series 2, WSP.

73. "Program for the Development of the Campaign"; William Sentner to Bill Chambers, Dec. 12, 1944; William Chambers to H. E. Klinefelter, Dec. 27, 1944; Naomi Ring to Bill McMurphy, Sept. 26, 1944, folder 1, box 1, series 2; Memorandum, Bill Sentner, William Chambers, Jan. 18, 1945, folder 17, box 2, series 2, WSP; Smith, "Missouri Valley Authority," 63–72; Carleton Ball, "What the M.V.A. Proposal Promises for America," *Social Action,* folder 795, JDP.

74. William Sentner to Francis Saylor, Mar. 31, 1945, William Chambers to William Sentner, Jan. 10, 1945, both in folder 17, box 2, series 2, WSP; *Post-Dispatch,* Feb. 20, 1945.

75. William Sentner to Frances Sayler, Mar. 31, 1945, folder 16, box 2, series 2, WSP; Smith, "Missouri Valley Authority," 67.

76. "Basic Information for Speakers on MVA," Jan. 1945, D-8/MVA, UEA; *Post-Dispatch,* Feb. 20, 1945.

77. *Post-Dispatch,* Mar. 22, 1945; Walter Packard to Jerry McConnell, unprocessed WSP.

78. Press release, Missouri Conference on MVA, Apr. 16, 1945; Raymond Tucker to James A. Davis, Apr. 30, 1945, in folder 794, JDP.

79. "Regional Conference on MVA, July 6–7, 1945," folder 795, as well as materials in folder 797, JDP; correspondence, leaflets, press releases, folder 8, box 1, series 2, WSP; "Sponsors of Regional Conference on MVA," and other materials in Missouri Valley Authority files, D-8 files, UEA; Spritzer, "One River, One Problem," 133.

80. "Political Significance of the MVA Movement," folder 1, box 2, series 2, WSP.

81. *Post-Dispatch,* Feb. 20, 1945; *Star-Times,* Feb. 17, 1945; Larry Allen Whiteside, "Harry S. Truman and James E. Murray: The Missouri Valley Authority Proposal," (master's thesis, Central Missouri State University, 1970), 77; Spritzer, "One River, One Problem," 129. William Sentner to Jack Becker, May 21, 1945, folder 8, box 1, series 2, WSP.

82. Spritzer, "One River, One Problem," 131.

83. *Post-Dispatch,* Nov. 29, 1944, Aug. 4, 1945; Sentner, "Political Significance of the MVA Movement," folder 1, box 2, series 2; Spritzer, "One River, One Problem," 132; Scheele, "Resource Development Politics," 41–43.

84. Jack (Becker) to William Sentner, Oct. 13, 1945, folder 7, box 1, series 2, WSP; *Post-Dispatch,* Oct. 24, 1945.

85. Spritzer, "One River, One Problem," 132; Scheele, "Resource Development Politics," 41–43; Marian Ridgeway, *The Missouri Basin's Pick-Sloan Plan: A Case Study in Congressional Determination* (Urbana: University of Illinois Press, 1955), 215; Sentner "Political Significance of the MVA Movement"; *Fairfield Iowa Ledger,* Sept. 18, 1945, in folder 7, box 1, series 2, WSP; *Kansas City Star,* July 8, 1945, in folder 8, box 1, series 2, WSP. For arguments that the MVA was a concerted step toward decentralized planning, see Patton quoted in unidentified newspaper article, Nov. 21, 1944, folder 4, box 1, series 2, WSP, and William Sentner to A. M. Piper, Sept. 1, 1944, folder 2, box 1, series 2, WSP.

86. Statement by James A. Davis before Congress, undated, folder 798; press release, Sept. 21, 1945, folder 800, both in JDP.

87. "Political Significance of the MVA Movement," folder 1, box 2, series 2, WSP; William Sentner to C. B. Baldwin, Nov. 3, 1945, folder 10, box 2, series 2, WSP.

88. James Matles to William Sentner, July 17, 1944, William Sentner, folder 3, box 1, series 6, WSP. "Political Significance of the MVA movement," folder 1, box 2, series 2, WSP. See Lisa Kannenberg, "The Product of GE's Progress: Labor, Management, and Community Relations in Schenectady, New York, 1930–1960" (Ph.D. diss., Rutgers University, 1999), for a discussion of the flourishing of community-based campaigns.

89. See chapter 6 and epilogue and conclusion in Feurer, *Radical Unionism in the Midwest;* Robert Bussel, "'A Trade Union Oriented War on the Slums': Harold Gibbons, Ernest Calloway, and the St. Louis Teamsters in the 1960s," *Labor History* 44:1 (2003): 49–67.

90. Becker correspondence, folder 8, box 1, series 2, WSP; Benton Stong to Members, Nov. 30, 1948, JDP; John Brophy to James A. Davis, Apr. 1, 1948, folder 819, JDP; John Brophy to All Industrial Union Councils, Feb. 27, 1947, folder 80, JDP; John Brophy to James A. Davis, Apr. 1, 1948, f 819, JDP; "CIO Committee for MVA, Feb. 22, 1947," and John Brophy to All Industrial Union Councils, Feb. 27, 1947, f 804, JDP. Throughout these legislative attempts, MVA supporters also blamed Truman for torpedoing positive prospects for the bill (Spritzer, "One River, One Problem," 132–36).

91. Lizabeth Cohen, *Making a New Deal: Industrial Workers in Chicago, 1919–1939* (Cambridge: Cambridge University Press, 1991); David Harvey, *Spaces of Hope* (Berkeley: University of California Press, 2000), Andrew Herod, *Labor Geographies: Workers and the Landscapes of Capitalism* (New York: Guilford, 2001); Andrew Herod, ed., *Organizing the Landscape: Geographical Perspectives on Labor Unionism* (Minneapolis: University of Minnesota Press, 1998). Wills quoted in Herod, *Labor Geographies,* 147; Crawford D. Goodwin, "The Valley Authority Idea—The Fading of a National Vision," in Hargrove and Conkin, *TVA: Fifty Years of Grass-Roots Bureaucracy,* 265.

3. The Fight for Fair Employment and the Shifting Alliances among Latinos and Labor in Cold War Los Angeles

KENNETH C. BURT

This essay suggests a major reevaluation of the dominant narrative around the impact of the Cold War among Latinos in Los Angeles, and California generally. The dominant narrative is articulated by Zaragosa Vargas in *Labor Rights Are Civil Rights: Mexican Workers in Twentieth-Century America:* "For America's minorities, anticommunism undermined interracial unionism, undid the civil rights–trade union alliance, and set back the fight for full citizenship because it strengthened Anglo hostility to minority demands for social, racial, and economic equality."[1] This essay suggests a more nuanced approach to the context of Latino politics. The marginalization of many of those in and around the Communist Party did not represent the end of the labor community–civil rights alliance nor did it set back civil rights reforms. The coalitions continued. What changed were the participants and their ideological orientation. The old (secretly) Communist-led coalitions advocating for fair employment laws were replaced by ones led, in part, by democratic socialists. The dominant civil rights coalition in the 1950s was the California Committee for Fair Employment. Those in the three key positions—the president and two staff people—were all products of the labor movement; moreover, two had ties to the Socialist Party, and the third was a Trotskyist who become a Social Democrat. All "men of the Left," they shared a distaste for the Communist Party and worked well with liberals, including the faith community. This new alignment was also more successful than the old Communist-led coalitions in getting the California State Legislature to enact fair-employment (and then fair-housing) laws. This finding is consistent with the work of labor scholar Robert H. Zieger, who states in *The CIO, 1935–1955,* that, "In state capitols CIO (and later AFL-CIO) legislative representatives played significant roles in the enactment of civil rights laws whose provisions are now commonplace but that were in the 1950s and 1960s great victories for human rights."[2]

This newer approach to the state's post–World War II civil rights politics also explains other seeming inconsistencies in the literature. For example, even in stating that the Cold War led to the crushing of Latino organizations, which is correct as far as it is applied to those within the Communist milieu, Chicano scholars have consistently praised the Community Services Organization. So how exactly did a militant group such as the CSO thrive in a hostile environment where "anticommunism undermined interracial unionism, undid the civil rights–trade union alliance, and set back the fight for full citizenship"? The answer to the apparent paradox lies in a fuller understanding of the CSO's affiliation with Saul Alinsky's Industrial Area Foundation and its labor and community ties. The two pillars within the original Los Angeles CSO representing organized labor were the International Ladies Garment Workers' Union (ILGWU) and United Steel Workers of America (USWA). These two unions were progressive in their support of organizing Latinos in their neighborhoods as well as on the job and in advocating for civil rights legislation in California. Jewish Socialists (whose comrades in Eastern Europe had been killed by Stalin) led the ILGWU. Catholic "labor priests" (whose fellow clerics met a similar fate at the hands of the Soviet Union) heavily influenced the USWA.[3] These two groups and their extended networks would form the core of post–World War II civil rights politics in California.

Much less studied than the forces around the Communist Party, these progressive tendencies nevertheless had a profound influence on civil rights generally and on Latino politics in particular. Moreover, their progressive politics never became a severe liability because, unlike the Communists, they never supported America's principle foreign enemy, the Soviet Union. The new coalition was also highly successful because of organizational skills and a reform politics that easily meshed with developing liberalism. These progressive forces also exhibited a comfort level with patriotism and religion that ran deep among Mexican Americans and the larger society in the 1950s and, before their Communist rivals, fully embraced the of idea of electing a Latino to the Los Angeles City Council. This new progressive alignment provided enhanced access to a range of important institutions in addition to labor, including the Catholic Church and the Jewish Community. After the purging of the Communists and Communist-line unions from the AFL and CIO in 1948–50, the ILGWU and the USWA assumed even greater roles within their respective umbrella organizations. The liberal and progressive-led AFL and CIO bodies voted to work through the CSO, just as the Communist-led unions had previously worked through the Congress of Spanish Speaking People. The ideological conflict that was to divide the CIO in Los Angeles in the late 1940s was also present at its inception.

The Birth of the Los Angeles CIO Council and the Conflict between Socialists and Communists

The inchoate CIO emerged as a dynamic force in Los Angeles in 1937, when workers at the Douglas Aircraft Factory in Santa Monica staged a sit-in strike. Other unions, led by ILGWU organizer Bill Busick, provided assistance. He was a former Socialist Party candidate who had been arrested for his orations and bailed out of jail by author and political activist Upton Sinclair, the 1934 Democratic candidate for governor. Within months of the short-lived strike, more than one hundred CIO unions were operational in Los Angeles. Latinos headed four of the union locals and further served as organizers, activists, and elected union leaders in some of the other groups.[4] Moreover, the ILGWU had the largest number of Mexican and Mexican American members and the CIO, under the guidance of chairman Busick, was granted a charter as the Los Angeles Industrial Council.[5] The CIO enjoyed legitimacy because of its close affiliation with President Roosevelt, who openly supported industrial unionization, and whom it had helped reelect in 1936 in the most class-based electoral conflict in American history.

Within a year, however, the ILGWU and the Socialists had lost control of the Los Angeles CIO Council to the Communists. This was due, in part, to International Longshoremen's and Warehousemen's (ILWU) President Harry Bridges's appointment as the Western Regional CIO Director. About the same time, the United Auto Workers assigned Communist Wyndham Mortimer to organize on the West Coast. This gave those in the Communist Party milieu control over two of the three largest CIO unions in Los Angeles, and the power to outvote the Socialist-led ILGWU. By the spring of 1939, the council settled on its third leader, with whom it would remain identified for the next decade: Philip Connelly. The CIO's executive officer was a parochial school-trained Irish Catholic, who bore the nickname "Slim" because of his girth. He started as a reporter with the *Herald-Express* and was the second president of the Los Angeles Newspaper Guild. "Phil was a [secret] Communist and a progressive guy," stated James Daughtery, a comrade and the organizer for the Utility Workers. "He would call us guys who were heading up various unions. . . . We mapped out a program to increase our members among Black people and among Mexican people."[6] Connelly's relationship to the Communist Party became less obtuse in 1947, when he married Dorothy Healey, head of the Communist Party in Southern California.[7] More important for internal labor politics, the withdrawal of the ILGWU from the CIO, in 1940, eliminated significant left opposition from within the Los Angeles CIO Council.[8]

The Communist-led Los Angeles CIO Council demonstrated its commitment to racial justice by organizing industries with large numbers of minorities, taking on community-related concerns, and consciously promoting leadership from within the ranks. "They had minority members on the payroll who worked very diligently among minorities," recalled Assemblyman Augustus "Gus" Hawkins, the lone African American in the state legislature, who would himself work for the CIO-PAC. "That was an open field for them, you see, and they exploited that support."[9] For his part, Hawkins adroitly navigated the intra-left fighting; he worked closely with Bridges and Connelly but formally reported to Sidney Hillman, president of the Amalgamated Clothing Workers, an old Socialist, but who was more comfortable working with Communists than was the ILGWU's President David Dubinsky. The Los Angeles CIO Council consciously sought to include Latinos, particularly those within the Communist milieu. Frank López, from the United Furniture Workers, Local 567, served as the vice president of the Los Angeles CIO Council. In addition to organizing factories with large numbers of minorities, the CIO also sought to integrate "all white" industries. For his part, Daugherty helped break open the utility industry, which refused to hire Mexicans even to dig pole holes for transmission lines. He negotiated a nondiscrimination clause in the first union contract and then pressured management to diversify the workforce. "The end result was that we got great support [for the union's program] from the Mexican workers," according to Daugherty.[10]

The CIO Council also supported efforts by Luisa Moreno, a Guatemalan-born organizer for the United Cannery, Agriculture, Packing, and Allied Workers of America (UCAPAWA), to establish a Latino organization that would work closely with the CIO. A former Communist, who still worked closely with those in the party, she took a year and organized the Congress of Spanish Speaking Peoples.[11] The Congreso represented the confluence of three social forces: Latinos seeking to organize themselves and form alliances outside the ethnic community; the CIO's hope of gaining access to the ethnic community for organizing purposes; and the Communist Party's desire to expand the network of anti-fascist, popular front organizations. The Congreso fit comfortably into the paradigm adopted by the Communist Party of the United States in 1938. It decided to adopt a reform agenda and to undertake "mass work among the national groups and organizations in the first place among Italians, Germans, Poles, Jews, and South Slavs, and Spanish-speaking people."[12]

The First National Congress of the Mexican and Spanish-American Peoples of the United States was held in Los Angeles in March 1939. The Congreso also benefited from its placement squarely within the New Deal and the election, in November 1938, of California Governor Culbert Olson, a Democrat who was backed by the liberal-left and politically active Mexican Americans. At the conclave, the delegates heard from Olson's son and top aide, Richard Olson, Lieutenant Governor Ellis Patterson, and Carey McWilliams, chief of California's Division of Immigration and Housing. Coalition partners, including the presidents of two CIO unions, led some of the breakout groups.[13] Reid Robinson, president of the International Union of Mine, Mill, and Smelter Workers, headed the labor committee; UCAPAWA president Donald Henderson assisted. The two unions had a sizable Latino membership and were part of the left wing of the militant new Congress of Industrial Organization. The Congreso passed resolutions supporting "legislation outlawing all racial distinctions against the Spanish-speaking people" and opposed efforts to weaken the National Labor Relations Act.[14]

In typical popular front fashion, the Congreso's president, Eduardo Quevedo, was a liberal progressive who came out of the Latino community, and the staff person, Josephina Fierro de Bright, had strong ties to the Communist Party. The eighteen-year-old lived in Beverly Hills with her screenwriter husband, John Bright, who was one of the original "secret four" members of the Hollywood Branch of the Communist Party.[15] This powerful alliance lasted less than one year. It was torn apart by the organization's decision to abandon its opposition to fascism in response to the shifts in Russia's position following the signing of the Hitler-Stalin Pact.[16] The Los Angeles CIO Council and its allies proceeded to attack President Roosevelt and Governor Olson—icons of the New Deal—for supporting war preparedness. They then sought to block Roosevelt's renomination by running a rival slate of delegates for the 1940 Democratic National Convention.[17] For his part, Eduardo Quevedo, like most Latinos, departed the Congreso, leaving behind those operating in CIO and Communist Party circles.[18] This development was parallel to developments in the African American community, where A. Philip Randolph, head of the Sleeping Car Porters Union, and with ties to the Socialist Party, resigned as president of the national Negro Labor Congress.[19]

Following the splintering of the Congreso as a broad-based organization, the Latino activists would focus their energies in two general directions.

Those close to the left-led CIO Council would focus on empowering workers though unionization, and would engage in a number of community issues, most notably taking leadership of the Sleepy Lagoon Defense Committee during World War II. In the political arena, they supported non-Latino CIO-endorsed candidates, despite the Second Congreso's stated commitment to "fight for political recognition" in "Federal, State, County, and Civic Life."[20] The Eduardo Quevedo-led cohort focused on increasing the number of Latino appointed and elected officials, assumed a leadership role in advocating for Latino youth, and joined with others in pushing for fair employment legislation. This included making permanent the federal Fair Employment Practices Committee created by President Roosevelt at the urging of A. Philip Randolph.

The Reemergence of a Socialist-led, Labor-Based Civil Rights

In 1946, the California CIO Council and others within the partially reconstructed popular front partnered with the NAACP and others to place Proposition 11 on the November 1946 ballot. The measure called for the outlawing of discrimination on the job and the establishment of a state Fair Employment Practices Commission. It was modeled after legislation twice introduced by Assemblyman Hawkins. Hawkins's bill did not even get out of committee in the Republican-controlled state legislature in 1943. In the next legislative session, in 1945, he reintroduced the measure as Assembly Bill 3. To improve its chance of passage Hawkins sought to make the issue bipartisan. Assemblyman William Rosenthal, from Boyle Heights, the legislature's lone Jewish member, cosponsored the bill with two moderate Republicans. The liberal community then sought to rally support behind the legislation, forming in Los Angeles the Southern California Committee for a State FEPC. Judge Isaac Pacht, president of the Los Angeles Community Council, chaired the group. The liberal-led committee placed discrimination in the context of World War II. "Enemy bombs and bullets don't discriminate between one American fighting man and another . . . the blood of Catholic, Protestant, and Jew, of Negro, Mexican, and a dozen other 'minority' groups has been spilled in the fight for democracy and freedom," stated one flyer. "It isn't going to make much sense to them if they are told, when they come home: 'You were good enough to FIGHT for us, but you can't WORK for us because you are a Mexican (or a Jew, or a Catholic, or a Negro, or . . .).'"[21] According to Hawkins, this was the first broad based, liberal-led, multicultural organization. It included liberal Mexican Americans such as Eduardo Quevedo, and leftist CIO leader Luisa Moreno. Religious community leaders also supported the bill in 1945. Los Angeles FEPC backers included Catholic Archbishop John J. Cantwell, Rabbi Edgar F. Magnin, Episcopal Bishop W. Bertrand Stevens, and Church Federation executive E. C. Farnham.[22]

The AFL California State Federation of Labor endorsed Proposition 11 at its summer 1946 convention. The dominant trade union movement in the state had long supported ending racial discrimination but had done little to agitate or educate around improving race relations. Moreover, the national AFL gave it no legal power to prevent discrimination among its affiliates.[23] However, the national AFL was committed to ending racial discrimination, and Proposition 11 provided an opportunity to act. Along with the national CIO, the AFL was working closely with the New York-based Jewish Labor Committee to establish civil rights committees within the major labor councils around the nation. This then would be the ideal time to start such a group within the Los Angeles Central Labor Council, which represented a half million workers (and which was five to ten times larger than the CIO Council).[24]

The Socialist-led ILGWU, which had helped start the Los Angeles CIO Council in 1937, now took the initiative in 1946 in forming and staffing a civil rights committee within the AFL Central Labor Council. The council formed a Labor Committee to Combat Intolerance under the direction of Zane Meckler. Meckler had joined the Young People's Socialist League while attending the Teachers College at Columbia University, and most recently worked for the CIO Textile Workers. The ILGWU-headed Jewish Labor Committee (JLC) donated his services to the AFL. Meckler had arrived in Los Angeles in July 1946 carrying letters of introduction from national AFL and CIO leaders. According to Meckler, AFL council head William Bassett quickly embraced the idea of establishing a local civil rights committee. Bassett's enthusiasm likely reflected a sincere desire to improve race relations, a predisposition to follow national union policy, and the JLC's approach of working through established local labor leaders.[25] "We do not even propose to give publicity to our own organization," Meckler told the *Los Angeles Times,* "but to name official CIO and AFL leaders to head a labor committee against intolerance and perform the basic education and publicity through these channels."[26]

Two days later, the *Los Angeles Citizen,* the AFL's weekly newspaper, announced the formation of the Labor Committee to Combat Intolerance. "The American Federation of Labor always has been opposed to intolerance and discrimination," stated Aubrey Blair, who also headed the council's Church, Civic, and Charities Committee. The paper focused on the practical implications of not being more forceful in attacking prejudice. This argument had two basic components: first, employers exploited historic antagonisms based on ethnicity, race, and religion to undermine support for unionization; and second, Communists were using legitimate grievances in this area to advance their larger agenda. "It was also announced that during the next few months the committee would sponsor a number of community-wide activities dramatically illustrating Labor's stake in the drive against intolerance."[27]

The "first public function" of the Labor Committee to Combat Intolerance was a luncheon for two hundred labor leaders at the Mayfair Hotel, with Will Rogers Jr. as the keynote speaker. Rogers was the Democratic candidate for U.S. Senate. He used the luncheon as a venue for his major civil rights speech. The AFL newspaper stated that the audience included guests from "community organizations that will cooperate closely with the program."[28] According to Meckler, while the AFL successfully reached out to African Americans and immigrant Jews, in 1946 there were no community-based Latino organizations with whom to ally.[29] This is because Quevedo, the Congreso's founding president and liberal Latino leader during World War II, had stopped his active political life to raise his children after the death of his wife. The Communist-led Congreso had also disbanded. For his part, Assemblyman Hawkins hired Jaime González to join the pro–Proposition 11 campaign staff. González was a former CIO activist who had a good relationship with Connelly but whose father, a former Mexican government official, was a Socialist, and his mother was active in the ILGWU.[30]

The AFL campaigned for Proposition 11 to create a Fair Employment Practices Commission.[31] So, too, did the CIO and the liberal-left. The opposition was based organizationally in the Chamber of Commerce and among agribusinesses. Opponents played on historic racial fears, enhanced by the movement of large numbers of African Americans to California during the war to take jobs in the shipyards and other defense work. Opponents also played the Red Card, stating in the official ballot argument that fair employment was "communistic." The daily press also opposed the initiative. In the end, the fair employment initiative failed by an almost three-to-one margin.[32]

The lopsided defeat of the Fair Employment initiative was a huge setback for the civil rights movement. It also reflected a strategic miscalculation because it is far easier to enact civil rights laws in legislative bodies than among voters. Yet 1946 would prove to be a pivotal moment because of the engagement of the AFL and the non-Communist left in civil rights through the initiative of the Socialist-led ILGWU. The Jewish Labor Committee staffers would continue to work through the AFL Central Labor Council and with CIO unions loyal to the national CIO leadership and in opposition to the

Communists leading the Los Angeles Council. This served to create an alternative civil rights and political network that included racial minorities.

The Community Services Organization: Progressive Labor and Community Empowerment

Shortly after the failed 1947 city council campaign of Edward Roybal, he and a group of supporters met to decide what to do next. They expressed anger at rampant discrimination and frustration at the absence of Latinos in public office and the reality learned during the campaign that most Mexican Americans in the progressive and cosmopolitan district were not registered to vote. The group decided to stay together to form a politically oriented group to fill the organizational void in the ethnic community. These indigenous community activists soon linked up with Saul Alinsky, the independent radical at the head of the Chicago-based Industrial Areas Foundation (IAF), and with Fred Ross, a community organizer looking to work in the Latino community. Out of this came the Community Services Organization that Ross agreed to work for, and Alinsky agreed to help by paying Ross's salary.[33]

The initial CSO officers reflected the organization's progressive positioning. Edward Roybal, around whose unsuccessful 1947 city council campaign the group came together, became CSO president. He was a health educator in the fight against tuberculosis. He was also a World War II veteran who had served briefly on the Los Angeles County Democratic Central Committee and during the war had endorsed a Popular Front event cosponsored by a number of Latin American consuls.[34] The vice president was Jamie González, who had chaired the CIO Council's Minority Committee during World War II, but had since become a YMCA youth counselor.[35] Treasurer María Durán, a member of the immigrant generation, was a board member of her ILGWU local and an independent radical (whose daughter had Trotskyist leanings).[36] A key original board member was United Steel Worker union leader Tony Ríos. As a teenager he had helped lead a farmworker strike; he identified with the national CIO and the Catholic Worker movement.[37]

The presence of rank and file leaders of the AFL International Ladies Garment Workers Union and the CIO United Steel Workers of America within the CSO's leadership team reflected the growing influence of Latinos within those two unions. The two unions shared a progressive, community orientation. Jews with ties to the old Socialist Party continued to lead the ILGWU. The United Steel Workers were close to labor priests and the progressive wing of the Catholic Church.[38] Simultaneous to the formation of the CSO, in 1947, both unions were involved in the founding and support of the Catholic

Labor Institute. The group encouraged Catholics to join unions and portrayed Christ as a working-class carpenter.[39]

The CSO leaders' latent suspicion towards Communists was reflected in the process by which the organization decided whether to accept Fred Ross as their community organizer. The group liked his ideas and analyses but insisted that he prove he was not a Communist. Not knowing how to prove what he was not, Ross called Alinsky, who in turn contacted Chicago Bishop Bernard J. Sheil, who served on Alinsky's board and headed the national Catholic Youth Organization (CYO). Bishop Sheil called Bishop Joseph Mc-Gucken in Los Angeles. McGucken had chaired Governor Earl Warren's commission that investigated the causes of the Zoot Suit Riots. As a result, Ross received an audience with McGucken, who agreed not only to vouch for Ross but to back the organizing effort, sending a supportive letter to area priests.[40]

Ross went to work to broaden and deepen the CSO's reach throughout the community, targeting the two groups with the largest number of Latino members: organized labor and the Catholic Church. He built on existing relationships, developing ties to parish priests and gaining the institutional support of the ILGWU and the Steel Workers, who shared a commitment to community organizing. "The work issues were wages, hours and working conditions, and industrial safety. The community issues were street lights, paved streets, and housing. And discrimination was a big problem. So you had to link the two together," recalled Cass Alvin, Polish American spokesman for Steelworkers District Council 38. "We used to tell people: 'You work at Bethlehem [Steel], but you vote in the community.'"[41] The ILGWU's Abe Levy added that the union had thousands of new members, most of whom were Latinas, and the union supported the CSO and the Catholic Labor Institute "to get connections from the community."[42] The union also hired organizer Hope Mendoza, who joined the CSO board.[43]

Ross also reached out to Latino professionals and small businessmen, and to non-Latinos, particularly Jews, but also white ethnics in the Boyle Heights neighborhood on the Eastside of Los Angeles. Having incorporated key power centers into the group, the CSO undertook building a membership from the ground up. It conducted nightly "house meetings," where supporters invited a group of friends and neighbors to their home to learn about the CSO. Those who showed interest were put on one of a number of committees, which Ross staffed during the day. Ross encouraged the CSO to welcome everyone willing to work for group-established, community-oriented goals, and not to bar Communists, as a number of liberal groups had started to do.[44]

While insisting on remaining above sectarian polemics, Ross remained acutely aware of the Communists' alternating efforts to draw CSO leaders into their orbit and to take over the organization. Henry Nava, who would become the CSO's second president, stressed that Ross "cautioned us" about how the Communists might try to take over the CSO.[45] "What I heard from my dad," recalls Fred Ross Jr., himself an organizer, "is that the [Communist] Party was dying to get a hold of the Latino leadership. They were hoping to take all these *new* leaders on their agenda."[46] Ross's approach could be summarized by one of his axioms: "Don't waste time fighting the competition; use that time to fight the issues and win and that will take care of the competition."[47]

Still, as an organizer, it was Ross's job to empower the indigenous Latino leaders to reach their own conclusions. In late summer 1947, the CSO drew the attention of those within the Communist Party milieu who were now organizing through the Mexican American Civil Rights Congress, which was essentially the latest incarnation of the Congreso. It was led by Frank López, now a UE Local 1421 organizer, Oscar Castro, with the Furniture Workers, and Leroy Parra, a Latino Communist on the board of the Progressive Citizens of America, the precursor to Wallace's Progressive Party. After a police beating of a Latino youth, the Mexican American Civil Rights Congress invited Edward Roybal, Margarita Durán, Tony Ríos, and Henry Nava to participate in a series of protest meetings under their auspices. Some of the CSO leaders agreed. "I saw it was orchestrated for a certain purpose, and it was not a community effort," said Nava. "They wanted to absorb respectability by listing our names in their mailings."[48]

In January 1948, with the CSO's activist base having reached several hundred, and house meetings bringing in still more, the organization convinced the Registrar of Voters to come to the Eastside to conduct its first-ever swearing-in of Mexican American volunteer registrars. Election officer Marcus Woodward swore in forty-nine registrars in the social hall of St. Mary's Catholic Church. With missionary zeal, they began, in Tony Ríos's words, to seek out individuals eligible to vote in "churches, markets, and door-to-door every day of the week."[49] The results were phenomenal. In three months, the CSO's volunteer registrars signed up eleven thousand new voters. This doubled the total number of Latino voters in Los Angeles and dramatically impacted the political dynamics in the Boyle Heights and East Los Angeles neighborhoods where the CSO had focused its efforts.[50]

The CSO grew out of the desire of indigenous Latino activists to improve their lives and their community. The garment and steel unions joined this effort out of a progressive desire to organize on the job and in the community, to help their Latino memberships, and to organize additional members. The issue of Communism was never part of this equation. Yet the effect of organizing a robust community-based Latino organization was to reduce the political space available for Communists and their allies to gain ground based on exploiting unaddressed grievances. Yet ironically, because the CSO never "red baited," the presence of this new block of progressive Latino voters was available for courting by those who expressed sympathy for Latino interests.

The Labor-Left Changes Strategy and Embraces Latino Candidates

The CSO's growing prowess and the dramatically expanded Mexican American voter base caught the attention of the CIO Council and their allies within the Los Angeles Communist Party, the largest outside of New York City. These forces had broken with President Harry Truman, the national CIO, and the Democratic Party. This provided for bitterness between former friends not seen since the Hitler-Stalin Pact. And, like the earlier rupture, the organizational issues were intertwined with foreign and domestic politics. The Soviet Union opposed the Marshall Plan to rebuild war-torn Europe and supported the formation of the Progressive Party in the United States. This third party was widely expected to take away enough Democratic votes in 1948 to ensure the election of a more isolationist and more anti-labor Republican president. It was also expected to make it impossible for the Democrats to recapture Congress.[51]

The Los Angeles CIO Council backed this move and, in early 1948, was looking for allies to help assemble a third political party to maintain control of the CIO Council in the face of increasing pressure from the national CIO to conform or lose its power. Anticipating the internal struggle for control of the Los Angeles CIO Council, the state CIO developed a strategy of increased emphasis on minority rights. "The [Nov. 1947] Santa Cruz Convention set up machinery with which to carry out a hard hitting program for minority groups," read the minutes of the California CIO executive committee, capturing the purposefulness of the industrial union movement's activities. "Those organizations which have gone ahead and done something about this point have strengthened their position instead of weakening it. . . . When the heat comes on we will have to look to minority groups for support."[52]

The CIO Council and Communist Party Left recognized that the newly registered Latino voters were open to the Progressive Party because they had no history of voting for Democrats, and its presidential candidate was former Vice President Henry Wallace. He was popular among Latinos because he spoke Spanish and had represented President Roosevelt in Los Angeles and in Latin America during World War II. (Those within the Communist milieu conveniently forgot that they had attacked Wallace, along with Roosevelt, during the 1940 election, during the period of the Hitler-Stalin pact.) The point person in this new initiative was Frank López. The former CIO Council and Congreso officer was now the third party's Latino staffer and organizer of Amigos de Wallace in Los Angeles. He worked closely with the CIO Council and helped to organize a "Leadership School" on "How to Fight Discrimination in the Shop and in the Community."[53]

The Progressive Party's most notable inroads into Latino Los Angeles, however, came with the recruitment and support of CSO member José Chávez and CSO advisor Richard Ibañez to run for elected office. José Chávez had run for office two years earlier against Assemblyman Elwyn S. Bennett, an Anglo incumbent with a 100 percent CIO voting record. At that time, the CIO Council rewarded the legislator for his consistent support for labor; loyalty to labor was now submerged by a more pressing goal: to develop an alliance with the Mexican American community. "Chávez's endorsement should be based on his progressive pro-labor record and the need for representation in the State Assembly of California's largest national minority," stated a Los Angles CIO Council internal document.[54] Attorney Richard Ibañez ran for the Superior Court.[55] John Allard, a member of the Council's PAC, and president of UAW Chrysler Local 230, added that Connelly was reaching out to Latinos "with zest, with zeal" because "there was strength" in the rapidly developing community.[56]

The CIO Council's support for José Chávez also served to differentiate the council's leftist leadership from growing internal opposition, which was coalescing around the newly organized California National CIO-PAC. This group was receiving backing from newly appointed CIO Regional Director Irwin DeShetler and from the larger international unions, such as steel, rubber, auto, and oil; together they represented a majority of the CIO members in Los Angeles. His selection, moreover, reduced Harry Bridges's scope of influence, and he became CIO director for Northern California. This led to the unusual situation where both the Los Angeles CIO Council and the National CIO-PAC functioned as CIO-sanctioned institutions even as they competed with each other for the hearts and minds of the industrial union movement.[57]

The underlying tensions between the warring factions within the LA CIO Council broke out into the open and engulfed the two Latino campaigns. In a directive to all CIO Councils, but specifically targeting Los Angeles and

New York, the largest bodies under Communist Party control, the national CIO demanded that councils pass a resolution condemning the Progressive Party and supporting the Marshall Plan. When the Los Angeles CIO Council refused, unionists loyal to the national organization walked out of the organization and charged that the municipal council was more interested in following the Communist Party line than in protecting U.S. workers.[58]

The Los Angeles CIO Council retaliated by playing the race card: seventy-five African American and Mexican American CIO activists charged that members of the National CIO-PAC "gave almost no consideration to the aspirations of Negro and Mexican people for representation in public office." According to the minority union activists, "These endorsements indicate the degree to which [the rival] group is fronting for anti-labor, anti-minority elements." By contrast, they asserted, the Los Angeles CIO Council "demonstrated an awareness of the responsibility of labor to the coalition, important segments of which are the Negro- and Mexican-American people."[59]

The facts were more nuanced than the incendiary language. The National CIO-PAC had endorsed African American Democratic Assemblyman Augustus Hawkins and nonpartisan judicial candidate Richard Ibañez, the most prominent minority candidates. But they had not backed José Chávez or any third-party candidates running for partisan office. Still, the racism charge carried a wallop and provided a stark contrast: the CIO Council and the Communists supported a Latino for the legislature; the National CIO-PAC and progressive anti-Communists did not.[60]

On June 1, 1948, thousands of newly registered Mexican American voters went to the polls. The result was electrifying. The two Latino candidates achieved a record number of votes in their surprisingly strong, if ultimately unsuccessful, campaigns. "[A] democratic development has taken place almost unnoticed," editorialized the Los Angeles Daily News, adding, it "hasn't taken place by accident but because a group known as the Community Service Organization has worked to encourage it." The paper added: "The fact that a pro-Wallace spirit may have animated some of the election interest nevertheless doesn't invalidate the deeper significance of what took place."[61]

The CSO created a new block of progressive voters and thus changed the political calculus for the Latino community and those wishing to relate to the community. The CSO's goal was to get the attention of local government officials, but those within the CIO Council and the Communist milieu also took notice. This group, which had previously related to Latinos as workers and community members, now also saw them as voters. Despite the powerful use of race as an organizing tool, and the good will that went with an association with former Vice President Henry Wallace, there were limits to their ability to pick up additional adherents because of the presence of the CSO as the dominant Latino organization. To their credit, the ILGWU and the USWA never pressured the CSO to adopt their own political agenda. The CSO remained above the partisan fray even as the two unions bitterly attacked Henry Wallace in their narrowly successful effort to carry California for President Truman, and thus ensure his come-from-behind reelection.

Edward R. Roybal: Latino Mobilization and Coalition Politics

"Next year there will be an excellent chance to form a new coalition," wrote former California Attorney General Robert Kenny, a Wallace partisan, in the *Nation*. "A municipal election will be held in Los Angeles in the Spring of 1949."[62] The district in which the liberal-left held greatest sway was the ninth, which was based in Boyle Heights, with its radical traditions, large Jewish and Latino communities, and smaller number of African Americans, Japanese Americans, and white ethnics. The ailing seventy-eight-year-old incumbent was an icon on the Left. Parley P. Christensen was the 1920 presidential candidate of the Farmer-Labor Party. Despite repeated statements that he might retire, the progressive warrior refused to leave the stage so that a minority candidate could run for the Los Angeles City Council that then consisted of fifteen white men, all but one of whom were Protestants; diversity consisted of a lone Irish Catholic.

The best person situated to challenge Councilman Christensen was CSO President Edward Roybal. Over the course of eighteen months he had helped create and lead the first broad-based organization within the Mexican American community. The group had developed an independent political base that incorporated hundreds of activists, a thousand members, and fifteen thousand new voters (although they were not all in the district). Moreover, the CSO was near the center of the liberal-left ideological spectrum in the district, and had established ties to organized labor, the Catholic Church, the Jewish community, and to individuals in both the Democratic and Progressive parties. The CSO also benefited enormously from the steady hand, adroit skills, and tireless efforts of its organizer, Fred Ross. His strategy was simple: mobilize Latinos, and build alliances to other important voter blocks, particularly Jews and union members.

Edward Roybal announced his candidacy for city council and resigned as CSO president in January 1949.[63] He started with the backing of the AFL garment workers and CIO Steel Workers. The steel workers also helped line up support from the National CIO-PAC and other CIO unions loyal to the national organization. The ILGWU helped line up support among progressive Jews, including members of the Jewish Labor Committee and the Workmen's Circle, a large fraternal society within the Socialist Party milieu that included a growing number of professionals and business owners. Roybal and his campaign manager, Roger Johnson, the first president of the Los Angeles Newspaper Guild, spent a lot of time with Jewish community leaders. As a result, the Jewish community did not run a candidate of its own against Christensen, making it easier for Yiddish-speaking voters to back Roybal. Roybal also picked up support from three heavily Latino unions, the AFL Laborers Local 300, the CIO Amalgamated Clothing Workers, and the independent railroad brotherhood-affiliated Maintenance of Way local.[64]

Obtaining support from the two big labor councils would be more challenging. The AFL Central Labor Council ultimately stayed with Christensen, rewarding the incumbent for his pro-labor record.[65] The Los Angeles CIO Council had a more difficult decision. They could do as they did in 1947, and join with the AFL to back an old friend—Christensen—or they could back a challenger with whom they shared progressive allies. In a very profound way, the CIO Council's options had been reduced by decisions made the previous year, when in an effort to gain a competitive advantage over its rivals within the CIO, it had deviated from the general practice of backing pro-labor incumbents. The CIO Council then went further and accused the National CIO-PAC of being racist for not supporting a Latino candidate running on the Progressive ticket. A decision not to support Roybal thus risked exposing the CIO Council to race-based attacks from the National CIO-PAC, as well as isolating the Council from the most dynamic social force in Los Angeles.

The CIO Council decided to go with Roybal. "So by 1949, Phil Connelly knew that things had changed a lot," quipped Tony Ríos.[66] "It was an exciting flip," stated James Daugherty, describing the CIO Council's decision to back Roybal. The longtime Connelly confidant, who was now head of the California CIO Council, added that the decision was not universally supported. "There was a lot of criticism," both from Connelly's "enemies" and from longtime "Christensen supporters" in the council.[67]

After deciding to go with Roybal, the CIO Council urged its affiliates and allies to do the same. The Independent Progressive Party, the leftist CIO unions with large Latino memberships, and the African American *California Eagle*—all of whom had campaigned for Christensen two years earlier—joined the CIO Council in backing Roybal. The *Labor Herald* later stated that Roybal "was vigorously supported by several CIO local unions with heavy membership in his district, namely Furniture Workers Local 576,

ILWU Warehousemen's local 26, Electrical Workers local 1421, FTA local 25 and Mine-Mill local 700."[68] The Left's decision to back Roybal also increased enthusiasm within a number of allied AFL unions with a strong left-wing membership in the district.

The CIO Council did not join the Roybal campaign, however; it chose instead to organize its own door-to-door efforts in conjunction with the Independent Progressive Party. CIO Council delegate and Communist Party chief Dorothy Healey stressed that "the C.I.O. always ran its campaigns independently."[69] For his part, Roybal appreciated the help but remained highly cynical about their motives. He stated that Phil Connelly and company joined the campaign only after Monsignor O'Dwyer and "everybody else was in there." "They didn't want a pro-Roybal campaign as such," stressed Roybal. "They wanted to use my name and the CSO as a vehicle to build [the Independent Progressive Party]."[70]

The support for Roybal by the CIO Council, even if qualified, caused a stir in some quarters. The AFL Labor League of Hollywood Voters, a federation of twenty-odd Hollywood unions, issued a statement two weeks prior to the March election that lauded Christensen and attacked Roybal for accepting support from the CIO Council and its allies in the community. "It is the position of the League of Hollywood Voters that 'Stalinists' constitute the main menace to full democracy and complete civil rights at home and abroad, and any candidate who accepts their support is automatically an opponent of free labor and good citizens alike."[71] The strong statement is likely a reflection of the ideological transformation of its chairman, actor Ronald Reagan, from a Popular Front supporter to a liberal anti-Communist during the bitter jurisdictional struggle between the International Association of Theatrical and Stage Employees (IATSE) and the left-led and CIO-supported Conference of Studio Unions.[72]

Despite such opposition, Roybal had built a formidable coalition that reached into every segment of the diverse district. On Election Day, fourteen of the fifteen city councilmen easily won reelection. Only Christensen failed to win outright. It was not that he had lost support in the district. His actual gain of more than 7 percent over his previous total just wasn't enough to secure the election. The big change was Roybal. His support increased almost four-fold, due in large measure to the successful CSO voter registration and get-out-the-vote drive, and overwhelming support from the Jewish precincts in Boyle Heights. Roybal won in the runoff by a two to one margin.[73]

In two short years, Edward Roybal and the CSO had transformed politics on the Eastside and within progressive Los Angeles. His relatively tall frame and upraised hand against the marble pillars and wood dais of the council chamber provided a powerful and dignified image. The July 1949 swearing-in made Roybal an important ethnic symbol, emblematic of a community on the move. Roybal was the only Mexican American to hold a major office in California. The thirty-three-year-old councilman was also a source of pride for supportive coalition partners, including many within organized labor. Soon after the election, the AFL Central Labor Council, which had backed the loser, pledged their loyalty to the new councilman. Philip Connelly, who had delivered the CIO Council for Roybal, ironically never got a chance to bask in the reflected glory. He was forced to resign in March 1949 as head of the CIO Council. It was a severe blow to the Communist Party Left, in part because the CIO had been used to form civil rights and political coalitions.[74]

The Fight for a Fair Employment Ordinance

One of Roybal's first official acts was to assume the leadership of the civil rights forces inside the council and out in the community who were support-ing a municipal ordinance to ban discrimination in employment. It would be a tough sell in Los Angeles because two years earlier a similar measure had failed to pass on a seven to eight vote, and the political dynamic within the council had not changed. Roybal had replaced another civil rights cham-pion and the other fourteen members had remained the same. The issue had gained a new sense of urgency among minority advocates because the Republican-controlled California legislature had turned down Hawkins's Fair Employment Practice Commission bill and a weaker proposal to study the issue that was backed by moderate Republican Governor Earl Warren. Similar measures were defeated in Congress by a coalition of conservative Republicans and Southern Democrats.[75]

Despite freshman standing, Roybal was a natural to take the lead on the council and to work with a broad array of community-based organizations. He was the only identifiable "minority" on the council. Roybal also had more freedom to focus on civil rights because voters in his liberal-left district ex-pected its representatives to fight for social justice. Still, he was faced with a challenge. He needed to establish a rapport with his colleagues even as he asked for help on a controversial measure in which councilmen had already staked out clear positions. Roybal, moreover, needed to stay focused on his district even as he dove into council business. As a newly elected politician, Roybal went in with tremendous goodwill in the community, but he would need to rapidly consolidate his support because the council term was only two years. In effect, Roybal decided to make the uphill fight for fair employ-ment his signature issue.

Councilman Roybal began to organize within and outside of the council. Working with organized labor and the Jewish community, he lined up council colleagues to cosponsor the measure and helped assemble a broad-based coalition to advocate for its passage. The Council for Equality in Employment served as an umbrella organization of labor, liberal, religious, and minority organizations. Milton Sean, director of the Anti-Defamation League, a Jewish defense group, served as the temporary chair. Key partners included the AFL Central Labor Council and the CIO Industrial Union Council. The group drafted the proposed ordinance based on language developed two years earlier and models developed in other cities. The Council for Equality in Employment also developed plans to aggressively shape public opinion behind the proposal in the hopes of gaining the eight votes.[76]

The strategic challenge was that the eighth vote would have to come from a member of the council's conservative, anti-civil rights majority. The most likely supporter, if one was possible, was Councilman Ed Davenport. Davenport represented a politically liberal district that included much of central Los Angeles, with a sizable Mexican American and Filipino American population. He had gotten elected with liberal-left backing and a promise to support fair employment, but he had proved to be a conservative Democrat and a rabid anti-Communist. Reaching him would require a reframing of the issue in terms of equality of opportunity and how eliminating discrimination would strike a blow to the Communist Party Left.[77]

These largely behind-the-scenes activities were shaken three weeks into the council session with the intervention by groups associated with the Communist Party. They proposed their own ordinance and established a separate coordinating council, with the California Legislative Conference acting as a primary coalition vehicle. Paul Major, president pro tem of the Men's Division of the American Jewish Congress, headed the group, which included many of those associated with the failed Wallace campaign. Some fifty delegates from a variety of community groups met on July 21 at the Alexandria Hotel. They kicked-off a planned signature drive in each district with a barbecue at the Commonwealth Club in Central Los Angeles.[78]

Assemblyman Hawkins, who maintained good relations with both liberals and leftists and had worked for the CIO-PAC during World War II, provided the principal remarks. The *California Eagle,* the Left's principal voice in the African American community, sought to demonstrate the group's appeal across racial divides by listing one of the attendees as "Jaime González, of the Community Services Organization." González, no longer a CSO officer, recalled that he attended the event as an individual. The participation of Hawkins and González demonstrated the reality of overlapping networks and the still-fluid political situation. The leftists failed, however, to convince a single city councilman to introduce their alternative fair employment measure.[79]

On August 9, 1949, Councilman Roybal and six colleagues jointly introduced a fair employment measure dubbed the Equal Opportunity Ordinance. The measure was referred to Roybal's Public Health and Welfare Committee and the Personnel Committee chaired by Councilman Ed Davenport. The proposal would be heard by a joint special committee.

Roybal's primary ally in the civil rights and labor community, the Council for Equality in Employment, meanwhile, positioned itself as a "constructive voice" and sought to marginalize those on both the racist Right and the Communist Left. In so doing they placed their civil rights agenda—and by extension, President Truman's Fair Deal—in the context of the Cold War. "The evils and injustices arising from discrimination in employment because of race, creed, color, or national origin form a fertile breeding ground within our City for communistic influences," wrote the Council for Equality in Employment. "To fail to take constructive action now will give further credence to the belief that racial and religious discrimination is too thoroughly established in our economy to be outlawed." The coalition sought to reassure the city council that its proposal was mainstream, emphasizing that similar measures had been passed by municipal governments in Chicago, Phoenix, Philadelphia, Milwaukee, Minneapolis, and such western states as Washington, Oregon, and New Mexico.[80]

The Council for Equal Opportunity strategy also played into the individual tactical needs of its coalition members. The efforts to marginalize the Communist Party Left to get the critical eighth vote from a conservative Democrat on the city council converged with the efforts by liberal and progressive unionists who were in pitched battles for control of their organizations. In the Los Angeles CIO Council, the national CIO forces had helped force Connelly's resignation but had not yet assumed control of the council. The national CIO was considering the expulsion of Communist-line national unions from its ranks. The AFL was also in the midst of battling Communists within its respective locals. The same process was occurring within the Jewish and African American communities in Los Angeles.[81]

The liberal labor and minority coalition then developed a more formal organizational structure. Judge Isaac Pacht agreed to serve as chair of the Council for Equal Opportunity. He was president of the Jewish Community Council. A functioning steering committee included representatives from every sector of the city, including CSO President Henry Nava, representatives from the NAACP and the Japanese American Citizens League, along with organized labor. The group sought and obtained a list of prominent citizens to serve as group "sponsors," thereby providing additional credibility. They included James Roosevelt, the late president's son, and former Congressman Will Rogers Jr., son of the cowboy comedian.

With prominent endorsers providing credibility and affiliated groups providing organization, the Council for Equal Opportunity embarked on an unprecedented citywide organizing drive to build neighborhood-level support of the proposed ordinance. It then established an organization within each of the fifteen council districts and began to lobby the respective councilmen. Participating organizations provided staff for the project, with one to three full-time staff assigned to drive the campaign in each council district. In addition to identifying pressure points with each councilman, the staff liaison was responsible for building a broad coalition and coordinating activities with the Council for Equal Opportunity command center.[82]

The fight for fair employment was particularly intense in two districts, although for different reasons. In Roybal's district, the Council for Equal Opportunity assigned three organizers to direct and help keep control of the debate. CSO organizer Fred Ross was assigned to oversee the campaign in Roybal's political base in Boyle Heights. Ross achieved what no other Council for Equal Opportunity designated coordinator would have dared try: the integration of the Communist Left and their allies into a united front. This was finessed by the creation of a new organization, the Ninth Council District Independent Citizens Council for an FEPC Ordinance. According to Ross, "We have been able to persuade the leadership in every group to make compromises in the interest of united action for FEP." The groups included the Boyle Heights and Lincoln Heights CSO and such core Council for Equal Opportunity affiliates as B'nai B'rith, United Steel Workers Local 1981, and the International Ladies Garment Workers' Union. They also included the Independent Progressive Party and the Mexican American National Association (ANMA), an outgrowth of Amigos de Wallace.[83]

The most important district in terms of the final council vote was the twelfth, home to Councilman Davenport, whose downtown constituents included a sizable number of Mexican Americans. The campaign reached out to labor, church, minority, civic, and veterans groups within the district. The multitask campaign operated on a number of levels. Opinion leaders in the district were contacted and encouraged to contact the councilman, and editors of neighborhood papers were asked to carry supportive material. Organizations were approached and asked to pass a resolution of support at their next meeting, at which time organizers distributed postcards. The cards were then collected, stamped, and mailed to Davenport. Supportive organizations likewise mailed information to their members, and public events were used as opportunities to promote the ordinance and to generate additional postcards.[84]

Labor Day 1949 celebrations provided ideal forums. The first major event of the day was the Catholic Labor Institute's annual Mass and breakfast, where CIO Director Irwin DeShetler shared the stage with Archbishop Francis McIntyre and AFL Council President Thomas Radford. This was followed by the Los Angeles CIO council's citywide picnic at Streamland Park in the Eastside community of Pico Rivera. Some seven thousand unionists participated in the family-oriented event. At fifteen-minute intervals, participants were directed from the podium to the civil rights table to write a postcard to their councilman.[85]

Two weeks later, the vote nearing, the Council for Economic Equality impelled Councilman Roybal to speak at the September 16 Mexican Independence Day celebration in Davenport's district. The event was expected to draw between 1,000 and 1,500 people, and organizer Max Mont attended to encourage them to send postcards to their councilmen. Roybal's appearance was particularly noteworthy because it signified his ability to appeal to Mexican Americans throughout the city and his willingness to go into a colleague's district for the purpose of generating interest for an upcoming vote. Roybal and the liberal civil rights coalition went all out to pressure Davenport.[86]

While the Communist Party Left had made a tactical decision to work with the CSO and the liberal civil rights coalition in the ninth council district, it continued to build its independent political base among labor and minority activists, particularly Mexican Americans. For the sixteenth of September, the Progressive Party sponsored a "Fiesta for Freedom." The event took place at the CIO Building that remained under the control of the leftists despite their losing control of the council. The event attracted eight thousand people and included Ignacio López, a prominent Mexican American publisher, who "urged fiesta guests to get into action behind the fight to pass fair employment legislation."[87]

Countervailing pressure came from conservative and right-wing members of the community. On September 23, 1949, the Los Angeles Times weighed in, editorializing against the proposed ordinance. The Times argued that such a measure "tends to rob an individual of his freedom to choose his associates in work, as business partners or employees, and stirs up a train of resentments and conflicts." The powerful paper reiterated the charge that the Communists supported the measure. Then came a new argument. In a creative use of the maxim that "all politics are local," the paper extrapolated data from the failed

1946 state fair employment initiative to demonstrate that voters in fourteen of the fifteen council districts opposed the idea of a fair employment law. The *Los Angeles Times* stressed that Roybal alone "supports the wishes of a majority of the people whom he represents."[88]

Four days later, on September 27, 1949, the Los Angeles City Council voted against the proposed ordinance eight to six, with one supporter absent. Despite the unprecedented mobilization of community groups and thousands of voters who sent postcards to their representatives, nothing changed. It is unlikely that a different strategy would have prevailed in a context where the council majority had already voted against the idea, the majority of the voters had expressed their opposition, and where conservative economic and opinion leaders like the *Los Angeles Times* helped animate the opposition.[89]

Conclusion

The disappointing defeat for the Roybal-authored fair employment ordinance was still a victory for the councilman, for the CSO, and for liberal labor. The campaign elevated Roybal's political profile and hastened the CSO's integration into the city's developing minority-liberal-labor alliance while protecting itself from criticism of those in the Communist milieu, which still had a strong presence in the ninth council district. The annual report of the Japanese American Citizens League talked about its membership in the Council for Economic Equality and their work with Roybal and the CSO. More importantly, Japanese American civil rights organizations stressed the continuing dialogue between minority and labor groups.[90]

The following spring, in April 1950, the renamed Greater Los Angeles CIO Council formally "pledge[d] complete physical and moral support to the Community Services Organization."[91] This was possible, in part, because— with the ouster of the Communist-led unions—those CIO leaders close to the CSO, particularly in the Steelworkers, assumed positions of prominence in the reconfigured organization. So, too, the AFL Los Angeles Central Labor Council endorsed the CSO and encouraged its affiliates to support the organization. This dramatically improved Latino-AFL relationship reflected the importance of Councilman Roybal to the unions, and the emergence of ILGWU organizer Hope Mendoza as the key liaison between the AFL and CSO and the larger Latino community.

But, on a more subtle level, the changes in the Latino-labor relationship also reflected the ILGWU's multi-pronged investments in civil rights. The garment union was a pillar in both the Community Services Organization and the Jewish Labor Committee, as well as a force in the Central Labor

Council, Catholic Labor Institute, and Jewish Community Relations Council. It also remained central to the small but influential network of Socialists and Social Democrats. The garment union thus provides much of the behind-the-scenes social cohesion for the overlapping progressive networks. It was ironic that the ILGWU, which had had its Socialist leader removed as the head of the inchoate Los Angeles CIO Council by a Communist, would a decade later be involved in reducing their rival's influence. Moreover, this new influence would be institutionalized because the JLC's Max Mont, building on the pioneering work of Zane Meckler, would become the civil rights point person for both the AFL Central Labor Council and the Greater Los Angeles CIO Council.

Councilman Roybal would try several more times to pass a fair employment ordinance in Los Angeles, but to no avail. Roybal and the other liberal, labor, minority, and religious coalition partners, including Rt. Rev. Msgr. Thomas O'Dwyer, came together with like-minded people in Northern California to push for a state Fair Employment Practices Commission. Councilman Roybal served as a co-chairman of the California Committee for Fair Employment, and Steelworker Tony Ríos, CSO's third and longest serving president, assumed an active role on its board. Within the California Committee for Fair Employment, four progressives with "anti-Stalinist" attitudes provided critical leadership.[92] C. L. Dellums, the West Coast head of the Brotherhood of Sleeping Car Porters, and a top NAACP official, chaired the California Committee for Fair Employment. His boss, A. Philip Randolph, the father of the World War II national Fair Employment Practices Commission, was a Socialist who had resigned as president of the Negro Labor Congress after the Hitler-Stalin Pact. Moreover, the Communist-led "Progressive Caucus" opposed Dellums's election to a central labor council post because he was "not progressive enough."[93] The two full-time staff people came from the Jewish Labor Committee. The California Committee for Fair Employment's secretary and lead lobbyist was William "Bill" Becker. He had staffed the labor desk for Norman Thomas's 1948 Socialist Party presidential campaign before coming to California to organize farmworkers with Ernesto Galarza under the banner of the Socialist-led AFL National Farm Workers Union. The coordinator for Southern California was Max Mont. Mont was a former Trotskyist (a follower of Max Shachtman) who had fought the Communist leadership within the United Electrical Workers (UE), and then became a Social Democrat. A third individual, Earl Rabb, with the San Francisco Jewish Community Relations Council, functioned as a de facto staffer. He knew Becker and Mont from his college days in New York, where he was a follower of Shachtman. Dellums, Becker, Mont, and Rabb—all men of the

Left—shared both the anti-Stalinist attitudes that ran throughout liberal labor and the larger society, and possessed an abiding passion for civil rights.[94]

Finally, in 1959, ten years after Roybal first introduced his proposed municipal ordinance, and under continued pressure from the California Committee for Fair Employment, the California Legislature passed a state Fair Employment Practices Act. Newly elected Democratic Governor Edmund G. "Pat" Brown signed the bill as his first major legislative achievement. Three years later, Edward Roybal was elected to Congress as the first Latino from California; Augustus Hawkins was elected as the state's first African American member of Congress. That same year, 1962, the CSO birthed the United Farm Workers under the leadership of César Chávez and Dolores Huerta, both of whom were trained by Catholic labor priests prior to developing their organizing skills as top CSO leaders. In yet another remarkable connection, Dolores Huerta went on to became the national honorary co-chair of the Democratic Socialists of America, the descendent of the old Socialist Party whose members had helped shape postwar labor and civil rights politics in California.[95]

Notes

1. Zaragosa Vargas, *Labor Rights Are Civil Rights: Mexican Workers in Twentieth-Century America* (Princeton, N.J.: Princeton University Press, 2005), 284.

2. Robert H. Zieger, *The CIO: 1935–1955* (Chapel Hill: University of North Carolina Press, 1995), 375.

3. George G. Higgins, *Organized Labor and the Church: Reflections of a 'Labor Priest'* (New York: Paulist Press, 1993); Kenneth J. Heineman, *A Catholic New Deal: Religion and Reform in Depression Pittsburgh* (University Park: Pennsylvania State University Press, 1999).

4. Four of the new CIO unions were headed by Latinos: Carlos Panchez, Shoe Workers Local 112; Bob Morales, Steel Workers Organizing Committee (SWOC), Lodge 1447; Rocque Torrea, SWOC Lodge 1502; and Pablo Romero, Mine-Mill Local 370, based in Wilmington. Los Angeles IUC: Affiliated Unions List, 1937, Los Angeles County Federation of Labor Papers, Urban Archives Center, California State University, Northridge (UAC, CSUN).

5. For more on the founding of the CIO Council, see Kenneth C. Burt, "Los Angeles Council, Congress of Industrial Organizations," in Mari Jo Buhle, Paul Buhle, and Dan Georgakas, eds., *Encyclopedia of the American Left,* 2d ed. (New York: Oxford University Press, 1988), 459–61, and CIO Papers, box 6, Los Angeles file, Catholic University of America.

6. Author's interview with James L. Daugherty, Lynwood, California, Feb. 11, 1995. See also "'Slim' Connelly New Secretary of LA Council," *Labor's Herald,* May 18, 1939, 4.

7. Dorothy Ray Healey and Maurice Isserman, *California Red: A Life in the American Communist Party* (Urbana: University of Illinois Press, 1993), 116.

8. For more on the Communist Party, whose membership in Los Angeles rose to five thousand, see Maurice Isserman, *If I Had a Hammer: The Death of the Old Left and the Birth of the New Left* (New York: Basic Books, 1987), 3–28.

9. Author's interview with Augustus Hawkins, Washington, D.C., June 28, 1998.

10. James Daugherty interview.

11. Moreno briefly joined the Communist Party in New York. See Deportation and Related Activities, Luisa Moreno Benis, box 7, file 53 and 58, Robert W. Kenny Collection, Southern California Library for Social Studies and Research (SCLRSS).

12. "Draft Convention Resolutions," *The Communist* 17:4 (Apr. 1938): 351–58.

13. "Digest of Proceeding, First National Congress," box 13, file 9, Ernesto Galarza Papers, Special Collections, Stanford University; "U.S. Latins Open 3–Day Congress," *People's World,* Apr. 28, 1939, 3; "Southwest Congress Raises Minorities' Problems, Spurs Unity," *People's World,* May 1, 1939, 3.

14. "Digest of Proceedings, First National Congress"; "U.S. Latins Map Defense of Democracy: Southwest Congress Raises Minorities' Problems; Spurs Unity," *People's World,* May 1, 1939, 3.

15. Patrick McGilligan and Paul Buhle, in *Tender Comrades: A Backstory of the Blacklist* (New York: St. Martin's Press, 1997), 128–54.

16. The change in position can be seen by comparing Congreso resolutions at the national Congreso in Los Angeles in Apr. 1939, and the Dec. 1939 state gathering in Los Angeles. The first Congreso had endorsed the "Lima Conference for its efforts to block Nazi and Italian fascist domination of the economies of Central and South America." Now the Congreso declared the "European War has as its aim the redivision of the colonial countries and the conquest and reconquest of the markets and the resources of the world" and "the peoples of the United States, Mexico and all Latin America desire peace and complete neutrality," 13/9, Ernesto Galarza Papers, Special Collections, Stanford University.

17. Robert E. Burke, *Olson's New Deal for California* (Berkeley: University of California Press, 1953), 207–8; Harvey Klehr, *The Heyday of American Communism: The Depression Decade* (New York: Basic Books, 1984), 403; Minutes, Los Angeles CIO Council, Apr. 5, 1940, p. 1, Los Angles County Federation of Labor, UAC, CSUN; Statement of Vote, 1940, California State Archives.

18. Eduardo Quevedo became president the Los Angeles-based Spanish American Voters of California and functioned as the leader of the Mexican American community.

19. Harvey Klehr, *The Heyday of American Communism,* 402–3. A similar process occurred in the student movement. See chap. 9, "From Popular Front to Unpopular Sect," in Robert Cohen, *When the Old Left Was Young: Student Radicals and America's First Mass Student Movement, 1929–1941* (New York: Oxford University Press, 1993), 278–321.

20. Special Bulletin, Preparation for the Second Congress of Spanish-Speaking People in California," box 13, file 9, Ernesto Galarza Papers, Special Collections, Stanford University.

21. Leaflet, "Don't Mess It Up Now, Buddy!" FEPC, Pamphlet File, SCLRSS.

22. Augustus Hawkins interview; "Campaign Opened for California FEPC Act," *California Jewish Voice,* May 18, 1945, 3; "Clergy Cooperates on State FEPC Bill," *California Jewish Voice,* June 8, 1945, 2; "Continue Fight for State FEPC," *California Jewish Voice,* July 13, 1945, 2.

23. "Cal. Federation Recommendations, Propositions to Be on Nov. 5 Ballot," *Los Angeles Citizen,* Sept. 9, 1946, 1; Philip Taft, *Labor Politics American Style: The California State Federation of Labor* (Cambridge, Mass.: Harvard University Press, 1968), 177–78.

24. Author's interview with Emanuel Muravchik, telephone, Sept. 29, 2002; author's interview with Zane Meckler, Malibu, California, Mar. 29 and April 5, 1996; author's interview with William Becker, St. Helena, California, Sept. 8, 1993 and April 12, 1996.

25. Zane Meckler interview.

26. "Jewish labor Maps Campaign against Bigotry," *Los Angeles Times,* July 17, 1946, in part 2, p. 3.

27. "Committee to Fight Intolerance Named by Labor Council," *LA Citizen,* Aug. 8, 1946, 3.

28. "Will Rogers CLC Committee Meeting Guest," *Los Angeles Citizen,* Sept. 13, 1946, 4.

29. Zane Meckler interview.

30. Author interview with Jaime González Monroy, Monrovia, California, June 22, 1997.

31. "Cal. Federation Recommendations, Propositions to Be on Nov. 5 Ballot," *Los Angeles Citizen,* Sept. 9, 1946, 1.

32. Ballot Pamphlet and Statement of the Vote, 1946, California State Archives.

33. Kenneth C. Burt, "Latino Empowerment in Los Angeles: Postwar Dreams and Cold War Fears, 1948–1952," *Labor's Heritage 8:1* (Summer 1996): 4–25; Stanford D. Horwitt, *Let Them Call Me Rebel: Saul Alinsky, His Life and Legacy* (New York: Vintage Books, 1989), 222–35.

34. Author's interview with Edward Roybal, Pasadena, Mar. 10, 1995; "Earl Robinson to Emcee Pan-American Festival," *California Eagle,* Jan. 25, 1945, 12; Members of County Central Committees, May 1944, Los Angeles County Registrar of Voters; Himilce Hovas, *The Hispanic 100: A Ranking of the Latino Men and Women Who Have Most Influenced American Thought and Culture* (New York: Citadel Press, 1995), 81–85.

35. Jamie González Monroy interview.

36. Author's interview with Margarita Durán Méndez, Norwalk, California, Mar. 11, 1995.

37. Author's interviews with Anthony "Tony" Ríos, Los Angeles, 1994–97; "Anthony Ríos Dies; Built Latino Political Power," *Los Angeles Times,* May 22, 1999, B1.

38. See Heineman, *Catholic New Deal.*

39. Author's interviews with Cass Alvin, Downey, California, June 27, 1994, and Los Angeles, May 6, 1995; Tony Ríos interview; author's interview with Abe Levy, Los Angeles, May 31, 1996; author's interview with Msgr. William Barry, Newport Beach, California, Nov. 2, 1994. Catholic Labor Institute Papers, Archival Center, Archdiocese of Los Angeles.

40. P. David Finks, *The Radical Vision of Saul Alinsky* (New York: Paulist Press, 1984), 40–41; Fred Ross, untitled manuscript, 15, 21/8, Fred Ross Papers, Special Collections, Stanford University.

41. Cass Alvin interview.

42. Abe Levy interview.

43. Ibid.; author's interview with Hope Mendoza Schechter, Sherman Oaks, California, Sept. 3, 1994, and subsequent conversations.

44. Tony Ríos interview; author's interviews with Fred Ross Jr., 1996–2001; Hope Mendoza Schechter interview; Dorothy Ray Healey and Maurice Isserman, *California Red*, 135–36, recalled that Communist Party leader Henry Steinberg had "helped organize" CSO. This openness is also reflected in the views of the Trotskyist Socialist Workers Party. It's "for members only" internal bulletin described CSO as "non-sectarian" and labeled its policies as "progressive." The SWP also noted that: "The Stalinists have not made any deep inroads in the CSO though some leading members have Stalinists leanings. The [so-called] right-wing union leaders are considerably more influential and obviously regard the CSO as an important field for work." "On the Mexican Question," in SWP, Internal Bulletin, no. 3 (Jan. 1949), Los Angeles City Convention Issue, 1–8, Holt Labor Library, San Francisco.

45. Author's interview with Henry Nava, Monterey Park, California, Feb. 9, 1995.

46. Fred Ross Jr. interview.

47. Fred Ross, *Axioms for Organizers* (San Francisco: Neighbor to Neighbor, 1989), 4.

48. Henry Nava interview; Tony Ríos interview; Fred Ross Jr. interview; Ed Roybal interview; "Mexican Group Hold Dance," *Eastside Sun,* Sept. 5, 1947, 1; CRCLA, Mexican CRC Dance, 1947, 8/36, SLSSR; CRCLA, Mexican Civil Rights Congress, 1947–48, box 13, file, 5, SLSSR. The Communist Party made a decision in June to increase its work among Latinos. "Southern California: Party Building Conference," June 14–15, 1947, Subject File, CP 1947, SCLRSS.

49. Tony Ríos interview.

50. "Latin Vote Registration Doubled, Group Announces," *Belvedere Citizen,* Apr. 30, 1948; "Spanish-Speaking Group Spurs Vote Registration," *Los Angeles Times,* Mar. 15, 1948; "X-Ray Used in Registration of Voters and Tests for TB," *Daily News,* Mar. 6, 1948; "Latin Area Vote Increased," *Daily News,* Apr. 28, 1948; Sanford D. Horwitt, *Let Them Call Me Rebel,* 234.

51. Zieger, *The CIO,* 253–93; John C. Culver and John Hyde, *American Dreamer: A Life of Henry A. Wallace* (New York: W. W. Norton & Company, 2000), 426–70.

52. California Industrial Union Council, Executive Board Minutes, Feb. 13–15, 1948, 60–61, CIUC, 301/Box 24, Irwin DeShetler Papers, Archives of Labor History and Urban Affairs, Wayne State.

53. "CIO Minority Rights Program Gets Underway," *Labor Herald,* Feb. 10, 1948, 1; LA CIO Council-Committee, Minorities/Fair Practices Committee: CIO Leadership School on Discrimination, Feb. 29, 1948, and LA CIO Council-Committee, Minorities/Fair Practices Committee: Announcements, correspondence, reports, 1948, LACFL Papers; LA Council CIO-PAC, Library and Archives, International Longshore and Warehouse Union.

54. Tony Nicol, Remarks, Apr. 2, 1948, LA CIO Council, LA CIO Council—PAC, 1946–49, Box 9, UAC, CSUN.

55. Author's interview with Richard Ibañez, Los Angeles, July 19, 1997.

56. Author's interview with John Allard, Artesia, California, Dec. 12, 1996.

57. "Murray to California," *CIO News,* Apr. 12, 1948, box G, file Murray, Library and Archives, International Longshoremen's and Warehousemen's Union, San Francisco.

58. For insights into the power struggle within the Los Angeles CIO from the Left's perspective, see the *Labor Herald,* particularly Feb.-Mar.1948, and Healey and Isserman,

California Red, 112–13. See also the Phil Connelly Papers at the Special Collections, University of California, Los Angeles; Los Angeles Country Federation of Labor, UAC, CSUN Center; and the California CIO Council Papers at the Southern California Library for Research and Social Studies, and material at the Library and Archives, International Longshoremen's and Warehousemen's Union. For the national CIO's perspective, see the *CIO News,* the Irwin DeShetler Papers, and the United Auto Worker Papers, all at Archives of Labor History and Urban Affairs (ALHUA), Wayne State. The United Steel Workers Papers are at the Historical Collection and Labor Archives, Penn State.

59. "CIO Charges Rump Bloc Endorses Anti-labor Men, *Labor Herald,* May 11, 1948, 2; "Negro and Mexican-Americans Denounce Leaders of Walk-Out," *California Eagle,* May 20, 1948, 1; "Statement Condemning CIO Regional Action Has Additional Signers," *California Eagle,* May 20, 1948, 1.

60. "CIO Charges Rump Block Endorses Anti-Labor Men," 2; "Negro and Mexican-Americans Denounce Leaders of Walk-Out," 1; "Statement Condemning CIO Regional Action Has Additional Signers," 1; "Broad Coalition Backs Superior Judge Candidate," *People's World,* May 11, 1948, 2; "Negro, Mexican Leaders Hail CIO Council Stand," *People's World,* May 21, 1948.

61. Editorial, "Process of Democracy," *Daily News,* June 9, 1948, 48.

62. Robert Kenny, "A Californian Looks Ahead," *Nation,* Oct. 23, 1948, 460–61.

63. "Elect Henry Nava Head of Community Services Organization," *Belvedere Citizen,* Feb. 4, 1949.

64. Author's interview with Roger Johnson, Hollywood, California, Dec. 19, 1981; Tony Ríos interview.

65. "Voter League OKs Candidates for Apr. 5 Ballot," *Los Angeles Citizen,* Mar. 4, 1949, 1.

66. Tony Ríos interview.

67. James Daugherty interview.

68. "Roybal Wins City Council Race in L.A.," *Labor Herald,* June 14, 1949, 3.

69. Letter, Dorothy Healey to the author, Mar. 10, 1995.

70. Edward Roybal interview.

71. "Hollywood Labor Group Backs Christensen," *Sentinel,* May 19, 1949, A4. See also "Christensen Endorsed by Labor League of Hollywood," *Eastside Sun,* Mar. 18, 1947, 1; "Voter League OKs Candidates for Apr. 5 Polls," *Los Angles Citizen,* Mar. 4, 1949, 1.

72. Author's interview with Roy M. Brewer, Tarzana, California, Mar. 12, 1995. The West Coast head of IATSE was a Truman Democrat and vice chair of the Hollywood League. Stephen Vaughn, *Ronald Reagan in Hollywood: Movies and Politics* (Cambridge: Cambridge University Press, 1994), 158.

73. Tabulation of Returns, Council District 9, Apr. 5, 1949, and Tabulation of Returns, Council District 9, May 31, 1949, City of Los Angeles Election Division. The author calculated the levels of support for Roybal by precinct and then applied those levels to a precinct map, using known demographic information, such as the fact that Jewish voters were concentrated around and north of Brooklyn Avenue. See also Katherine Underwood, "Process and Politics: Multiracial Electoral Coalition Building and Representation in Los Angeles' Ninth District, 1949–1962" (Ph.D. diss., University of California, San Diego, 1992).

74. "'Slim' Connelly Steps Down; Gets Ovation," *Labor Herald,* Mar. 22, 1949, 8; Healey and Isserman, *California Red,* 117.

75. Editorial, "Republicans Flunk Test," *Daily News,* Apr. 27, 1949; "Warren Loses Inquiry on Racial Bans," *Daily News,* Apr. 27, 1949; "Fair Employment Practices Bill Loses in Committee," *Daily News,* May 12, 1949; Minutes, Program Planning Committee, June 13 and July 11, 1949, 5/5, Fred Ross Papers, Special Collections, Stanford University.

76. Editorial, "An FEP Ordinance," *B'nai B'rith Messenger,* Sept. 2, 1949, 4; Max Mont, Weekly Reports, Aug.-Sept. 1949, in author's files.

77. "James Roosevelt Charged with 'Double-Crossing' His Party," *Merced Sun-Star,* Apr. 16, 1948; 10/CEE 1948–49, Jewish Community Relations Committee, UAC, CSUN; Max Mont, Weekly Reports.

78. "City FEPC Planned at Meet," *California Eagle,* July 28, 1949, 7; "FEPC for LA Planned Last Sun. at Bar-B-Q," *California Eagle,* Aug. 4, 1949, 1.

79. "City FEPC Planned at Meet," 7; "FEPC for LA Planned Last Sun. at Bar-B-Q," 1; Jaime González Monroy interview.

80. "City Council," *California Eagle,* Aug. 11, 1949, 2; "Grass Roots Support for FEPC," *California Eagle,* Aug. 25, 1949, 18.

81. Author's interview with Zane Meckler, Mar. 29 and Apr. 5, 1996.

82. Letter, Isaac Pacht, CEE, to Henry Nava, CSO, Aug. 18, 1949, with attachments, 5/12, Fred Ross Papers, Stanford University; "Write Your Council Representatives to Pass FEPC Resolution," *B'nai B'rith Messenger,* Sept. 2, 1949, 1; Jewish Community Relations Council, CEE 1949–50, UAC, CSUN; Max Mont, Weekly Reports.

83. Fred Ross to Fred Herzberg, Sept. 23, 1949, with attachment, CRC, Box 10, file CSO 1948–49, UAC, CSUN.

84. Max Mont, Weekly Reports.

85. "Big CIO Picnic," *The Beam,* USWA Local 2058, USWA Reel 855, James Thimmes Correspondence, Charles Smith, 1049, USWA, Historical Collection & Labor Archives, Penn State; Max Mont, Weekly Reports.

86. Max Mont, Weekly Reports.

87. "Court Sets CIO Bldg. Pleas Today," *People's World,* Sept. 14, 1949, 3; "8,000 Pay Homage to the 'Queen,'" *People's World,* Sept. 20, 1949, 3.

88. Editorial, "The Council and FEPC," *Los Angeles Times,* Sept. 23, 1949; Minutes, Greater LA CIO Council, Oct. 4, 1949, 6/Local Industrial Council, Correspondence (1935–55), Reel 1, Los Angeles, George Meany Memorial Archives.

89. Don Parson, "'The Darling of the Town's New-Fascists': The Bombastic Political Career of Councilman Ed J. Davenport," *Southern California Quarterly* 81:4 (Winter 1999): 478.

90. Memo, Harry Honda to author, Jan. 4, 2001, with attachment, Sam Ishikawa, "Report of the Pacific Southwest Regional Office," Japanese American Citizens League, Oct. 1, 1948–Dec. 15, 1949.

91. Letter, Albert Lunceford, Greater Los Angles CIO Council, to Committee to Abolish Discrimination, CIO, Apr. 18, 1950, with attachment, Resolution, Community Services Organization, adopted Apr. 4, 1950, 197/(Calif.) LAIUC, CIO Sec.-Tres., ALHUA.

92. William Becker interview; C. L. Dellums, "International President of the Brother-

hood of Sleeping Car Porters and Civil Rights Leaders," p. 119, Oral History, University of California, Berkeley; Tony Ríos interview.

93. C. L. Dellums, "International President of the Brotherhood of Sleeping Car Porters and Civil Rights Leader," p. 58, Oral History, University of California, Berkeley.

94. William Becker interview; C. L. Dellums, Oral History, p. 119; author's interview with Atara Mont, Los Angeles, Apr. 7, 1996; author's interview with Earl Rabb, San Francisco, Feb. 14, 2004.

95. For Huerta and Democratic Socialists of America, see DSA website. For more on labor and Latino politics, see Kenneth C. Burt, *The Search for a Civic Voice: California Latino Politics* (Claremont, Calif.: Regina Books, 2007).

4. From Fellow Traveler to Friendly Witness: Shelton Tappes, Liberal Anticommunism, and Working-Class Civil Rights in the United Auto Workers

DAVID M. LEWIS-COLMAN

Not long ago our union was badgered by Communists and their stooges who tried to exploit racial and religious antagonisms as a means of seizing control. But we defeated these elements. First, by building a militant union that fought for the just demands of the workers. Second, by seeing to it, through a UAW Fair Practices and Anti-Discrimination Department, that all union members received fair and equal treatment. Thus, by practicing the ideals to which the Communists paid hypocritical lip service, we undermined their own propaganda.[1]

—Walter Reuther, ca. 1952

On March 12, 1952, in the federal building in Detroit, a black UAW international representative named Shelton Tappes took the stand to testify before the House Un-American Activities Committee. HUAC had come to Detroit to hold hearings on Communism in the Detroit area. The committee focused much of its attention on UAW Local 600 at Ford's massive River Rouge plant in Dearborn. Tappes was uniquely qualified to testify about left-wing politics in Detroit and at the UAW's largest local, which represented over eighty thousand workers by 1945. Born in 1911 in Omaha, Nebraska, Tappes moved to Detroit in 1928 and began working in the Briggs plant on Mack Avenue and later found work at the Rouge plant. Although Tappes never joined the party, Communist activism shaped his political outlook and individual party members gained his trust and respect. Tappes developed a close relationship with Scottish immigrant, Rouge employee, and Communist Bill McKie. Tappes joined the CP led Auto Workers Union in the early 1930s, which McKie had helped organize to bring a union to auto workers in Detroit. Tappes also became active in the Unemployed Councils McKie helped build to enable the poor to fight evictions and demand more government relief during the Great Depression. Tappes worked closely with black Communist Rouge workers like Nelson Davis and Dave Moore in popular front civil rights groups like the National Negro Congress and in helping organize the United Automobile Workers. Tappes's ties with Communists proved useful in his bid for electoral office in Local 600 in the early 1940s. With the backing of the well-organized party chapter at the Rouge plant, Tappes was elected recording-secretary in 1942, becoming the only black executive board member in the local. Tappes held the position, with Communist support, for three years.[2]

Tappes, however, did not come to the federal building in March 1952 to defend his comrades or, like many subpoenaed witnesses during the second Red Scare, to refuse defiantly to answer HUAC's questions. Instead, Tappes named names. He discussed the past and present party affiliation of a number of Local 600 activists, in particular black Rouge activists such as Nelson Davis, Veal Clough, Civil Rights Congress president Art McPhaul, and Local 600 recording-secretary and National Negro Labor Council president, William Hood. Tappes distanced himself from his past association with the Communist Party. He admitted attending several party meetings in the early 1940s but merely as an outside speaker. He also claimed that he resigned from CP front groups like the National Negro Congress as soon as he found out they were led by the party. In his testimony, Tappes confirmed HUAC's assertion that the party exploited the "Negro issue" and that by manipulating parliamentary procedure, a small but disciplined Communist cadre was able to greatly influence Local 600 politics.[3]

Tappes's political transformation from fellow traveler to friendly witness reveals much about the effects of Cold War anticommunism on the Congress of Industrial Organizations and working-class civil rights struggles in the United States. A number of scholars have persuasively argued that the Red Scare narrowed the CIO's broad social vision, which in the 1930s and early 1940s embraced militant civil rights activism. Determined to survive the postwar conservative shift, which increasingly linked racial equality and Communism, the CIO distanced itself from civil rights issues, expelled the CP-led unions, and purged the Communists that had been in the forefront of the labor-based struggle for racial equality. According to these scholars, the labor movement in the second half of the twentieth century focused on the relatively safe issues of wages and benefits, and the mantle of civil rights leadership passed from workers to middle-class black leaders, who emphasized integration over economic justice. In this narrative, labor's white leadership is often absolved of responsibility for this shift, depicted instead as enlightened leaders forced to balance their liberal commitments with the imperative for institutional survival in the face of white workers' racism, the Red Scare, and business hegemony.[4]

The political trajectory of Shelton Tappes, however, suggests that the impact of the Cold War on working-class racial politics involved more than simply the abandonment of civil rights by labor liberals hemmed in by new political forces. First, Reuther, like many labor liberals, did not simply retreat from civil rights in the postwar years. Instead, Reuther became a vocal advocate for civil rights, expanding the UAW's Fair Practices Department and hiring a number of staff to focus solely on civil rights issues. Reuther's civil rights stance grew partly out of his own commitment to oppose any kind of racial, ethnic, or religious bigotry that undermined class unity. But he also became a civil rights proponent because, like many liberal anticommunists, he viewed civil rights as a key Cold War battleground. Reuther believed that the Soviet Union and its agents around the world exploited the issue of racism to undermine the labor movement in the United States and American power globally. He asserted that the only way to counter Communist propaganda and win the hearts and minds of the world's population was to close the gap between the ideal of equality and the reality of racial inequality.[5]

Second, black labor radicals and civil rights activists were not all purged from the CIO or lived on in the margins as union dissidents. A number of these activists, including Tappes, accommodated labor's anticommunism in the late 1940s and early 1950s, helping to transform the political culture of the black working class. This accommodation by some black workers emerged largely as a pragmatic response to the conservative postwar political climate. Determined to sustain the struggle for civil rights in some form in the union, Tappes aligned himself with the triumphant liberal wing of the union led by Reuther and appeared before HUAC. Personal considerations also certainly shaped Tappes's decision to embrace Cold War racial pragmatism. Political survival in the union and the promise of a job in the union hierarchy appealed to many individuals. And the threat of losing a job, family, and friends in the face of red-baiting proved powerfully coercive and prodded many fellow travelers to acquiesce to HUAC. Tappes's alliance with the party had also always been tenuous, built partly by Tappes as a pragmatic way to advance black interests. The frustrations of this pragmatic alliance led to feelings of distrust and betrayal on Tappes's part well before the postwar Red Scare.

Tappes's decision to accommodate anticommunism represented a broader shift occurring inside labor that had serious consequences for how the country resolved race and class conflicts in the postwar years. The shift did not represent, as some scholars have suggested, a retreat from civil rights but instead a transformation of the politics of civil rights inside the labor movement. In the early 1940s, Tappes helped forge a network of autonomous black caucuses in the UAW that advocated direct and affirmative action to achieve racial equality in employment and in the union. This labor-based wartime civil rights movement demanded that equality between white and black workers be immediate and measurable. The black caucuses' workplace and union-centered activism became a kind of "civic" unionism, often overflowing into militant challenges to the racial structure of Detroit's neighborhoods, leisure spaces, and politics. The support and sympathy of an ascendant white Left in the UAW during World War II allowed independent black activism to flourish.

In the late 1940s, the triumphant liberal anticommunist UAW faction denounced and ultimately dismantled the black caucus movement Tappes had helped build in Detroit's UAW. The Reuther faction did not attack the black caucus simply in response to the urgency of institutional survival in racially conservative times. Liberals like Reuther sought to replace black caucuses with a civil rights program more consistent with their ideology and more favorable to their institutional interests. The black caucus's militancy undermined Reuther's attempt to build stable bargaining relationships with employers in the postwar years and to consolidate his control over union affairs. The racial consciousness of the caucuses also challenged Reuther's class-first politics, which were rooted in the older Socialist "Black and White, Unite and Fight!" belief that African Americans would advance through a united labor movement built around a common class identity. Reuther replaced the black caucuses with a civil rights program that emphasized gradual change through education and bureaucratic antidiscrimination procedures. This liberal civil rights program proved inadequate. The attacks on the black caucus left lasting resentments and distrust in the black community toward organized labor, and liberal civil rights lacked the capacity for grassroots mobilization and militancy required to eliminate racism. Despite these limitations, many black workers like Tappes believed that Cold War civil rights were better than no civil rights and began to work within the UAW's civil rights bureaucracy.

Organizing Black Workers at Ford

Tappes's rise to power in the UAW began in the fall of 1940. As a twenty-nine-year-old foundry worker in the River Rouge plant, Tappes joined the UAW's renewed attempt to organize the Ford Motor Company. He helped lead a committee the CIO created to organize black Ford employees. The committee had a large contingent of Ford employees, primarily men, who spearheaded the organizing of black workers in the plants. Tappes, along with other black trade unionists, built an especially strong union base among the thousands of black workers employed in the foundry of the River Rouge complex. The committee established ties to the city's black community and mobilized the support of black newspapers, churches, and civil rights groups. Black unionists worked tirelessly to mobilize community support for the labor struggle. The National Negro Congress, under the leadership of LeBron Simmons and the minister of the Hartford Avenue Baptist Church, Charles A. Hill, provided important support for the drive. Black women in the CIO committee's women's auxiliary convinced their male relatives and the reluctant wives of autoworkers to support the union. They distributed pro-union literature and organized luncheons and public meetings to win support from Detroit's black community.[6]

Black unionists shared the CIO's commitment to integration through working-class advancement in the labor movement. Like the CIO's white liberals and progressives, black unionists believed in the power and necessity of uniting all workers regardless of race or ethnicity. Party member Dave Moore fondly recalled the sense of "togetherness" and "close-knit brotherhood" that developed in Local 600 at the Rouge. Moore recalled white Communists playing a key role in creating this culture of unity, telling workers "We should not be divided based on race. What happens . . . to Dave Moore as a black man happens to Sally Jones as a white woman." Interracial unity proved important to Shelton Tappes, who had been deeply moved by the interracial spirit of the 1932 Ford Hunger March in Dearborn, where he witnessed Ford security men and Dearborn police violently attack black and white workers who had joined together to demand jobs and relief. Tappes recalled that one of his "best" experiences during the 1941 Ford drive was visiting the homes of a Polish and Mexican worker who expressed interest in the UAW but were not sure if they were eligible as noncitizens.[7]

The appeal of unionism to black autoworkers, however, proved more complex than simply a commitment to working-class advancement through an integrated labor movement that transcended racial identity. The appeal of interracial cooperation that animated the founding generation of black UAW members coexisted, sometimes uneasily, with a deep sense of racial pride and a belief that the union should advance the interests of the entire black community.[8] The popularity of nationalist groups like the Nation of Islam and Development of Our Own in Detroit's Depression-era black community certainly reinforced the appeal of race-based politics among black union organizers. In Detroit, Shelton Tappes emerged as a symbol of civil rights unionism. Tappes's father instilled in him a militant sense of racial pride that carried over into his union activism. Sent away from Mississippi by his family at the age of fourteen because he was "too outspoken," Tappes's father "hated the word Negro." Forty years before Willie Ricks popularized the slogan "black power," the senior Tappes told his son "You are black." Tappes believed that the UAW "had an extra appeal" to blacks—"Equality and a chance to advance, where to whites, it was more economic." Racial advancement also shaped black party members' labor organizing. Horace Sheffield recalled black Communist and Ford drive organizer Dave Moore as being "strong on the black liberation thing."[9]

Black Ford organizers also saw the UAW as a vehicle to transform a system of racialized capitalism that had historically relied on white supremacy to denigrate and exploit cheap black labor. In this sense, black workers could accept the idea that "What happens to Dave Moore as a black man happens to Sally Jones as a white woman," up to a certain point. The slogan functioned as an inspiring rallying cry by emphasizing the common humanity and general lack of power and poor conditions all workers experienced. But black labor activists pointed out that historically black labor occupied a distinct position in the working class, confined through racism, to the most menial, insecure, and lowest-paid jobs in agriculture or servicing whites' emotional and physical needs. The UAW's black activists linked their activism to the struggle to bring dignity to black labor. In a 1940 NNC pamphlet, Chris Alston urged all black Ford employees, including the skilled, to reject Ford's paternalism and support the union because "the price that the mass of Negroes working in the foundry have to pay in order for a few of their brothers to work at skilled jobs is too great a price to pay for a race whose contribution to American life has always been that of labor without honor." Alston promised black Ford employees that the UAW would encompass black workers' broad quest for freedom and dignity and lead the struggle for equal seniority rights, a day off on Emancipation Day, and against the poll tax in the South.[10]

Most black Ford workers rejected the CIO's organizing appeals and continued to oppose the UAW. Some black Ford workers vigorously opposed the UAW and often in alliance with Ford security and the CIO's management backed the AFL rival, instigating violent attacks on CIO organizers. The violence came to a head in the first two weeks of April, 1941, when the UAW-CIO called a strike shutting down Ford's facilities, including the River Rouge plant. Just after sunset on April 2, a major battle broke out between around two hundred black workers and CIO pickets at Gate 4 of the long factory building on Miller Road. After exchanging taunts, black workers inside the plant rushed the interracial but predominately white crowd of CIO pickets who had gathered on the stairways of the Miller Road overpass. Moving across the overpass and the street, some of the attackers beat the pickets with long, heavy pieces of forged steel while others launched steel bars, rods, and bolts from the overpass into the crowd of pickets below. The pickets repulsed the attack only to have the battle repeated two hours later. The violence spilled over into Detroit's black community, where over the course of two weeks AFL and CIO men clashed in North Detroit, West Side Detroit, Ecorse, River Rouge, and Inkster.[11]

Most black workers remained neutral, seeking to navigate carefully the fluid and uncertain terrain of shifting power relations inside Ford's plants. Black workers who depended on Ford's goodwill for their jobs and had been historically excluded from unions waited to see if the UAW or Ford would emerge victorious from the battle. The vast majority of these neutral black workers waited in their homes away from the conflict, but some 1,500 of them waited nervously, trapped inside the plant. Fearful of being assaulted by white CIO pickets who still nursed racial resentments and wounds from earlier battles with black strikebreakers, many black workers trapped in the plant refused to leave. In perhaps its finest hour, the CIO's committee to organize black workers mobilized to end the stand off. In a much-celebrated incident, Horace Sheffield, a black Rouge worker, Trotskyist, and NAACP youth activist, used a UAW sound car (an automobile with loudspeakers) to persuade black workers to leave the plant and to reassure white pickets that African Americans supported the union. Without the approval of the anti-union Detroit NAACP, Sheffield attached a sign to the back of the sound car that read "Detroit Youth Council of NAACP." At one point NAACP head Walter White flew to Detroit to urge the black strikebreakers to leave the River Rouge plant and to persuade the local chapter of the NAACP to back the union. Some semblance of racial unity prevailed and the strike ended on April 11, after Ford agreed to an election supervised by the National Labor Relations Board. Several weeks later, the UAW-CIO faction won an over-whelming victory against the UAW-AFL faction in the NLRB elections.[12]

A significant number of black workers, although still a minority, voted for the UAW-CIO, thereby helping it win recognition from Ford on May 21, 1941. The Ford victory broke the firm grip Ford and the company's conserva-tive black allies in Detroit had over employment opportunities for African Americans in Detroit. African American workers at Ford quickly adjusted to the newfound power of the UAW and joined the union. Walter Hardin, who headed the CIO's committee to organize black Ford employees, reported that several days after the UAW's NLRB victory, "Negro applications were coming in to the local office at the rate of one hundred per day," and "receipts for the two offices averaged around $800 per week." Even Horace Sheffield's father, Horace Sheffield Sr., eventually joined the union. Sheffield Sr., who worked as a foundry foreman, had refused to leave the plant during the strike and remained loyal to Ford, believing that "God had used Henry Ford to provide black people with an opportunity to gain middle-class status." But like many black autoworkers, Sheffield certainly understood that the UAW represented something new, permanent, and potentially liberating for the city's black working class.[13]

The Ford victory had a significant impact on Tappes's career. In less than two years Shelton Tappes had become one of the most recognizable names in Detroit. In 1941, Tappes became president of Local 600's foundry unit. He also became a member of the UAW's Ford negotiating committee and helped negotiate the union's first contract with Ford, which included a no-discrimination clause. In 1942, Tappes was elected Local 600 recording-secretary and became the union's first black worker to sit on the local's executive board.[14] In addition to his role as a militant trade union official, Tappes assumed the role of independent political activist and led struggles in the plant, community, and union hall to advance black workers' interests. Tappes's activism catapulted him into the role of the UAW's unofficial black international officer in a union with an all-white international leadership and a spokesperson for Detroit's black community.

Tappes and the Anti-discrimination Campaign in the Workplace

As African Americans entered the industrial workforce during the war, they encountered a deeply entrenched system of employment discrimination. Black workers often had difficulty just getting a job in the defense industry. Even in the face of labor shortages, plant managers regularly refused to hire black workers, particularly women. At the end of 1942, Ford, the city's largest employer of black labor, stopped "recruiting" African Americans at its new defense plants. Black women were more likely to be excluded from defense work than men. By late 1942, only one hundred black women worked in the city's defense plant out of a total of fifty-eight thousand women working in war production. When defense plants hired African Americans, they did so in ways that maintained segregation and inequality. Most black men found themselves working in the least desirable jobs in the foundry, spray-painting, and maintenance departments and women ended up in custodial positions or in service jobs such as cafeteria work. These jobs paid less and were often more dangerous, particularly for workers in the spray-painting department, who inhaled toxic fumes on a daily basis.

Employers made it almost impossible for black workers to move out of these positions into better-paid classifications. Foremen regularly denied black workers' promotions, in many cases ignoring their seniority rights. And because employers only began hiring black workers in significant numbers during World War II, most black workers had less seniority than white workers and were the first to be laid off. White workers and the UAW were complicit in sustaining inequality in plants. White union members often held hate strikes protesting employers' decisions to promote black workers into previously all-white departments, and local union officials often refused to handle black workers' grievances. Union contracts sustained the racial job structure inside the plants. Most contracts required seniority to be based on department rather than on a plant-wide basis, locking black workers into segregated departments. Initially, some black workers welcomed this as protection against competition from white workers but they increasingly viewed it as a barrier to promotion.[15]

The right to defense jobs quickly emerged as a central civil rights demand during World War II. Black working-class leaders built a national movement demanding federal action to end racial discrimination in defense industries. The movement adopted the slogan of double victory, symbolizing a military victory abroad and a victory against racism at home. Brotherhood of Sleeping Car Porters President A. Philip Randolph called for a march on Washington to pressure President Franklin Roosevelt to ban discrimination in the defense industry. All-black March on Washington committees spread in African American communities around the country, raising money, recruiting marchers, and arranging transportation for the planned march. Pressure from these grassroots committees in dozens of cities around the country forced Roosevelt to sign executive order 8802, which banned racial discrimination in the defense industry and created the Fair Employment Practices Committee (FEPC) to investigate cases of discrimination.

The spirit of the March on Washington movement did not end after Roosevelt created the FEPC. Tappes, along with the cadre of black Ford organizers, began to build a network of black caucuses inside the UAW to translate the executive order into real gains for black workers. Local 600 emerged as the center of black caucus activism in the UAW. Seventeen percent of the Rouge's eighty-five thousand employees were black and 15 percent of the UAWs one hundred thousand black members worked inside the Rouge.[16] As recording-secretary, Tappes was strategically placed to use his office to coordinate much of the anti-discrimination activity of Detroit's black autoworkers. The Local 600–led anti-discrimination campaign was reinforced by a sensitive and sizable white left. The Communist Party had a strong presence in the Rouge and helped create a climate of interracial solidarity supportive of anti-discrimination activism. And ambitious white trade unionists responded to black workers' issues, partly in recognition of black political power in the local. As early as 1942, the local's newspaper, the *Ford Facts,* printed the photographs of the local's left-wing and all-white executive-board, with a banner declaring the board's unanimous support for the "FIGHT FOR NEGRO WOMEN IN WAR INDUSTRY."[17]

Black caucuses, often known as victory committees, soon emerged in other UAW locals around Detroit. By 1943, Tappes led an effort among black unionists to coordinate the activities of the black caucuses at a city and a regional level. In late 1943 or early 1944, black unionists from Local 600 and Locals 7, 22, 205, 208, 155, and 742 formed the Metropolitan Detroit Negro Labor Council (MNLC). The Labor Council retained strong ties with black workers and white supporters around the Midwest and parts of the South in cities such as Saginaw, Toledo, Indianapolis, Memphis, Cincinnati, and Chicago. The Labor Council's first officers were mostly men from the ranks of the UAW's Ford drive. Tappes became the group's president in 1944. Three of the Labor Council's officers were women autoworkers who had recently entered defense work. Lillian Hatcher, an executive officer of Local 742, became vice president; Hatcher's friend and co-worker Lena Rita Roberts was the group's treasurer, and Margaret Frierson from Local 22 became the corresponding secretary.[18]

The black caucuses and Labor Council used a variety of tactics to eliminate employment discrimination, and in the words of Tappes, to make sure "the Negro question" remained "a crisis issue within the union at all times." They pressured the FEPC to hold hearings in Detroit and worked with FEPC officials in the city to negotiate grievances with employers. In 1943, black caucus activists successfully pressured the UAW to establish its own Fair Practices Committee. Under the leadership of George Crockett, a former government labor investigator and future congressman, the committee led aggressive investigations into racial discrimination in the workplace.[19] Crockett also urged the UAW to commit itself to protecting the seniority black workers were gaining during the war. Crockett, along with the Labor Council and white allies in the Communist Party, proposed the idea of proportional seniority. Proportional seniority would require defense employers to employ the same percentage of black workers after the war as they employed during the war.[20]

The Labor Council mobilized the support of the community in their struggle to get black men and women hired and promoted. The local chapter of the National Negro Congress became a key black caucus ally. A number of black caucus leaders, including Shelton Tappes, became NNC leaders. Tappes co-chaired the group's Trade Union Committee, which sought to mobilize community support for workers' issues. The Labor Council's women's auxiliary organized numerous pickets against discriminatory employers and complicit local unions. Rose Billups, wife of black Communist autoworker Joseph Billups, headed the Labor Council's women's auxiliary and recruited its members to staff the picket lines. Billups organized picket lines, led mostly by black women, at Ford's Highland Park plant, the Plymouth plant, and the River Rouge facility.[21]

The Labor Council and black caucuses gained the support of the black rank and file by aggressively advocating for their interests and embracing their militancy. Many victory committees began to function as black unions designed to "settle all specifically Negro disputes." Lillian Hatcher recalled being impressed by the "victory men" who challenged a white union official who had discouraged her from joining the union. Hatcher also remembered the predominately male black caucuses taking up the cause of black women, who found it difficult to find defense jobs despite the influx of tens of thousands of white women into defense plants. Black caucus men, however, generally did not seek to break down sex segregation in jobs, instead agitating for black women to gain access to jobs reserved for white women. The willingness of caucus activists to support and in some cases organize work stoppages and wildcat strikes also certainly appealed to the thousands of black workers, including many southern migrants, entering defense work. Even black Communists like Chris Alston violated party support for the no-strike pledge and led black workers out of factories during the war.[22]

Civic Unionism: The Black Caucus and Community Justice

Tappes and other black UAW activists did not confine their struggle against discrimination to the workplace. Tappes helped lead a fight to confront the housing shortage in wartime Detroit and the exclusion of black workers from newly built public housing. Black unionists became involved in the battle over the Sojourner Truth housing projects, which polarized Detroit's black and white residents and symbolized the problem of discrimination in a city that faced a serious wartime housing shortage. Between January and April 1942, black UAW members, mostly from the Rouge foundry, mobilized to keep the Sojourner Truth housing projects open to black occupancy. City and federal officials had succumbed to pressure from white residents who lived near the projects and decided to exclude African Americans. The UAW activists quickly organized to reverse the government's decision. Shelton Tappes and Horace Sheffield helped lead the Sojourner Truth Citizens Committee and rank and file union members picketed and sent thousands of postcards to Roosevelt protesting the decision to keep the projects all-white. By the end of April, black workers began moving into Sojourner Truth. Throughout the war, Tappes took a leadership role in housing struggles.[23]

Fairness in leisure became an important arena of struggle for black autoworkers who wanted to take advantage of the city's opportunities for play after a hard day's work inside a factory. Black autoworkers led an important struggle against one of Detroit's most popular working-class leisure spaces, the Bob-lo Island. Bob-lo was a picturesque Canadian island located eighteen miles south of Detroit on the Detroit River near Lake Erie. At the turn of the century, a growing number of Detroit's residents visited the island to enjoy its picnic areas, carousel, and the Ford-built dance hall, which earned the reputation as the second largest in the world.[24] During the war, the Bob-lo became a source of tension between black and white unionists. Although Jim Crow did not exist on Bob-lo Island, the companies that ran the excursion steamers refused to allow African Americans to board the ships. At the Graham-Paige plant, black workers in alliance with the Metropolitan Negro Labor Council forced the local union to cancel its planned excursion to Bob-lo Island. At a general meeting, black workers demanded that the local cancel its plan to use their recreation dues to rent one of the steamers to go to Bob-lo. They declared it was a violation of their rights and the principles of interracial solidarity. The threat of a picket line at the local union hall, combined with Negro Labor Council pressure on UAW president R. J. Thomas, forced the local to cancel its plans.[25]

The international proved more reluctant to challenge segregation in bowling, a more widespread and routine form of leisure among their members. Unlike the Bob-lo, bowling was a central form of recreation and bonding for the union's predominately male workforce. Bowling had deep roots in Detroit's working class. The city's breweries, such as the Stroh brewery, often sponsored teams and leagues, which were regularly covered by the local newspapers.[26] During the 1930s, the CIO began to sponsor its own bowling teams as part of its effort to build working-class solidarity and union loyalty. During the war, many UAW locals sponsored teams that participated in league play sanctioned by the American Bowling Congress. The ABC controlled league play around the country, and most bowling alleys sought to sponsor ABC bowling. African Americans, however, found it difficult to gain access to bowling. The ABC had a whites-only clause in its constitution that barred blacks from participating in its leagues. Fearful of losing ABC sanction, bowling alleys also excluded African Americans. Many alleys excluded blacks during off-season bowling as well. Black bowlers who sought to gain access to alleys reported having their bowling bags, which included shoes and ball, thrown in nearby rivers.[27]

During the war, black caucuses took the lead in the struggle to integrate bowling. In the mid-1940s, Local 600 activists began to protest the union's decision to participate in ABC bowling. For the 1944–45 season, the local's executive board passed a motion that banned its members from participating in ABC sanctioned bowling. As head of the union's Fair Practices Committee, George Crockett supported aggressive action against union participation in ABC leagues, which he claimed was a clear violation of the UAW's constitutional ban against discrimination. Crockett, along with UAW legal counsel Maurice Sugar, tried to get the international to take a strong stand against the ABC. They wanted the UAW to lead a boycott of the ABC and if that failed, have the UAW set up its own leagues. Crockett believed that he could convince bowling alleys to agree to mixed matches, despite the potential loss of ABC affiliation. The local NNC, with its strong ties to the auto plants, also became involved in pressuring the UAW to take action against the ABC. Fearful of the effects a bowling ban would have on the loyalty of its members, the UAW's all-white executive board refused to support a boycott of the ABC and forced Local 600 to rescind its ban. The UAW, however, promised to complain to the ABC about its exclusionary clause. And in a move that insulted rather than appeased its black members, the UAW set up a separate black bowling tournament.[28]

Black Power in the Union

Tappes, along with other black caucus leaders, tied the success of their struggles in the workplace and community with their ability to gain power inside the UAW. During the war, black autoworkers found themselves excluded from political power in the UAW. The number of black members who held elected office, according to historians August Meier and Elliott Rudwick, "was tiny in proportion to their numbers in the UAW." In 1940, the UAW had only three black presidents of local unions. None of these locals were in Detroit. Three locals in Detroit did elect African Americans vice president in 1940, and Local 600, the UAW's largest local, had elected Shelton Tappes recording-secretary in 1942. But most black elected officials were confined to committee positions in the foundry and other predominately black units. Most distressing to black autoworkers was the lily-white UAW executive board.[29]

Throughout the war, black autoworkers unleashed their political energies and ambitions in a campaign to integrate the UAW's executive board. Black workers demanded a black seat as early as 1939, but the demand did not become viable until 1943.[30] At the convention, a Tappes-led black caucus submitted a resolution to establish a Minorities Affairs Department with an elected director who sat on the UAW executive board. The caucus called for the new director to be a black man. Tappes was picked as one of the likely candidates for such a position. Black UAW members were optimistic about their ability to gain an executive board seat with a record-high delegation of 194 black members attending the convention. The black caucus also had gained support for its proposal from the UAW's non-Communist left-wing secretary-treasurer George Addes and Vice President Richard Frankensteen and their allies in the Communist Party. The Communist member of the convention resolutions committee, Nat Ganley, introduced the caucus proposal to the convention.[31]

The proposal triggered heated opposition on the convention floor. The union's Reuther caucus vigorously opposed the proposal. Reuther and his allies objected to the proposal partly because of the black UAW members' support for the union's left wing. The Reuther-led faction believed that a black executive board member would shift the balance of power in the union to the left. The Reuther faction also opposed the proposal on ideological grounds, arguing that the proposal undermined the class basis of solidarity. As Victor Reuther asserted, "You are establishing, if you adopt the minority report, a dangerous practice of Jim Crowism in our own plant . . . we should not establish the practice of giving special privileges to special groups, because that is a Jim Crow privilege and will rebound and kick in the teeth the very people it is trying to help."[32]

Several black delegates also broke with the black caucus and opposed the proposal. Horace Sheffield spoke against the minority report. Some caucus leaders, like Hodges Mason, claim that Sheffield sold out the caucus for a promise of a job by Walter Reuther. And although Sheffield worked with Tappes and the black caucus around some issues, this relationship proved tenuous. Personal rivalry and ambition sometimes put Sheffield at odds with Tappes. Sheffield's Trotskyist and Reuther-faction sympathies also placed him on the margins of black union politics, which were decidedly left and anti-Reuther. Sheffield believed that the party often exploited the race issue and was not a reliable ally for black workers. This point seemed to be confirmed for Sheffield at the convention when the party lobbied Tappes to accept a compromise that would have weakened the voting power of the new executive board member. In a thinly veiled attack on the party, Sheffield claimed that "The Negro in this convention has been made the victim of political demagoguery. . . . I resent human misery being exploited, and that has been done in this convention." In the postwar years, Sheffield's political isolation would lessen, and he would emerge as the dominant voice of black politics in the UAW.[33]

Postwar Challenges to Tappes and the Black Caucus

In the immediate postwar years, the black caucus continued to achieve some success in building an anti-racist movement in the UAW. At the UAW's convention in 1946, Tappes, along with George Crockett, led a successful effort to pass a resolution establishing a Fair Practices Department. The department, which replaced the Fair Practices Committee, could not be abolished at the whim of a hostile executive board. Two months after the convention, black UAW activists helped organize a successful Tenth Annual Convention of the National Negro Congress. The one thousand delegates—many of whom came by car, plane, and bus in solidarity with the striking railroad workers—committed themselves to work with labor organizations to "stamp out discrimination." The positive response to the convention by liberal politicians and labor leaders generated a sense of optimism among Detroit's black trade unionists. UAW secretary treasurer George Addes addressed the convention and CIO President, Phillip Murray, sent his "best wishes . . . with the hope that your important deliberations will represent a constructive contribution toward the goal we both believe in." Even the less racially liberal mayor of Detroit, Edward Jeffries, lent support to the convention. In response to a request by the NNC, Jeffries signed an official proclamation that declared May 17 as "Death Blow to Jim Crow Day." In his proclamation, Jeffries called upon the citizens of Detroit to "join with the members of the National Negro Congress in the endeavor to kill Jim Crow practices throughout America."[34]

Tappes also remained politically active inside the union, advocating a continuation of the black caucus movement and its broad-based civic unionism. In 1946 and 1947, Tappes, along with veteran caucus activists, helped organize the Committee for a Negro Vice President. The committee led an unsuccessful bid to elect a black worker to a top spot in the Michigan CIO and elected black leftist Coleman Young as director of organization of the Wayne County CIO.[35] The Committee's "main objective" was "to get a Negro in top office of the UAW." It chose Tappes as its candidate for UAW vice president at the 1947 convention. Tappes's campaign emphasized racial equality and developed a progressive platform designed to appeal to all workers. The campaign ran on the TAPPES PLAN FOR ANNUAL WAGE, which was a guaranteed number of working days in each contract, a thirty-hour work week for forty hours pay, and a ceiling on individual man-hour production.[36]

Black caucus activism, however, proved more difficult to sustain in the postwar years in the face of an increasingly assertive right-wing faction—a coalition of Socialists, trade unionists, and white southerners. The leader of the faction, Walter Reuther, became president in 1946, and the following year his faction took control of the executive board. Some historians, like Reuther biographer Nelson Lichtenstein, have acknowledged the tension between black leftists and the right-wing faction, but do not adequately acknowledge the centrality of anti-black caucus politics to the Reuther faction or its negative impact on black self-organization in the union.[37] For a variety of reasons, the newly empowered Reuther faction made undermining the black caucus a priority. The faction's southern white base of support limited Reuther's ability to act on civil rights issues. "Walter's supporters from the South," Tappes asserted, were "interested principally in the question, How far are you going to let the Negroes go? What is going to be your position on that?"[38]

The black caucus also represented a threat to Reuther's ability to consolidate factional control over the union. The black caucus had been an important ally of Reuther's left-wing faction opponents, who had run the executive board during the war. The caucus also had developed sustained criticisms of Reuther that weakened his image among black workers and had stung him personally. In 1946, the caucus, led by George Crockett, organized a No-Reuther campaign to prevent his election as UAW president. Crockett wrote in his *Michigan Chronicle* column that "the best interest of the Negro in the UAW was not being served by promoting Walter Reuther to power." He pointed to the Reuther faction's opposition to "energetic investigation" of the Fair Practices Committee under Crockett's leadership and to his attempt to build ties between the FPC and outside civil rights groups.[39] And Crockett reminded black workers that Reuther had failed to make a no-discrimination clause a priority during the union's strike against GM in 1946.[40]

Reuther's class-first politics also put him at odds with the black caucus. Reuther believed that racial divisions and inequality resulted from an exploitative economic system. A color-blind class struggle that focused on generating more wealth and distributing wealth more equitably could overcome racial divisions. In a widely circulated article titled "Tolerance is Not Enough," written a year before assuming control of the UAW, Reuther argued that minorities would advance when there was "a higher national and world output," and when this output was distributed "equitably."[41]

The political climate of the early Cold War shaped and facilitated the Reuther faction's attacks on the caucus. Although the black caucus remained independent of the party, and even though some black Communist caucus members had placed racial loyalty over party policy during the war, Reuther and his allies effectively linked black caucus politics with Communism. Reuther referred to caucus activists as Communist "stooges" who exploited "racial and religious antagonisms as a means of seizing control."[42] Black caucus opponents' red-baited initiatives like the demand for a black executive seat, which the party supported but certainly did not inspire or coordinate. At the 1946 convention, resolutions committee member, Ben Harrison claimed that a resolution by Tappes to secure a black board seat "stinks! Plain, pure and simple," of Communist influence. Some black anticommunist leaders in Detroit, like NAACP leader, Gloster Current, shared Harrison's opinion, stating the Tappes's plan was "the communist approach of dubious special consideration." The following year, when Tappes ran for UAW vice president, he faced "bitter opposition among those who charge he is being sponsored by extreme leftists and Communists."[43]

The UAW's new administration acted quickly to purge the core leadership of the black caucus from staff positions and elected positions. Reuther discharged black UAW staff members John Conyers, William Bowman, John Buchanan, and Arto Johnson, all of whom had been active in the Metropolitan Negro Labor Council. UAW international representative William Lattimore survived Reuther's purge but was reassigned to maintenance work at the FDR training school in Port Huron, Michigan. These staff positions had provided the caucus with important resources for maintaining an infrastructure and some sense of institutional support for black activism. The Reuther faction also targeted caucus strongholds during local union elections, diminishing black caucus control over its traditional bases of power in Local 600 and the Wayne County CIO.[44]

The black caucus could no longer look to traditional left-wing faction allies for help. A Red-Scare driven by factional feuding gripped the union in the late 1940s, weakening its increasingly defensive left, which was a coalition of black workers, Communists, and non-Communist white progressives. Reuther tried to use Section 8 of the UAW's constitution to ban Communists from elected office and removed several leftists from the staff. Red-baiting campaigns helped Reuther's supporters defeat Communist-backed candidates at Local 155 and undermine the left leadership of Local 248 during its strike against Allis-Chalmers in West Allis, Wisconsin. Reuther, along with national CIO leaders, helped oust the left-wing leaders of the Wayne County CIO, including Coleman Young.[45] In early 1948 the Reuther caucus helped its supporters gain control of the top four offices in the Local 600 black caucus stronghold by exploiting the refusal of the local's left-wing officers to sign the Taft-Hartley anticommunist affidavits. Refusal to sign the affidavits barred workers from holding union office.[46]

Police repression also weakened the union's left. White and black leftists faced widespread persecution following the attempted assassination of Walter Reuther in April 1948. Detroit's chief of police and former Ford attorney Harry S. Toy used the shooting to break left-wing influence at the Rouge, where an active Henry Wallace campaign led by black leftist Nelson Davis had emerged. The anticommunist Toy, whose reputation for police brutality earned him the nickname "Shoot first Harry Toy,"[47] had called for "shooting, jailing, and deporting all citizens who support Henry Wallace." Toy arrested a number of left-wing leaders at the local, including W. G. Grant, Percy Llewellyn, Nelson Davis, William Johnson, and Shelton Tappes. Tappes's face appeared on the front page of a Detroit newspaper, where he was described as a "consistent follower of the Communist Party line." The UAW's executive board did little to defend the arrested unionists.[48]

The political climate put the union's non-Communist left on the defensive and eroded the popular front-style politics that had supported independent black activism. The UAW's non-Communist left-wing board members, led by George Addes and Leonard Thomas, endorsed the use of Section 8 to exclude Communists from union office and were accused by the party of making "desperate . . . factional deals . . . in shops catering to white-chauvinist, anti-Negro groups."[49] At the 1947 convention the union's white leftists refused to provide even token support for Tappes. The non-Communists in the left-wing caucus believed that Tappes would spoil the election for their vice presidential candidates, R. J. Thomas and Richard Leonard, and lead to a right-wing take-over of the executive board. The persistent red-baiting of black caucus activism also certainly helped convince the non-Communist left to distance itself from Tappes.[50]

The Red Scare also heightened divisions in black Detroit and weakened the community networks the caucus had forged during the war. A growing number of African Americans in Detroit began to shift their support to Reuther, partly as a pragmatic response to early Cold War politics. The *Michigan Chronicle* endorsed Reuther because its editorialists believed that black autoworkers would benefit from the stability a Reuther regime would provide. The *Chronicle* asserted that "the so-called Negro issue had become such a political football in the union that no real, substantial gains for our workers was possible." The paper qualified its endorsement of Reuther by declaring, "While we do not regard Walter Reuther as another Abraham Lincoln or John Brown, we do believe that Mr. Reuther is best fitted . . . to advance our cause within and without the organization."[51]

Shelton Tappes found it increasingly difficult to maintain his status and influence in the union and community in the face of the Red Scare and rise of the Reuther faction. In early 1949, Tappes took over the leadership of the UOPWA strike against the Great Lakes Mutual Insurance Company, but the strike "petered out . . . faded from the scene." Several weeks after the strike, Tappes announced what would prove to be his unsuccessful candidacy for recording-secretary of Local 600. Charles Wartman of the *Michigan Chronicle* captured the marginalization of Tappes when he wrote that, "Although he was once one of the outstanding Negroes in the UAW . . . Tappes got caught in the vortex of union politics, and now finds himself seeking office without the sanction of the top officers in the UAW-CIO."[52]

The Rise of a Liberal Civil Rights Program

As Tappes and the black caucus movement became increasingly marginalized, Reuther forged a new approach to civil rights more consistent with his anticommunist and class politics. Reuther began by expanding the Fair Practices Department that had emerged in response to black caucus organizing. He quickly asserted control over the department, appointing himself and a black ally, William Oliver, co-directors. Like Sheffield, Oliver had been an early Reuther supporter. Elected recording-secretary in 1942 at the Ford Highland Park plant, Oliver proved loyal to Reuther during wartime factional struggles. Oliver had also earned a reputation as an unreliable ally of the black autoworkers. Many black autoworkers referred to him pejoratively as "Singing Sam," because of the expectation he would faithfully serve the white executive board's interests. The name played on the stereotype of the loyal slave, an image that was reinforced by Oliver's career in the 1930s as a singer in an all-black singing group, the Ford Dixie 8, sponsored by Ford for its sales program.[53]

The Fair Practices Department, which expanded in size in the postwar years, diverged from black autoworkers' wartime activism. The union's new leaders advocated a gradual approach to achieving racial equality that emphasized education and legislative reform. The department shifted its focus away from the daily shop-floor concerns of black workers and began to allocate the bulk of its resources toward lobbying at the state and federal level. In the late 1940s and early 1950s, the department sought to implement a series of legislative reforms including the "National Act Against Discrimination in Employment," the end to Senate Rule 22, which had allowed southern conservatives to filibuster civil rights laws, and various civil rights reforms included in Truman's Committee on Civil Rights. Along with grassroots letter writing campaigns organized by department staff, Oliver and Reuther testified before Congress, urging support for civil rights bills. In some cases, the department published this testimony as brochures distributed to UAW members.[54]

The department, however, often supported moderate legislation and used its power to derail civil rights mobilizations and legislation it viewed as too radical. In the summer of 1951, the department organized a campaign to defeat a petition drive by the Detroit Negro Labor Council to secure a referendum on the fall ballot for a tough fair employment practices ordinance in Detroit. The drive leaders, mostly black caucus veterans, sought to use the petition process to build a permanent grassroots coalition of local unions, churches, and community groups committed to ending employment discrimination. The Fair Practices Department denounced the referendum as a Communist effort to sow racial discord. Reuther said the drive was an "obvious attempt by the Communists to defeat the FEPC in Detroit, and to use this defeat in propaganda against democracy throughout the world." The UAW barred its elected officials from signing the petition and declared its support for a Detroit fair employment ordinance to be passed by the city council, not through mass mobilization. The department-supported ordinance was weaker than the proposed referendum. NLC activists claimed it was a "milk and water FEPC bill, which abounds in pious words but is short on penalties." The UAW's attacks on the NLC helped stall the drive and neither initiative led to a municipal ordinance. Black autoworkers in Detroit did not gain fair employment protection until 1955, when the state, after almost a decade of agitation, passed a bill banning employment discrimination. But even this bill lacked the resources and power to stamp out discrimination in Detroit auto plants.[55]

On occasion the department expanded its reach outside the legislative arena and tried to implement civil rights reforms through direct negotiations with employers or organizations accused of discrimination. The department's gradualism, penchant for top-down solutions, and hostility towards grassroots mobilization shaped these efforts as well. While the department acknowledged the persistence of racial discrimination on the shop floor, it sought to channel black workers' complaints away from militant self-organization and through the centralized and ostensibly color-blind grievance procedure that covered all workers. While the department encouraged local unions to establish fair practices committees, the executive board restricted the ability of these committees to act independently. In one instance, Oliver intervened in Local 29 in Detroit to convince black workers to disband their independent "Committee to Abolish Discrimination." Oliver made it clear that the days of the black caucus were over. In the future, black workers would follow union procedures "so that we can realize harmonious working relationships between the workers in the plant." Channeling black workers' complaints through the union grievance procedure, however, often left those workers at the mercy of regional directors, who often shared the racial prejudices of many rank-and-file white workers. Throughout the 1950s and 1960s, black autoworkers complained about the indifference of the department toward their issues in the plants.[56]

The department achieved some successes that helped convince a number of black and white workers that it had developed the most effective approach to civil rights in the early Cold War. After his election, Reuther revived the campaign against bowling discrimination by the ABC that he had opposed during World War II. Reuther still opposed banning union members from ABC bowling, arguing that such aggressive action would harden racist attitudes and drive white workers into company leagues. Through a combination of direct lobbying of the ABC, legal action, the formation of the national Fair Play in Bowling Committee, and sponsorship of integrated bowling tournaments, the UAW campaign helped convince the ABC to end its whites-only policy. The victory, however, was bittersweet, coming ten years after the wartime campaign to integrate bowling and at a time when Detroit's racial boundaries were being redrawn in ways that made it increasingly unlikely that black and white people would ever bowl at the same alleys.[57]

Tappes Testifies

As the Fair Practices Department became entrenched, Tappes slowly shifted his support away from the union's disintegrating left. At the union's 1949 convention, Tappes voted for black leftist William Johnson for UAW vice president but cast his second vote for Reuther's vice-presidential candidate, John Livingston. Tappes also voted to uphold the expulsion of Allis-Chalmers Local 248 leader, Harold Christoffel, who was accused by the UAW leadership of belonging to the Communist Party. Tappes's close political ally in the black caucus, Hodges Mason, recalled years later being "bitterly disappointed" by Tappes's vote on Christoffel.[58] The next year Tappes completed his drift toward the right when he allied himself with the Reuther candidate for Local 600 president, Carl Stellato. Stellato appointed Tappes to the local's bargaining committee and later appointed Tappes as the first African American to sit on the local's grievance review board. In January 1951, Tappes accepted a staff position in the UAW as an international representative.[59] Almost one year later, Tappes took the stand as a friendly witness in front of HUAC.

Tappes's testimony, however, did not represent a genuine conversion to liberal anticommunism. Tappes had become increasingly skeptical of the party and its alliance with black workers. He experienced firsthand that the party's interests, not those of black workers, were primary. In 1945, his Communist allies and friends in Michigan rebuked him publicly for his unwillingness to join the party. The next year the party withdrew its support for Tappes's bid for Local 600 recording-secretary and backed William Johnson instead, a black worker who had recently been discharged from the army.[60] But the party's decision proved less decisive in Tappes's shift than the changing political climate that shattered the union's left-wing coalition dividing Communists from non-Communists and non-Communists from militant black union activists. In this context, Tappes made a pragmatic decision to support the Reuther faction, hoping that he could sustain civil rights struggles in the union and survive politically and economically as hired staff in the UAW. Tappes succeeded to some extent, quietly working as an international representative assisting black workers who complained of racial discrimination.

The peace Tappes made with liberal anticommunism, however, had its costs. For the next decade and a half, the Fair Practices Department set the tone for the UAW's civil rights program, attacking residual black militancy inside the union and focusing primarily on legislative and some contractual reforms. Some of these civil rights efforts led to important reforms, like the elimination of discriminatory contract language and fair employment laws in Michigan. But these reforms did not fundamentally alter the condition of black workers, who remained confined to the lowest-paid work and underrepresented in the leadership of the union. In the early Cold War, the UAW's leaders had ironically undermined the grassroots movement that was best situated to generate the bottom-up pressure required to translate these formal victories into real gains for the city's black working class.

Notes

1. Suggested text for Walter Reuther, "What Are We Waiting For?" ca. 1952, UAW Fair Practices Department Collection, Box 61, Archives of Labor and Urban Affairs (ALUA), Wayne State University, Detroit, Michigan.

2. Thomas N. Maloney and Warren C. Whatley, "Making the Effort: The Contours of Racial Discrimination in the Detroit Labor Market, 1920–1940," *Journal of Economic History* 55:3 (Sept. 1995): 468; Louis Stark, "Green Bares Talk with Aide of Ford," *New York*

Times, Feb. 15, 1941; Judith Stepan-Norris and Maurice Zeitlin, *Talking Union* (Urbana: University of Illinois Press, 1996), 31, 32, 59. For more on the strength of the Communist Party at the River Rouge, see Robert Korstad and Nelson Lichtenstein, "Opportunities Found and Lost: Labor, Radicals, and the Early Civil Rights Movement," *Journal of American History* 75 (Dec. 1988): 796.

3. Oral interview, Shelton Tappes, Blacks in the Labor Movement Collection, ALUA; House Un-American Activities Committee, Hearings, Feb.–Mar. 1952, "Communism in the Detroit Area," Shelton Tappes testimony.

4. See Michael Honey, *Southern Labor and Black Civil Rights: Organizing Memphis Workers* (Urbana: University of Illinois Press, 1993); Robert Korstad, *Civil Rights Unionism: Tobacco Workers and the Struggle for Democracy in the Mid-Twentieth Century South* (Chapel Hill: University of North Carolina Press, 2003); Korstad and Lichtenstein, "Opportunities Found and Lost"; Nelson Lichtenstein, *Walter Reuther: The Most Dangerous Man in Detroit* (Urbana: University of Illinois Press, 1997); Ruth Needleman, *Black Freedom Fighters in Steel: The Struggle for Democratic Unionism* (Ithaca, N.Y.: ILR Press, 2003); Honey, Needleman, and Korstad hold labor leaders more accountable for their choices in the postwar years. Lichtenstein, in *The Most Dangerous Man,* tends to portray Reuther's compromises more sympathetically and does not thoroughly examine the limitations of his civil rights program or the deep resentments held by many black workers toward Reuther.

5. See Mary Dudziak for more on the politics of race during the Cold War; Mary Dudziak, *Cold War Civil Rights: Race and the Image of American Democracy* (Princeton, N.J.: Princeton University Press, 2002).

6. Report by Walter Hardin, "Section 5, Negro Organization at Ford's," [n.d.], Vertical File, UAW International Activities, Box 72, ALUA; Tappes interview, BLMC, ALUA; Aug. Meier and Elliott Rudwick, *Black Detroit and the Rise of the UAW,* (New York: Oxford University Press, 1981), 82–85.

7. Stepan-Norris and Zeitlin, *Talking Union,* 105, 116, 135.

8. As a number of scholars have shown, the fusion of labor and civil rights activism was not just confined to Detroit, but had deep roots in the country's black working class. There is an extensive body of literature on civil rights unionism. See Eric Arneson, *Brotherhood of Colors: Black Railroad Workers and the Struggle for Equality* (Cambridge, Mass.: Harvard University Press, 2001); Melinda Chateauvert, *Marching Together: Women of the Brotherhood of Sleeping Car Porters* (Urbana: University of Illinois Press, 1997); Michael Honey, *Southern Labor and Black Civil Rights;* Robin Kelley, *Hammer and Hoe: Alabama Communists during the Great Depression* (Chapel Hill: University of North Carolina Press, 1990); Robert Korstad, *Civil Rights Unionism.*

9. Victoria W. Wolcott, *Remaking Respectability: African American Women in Interwar Detroit* (Chapel Hill: University of North Carolina Press, 2000), 187–88; Stepan-Norris and Zeitlin, *Talking Union,* 103, 133; "Ford Turns 100: '41 Strike Divided Workers, a Family," Sheryl James, *Detroit Free Press,* May 12, 2003.

10. James, "Ford Turns 100."

11. Hardin report, ALUA; Louis Stark, "Pickets Leaving," *New York Times,* Apr. 3, 1941.

12. Meier and Rudwick, *Black Detroit,* 87–107; Louis Stark, "Ford C.I.O. Men Accept Peace Formula of Governor, Company Sets Conditions," *New York Times,* Apr. 11, 1941; Louis Stark, "Ford Strike Ends as Both Sides Bow to Defense Needs," *New York Times,* Apr. 12, 1941; Louis Stark, "C.I.O. Sweeps Poll in 2 Ford Plants: Seeks a Contract," *New York Times,* May 23, 1941.

13. Report by Walter Hardin, "Section 5 Negro Organization at Ford's," [n.d.], Vertical File, UAW International Activities, Box 72, ALUA; James, "Ford Turns 100."

14. Meier and Rudwick, *Black Detroit,* 106, 147.

15. Alan Clive, *State of War: Michigan in World War II* (Ann Arbor: University of Michigan, 1979), 28, 128; Meier and Rudwick, *Black Detroit,* 136–37.

16. Thomas Sugrue, *The Origins of the Urban Crisis: Race and Inequality in Postwar Detroit* (Princeton, N.J.: Princeton University Press, 1998), 132; "Current Notes," *Michigan Chronicle,* Dec. 2, 1944.

17. Korstad and Lichtenstein, "Opportunities Found and Lost," 796; Flyer, "THEY SUPPORT FIGHT FOR NEGRO WOMEN IN WAR INDUSTRY," 1942, Shelton Tappes Collection, ALUA.

18. *Michigan Chronicle,* Sept. 2, 1944; Tappes interview, BLMC, ALUA; Joseph Billups interview, BLMC, ALUA.

19. Meier and Rudwick, *Black Detroit,* 152; Minutes, UAW International Executive Board, Sept. 16, 1941, UAW International Executive Board Meetings Collection, box 2, ALUA; Meier and Rudwick, *Black Detroit,* 117–36; Minutes, UAW-IEB, Oct. 1–6, 1944, UAW-IEB Meetings Collection, box 3, ALUA.

20. "Metropolitan Labor Council Sponsors Meet," *Michigan Chronicle,* Sept. 2, 1944; Sugrue, *Origins of the Urban Crisis,* 104.

21. Herbert Hill, quoted in Billups interview, BLMC, ALUA; Tappes interview, BLMC, ALUA; Joseph Billups interview, BLMC, ALUA.

22. Charles Denby, *Indignant Heart: A Black Workers' Journal* (Detroit: Wayne State University Press, 1978), 96–97; Lillian Hatcher, Oral interview, Institute of Labor and Industrial Relations (University of Michigan-Wayne State University). Program on Women and Work Oral History Project, 1978–79, Bentley Historical Library, University of Michigan; "Current Notes," *Detroit Tribune,* Dec. 2, 1944.

23. For further discussion of the Sojourner Truth controversy, see Dominic Capeci Jr., *Race Relations in Wartime Detroit: The Sojourner Truth Housing Controversy of 1942* (Philadelphia: Temple University Press, 1984); Meier and Rudwick, *Black Detroit,* 176–80; Sugrue, *Origins of the Urban Crisis,* 73–77.

24. Jenny Nolan, "Bob-lo, island of the white wood," *Detroit News,* "Rearview Mirror"; Patricia Zacharias, "When Detroit danced to the big bands," *Detroit News,* "Rearview Mirror," June 23, 2001.

25. Shelton Tappes, quoted in Billups interview, BLMC, ALUA; "Current Notes," *Michigan Chronicle,* Feb. 2, 1946

26. Vivian M. Baulch, "Detroit's legends of bowling," *Detroit News,* May 12, 2001.

27. Althea J. White, "Letters to the Editor," *Ebony,* Apr. 1995.

28. James F. McNamara to George Addes, Nov. 21, 1945, UAW FPD Collection, box 1, ALUA; George Crockett to Vera Vanderburg, Oct. 12, 1945, UAW FPD Collection, ALUA;

George Crockett to George Weaver, Nov. 17, 1945, UAW FPD Collection, box 1, ALUA; Robert H. Mast, *Detroit Lives* (Philadelphia: Temple University Press, 1994), 168.

29. Meier and Rudwick, *Black Detroit,* 75.

30. Tappes interview, BLMC, ALUA; Mason interview, BLMC, ALUA; Proceedings, UAW Convention, 1942.

31. Proceedings, UAW Convention, 1943, ALUA. There was extensive press coverage of the debate about representation for black workers at the Buffalo convention; see Horace Cayton, "Factionalism Causes Negro to Get More Recognition at Union Convention," *Pittsburgh Courier,* Sept. 23, 1943; "Proposes Two Resolutions," and "Reuther . . . Slaps Addes for Stand on Race Issues," *Michigan Chronicle,* Oct. 2, 1943; "Negroes Split over UAW Executive Board Member," *Michigan Chronicle,* Oct. 9, 1943; Daniel L. Wells, "UAW Adds Union Title . . . the Most Unpredictable," *Detroit Free Press,* Oct. 10, 1943; Thomas Groehn, "Labor and Industry," *Detroit News,* Oct. 10, 1943; "Reuther Denies Eaton's Charge of Race Bias at UAW Meet," *Detroit Tribune,* Oct. 23, 1943.

32. Proceedings, UAW Convention, 1943, ALUA; "Reuther . . . Slaps Addes for Stand on Race Issues."

33. Horace Sheffield interview, BLMC, ALUA; "Reuther . . . Slaps Addes for Stand on Race Issue"; "Negroes Split over UAW Executive Board Members"; Proceedings, UAW Convention, 1943, ALUA.

34. "Communists to Speak at National Negro Congress," *Wage Earner,* Apr. 19, 1956; Minutes from an unidentified local union committee that sent delegates to the NNC convention, June 8, 1946, Vertical File, African Americans, Soc., A-Z, NNC,NALUA; "Asks U.N. Probe U.S. Anti-Negro Bias," *Michigan Chronicle,* June 10, 1946; Press Release, National Negro Congress Convention, May 25, 1946, ACTU Collection, box 29, ALUA; "Death Blow to Jim Crow Day is May 17," *Michigan Chronicle,* May 17, 1946; "Murray Greets NNC Detroit Convention," *Michigan Chronicle,* May 24, 1946.

35. "Report on Negro Vice-President in the UAW-CIO," by Arthur McPhaul, [n.d.], Nat Ganley Collection, ALUA.

36. Ibid.; "Tappes for Vice President UAW-CIO," Shelton Tappes election flyer, Nat Ganley Collection, ALUA; *Michigan Chronicle,* Nov. 1, 1947. For more on the CRC in Detroit, see chapter 3 in Edward Carl Pintzuk, "Going Down Fighting: The Michigan Communist Party after World War II " (Ph.D. diss., Wayne State University, 1992).

37. Lichtenstein, *Most Dangerous Man in Detroit*

38. Mason interview, BLMC, ALUA; Tappes interview, BLMC, ALUA.

39. "Report of the International UAW-CIO Fair Practices Committee, Third Quarter, 1945," Norman Matthews Collection, box 1, ALUA; "The Committee's Findings and Recommendations on Charges of Racial Discrimination in UAW-CIO Plants and Locals in Toledo, Ohio," UAW Fair Practices Department (FPD) Collection, box 1, ALUA; Minutes, UAW International Executive Board (IEB), Nov. 26–28, 1945, UAW-IEB Meetings Collection, box 3, ALUA; Tappes interview, BLMC, ALUA.

40. "Fair Practices Clause Absent in GM Contract," *Michigan Chronicle,* Mar. 23, 1946; series of letters between George Crockett and Walter Reuther from Aug. 21, 1945, through Feb. 8, 1946, George Crockett Collection, box 1, ALUA; George Crockett interview, BLMC, ALUA.

41. Article by Walter Reuther, "Tolerance Is Not Enough," [n.d., sometime in 1945], Crockett Collection, box 1, ALUA.

42. Suggested text for Walter Reuther, "What Are We Waiting For?" ca .1952, UAW FPD Collection, box 61, ALUA.

43. Proceedings, UAW Convention, 1946, ALUA; *Michigan Chronicle*, Apr. 20, 1946; "Shake-Up in UAW Looms as Reuther Wins," *Michigan Chronicle*, Nov. 15, 1947.

44. Tappes interview, BLMC, ALUA.

45. Roger Keeran, *The Communist Party and the Auto Workers Union*, (Bloomington: Indiana University Press, 1980), 261–87; *Michigan Chronicle*, Apr. 17, 1948; *Michigan Chronicle*, Aug. 14, 1948; *Michigan Chronicle*, Sept. 11, 1948.

46. Keeran, *Communist Party*, 286; *Michigan Chronicle*, Jan. 10, 1948; *Michigan Chronicle*, Jan. 24, 1948; William D. Andrew, "Factionalism and Anti-Communism: Ford Local 600," *Labor History* 20 (Spring 1979): 238.

47. Angela Dillard, "From the Reverend Charles A. Hill to the Reverend Albert Cleage Jr.: Change and Continuity in the Patterns of Civil Rights Mobilizations in Detroit" (Ph. D. diss., University of Michigan, 1995), 184.

48. *Michigan Chronicle*, May 1, 1948; *Daily Worker*, May 5, 1948; Newspaper headline, n.d., n.t., "Best of 40 Tips Are Acted On," Shelton Tappes Collection, box 1, ALUA; Lichtenstein, *Most Dangerous Man in Detroit*, 275; Local 600 Executive Board Meeting Minutes, Mar. 23, 1948; UAW Local 600 Collection, ALUA; *Michigan Chronicle*, Apr. 26, 1948.

49. Keeran, *The Communist Party and the Auto Workers Unions*, (Bloomington: Indiana University Press, 1980), 260–75; John Williamson, "Why Reuther Won in UAW," *Daily Worker*, Nov. 27, 1947.

50. UAW Convention Proceedings, 1947; Lichtenstein, *Most Dangerous Man in Detroit*, 268; *Daily Worker*, Nov. 27, 1947.

51. Editorial, "The UAW Convention," *Michigan Chronicle*, Nov. 22, 1947; Horace White, "The Facts in Our News," *Michigan Chronicle*, Nov. 22, 1947.

52. Charles Wartman, "On the Labor Line," *Michigan Chronicle*, Mar. 13, 1949; "Tom Thompson Holds Lead in Ford Elections," *Michigan Chronicle*, Apr. 2, 1949.

53. Minutes, UAW-IEB, Apr. 16–26, 1946, UAW-IEB Meetings Collection, box 3, ALUA; Crockett interview, BLMC, ALUA; Biographical Sketch of William H. Oliver, UAW FPD Collection, box 10, ALUA. For more on Oliver, see Kevin Boyle, *The UAW and the Heyday of American Liberalism* (Ithaca, N.Y.: Cornell University Press, 1998), 43–44.

54. William Oliver to Walter Reuther, Nov. 25, 1947, UAW FPD Collection, box 3, ALUA; *Michigan Chronicle*, Feb. 21, 1948; Minutes, UAW-IEB, Sept. 8–12, 1947, UAW-IEB Meetings Collection, box 4, ALUA; "Rejoins Staff for Permanent FEPC Law," *Chicago Defender*, Oct. 18, 1947; Boyle, *The UAW and the Heyday of American Liberalism*, 109–10.

55. Letter from top four officers of the UAW, co-directors of Region 1 and 1–A to local presidents, recording-secretaries, executive boards, and fair practices committees in Regions 1 and 1–A, July 3, 1951, Ken Morris Collection, box 14, ALUA; Charles Wartman, "On the Labor Line," *Michigan Chronicle*, Aug. 11, 1951; Asher Lauren, "CIO Wrangles over FEPC," *Detroit News*, n.d., ACTU Collection, box 37, ALUA; for further discussion of the FEPC referendum issue, see Dillard, "From the Reverend Charles A. Hill," 212–16, and Sugrue, *Origins of the Urban Crisis*, 170–73.

56. List of UAW local FPCs, June 6, 1949, UAW FPD Collection, box 27, ALUA; Minutes, UAW-IEB, Aug. 18, 1946, UAW-IEB Meetings Collection, box 3, ALUA; William Oliver to Jim Walters, May 7, 1947, UAW FPD Collection, box 14, ALUA. This conservative model for the fair practices committees partly reflected Oliver and Reuther's attempt to contain the race question and black caucus activism. But it also reflected Reuther's commitment to a centralized and bureaucratic method of resolving shop-floor disputes. Early in his career as union official, Reuther opposed the rank and file's use of wildcat strikes and work stoppages as "mobocracy." He believed that such militancy triggered corporate reprisals and internal factional struggles that undermined union strength. In 1940, as director of the UAW's General Motors department, Reuther helped implement a grievance arbitration procedure designed to create an "impartial" judicial approach to securing workers' rights in the workplace. By the early 1950s this system defined shop-floor relations in most other auto plants. This grievance procedure proved extremely flawed. It displaced the more responsive shop steward system with a lengthy system of written complaints, arbitrators, and umpires. Written grievances often took months to reach the highest levels of arbitration, companies won the right to file grievances against the union, union committeemen increasingly acted as "contract policemen" who sought to contain shop-floor militancy, and Reutherites who controlled the grievance machinery often refused to process grievances that might set a bad precedent for the union or grievances that were filed by political opponents. See Steve Jeffreys, *Management and Managed: Fifty Years of Crisis at Chrysler* (New York: Cambridge University Press, 1986), 95, and Lichtenstein, *Most Dangerous Man in Detroit*, 146–53.

57. UAW-IEB meeting, Dec. 9–18, 1946, UAW-IEB Meetings Collection, box 4, ALUA; Attendance List, "Conference to Promote Democratic Participation in Bowling," n.d., UAW FPD Collection, box 5, ALUA; William Oliver to Walter Reuther, Aug. 19, 1947, UAW FPD Collection, box 3; Biographical Sketch of William Oliver, n.d., UAW FPD, box 10, ALUA; "UAW Sponsors Tourney in Move against ABC," *Michigan Chronicle*, Nov. 11, 1947; Minutes, UAW-IEB, Sept. 10, 1947, UAW-IEB Meetings Collection, box 4, ALUA. For examples of the UAW's educational and legal approach, see William Oliver to Walter Reuther, Aug. 29, 1947, UAW FPD Collection, box 3, ALUA; Oliver to Betty Hicks, Aug. 29, 1949, UAW FPD Collection, box 3, ALUA; William Oliver to Walter Reuther, Nov. 25, 1947, UAW FPD Collection, box 3, ALUA.

58. Proceedings, UAW Convention, 1949; Mason interview, BLMC, ALUA.

59. *Michigan Chronicle*, May 27, 1950; *Michigan Chronicle*, June 30, 1950; *Michigan Chronicle*, Jan. 13, 1951.

60. Tappes interview, BLMC, ALUA; "Vote Counting Incomplete as W. Stone Leads," *Michigan Chronicle*, Apr. 14, 1945; "Tappes Says Housing Question Defeated Him," *Michigan Chronicle*, Apr. 21, 1945; "Leaders See Challenge in Tappes Defeat," *Michigan Chronicle*, Apr. 28, 1945; HUAC Hearings, Feb.–Mar. 1952, "Communism in the Detroit Area," Shelton Tappes testimony; "Labor Looks Ahead," *Michigan Chronicle*, May 11, 1946.

5. Putting the "I" before "UE": Labor's Cold War in Schenectady-GE

LISA KANNENBERG

The United Electrical, Radio, and Machine Workers' (UE) harrowing post–World War II experience illuminates very effectively the chilling effect of the Cold War on the climate of reform that had nurtured the CIO unions' earlier progress. To the UE—fighting off not just former CIO allies but Congress, the FBI, the courts, the press, the Catholic Church and last but not least, corporate America—the assault was utterly devastating. But for the anticommunist core of the CIO—and ultimately, the entire labor movement—the Cold War was equally if perhaps more subtly destructive. Historians have long acknowledged that the left-wing purge damaged the CIO, noting that skilled leftist organizers were eliminated just as the movement sought to expand beyond the basic industries into important new areas, such as the South and the white-collar workforce. Expansion in those directions might have diversified and strengthened the movement; instead, those efforts failed as the federation turned destructively inward. Even historians who approve of the purge acknowledge its deleterious effects. Robert Zieger, for example, described the purge as "damaging and even enervating" to the federation.[1] But the most lasting damage lay beyond these organizational issues. The Cold War altered the context of the struggle between labor and management swiftly and dramatically in the months and years following the war, with U.S. business the prime beneficiary.

As the largest and most influential of the CIO unions strongly influenced by the Communist Party, the UE became the chief target of the ferocious postwar offensive against left-wing labor. And as the largest and most influential union local in the electrical industry, UE Local 301 in the Schenectady–General Electric plant became a focal point of interest and attack. A look at Local 301's experience and its outcome can offer insight not only into the UE's travail, but also illuminate the larger movement's loss. UE Local 301 was a vital and dynamic organization, a stellar example of the CIO's best. At the time the local came under attack, it was working hard—and with some success—to carry the CIO's postwar program from the shop floor into the community. Local 301 grandly planned to build on the respect and legitimacy it had garnered in the course of the war to become a leading voice in the community, representing the city's working people. The local's leaders envisioned an expanded democracy, a polity attuned to the needs of the people. But the anticommunist onslaught, welcomed and subtly nurtured by General Electric, put an end to that exercise, forcing Local 301's energies into far narrower channels. The local's foray into politics and forced retreat back to the shop floor prefigure the similar fate of the mainstream labor movement.[2]

At first glance, Schenectady would seem to be an odd locale to nourish a "hotbed" of Communism. But in fact, the conservative upstate town had long been a venue for homegrown radicalism. Early in the century, Schenectady had boasted the highest percentage of organized workers of any town in the nation. It was an IWW stronghold by 1906, when GE workers pioneered the sit-down strike. Local politics, though, was alternately dominated by barely distinguishable Republican and Democratic machines quite friendly to the city's business class. That changed in 1911, when the Schenectady working class finally made its political mark. Led by the charismatic preacher-turned-politician George Lunn, Schenectady Socialists swept local elections. They put Lunn in the mayor's office and filled the city council with union men, including a respected British-born GE turbine inspector named William Turnbull. In just two years, the Socialists produced remarkable results. They built three new schools and raised teachers' pay. They constructed new playgrounds and parks and began municipal garbage collection. They organized a shelter for itinerant workers and a municipal unemployment bureau. The list goes on, and the work was very, very popular. It took an unprecedented fusion of Schenectady's Democrats and Republicans to squeeze out the Socialists, 54 percent to 44 percent, in 1913.[3]

The twenties were not a good time for radical Schenectady workers. Labor suffered a serious setback in the anti-radical aftermath of WWI. Those who managed to keep their jobs kept their heads down, until hard times in the 1930s undermined business supremacy and renewed a climate of reform. Still, when GE workers began to organize what became UE Local 301, William Turnbull, the old socialist, was at the center of the drive, offering advice to a band of local Communist Party members and their allies, including Julius Emspak and Leo Jandreau. Emspak left town to serve as the national UE's secretary-treasurer. Leo Jandreau stayed. Jandreau was a local boy of French Canadian background. Bright and talented, but with little formal education, Jandreau had "stolen" the machinist trade—learned it on the job, outside the official apprenticeship program. With a core group, including Communists and close supporters, he led Local 301 from the union's founding in 1936 through its defection to the IUE in 1954.[4]

The young Communists in Depression-era Schenectady had not personally experienced that first Red Scare, but it affected them deeply nonetheless. At no point did they operate fully and freely in the shop or the community as open members of the Communist Party; the twenties had foreclosed that option. A few Schenectady Communists always openly declared their affiliation. Some, like Sid Friedlander, were elected year after year to high leadership positions in Local 301. Others, like Jandreau himself, never acknowledged party membership. Overall, though, whether Communist or not, Local 301's homegrown leaders were decidedly left wing, and their competence earned them very strong support from the rank and file and even the grudging respect of local GE managers.[5]

In the hope-filled days at the end of WWII, Local 301 leftists dreamed of parlaying their newly acquired legitimacy into an active role in the community, for the first time since the socialists of 1911. Initially, they met some success, in the 1946 strike, and the elections that fall. But opposition coalesced swiftly, and ferociously. Within months the local was under attack, and its foray into mainstream politics was effectively squelched. An examination of those early postwar conflicts in Schenectady can enhance understanding of what was lost in the struggle: a "left-wing agenda" that happened to be the heart of the CIO's own.

The Postwar Debate over Wages, Prices, Profits, and Planning

In the waning months of World War II, the fragile, government-mediated cooperation between business and labor rapidly began to unravel as the nation contemplated the task of reconversion to peacetime production. Both sides drew heavily on the experience of depression and war in formulating proposals; they differed most dramatically in their general attitudes toward the role of the state and most particularly on the desirability of postwar economic planning. The CIO favored continued tripartite cooperation in a planned reconversion with the goal of creating a high-wage, full-employment economy. Consequently, they argued for programs to bolster employment and cushion the unemployed, raising wages and controlling prices to produce full employment through strong consumer demand. The CIO's policies embraced the essence of Roosevelt's "Second Bill of Rights": the right to a job at a living wage, the right to education, medical care, housing, and security in old age.[6]

American business generally did not share the CIO's vision of a planned prosperity and expanded social security. Strengthened by the war, business saw an opportunity to shake off the constraints of New Deal economic intervention and labor's claim to partnership, envisioning instead a return to the "free market" and the glorious autonomy of the twenties. Business pressed for swift price decontrol as the most effective incentive to spur the forces of production. The promise of profit, they argued, would promote a rapid transition and ultimately provide jobs.

Individual corporations and organizations like the National Association of Manufacturers (NAM) launched a concerted campaign to ensure that business and the "Free Enterprise System"—not labor and the New Deal state—would garner the lion's share of credit for the dazzling success of the wartime economic apparatus.[7] GE participated enthusiastically in this effort to shape perceptions and dictate postwar conditions, using the pages of its company paper, the *Works News,* to refurbish the Depression-battered image of the free enterprise system. In January 1945 the paper began with an eight-part series extolling the virtues of capitalism.[8]

GE then attacked the notion of government planning, widely disseminating a cartoon version of F. A. Hayek's *The Road to Serfdom* that disconnected planning from its popular association with New Deal social democracy and related it instead to fascist totalitarianism. GE used Hayek to snipe at the increasingly beleaguered wartime price-control agency, the Office of Price Administration (OPA).[9]

Leaders of Local 301 were deeply disturbed by GE's flood of pronouncements on the virtues of free enterprise and the evils of planning. Local 301 President William Wilkinson and Business Agent Leo Jandreau sent a scathing critique to GE President Charles Wilson in the fall of 1945. Wilkinson and Jandreau first took issue with a speech in which Wilson had denounced what he had called the "'fashionable belief' that everyone has a 'right to a job.'" The unionists knew that planning would be necessary to achieve labor's objectives, which they defined as "a job at a living wage, adequate unemployment compensation, a decent house . . . adequate medical care, reasonable prices for necessities—in a democratic country." The Schenectady leaders were particularly angered by the *"Road to Serfdom"* cartoon, rejecting Hayek's assertion that economic planning had led to dictatorship in Germany and Italy. "The whole world now knows," they wrote, "that it was the lack of planning in both these countries . . . which led to unemployment and hunger, and the breaking down of the spirits of the people." Wilson was presenting GE workers with "a hard and sad choice": "We are told that planning brings dictatorship. From bitter experience we know that no planning means no jobs. Do we have to choose between eating in chains or starving in 'freedom'?" "Apparently," they concluded presciently, "if any planning is to be done, GE wants to do it."[10]

This early exchange illustrates the manner in which the ability to manipulate language shaped relationships in the emerging Cold War. GE's critique of government planning, for example, turned on the linking of "Free Enterprise" and "liberty." GE sought to appropriate positive cultural values—liberty, democracy, individual opportunity—and link them to an idealized "free enterprise system," while simultaneously discrediting alternative ideas by associating them with culturally undesirable concepts like inefficiency, lack of choice, and "collectivism." The "Free Enterprise System" produced liberty; social planning destroyed freedom. The matter was that simple.[11]

The first conflicts of the postwar era were informed by such labor-management debates over first principles but soon came to focus on the more mundane question of the bottom line and workers' share of it. By August 1945, simmering tensions came to a boil. With the war over, layoffs increased, and the overtime that had softened the impact of the wartime wage freezes ended. Confronted with rank-and-file members angered by rising prices and shrinking pay checks, the UE, UAW, and Steelworkers—the CIO's "Big Three"—launched a concerted assault on the Little Steel formula that had frozen wages since 1942. But with the threat of inflation becoming a major concern, labor's demand for wage increases was vulnerable to attack as a potential contributor to the inflationary trend. The Truman administration's new wage policy permitted wage increases provided they did not result in rising prices; consequently, the question of continuing government's role in setting wages and prices became part of a hot debate, with labor favoring freeing wages while continuing price control and business advocating the reverse. Labor and management sparred on these issues through the strike wave that ushered in the New Year in 1946, through the debate that spring over extending the life of the OPA, and into the off-year elections that fall. UE Local 301 became a site of these defining struggles.[12]

The 1946 strikes first brought the issue to a head. In October 1945, Truman's economists boosted labor's position with an estimate that industry could increase wages 24 percent without raising prices and still earn profits at prewar levels.[13] Walter Reuther then issued his famous demand that GM "open the books" to prove that it could not afford to raise wages without raising prices.

The same discussion took place in the electrical industry, where GE joined the chorus insisting that continued price controls precluded any wage increase. The UE presented an arsenal of statistics to argue that General Electric could afford a sizeable wage increase without raising prices. To refuse, the union argued, would "pit [GE] against the interests of all GE workers . . . their families and the American people as a whole."[14]

E. D. Spicer, head of GE's negotiating team, followed the lead of GM management and curtly rejected the UE's effort to intrude on management's sacred ground. "We do not consider prices of General Electric a proper subject for negotiation," Spicer replied. "[We] do not propose to discuss . . . the Company's financial condition or its profits, past, current or prospective."[15]

Thus stymied, over two hundred thousand electrical workers joined the strike wave in mid-January, shutting down both the Westinghouse and GE chains in the first national strikes in electrical industry history. The GE strike was finally settled on March 13, 1946. Though the final wage settlement fell a bit short of the union's original "$2 a day" demand, it was significantly higher than the "10 percent or 10 cents" General Electric had first offered.[16]

For UE, the victory in GE proved truly bittersweet. It was, all agreed, a smashing victory for the union. Years later, General Electric managers still expressed a raw sense of shock at the depth of worker and community support for the strike; they viewed the outcome as "little short of a debacle."[17]

While the union was victorious, the victory was incomplete. Like the UAW, the UE failed in its critical effort to link wages to profits and to gain a voice in basic corporate decision making. Still, Schenectady union activists recall the strike as the high point of their union's existence. Never had they been so strong, so united; never was the community so receptive and supportive. The strike was extremely well organized; the union shut down the giant plant and kept strong picket lines at each of nine plant gates and two satellite plants through the worst months of a bitter Schenectady winter. Workers so thoroughly controlled the situation that essential maintenance and executive personnel had to apply to the strike committee for "passes" to enter the plant.[18]

Schenectady management was shocked and deeply angered by the community's support for the strikers. From politicians to ordinary citizens, Schenectadians overwhelmingly supported the union. George Churchill, the superintendent of streets, thoughtfully sent city workers to sand icy spots on the picket lines, and the police—many of whom had relatives in the shop—refused to enforce an injunction GE received that would have limited pickets to a handful per gate. Mayor Mills Ten Eyck chaired a community rally that drew six thousand supporters. Nineteen prominent citizens published an open letter to GE urging the company to settle on the union's terms. Over a thousand local merchants posted strike support placards in their windows, and 205 small businessmen and professionals sponsored a town meeting supporting the strikers. The Schoharie County Farmers Union contributed trucks of food and an 800–pound Holstein heifer that walked the picket line for a few hours before checking in to the strike kitchen. Citizens dropped off loads of wood for the burn barrels that warmed picketers, and the Schenectady Railway Company donated a trolley car to serve as a warming shed for the duration.[19]

The debate over wages, prices, and profits continued throughout the strike. Both GE and Local 301 used the local newspapers to carry on a spirited and often acrimonious campaign in the community. The company stressed that its wages were fair and its profits low, constantly linking wages to prices by reiterating its argument that the company could not grant the union's demand and continue to operate profitably without a corresponding price increase, then still blocked by the OPA. The union reproduced pay stubs to counter GE's claim to high and rising wages and published government statistics on company profits and reserves to support their argument that GE could easily raise wages without raising prices.[20]

Two weeks into the strike, GE sent orderly waves of engineers marching against the picket lines as a prelude to a plea for a court injunction in support of non-union workers' "right to work." The company's attempt to break the picket lines produced a wave of community support for the union that hastened the conclusion of the strike. The company won its injunction but was unable to enforce it; the next day over five thousand strikers showed up at the picket lines to defy the court order.[21]

The strike thus ended on a note of triumph for Local 301, and inspired the union to expand its reach into city politics. Declaring "We shall use our organized strength for the welfare of the city," the union vowed to accept its "special responsibility" to "debunk the fallacy that higher wages cause higher prices." Having won the contest for higher wages, Local 301 promised to carry the fight for price control into the community. At the victory celebration, Local 301 Vice President William Kelley announced the opening of a new Thirteenth Ward political action committee headquarters, the first of fourteen projected ward headquarters that the union envisioned as a "physical and practical means of carrying on community action." Local 301 became part of the national CIO-PAC campaign to consolidate the labor vote and maximize community influence in the 1946 midterm elections.[22]

Local 301's "fight for price control" was all but lost before it even began. By March of 1946 the OPA was on the ropes, struggling to hold the price line against a hostile Congress and a $3 million NAM public relations campaign later described as "spectacularly successful."[23] In this climate Local 301 took the fight for price control to the community as promised, but with singularly disappointing results. In late April, as Congress debated whether to extend the OPA or gut it, Schenectady unions organized a rally to "Save Price Control." Less than one hundred citizens showed up. In early May, a "giant telegram" directed to Congressman Kearney fared better. A coalition of labor and community organizations set up the telegram on busy State Street and gathered thousands of signatures. Local 301 also sent shop steward John Saccocio and his family to Washington, where Saccocio testified before the Senate Banking Committee in support of continued price control, using his own family budget to dramatize his testimony.[24]

GE countered with an offensive of its own, arguing that high prices and shortages were the result of government controls and labor's greed. Wilson's speeches struck at the twin evils: "Labor has no . . . right . . . to starve, endanger, or destroy the society of which it is a part," he thundered, and government had no right to "dam [the] stream" of production.[25] Inside the company, GE used the *Works News* to counter union arguments in the price-control debate, reinforcing the association between economic planning and state coercion GE began with "*The Road to Serfdom.*"[26]

It is impossible to precisely assess the local impact of the price-control debate between General Electric and Local 301, but anecdotal evidence suggests that GE's publicity efforts had some impact. In October 1946, when a national strike by cattlemen protesting the reimposition of OPA ceiling prices produced a critical shortage of meat supplies, the Schenectady *Union-Star* conducted an informal supermarket poll asking shoppers if they thought price controls should be removed. Even after months of vicious attack, the OPA was still very popular. As Meg Jacobs has noted, nearly 75 percent of Americans still supported the agency. The *Union-Star* poll supports Jacobs's findings: most of the twenty-seven respondents considered price controls a legitimate way to ensure continued inexpensive supplies. But seven articulated—in strikingly similar language—an ideological opposition to government controls; five of the seven were the wives of GE employees. "[In] a free market," said one, "we have our choice of whether to buy or not . . . natural competition will adjust prices." Another cited "the theory of supply and demand" as the best guarantor of fair prices. All expressed just the sort of faith in the "free market" that GE was working hard to create.[27]

Continuing price control was thus an uphill battle, but it did provide a focus for political action among Schenectady's CIO unions. By the fall of 1946 Local 301 had PACs operating in all fourteen wards. As the price-control issue sizzled through the summer, the CIO-PAC began to put more emphasis on the upcoming November elections.[28]

The '46 Election

The emerging Cold War deeply inflected the 1946 midterm election, nationally and in Schenectady. Heightened fears of the new "Red menace" marked domestic politics and sidelined the labor-management debate on wages, prices, and profits. The new belligerence boded ill for the American left—in politics and in the CIO. By the fall, the Republicans had fastened on the Red menace as a viable campaign issue and had begun to "[use] 'CIO' and 'PAC' as near-synonyms for 'Communist.'"[29] The new salience of the issue—now reaching into the domestic political scene—began to severely strain the left-center coalition in both party politics and the CIO.

In Schenectady, the CIO-PAC was nominally nonpartisan, though objectively their pro-labor criteria favored Democrats. Still, the first candidate to receive extensive consideration was Joe Dominelli, a charismatic young Republican who gained visibility as a leading activist in veterans' affairs. Dominelli chaired the Local 301 veteran's committee and held key posts in several other Schenectady veterans' organizations. In June, a nonpartisan group of veterans began a "Dominelli for Sheriff" campaign. Dominelli's opponent was William Dunn, majority leader of the city council and candidate of the Republican machine. Dunn was also a GE general foreman. Many Schenectadians viewed Dunn's run as sponsored by GE, as the company's retaliation for the alleged pro-union bias of the Schenectady County sheriff's department during the strike. The CIO-PAC quickly endorsed Dominelli's candidacy, but by the fall the PAC had switched its support to a strongly pro-labor businessman, William Sherry, who was running on the Democratic ticket. Dominelli withdrew and threw his support to Sherry as a more viable contender.[30]

The "Beat Dunn" campaign became the chief focus of CIO-PAC efforts in Schenectady. A second target was incumbent Republican Congressman Bernard Kearney. Schenectady CIO affiliates had endorsed Kearney in 1942 but were angered by his party-line votes against continued price control and for restrictive labor legislation. The unionists instead backed Carroll "Pink" Gardener, a popular former professional wrestler. Beyond the two big races, the CIO-PAC-endorsed candidates held joint spots on Democratic and ALP tickets. The criteria for PAC endorsement included candidates' acceptance of the national CIO-PAC's Fourteen-Point Program and the committee's judgment that a candidate "[would] actually work for [the] program." The

program began with a plank calling for "lasting peace . . . through the Roosevelt peace program" and continued through a list of domestic goals: full
employment at "decent" wages; price control; universal health care; veterans'
programs; equal pay for equal work; "an end to discrimination in all forms,"
including race and sex discrimination, and finally, protection for farmers
and small businessmen.[31]

The Communist issue played very strongly in Schenectady, fueled by national developments within the UE and the CIO. Nationally, Republican
attacks on the CIO led affiliates to turn on leftists in their ranks and on the
left-led unions like UE. Philip Murray, president of both the USW and the
CIO, began to purge left wingers from the Steelworkers in May. Though
Murray continued to defend rhetorically members' rights to hold diverse
political beliefs, his action signaled a new standard of political orthodoxy
that foreshadowed the expulsion of leftist unions in 1949.[32]

In the UE, intensifying pressures had an even more ominous outcome:
internal dissent that took organizational form for the first time with the
founding of the UE Members for Democratic Action (UEMDA) in August
1946. Leaders of ten UE locals that had been taken over by right wingers
organized UEMDA; it drew strength from several currents including anticommunist Catholics and Socialists. UEMDA's fortress was District One,
in Philadelphia, James B. Carey's old home turf. Though Carey had been
deposed as UE president in 1941, he retained his prominent position as secretary-treasurer of the CIO. UEMDA coalesced around Carey and made its
national debut in September at the UE National Convention in Milwaukee.
There, UEMDA constituted a small but vocal faction with two main issues:
anti-Soviet foreign policy and a proposed constitutional amendment to bar
Communists from union office. Both were soundly rejected, and the UEMDA
slate lost to incumbent leftists by margins of six to one.[33]

These national developments had repercussions in Schenectady for Local
301 and the CIO-PAC. Schenectady newspapers gave page-one coverage to
the faction fight in Milwaukee. Soon a petition protesting Communist influence in the union circulated through several GE buildings. Results were
singularly unimpressive; only 166 workers in a workforce of over 10,000
signed. But it was the beginning of organized, ideologically driven factionalism within Local 301.

The new dissidents were—and remained—a tiny minority in the plant,
but the rapidly chilling climate hugely magnified their impact. The most
immediate effect was on the CIO-PAC's electoral work. On October 3, just
two weeks after the right-wing faction emerged in Local 301, CIO-PAC
launched its final push toward the November election by announcing its

endorsements and beginning to campaign in earnest. The unionists immediately ran into heavy flack from the Republicans, from the new UEMDA,
and from GE. Amadeo Volpe, a Democrat-turned-Republican running for
city council, led the charge for the Republicans. Local unionists had recommended Volpe as the only Republican friendly to labor, and the PAC committee had interviewed him. But when Volpe refused to embrace the PAC
program, the committee withheld its endorsement. Volpe responded to the
rebuff by conflating CIO-PAC, the Democratic Party, and the Communist
Party, charging that "an ideology that conflicts with American ideals" had
"crept into" the Democratic Party. Volpe claimed that during his 1944 run
for office on a Democratic-ALP ticket he had encountered activists "with
views that sounded as if they had come directly from Moscow." Republicans
amplified the theme, charging that "the Democrat-ALP-PAC bloc stands for
Communism dictated from Moscow." Price control and all other issues fell
by the wayside as Schenectady Republicans recast the election as a critical
contest "[pitting] Americanism against Communism."[34]

Volpe's lurid firsthand account of his brush with Communism in the
Democratic Party was echoed and reinforced from within Local 301. John
Saccocio, who had traveled to Washington with the CIO-PAC to testify in
favor of extending price control, broke with the Local 301 PAC and publicly
charged that the PAC was "definitely Communist controlled." Since his Washington testimony, Saccocio had traveled a great distance. He had been elected
to the Local 301 Executive Board and had helped to found the Schenectady
UEMDA. When the Local 301 Executive Board endorsed the CIO-PAC's
slate, the Republican Saccocio issued a "minority report" complaining that
the PAC slate favored Democrats even when their pro-labor sentiments were
questionable. He then angered the executive board by releasing his report
to the Schenectady press. A voice from the 301's past, Sal Vottis, former Local 301 financial secretary and self-proclaimed ex-Communist, supported
Saccocio's indictment of the CIO-PAC as "Communist controlled." Vottis
emerged from his new smoke shop—he had left the union to go into business—to add credence to Saccocio's claims, which he himself had raised when
the CIO-PAC was first organized in 1944.[35]

GE also took steps to limit the union's impact on the Schenectady political
scene that fall, though they did not overtly join in the anticommunist chorus.
Instead, GE tried to keep the local from mobilizing members and getting
them to the polls. When the CIO-PAC tried to distribute a nonpartisan
leaflet urging workers to register to vote and providing the necessary form,
plant guards were instructed to confiscate the flyers if they were distributed
on company property. This directive suppressed distribution at seven of the

nine plant gates. GE also refused to grant workers the paid two-hour break to leave the plant and vote mandated by the New York State Election Law, insisting instead on a half-day unpaid shutdown. The union suspected that GE hoped workers would go straight home, rather than to the polls, and thus keep down the working-class vote. The 301 Executive Board took the case to the district attorney, charging GE with evasion of the law and with "imposing a severe penalty" on workers "for exercising their citizen's duty." District Attorney Nicoll, a Republican running for reelection, agreed that GE was "clearly violating the spirit of the law" and acting in bad faith toward its employees. Nicoll announced that he would attempt to amend the law to make such actions "presumptive evidence of an intent to violate this law." The fact that Nicoll backed Local 301's charges in spite of GOP and GE opposition suggests that the CIO-PAC presented a formidable electoral force, one candidate Nicoll was loathe to cross.[36]

Despite such obstacles and the barrage of anticommunist rhetoric, PAC volunteers worked intensively to get out the message and the vote. They held nightly ward meetings and rallies, canvassed door-to-door, and traveled the streets with sound trucks on Election Day to get the people to the polls. Indeed, the CIO-PAC did quite well on its first real incursion into local politics, especially considering the salience of the Communist issue. In the year of the historic nationwide Republican landslide, Schenectady's Republican machine kept its hold on the town, but the CIO-PAC forced several candidates to run a great deal harder than they had expected.

Both of the PAC's chief targets—Kearney and Dunn—won their races, prompting the pro-Republican *Schenectady Gazette* to celebrate "the weakness of PAC." The "labor vote," the *Gazette* editorialized, "is not deliverable."[37] But a closer scrutiny of the election results gives a slightly different picture than the *Gazette*'s dismissive editorial suggests. Kearney won reelection to Congress, but lost in Schenectady County; in 1942 he had carried the county by fifteen thousand votes. Dunn, the majority leader in the city council and a powerful figure in the Republican machine, barely won the sheriff's race and lost in the city. Even the *Gazette* acknowledged that the Democrats had made serious inroads in some "rock-ribbed Republican strongholds."[38] The Fourth, Seventh, Eighth, and Ninth Wards and the contiguous Town of Rotterdam—all working-class areas heavily populated with GE workers—went solidly for Gardner and Sherry and gave strong support to the entire PAC-endorsed slate. In its final election analysis, the CIO-PAC noted these results with satisfaction, concluding that the organizations established in each ward would provide a "solid foundation" for continued political action toward "the vital 1948 presidential election."[39]

However difficult 1946 was for the Local 301—beginning with the long strike, continuing through the skirmishes over price control, and ending with the virulent revival of the spectral Red menace—the events of the year were but a sampling of things to come. For the next eight years—until Local 301 finally capitulated and went over to the anticommunist IUE in 1954—the local was subjected to ever-intensifying pressures as the Cold War gripped the nation.

The Committees Come to Town

The new Republican-dominated 80th Congress arrived in Washington determined to make its mark on the labor movement's hide. Legislators signaled this intent with a glut of punitive labor bills introduced in the first two weeks of the session—twenty-one in the Senate, thirty-seven in the House—which coalesced in the Taft-Hartley Act, passed in June over Truman's veto.

Taft-Hartley and a companion event—new hearings by the revivified House Un-American Activities Committee (HUAC)—ratcheted the union's problems to a new level. Taft-Hartley's Section 9(h) required elected union officers to sign affidavits declaring that they were not members of the Communist Party; the provision dovetailed neatly with the UEMDA's campaign to amend the UE Constitution to ban Communists from holding office. In July 1947 HUAC called in several UE right wingers, including 301's Sal Vottis, to testify about Communist influence in the UE. Anticommunist dissidents suddenly found themselves with a new forum and powerful new allies. As Ellen Schrecker has argued, the role of the state in the anticommunist crusade was central and essential to its success; the government's involvement "legitimated the efforts of other groups, bringing public support and the blessing of patriotism to hitherto private efforts."[40]

Schrecker's argument certainly held true for the UE, which soon found itself beset by a swarm of attackers. Right-wing controlled UE locals embraced the affidavits, purging leftists and beginning a movement to secede from the UE and affiliate with complying unions. Unions that refused to sign the affidavits were barred from using NLRB machinery, including board-supervised elections, leaving them wide open to raids from other unions. Though the labor movement had historically condemned raiding, it now assumed an aura of patriotism and the UE was soon besieged. By 1949, when UE officers finally submitted, more than five hundred shops had been raided and thirty-four thousand members lost.[41]

In the fall of 1948, the political attack on Local 301 began in earnest. For the remaining six years of the local's existence in the UE, investigative hearings and intra-union raids played a bitter counterpoint in Schenectady. On September 27 of that year, the Atomic Energy Commission (AEC) ordered General Electric to rescind recognition of UE as the bargaining agent at its atomic facilities, including the Knolls II Atomic Power Laboratory in Schenectady, a government-funded and -owned facility then under construction and slated to be operated by GE. The AEC ruled that UE constituted a security risk, basing its assessment on reports of the "alleged Communist affiliation" of UE's national officers and their refusal to sign the non-Communist affidavits demanded by Taft-Hartley. GE complied, but took the opportunity to suggest that the AEC's procedures were not stringent enough to ensure real security, since workers "were still perfectly free to belong to the UE" and could continue to associate with the suspect officers. The real solution, as GE would later argue, was for the government to identify and remove all Communists from potentially sensitive positions in unions and in the workforce.[42]

Local 301's officers and executive board wrote a very dignified rebuttal of the AEC's charges, emphasizing the local's "long and honorable record of devotion to the highest interests of the country." They protested charges of subversion, arguing that local officers were "solemnly pledged to defend the United States and its Constitution" against "those such as you" who threatened to subvert its protections. "We do not regard the Constitution of the United States," they concluded, "as lightly as you do."[43]

Schenectady unionists soon had a chance to elaborate on their devotion to the Constitution. Coinciding with the highly publicized AEC directive, Rep. Charles Kersten (R-WI) announced that his subcommittee of the House Committee on Labor and Education would conduct an investigation of Communist infiltration of the UE. The Kersten Committee began by grilling the UE's national officers in Washington, adding fuel to the faction fights then occurring at the 1948 UE national convention in New York City. Then Kersten dropped in on Local 301. On September 30 and October 1, Kersten interrogated Local 301 officers to determine the extent of Communist infiltration in the local and to help to restore "proper trade-unionism." Kersten rejected the argument that the UE constitution properly protected members' political rights. The Communist Party was not, he insisted, a political party but "an underground world-wide conspiracy dedicated to the overthrow . . . of trade unionism . . . [and] . . . all of the institutions of this country." It was in the rank-and-file's interest, he argued, to root out Communists lurking in the leadership. Thus Kersten took aim at the UE constitution; his interrogations sought to both identify the political affiliations of subpoenaed officers and to pressure them to amend the union constitution to bar Communists from leadership.[44]

Kersten began with testimony from several purportedly "friendly" witnesses, with very unsatisfactory results. They gave Kersten little help: the witnesses proved to be as wary of potential attacks on their union as they were to the presence of its Communists. Tom Riggi, a former Communist Party member, affirmed that though he now hated Communists he was also "strictly 100 percent trade union." Hitler, Riggi observed, had started by rooting out Communists and ended up destroying trade unions and democracy. "I hope to God," Riggi said, "[that] you fellows don't try to use this evidence to destroy our unions!" Though he asserted that the Communist Party had achieved "a complete stranglehold" on Local 301, Riggi refused to "name names."[45]

One reason the friendly witnesses failed to come through for Kersten was because, as Riggi noted, they lived and would continue to live in Schenectady. Kersten was asking them to testify against neighbors and co-workers they had often known since childhood. Many working-class Schenectady citizens had, at some point in their lives, taken a turn in the party; it had been a presence in the city since the early 1930s. The witnesses' reluctance suggests that in 1948 the Communist Party was not yet perceived as so great a menace and had not yet been placed so thoroughly beyond the pale that the need to destroy it could overrule the claims of community. But Riggi's testimony also supports Gerald Zahavi's argument that the nature of Communist Party participation in Local 301 had begun to change. The Communists in Local 301 had indeed been intimately involved in the affairs of the union, and their work attracted support from many militant Schenectady trade unionists. The party's work had been good, solid trade union work performed in the name of the union, not the party; most of the Communists did not function openly as party members. But in the postwar years, when the Communist Party and organizations it influenced were besieged, institutional loyalties became strained and confused. As Communists within the important Local 301 came under attack, more party members arrived—outsiders, "colonizers"—to help defend the union and implicitly the party's position within it. In doing so, they made the Communist Party as such more "visible" than it ever had been. And as Zahavi notes, some of the outsiders brought a cultural sensibility and agenda that often put them on a collision course with local Schenectady trade union Communists and the citizenry as a whole. The Communists became more "alien" and more vulnerable to isolation and attack as strangers arrived and local radicals dropped out.[46]

The 301 officers, however, were the central focus of Kersten's inquiry. Treated as hostile witnesses—Kersten was acting on the assumption that the local was indeed "Communist controlled"—they presented a united front and offered a spirited defense of the union. All refused to discuss their own or anyone else's politics; all staunchly defended the union constitution, at times eloquently. Helen Quirini, the Local 301 recording-secretary, gave Kersten a particularly hard time. When Kersten, early in his questioning, asked Quirini what sort of work women did in the plant, she got in a plug for her most passionate cause and a bit of a dig at GE: "They do all kinds of work," Quirini said. "A lot of the women are doing men's jobs, and we have to fight like hell to give them men's wages, and we are terrifically battling down there to give them an equal break." Later, when Kersten pressed her to repudiate the UE constitution's political tolerance, Quirini lectured the congressman. "When you became a Congressman," she said, "you took an oath to uphold the Constitution. When I became an officer I took an oath to uphold our Constitution, and I will not cooperate with you in violating your oath or my oath." Quirini's testimony ended after the following exchange with Kersten's colleague, Congressman O. Clark Fisher of Texas:

> Mr. Fisher: One question. Do you share the view that to expose Communists in local 301 would result in the union being busted?
>   Miss Quirini: I believe very strongly in our constitution, because you are starting with communism; tomorrow it will be married women; next day Jews; next day Negroes; next day Italians; next day Poles—[47]

Beyond presenting a united front in the hearings, the union leaders also ran a typically well-organized campaign, coordinated with the international headquarters, to demonstrate support in the shop and in the community. The effort included radio broadcasts, special flyers, petitions, and hearing rooms packed with supporters. Despite their efforts, however, these attacks, coupled with the AEC's, struck deep and took a toll. Joe Mangino, a rising young leader in the union, recalled the impact. The hearings, he said, "built up such a hatred. People were standing there saying 'There goes a bunch of Reds!' and 'Hang those Communists!' . . . it got pretty hot." Local 301's president, Andy Peterson, was particularly and poignantly affected by the pressure. Peterson's invalid wife was so distressed by Kersten's threat to cite the officers for contempt of Congress that Peterson felt "compelled for the sake of her personal peace" to swear out a deposition declaring that he was not and never had been a member of the Communist Party. Peterson concluded his bitter deposition, "I deeply regret that I am compelled by the force of personal circumstances to submit to a political inquisition which I believe to be dangerous, unlawful and evil in purpose. I shall continue . . . to defend our union against the attacks of your sub-committee and of the company and to uphold all of our members' rights as union members and as citizens." Two months later Peterson was swept out of office by a right-wing slate, along with most of the 301 officers. Buoyed by the spotlight trained on their adversaries, right wingers finally managed to make serious inroads in the local. For the first time, they ran and won key offices, including Frank Kriss as president, Steve Watts as chief steward, and Frank Fiorello as record-ing-secretary. Of the left-wing officers, only the redoubtable Business Agent Leo Jandreau and Vice President Bill Hodges survived.[48]

Even with all the assistance, though, the victory was narrow. The right-wing slate included a nucleus of UEMDA members, now renamed the Member-ship Committee. There was no striking distinction between workers who supported right wing or left; both sides reflected a cross-section of the work-force—men and women, Italians and Poles, Catholics and Protestants. The insurgents produced a six-page "Program for Action" that represented an evolution of the right-wing argument. Right wingers now argued that the Communists should be repudiated for pragmatic reasons: because they were dividing the CIO and because their presence weakened the union in its deal-ings with management.

Local 301 thus entered 1949 with a leadership group split down the middle between left and right wings. The membership committee held seven of twelve local offices, but the left wing held thirteen of sixteen seats on the executive board, whose members were elected by the shop stewards of each division. Objectively, the left still held the key posts, since the board and the shop stewards together formed the nervous system of the union in the shop and controlled the all-important daily functioning of the local. Still, the right wing had achieved its greatest success to date, and the resulting split made for a year filled with infighting that frequently spilled over into the public view. The new officers' first action, for example, was incendiary: they invited James Carey, still cornerstone of the right-wing opposition in UE, to address the January membership meeting. Carey wisely declined to appear in person but sent a recording denouncing "stooges for the Kremlin" trying to sow "confusion and chaos" in the CIO. Schenectady's press had a field day, providing extensive coverage of every contretemps.[49]

The Final Conflict

The right wing in Local 301 thus had considerable momentum going into what became the most critical year of the UE's existence. At the end of 1949, tension within the CIO came to a head; the UE and ten other left-wing unions were expelled from the federation. The CIO immediately chartered a new union for the electrical industry, the International Union of Electrical

Workers (IUE), with James Carey appointed president. UE locals controlled by the right wing immediately seceded and affiliated with the IUE. Many employers took advantage of the upheaval to cancel their contracts with the UE, a move technically illegal but permitted by the NLRB in this special circumstance. GE exercised its right under Taft-Hartley to petition for a new representation election in all of its plants, claiming a desire to help its workers make this critical decision. The NLRB scheduled elections in the three major chains—GM's electrical division, Westinghouse, and GE—for the spring of 1950.[50]

Curiously, the birth of the IUE had a deleterious effect on the right wing in Local 301, disrupting what momentum the insurgents had built. The right-wing officers felt compelled to withdraw from the UE and reconstitute themselves as a new "Local 301–IUE-CIO." Since their positions as Local 301 officers had been largely ceremonial, however, the new IUE leaders found themselves heading up a shadow organization without an organized political base in the shop and without access to the levers of real influence, still controlled by the incumbent left-wing UE organization. Kriss, Fiorello, and the seventy-one rank-and-file workers who did sign IUE cards were promptly expelled from the UE, and the campaign for NLRB certification was on.[51]

The national IUE, or "Imitation UE" as it was quickly dubbed by the UE, began as a "paper" organization. It had to prove itself and acquire members by competing nationally with the seasoned UE organization. But the IUE also had some formidable advantages. No union in American history ever came on to the scene with more fanfare or official goodwill. CIO President Philip Murray and Secretary of Labor Daniel Tobin blessed the IUE at its inaugural convention, and Truman sent his warmest regards. The CIO bankrolled the new union and offered veteran organizers to help in the campaign. The anticommunist nature of their enterprise gave IUE rallies a somewhat bizarre flavor that spring; they often featured an unusual cast of supporters: local politicians, Catholic priests, military men, even FBI agents, had spots on the IUE speakers' platforms.[52]

GE professed to play no favorites in the contest but its actions objectively damaged the UE. Claiming not to know which union its workers preferred, for example, GE refused to turn over union dues to the cash-strapped UE. Local 301 turned that crisis to opportunity, transforming the issue into a demonstration of rank-and-file support for the UE. Schenectady members promptly re-signed check-off authorizations. Local 301 delivered over ten thousand newly signed forms to the company in two days, stunning IUE organizers but not persuading GE to restore the sequestered funds. GE's kind offer to petition for a company-wide representation election also potentially hurt the UE by getting the IUE onto the ballot even in shops where the new union had no members at all. In Schenectady, GE management allowed the IUE to distribute political leaflets—one flyer entitled "Jandreau Communist Party Tie-in Exposed," especially roused UE ire—even as the company systematically confiscated political leaflets put out by Local 301. Despite these UE-undermining actions, however, GE did nothing to encourage Carey and the IUE directly or publicly. GE management politely rebuffed Carey's suggestion that the company endorse the right-wing cause as a patriotic gesture. The company strategy seems to have been to help destroy the left-wing UE without unduly strengthening its likely successor, the IUE.[53]

The results of the nationwide elections of spring 1950 devastated but did not destroy the UE. The union lost the entire GM electrical division and most of the Westinghouse chain and the smaller Sylvania and RCA corporations. The UE did best in GE, where the older union maintained its position in two of the company's three largest plants, including the crown jewel, Local 301. All told, the UE lost at least 152,000 members to the IUE and other unions but retained at least double that number, insuring its immediate survival and its continued influence in the industry.[54]

In Local 301, the UE won by a vote of 7,761 to 5,847. The comfortable victory in the face of the trauma of the preceding two years was due in part to the weakness of the IUE forces and in larger part to the remarkable confidence Local 301 members invested in Leo Jandreau. National IUE representative Joe Swire reported to his superiors that Schenectady IUE leaders lacked the "drive, initiative and imagination" to win over the workers. They had, Swire reported, made "serious blunders" in the opening days of the drive, including the false claim that they had signed up eight thousand supporters. Bad leadership thus did much to offset the advantages that accrued to the anticommunist IUE in its quest to slay the Red menace.[55]

But the chief factor accounting for the UE's success seems to have been the loyalty Local 301 members exhibited toward Leo Jandreau. Jandreau had been the key leader in the local from its inception in the mid-1930s and he enjoyed nearly universal respect. He was, as Joe Mangino put it, "our Communist," a man whose abilities put him "head and shoulders above everybody around." Even management respected Jandreau, considering him not only extremely talented but also a man of integrity. In the contest between UE and IUE, as Leo Jandreau went, so went Local 301. For the moment that meant the keystone local in the electrical industry remained in the UE.[56]

The elections of 1950 did not settle the matter, though. Many UE locals, including Local 301, endured not one but several raids in ensuing years. The IUE took another shot at Local 301 in September 1951, with results even less satisfying. The 1950 defeat had discouraged many of the Schenectady IUE activists; IUE officers resigned and the executive board disbanded. Dues paying IUE membership, never impressive, fell from a high of 133 in April 1950 to around a dozen throughout 1951—this in a shop of over 15,000 workers! Still, by June 1951 IUE organizer Julius Uehlein optimistically reported that the situation was improving. He thought the local activists could produce enough membership cards in July to petition for an NLRB election. With a little luck, a few strategic defections, and especially, a visit by the House Un-American Activities Committee, Uehlein believed the IUE could pull out a victory. But this time the UE won by an even bigger margin: 11,542 to 4,851.[57]

The magnitude of the 1951 victory was enormously comforting for the beleaguered Local 301. For a time, it seemed to insulate the local from further attacks, permitting the unionists to turn their attention once again to the nuts and bolts of their job. Schenectady's left-wing activists continued to be individually harried by surveillance agencies from the FBI to GE's own security apparatus, but the public attacks subsided. It was a brief respite.

In October 1952, a popular mass-circulation magazine, the *Saturday Evening Post,* published a sensational article by Lester Velie, "Red Pipeline into Our Defense Plants," starring Leo Jandreau and Local 301. The piece began with a photo of Jandreau testifying before a congressional committee. The caption identified him as "boss of Local 301" and a Communist since 1936. Velie described Local 301 as "a soviet in microcosm" controlled by Jandreau and his "politburo," the executive board. Curiously, the Local 301 Velie describes could also be read as a vibrant, effective, democratic trade union, strongly supported by the ranks. Velie had talked to hundreds of workers, finding them "eager to defend their union . . . [and] . . . convinced their leaders were being persecuted for their aggressive fight for better conditions." A Catholic worker told Velie, "The more the church and press are against our union, the more we're for it." Velie concluded that the UE was "so firmly embedded in our most important electrical plant that no rival union can blast it out."[58]

Velie was right: the UE was too embedded in Local 301 to be dislodged by a rival. Instead, Leo Jandreau led the local into the IUE, completing the process in March 1954. Jandreau's precise motives remain unknown. The national UE claimed that Jandreau crumbled under the pressure, and "sold out" Local 301 in exchange for relief from persecution. Senator Joe McCarthy had come to town in the fall of 1953, the biggest gun yet to be trained on Local 301 and Leo Jandreau, and McCarthy's visit had emboldened GE to do its own housecleaning. In conjunction with the hearings, then-GE president Ralph Cordiner had announced the "Cordiner Doctrine": GE workers who invoked the Fifth Amendment would be fired. Seven Schenectady Communists lost their jobs. It was in the midst of these events that Jandreau announced his intent to take the local into the IUE, and Jandreau was not called to testify before McCarthy.[59]

Mounting pressures certainly played a strong role in the decision. Jandreau had been quietly distancing himself from the Communists since the outbreak of the Korean conflict. Local 301 broke ranks with the national UE to support the U.S. effort there. He had maneuvered to remove party members from paid positions on the Local 301 staff. But he had also divorced his first wife to marry Ruth Young, the first woman to serve on the national UE Executive Board and a trade union leader in the Communist Party. Young moved into Schenectady and out of the party, trading her life as an activist for domestic tranquility and a new career as wife and mother. Young's Communist past, however, increased the Jandreaus' vulnerability. She too had been featured in the *Saturday Evening Post* article, identified as a "high-ranking party member."[60]

Whatever forces affected Jandreau's decision, the reasons he himself offered for the switch to the IUE are compelling enough at face value. The long siege of the UE had gravely weakened the union. The UE's energies and resources were increasingly absorbed by the sheer struggle to survive. The national weakness of the electrical workers, rooted in the schism, had made substantial progress impossible. Jandreau argued that the UE's national weakness had "begun to reflect locally"—GE was successfully undermining standards won in better days. Most seriously, the local had been unable to deal effectively with GE's new decentralization program. The company was moving work to new plants and the UE, Jandreau noted, "had not organized a new GE plant in years." The only solution Jandreau saw was to reunite electrical workers, local by local, in a single union. Significantly, Jandreau never joined the anticommunist chorus, never attacked the UE for its politics. His stated reasons for defecting were purely pragmatic.[61]

Even Jandreau's prestige in Local 301 did not make the switch an easy one. Many of his closest allies balked at the notion of going over to the "Imitation UE." They had, after all, been battling Carey and his union for years. In the end, Jandreau won over his supporters with the argument that nothing in Local 301 would change. The agreement with the IUE included a strong provision for local autonomy. The local would continue to run its own affairs but gain strength and credibility from its new affiliation. All they would be doing, Jandreau argued, was "putting the 'I' before UE." In the end, Jandreau carried the day, though over five thousand of the fourteen thousand votes went to the UE, a tribute to that union's remarkable resilience and the loyalty it inspired.[62]

Local 301 had traveled a long way since its decision to step into the community and take a role in Schenectady affairs following the 1946 strike. The confidence and sense of entitlement were long gone. In joining the mainstream movement, Local 301 also adopted its increasingly narrow focus. IUE Local 301 no longer claimed to speak in the interests of all citizens. The political travail of the Cold War years had nearly transformed the unionists into pariahs instead. In the years following Jandreau's defection, jobs continued to drain steadily away from Schenectady. The IUE was never able to mount an effective response. Jandreau was right in arguing that putting the "'I' before 'UE'" would allow the local to survive, but doing so did not make it thrive.[63]

Notes

1. Robert H. Zieger, *The CIO, 1935–1955* (Chapel Hill: University of North Carolina Press, 1995), 374.

2. For the Cold War attack on the UE and left-wing labor, see Ronald Filippelli and Mark McColloch, *Cold War in the Working Class: The Rise and Decline of the United Electrical Workers* (Albany: State University of New York Press, 1995); Ronald Schatz, *The Electrical Workers: A History of Labor at General Electric and Westinghouse, 1923–1960* (Urbana: University of Illinois Press, 1983); Steve Rosswurm, ed., *The CIO's Left-Led Unions* (New Brunswick, N.J.: Rutgers University Press, 1992).

3. Sandra Opdyke, "Building the Cooperative Commonwealth in Schenectady, NY" (master's thesis, Columbia University, 1990), 5–6, 15, 34. See also Karl Saidon, "A Social Portrait of Socialist Schenectady" (master's thesis, Columbia University, 1977).

4. For Local 301's formative years, see Schatz, *Electrical Workers*, 67–72; Lisa Kannenberg, "The Product of GE's Progress: Labor, Management and Community Relations in Schenectady, NY, 1930–1960" (Ph.D. diss., Rutgers University, 1999), chap. 2.

5. Gerald Zahavi offers a valuable study of the cultural dimension of Schenectady Communism in "Passionate Commitments: Race, Sex, and Communism at Schenectady General Electric, 1932–1954," *Journal of American History* 83:2 (Sept. 1996): 514–48. See also his "Uncivil War: An Oral History of Labor, Communism, and Community in Schenectady, New York, 1944–1954," in Robert W. Cherny, William Issel, and Kieran Walsh Taylor, eds., *American Labor and the Cold War: Grassroots Politics and Postwar Political Culture* (New Brunswick, N.J.: Rutgers University Press, 2004).

6. "Living Wage, Postwar Jobs Go Hand in Hand—Jandreau," Labor Day broadcast, reprinted in *EU [Electrical Union] News*, (hereafter *EU News*) Oct. 23, 1944. FDR's "Second Bill of Rights" became the template for the CIO's postwar agenda and also strongly influenced the UE's national program. See CIO Political Action Committee (CIO-PAC), "The Answer Is Full Employment," undated [1944], Series PA, file folder 107, United Electrical, Radio, and Machine Workers of America Archives, Archives of Industrial Society, University of Pittsburgh (hereafter UEA); UERMWA-CIO, "Jobs—Today and Tomorrow. Report of the General Officers for 1944–45," copy in author's possession.

7. Elizabeth Fones-Wolf, *Selling Free Enterprise: The Business Assault on Labor and Liberalism, 1945–60* (Urbana: University of Illinois Press, 1994), 26–29.

8. "Eight Answers to the Question . . . What Is Free Enterprise?" *Works News—Schenectady* (hereafter *WN-S*), Feb. 8, 1945; "Capital Helps Us Make the Most of Our Opportunities," *WN-S*, July 27, 1945;"Victory for a System," *WN-S*, Sept. 29, 1944.

9. "The Road to Serfdom," *General Electric Commentator*, Aug. 1945, was widely distributed to GE's employees, customers, and community "thought leaders."

10. William T. Wilkinson, president, and Leo Jandreau, business agent, to Charles E. Wilson, Oct. 23, 1945, box G1478, file folder CB-GE 824, UEA.

11. Corporations and business organizations very consciously went after that linguistic high ground. The NAM, for example, premised its highly successful 1946 public relations campaign on the following notion: "NAM . . . should be consistently FOR things rather than AGAINST things; it should . . . identify itself with the good ends desired by the American people and propose BETTER means to these ends than those proposed by the advocates of Collectivism." "The Public Relations Program of the National Association of Manufacturers," 1946, pamphlet in UEA (copy in author's possession), p. 6.

12. Joel Seidman, *American Labor from Defense to Reconversion* (Chicago: University of Chicago Press, 1953), 222–41; Barton J. Bernstein, "The Truman Administration and Its Reconversion Wage Policy," *Labor History* 6 (Fall 1965): 214–31.

13. Seidman, *American Labor from Defense to Reconversion*, 220–21.

14. Joseph Dermody to E. D. Spicer, Oct. 27, 1945, Series CB-GE, file folder 192; James Matles to C. E. Wilson, Dec. 26, 1945, Series CB-GE, file folder 193; both in UEA. Quote from Matles to Wilson.

15. E. D. Spicer to James Matles, Dec. 31, 1945, Series CB-GE, file folder 193, UEA.

16. Schatz, *Electrical Workers*, 167–70.

17. As quoted in Arthur Leff, Trial Examiner, "Intermediate Report," Case no. 2–CA-7581, National Labor Relations Board, Apr. 1, 1963, 6.

18. Interview by the author with Helen Quirini, James C. Carey, and Henry Antonelli, June 20, 1995, tape 1. Copy in author's possession.

19. Quirini, Carey, Antonelli interview, tape 1. The following account of the 1946 strike as it played out in Schenectady is from Kannenberg, "Product of GE's Progress," chap. 4.

20. Kannenberg, "Product of GE's Progress," 137.

21. Ibid., 139–40.

22. "To Schenectady . . . Thanks from the GE Workers," *Schenectady Gazette* (hereafter *SG*), Mar. 18, 1946; "Victory Message from Jandreau," *EU News*, Mar. 15, 1946; "Strike Settlement Gets OK by UE Conference," *SG*, Mar. 15, 1946; "CIO Prepares to Launch Vast Political Drive," *SG*, Mar. 16, 1946.

23. Fones-Wolf, *Selling Free Enterprise*, 32–40; Harvey C. Mansfield et al., *A Short History of the OPA* (Washington: Office of Price Administration, General Publication no. 15, 1947), 9–11, 90–101; National Association of Manufacturers (NAM), "The Public Relations Program of the National Association of Manufacturers," Oct. 1946, 7. Meg Jacobs offers a study of the grassroots dimensions of the OPA in "How about Some Meat?": The Office of Price Administration, Consumption Politics, and State Building from the Bottom Up, 1941–46," *Journal of American History* 84: 3 (Dec. 1997): 910–41.

24. "City Rallies to Save Price Control," *EU News*, Apr. 25, 1946; "100 Rally to Save OPA," *SG*, Apr. 26, 1946; "Joins Thousands to Sign OPA Telegram," *EU News*, May 2, 1946; "Union Leads Fight for Price Control," *EU News*, Apr. 4, 1946; "Saccocio Gives Dose of Facts to U.S. Senators," *EU News*, May 2, 1946.

25. Charles E. Wilson, "What's Ahead for Business?" address delivered before the Economic Club of Chicago, insert, *WN-S*, Nov. 8, 1946.

26. See, for example, *WN-S*, Apr. 26, 1946; Aug. 16, 1946; and July 19, 1946.

27. "Voice of Schenectady: Poll Voters Oppose OPA Controls on Meat," Schenectady *Union-Star*, Oct. 4, 1946; Jacobs, "How About Some Meat?" 928 n. 44.

28. "CIO-PAC on the Move," *EU News*, Apr. 4, 1946; "Political Action," *EU News*, Apr. 18, 1946.

29. James Boylan, *The New Deal Coalition and the Election of 1946* (New York: Garland, 1981), 106–16, 137.

30. Antonelli, Carey, Quirini interview, tape 1, side 2; "Dominelli Heads Vets Delegation to Demand City Act on Housing," *EU News*, June 13, 1946; "Dominelli Enters Sheriff Contest," *EU News*, June 27, 1946; "PAC Indorses Sherry; Plan 'Beat Dunn' Drive," *SG*, Oct. 3, 1946. For an interesting description of CIO-PAC organizing for Dominelli's primary campaign, see "Vote for Dominelli Dents GOP Machine," *EU News*, Aug. 29, 1946.

31. "PAC Committee Recommends List of State, Local Candidates," *EU News*, Oct. 3, 1946.

32. Filippelli and McColloch, *Cold War in the Working Class*, 89.

33. Ibid., 91–94.

34. "GOP Candidates Say Rivals Leaning to Left," *SG*, Oct. 9, 1946.

35. "Union Endorses All Candidates on PAC Slate," *EU News*, Oct. 10, 1946; "PAC Indorses Sherry; Plan 'Beat Dunn' Drive," *SG*, Oct. 3, 1946; "301 Board Hits Latest Attacks against Union," *EU News*, Oct. 31, 1946.

36. "Company Stops 301 Distribution of Union Registration Leaflets," *EU News*, Oct. 17, 1946; "Union Attacks Company Plan to Shut Down Plant for Half-Day on Election Day, No Pay," *EU News*, Oct. 24, 1946; "Union Battles GE Shut-Down," *EU News*, Oct. 31, 1946; "DA Says GE Violates Spirit of Election Law," *SG*, Nov. 2, 1946.

37. "CIO-PAC Workers Busy through Nov. 5," *EU News*, Oct. 31, 1946; "Local Election Showed Weakness of PAC, Satisfaction with GOP," *SG*, Nov. 7, 1946.

38. "Local Politicos Study Election's Significance," *SG*, Nov. 7, 1946. For election results reported by ward and district, see tabulations in "City, County Vote for State Officers;" "Vote for Representatives and County Officers"; and "Vote for Councilmen," *SG*, Nov. 6, 1946.

39. "Schenectady CIO-PAC Cuts Down GOP Vote," *EU News*, Nov. 14, 1946.

40. Ellen Schrecker, "McCarthyism and the Labor Movement," in Rosswurm, *The CIO's Left-Led Unions*, 139. For the HUAC hearings of July 1947, see Filippelli and McColloch, *Cold War in the Working Class*, 102–3. The HUAC hearings and charges were heavily covered in the Schenectady press. See "Local 301 Leader Denies Union Is Controlled by Reds," *Union Star*, Aug. 1, 1947.

41. Filippelli and McColloch, *Cold War in the Working Class*, 105, 110–12; Schatz, *Electrical Workers*, 178–80.

42. David E. Lilienthal, U.S. Atomic Energy Commission, to Charles Wilson, Sept. 27,

1948; L. Boulware to Lilienthal, Sept. 28, 1948, box N546/R146, file folder "GE—Attacks on Unions—Atomic Energy," UEA.

43. Executive Board [Local 301] to David Lilienthal, Oct. 25, 1948, D/L Series, L301, file folder 196, UEA.

44. U.S. Congress, House of Representatives, Special Subcommittee of the Committee on Education and Labor, "Investigation of Communist Infiltration of UERMWA," 80th Congress, 2d Session, 1948, 218–19.

45. Ibid., 191–217, 237–42, 244.

46. Ibid., 245; Zahavi, "Passionate Commitments," 514–16.

47. "Investigation of Communist Infiltration," 261, 263, 265–66.

48. Joseph Mangino, interview with the author, June 16, 1995, tape 1; Marshall Perlin to James Matles, Oct. 22, 1948, with attached deposition by Andrew Peterson, Series CB-GE, file folder 947, UEA.

49. For vote totals in the officers' and executive board elections, see unsigned [Frank Fiorello] to Jim [Carey], Jan. 3, 1949 and Jan. 5, 1949; Membership Committee, "Program of Action," undated [stamped Dec. 30, 1948], 1, 3; Transcript, "Recording of James B. Carey," Dec. 31, 1948, 4. All in box 2021, "UE D/L Files/Finnegan Files, L301, 1941–50," IUE Archives, Rutgers University, International Union Of Electrical Workers Archives, Rutgers University (hereafter IUEA). For examples of Schenectady press coverage, see "Local 301 Authorizes Probe of Left Wing Activity of Members," and "'Freedom Trailer' Carries Message of UE Anti-Reds," *Union Star*, Jan. 4, 1949. Accompanying these articles was a photo of "a pipe-smoking replica of 'Uncle Joe' Stalin" who invaded the membership meeting and sat in the front row.

50. Filippelli and McColloch, *Cold War in the Working Class*, 141–49; Schatz, *Electrical Workers*, chap. 8.

51. "Local 301 Expels 71 for Anti-UE Acts," *EU News*, Dec. 23, 1949.

52. Filippelli and McColloch, *Cold War in the Working Class*, 141–43.

53. "UE 301 Doing the Job for GE Workers, Carey Group in Company Union Role," *EU News*, Nov. 25, 1949; "GE Double Dealing Aimed to Aid Carey," *EU News*, Dec. 23, 1949; telegram, Joseph Dermody to Philip Van Gelder et al., Jan. 11, 1950, box G 1479, file folder CB-GE 936, UEA; Jandreau to L. J. Male, Works Manager, Jan. 25, 1950, box G 1478, file folder CB-GE 839, UEA; Filippelli and McColloch, *Cold War in the Working Class*, 131.

54. Schatz, *Electrical Workers*, 225–26; Filippelli and McColloch, *Cold War in the Working Class*, 141–49.

55. Memorandum, Joe Swire to James B. Carey, "Schenectady Situation," Feb. 20, 1950, RG I, box 2021, "UE D/L Files/Finnegan Files, L301, 1941–50," IUEA.

56. Joe Mangino, interviewed by Gerald Zahavi, Sept. 6, 1991, tape 1, side 2, Schenectady GE Oral History Project; A. C. Stevens [former Works Manager], interviewed by the author, June 20, 1995.

57. For a good overview of the campaign against UE, see Filippelli and McColloch, *Cold War in the Working Class*, chap. 6. John Sears explores Local 301's experience in "Labor Opposition to the Cold War: The Electrical Unions and the Cold War Consensus" (Ph.D. diss., Temple University, 1988), chap. 5. For the 1951 IUE campaign in Schenectady, see Julius Uehlein to James B. Carey, "Organizational Report: General Electric Schenectady Works," Feb. 21, 1951, and Uehlein to Carey, June 10, 1951, with attached

"Organizational Report on GE Schenectady Works," both in RG I, box 2083, file folder 28: "FR Correspondence, Julius Uehlein, 1951," IUEA. Schenectady IUE membership figures are from Frank Fiorello to James B. Carey, Nov. 27, 1951, RG I, box 2078, file folder 4: "FR Correspondence, F. Fiorello, 1949–52," IUEA.

58. For an example of the daily harassment Schenectady Communists endured, see the Irving Horowitz interview in Zahavi, "Uncivil War," 43–46. Lester Velie, "Red Pipeline into Our Defense Plants," *Saturday Evening Post,* Oct. 18, 1952, 19–20, 110ff.

59. Schatz, *Electrical Workers,* 229–30; Zahavi, "Passionate Commitments," 546–47.

60. Zahavi, "Passionate Commitments," 545–46; Velie, "Red Pipeline," 20; transcript, Ruth Young Jandreau interviewed by Meredith Tax and Ruth Milkman, Aug. 29, 1985, 52–53. My thanks to Ruth Milkman for sharing this interview.

61. IUE, "Exchange of Letters between IUE-CIO President Carey and Officers of UE Local 301," packet dated Mar. 10, 1954, RG I, box 2030A, file folder "UE L301, 1953–1955," IUEA. Quotes are from section entitled "The Record," 1–2.

62. Antonelli, Carey, and Quirini interview with the author, tape 2, side 1; Joe Mangino interview with the author, tape 1, side 2.

63. A. C. Stevens, "An Open Letter," *GE Schenectady News* (formerly, *Works News-Schenectady*), June 25, 1954, 12; Stevens, "A Statement to the Community," *GE-SN,* July 9, 1954; "4,000 May Be Affected in Schenectady," *Local 301 News* (formerly *EU News*), Aug. 2, 1954. For Local 301's hapless attempts to maintain jobs, see Kannenberg, "Product of GE's Progress," chaps. 4–5.

6. Housing, Race, and the Cold War in a Labor City

ERIC FURE-SLOCUM

Vying for the attention of city residents who waited in line to pay their taxes on the morning of January 9, 1951, public housing supporters and opponents confronted one another in Milwaukee's City Hall. Three members of the Milwaukee County Property Owners' Association and an allied group seeking to stall public housing construction entered City Hall to collect signatures for a municipal referendum. Claiming to have obtained permission from the mayor, they went into the city treasurer's office to talk with taxpayers. After the treasurer ordered them out of his office, they began collecting signatures in the lobby. A morning's work yielded over one hundred signatures.[1]

A delegation of Congress of Industrial Organizations (CIO) members arrived shortly before noon to protest the proposed referendum and to challenge this city hall petition drive. Milwaukee CIO leader Fred Erchul argued that the petitioners had provoked a confrontation, knowing "in advance that the CIO would of necessity have to defend its stand."[2] As the anti–public housing petitioners worked to persuade taxpayers, the CIO members held signs warning "For a Better Milwaukee Don't Sign." A property owners' spokesman complained that the labor union members not only disrupted and "jostled" the signature collectors, but used "vile and indecent language" in the presence of female petitioners.[3] Milwaukee's City Hall, a grand structure with an open central atrium rising eight stories, reverberated with the sounds of this contest until police removed both groups, "end[ing] the tramp of marching feet and exhortations by both sides."[4]

This City Hall clash illustrates the intense debate over housing in postwar Milwaukee and other urban areas. On that January 1951 morning, public housing opponents were close to securing a place for their referendum on the spring ballot. Soon after, a counter-referendum backing public housing and slum clearance made its way onto the ballot. The conflict over these competing referenda and intertwined debates over race, redevelopment, and growth helped to recast the city's postwar political culture and policies. Further, the domestic Cold War shaped postwar housing politics, especially through the pressures exerted on organized labor and the mid-century labor-left coalition. Varieties of conservative and liberal anticommunism narrowed the political space in which housing proposals were developed, debated, and enacted. Proposals for an interracial public housing program serving a broad working-class population lost ground. Milwaukee's Cold War, in short, helped to forge an increasingly racialized public housing program that was subsumed by the priorities of metropolitan development and growth, further marginalizing non-market approaches to housing working-class city residents.

Milwaukee had long been a working-class city in which organized labor played an important role. The city entered the 1940s with a vibrant working-class political culture and a sizable industrial economy. Over 38 percent of the city's workforce was employed in manufacturing in 1940. World War II–related production reversed, if only temporarily, earlier signs of decline in Milwaukee's manufacturing sector. By 1950, 42 percent of the city's employed workers were engaged in manufacturing. The occupational distribution of Milwaukee's workforce reinforces this picture of industrial strength. Operatives, or "semi-skilled" factory workers, constituted the single largest group, expanding from just under 20 percent of the labor force in 1940 to almost a quarter of it in 1950. About one fourth of Milwaukee's operatives in 1940 and 1950 were women, although that number rose during the war. While the employment structure resembled that of other Great Lakes and Eastern cities, Milwaukee led its peers in manufacturing employment.[5]

The CIO's emergence provided the impetus for the explosive growth in organized labor's ranks during the 1930s and 1940s, as both the CIO and the American Federation of Labor (AFL) competed to bring in members. The CIO's industrial unionism and vigorous organizing enabled it to build strong organizations in Milwaukee's large factories and other workplaces, including those of city and county workers. In 1932, Milwaukee unions counted about 20,000 members; by the end of the 1930s the total membership reached over 100,000. Milwaukee's skilled and semi-skilled workers were well organized, and labor unions continued to grow throughout the war. When the Milwaukee central labor bodies merged at the end of the 1950s, the local AFL-CIO represented 125,000 workers. Milwaukee deserved its reputation as a strong labor city.[6]

Working-class activity in the mid-century city also was reflected by the sharp increase in strikes and work stoppages. Beginning in 1934, thousands of Milwaukee workers took part in strikes, often focused on basic demands for union recognition. In 1937, Milwaukee workers joined others around the country in sit-down strikes.[7] Strike activity waxed and waned during these years, but remained at a high level until the war, when many unions pledged to refrain from strikes. Workers on the home front responded to patriotic calls, and many unions sought to secure a place as leaders in wartime production. However, militant unionists, both Communist and non-Communist, continued to pressure management through aggressive shop steward and grievance strategies or informal work stoppages and slowdowns.[8]

The approach of the war's end precipitated an unprecedented wave of strikes nationally and locally. While some cities witnessed general strikes, others, such as Milwaukee, experienced both a large number of strikes and labor actions hitting specific employers with large workforces. In 1946, about 16,700 Milwaukee workers were involved in strikes, accounting for a peak of 367,000 "worker-days idle." Milwaukee was the site of a round of especially prolonged strikes in this era before the passage of Taft-Hartley.[9]

Milwaukee labor had a hand in housing issues for many years. In the early 1920s, the Federated Trades Council (FTC) actively supported the Socialist administration's Garden Homes. This city-sponsored project began as co-operative housing for working-class families, aiming to relieve the post–World War I housing shortage.[10] In the 1930s, labor unions and allied organizations pushed for Milwaukee's first federally financed public housing, the Parklawn project. The CIO and the FTC also worked with a coalition of liberal and left-wing groups to lobby for the establishment of a Housing Authority in Milwaukee, to ensure that public housing would have an institutional presence in the metropolis.[11] When the Milwaukee Common Council undermined a 1938 proposal to establish the Housing Authority, the CIO newspaper responded angrily: the aldermen "rode ruthlessly over the demands of the city's population, of the trade unions—AFL, CIO, and Railroad—of the merchants, and sunk the Housing Authority on the bottom of Lake Michigan." The CIO maintained that the city leaders had been "instructed by the Association of Commerce, the big real estate operators and bankers" to vote against the authority.[12] By the end of the war, labor and its allies succeeded in their battle for a housing authority.

The labor-left coalition's early housing victories were modest. For the city's business and real estate leaders and conservatives more generally, however, the politics of public housing echoed the challenges to private enterprise heard from the city's Socialist administrations and Depression-era politics.

The scope and power of the 1930s labor movement proved most threatening to these leaders, as they battled the newly organizing CIO unions and resurgent AFL unions. During 1937 and 1938, the city's conservatives fought new public housing projects and the passage of a national public housing act at the same time they witnessed a flurry of sit-down strikes that idled factories and other workplaces. These workplace and housing conflicts, amidst the political turmoil of the period, heightened conservatives' concerns about the organizational and institutional strength of the urban working class. The rapidly growing CIO unions, in particular, had broadened the base for organized labor. Would public housing become another foundation for working-class social and political power?[13] Critics may have captured this possibility best when they sought to raise fears about public housing by labeling it "political housing."

The housing shortage during World War II and the following years proved to be one of the most contentious and consequential local issues. The CIO, and to a lesser degree the AFL, played an active role advancing proposals for defense housing, public housing, and other programs to assist workers and lower-income Milwaukeeans in finding decent shelter.[14] As in most cities, private housing and apartment construction had slowed significantly during the Depression. The wartime emergency also stalled private building, with the central city wards seeing virtually no residential construction. As defense production geared up, more workers seeking decent, affordable housing arrived in the city. Hardest hit by the wartime housing shortage were African American residents of city's near north neighborhoods and black workers who came to the city for defense work.[15]

African Americans made up just 1.6 percent of Milwaukee's population in 1940. That number increased by almost 150 percent in the following decade as the wartime and postwar demand for labor intensified.[16] In 1940, most of Milwaukee's black residents lived in the western precincts of the Sixth Ward and the southeastern corner of the Tenth Ward, just north of downtown (see fig. 6.1, p. 167). Previous and subsequent efforts to move into other sections of the city were blocked by restrictive covenants, white neighborhood and real estate leaders' resistance, and government policy. Milwaukee's African Americans would continue to confront and challenge segregation, as the city's growing black population slowly found housing northwest of and adjacent to the earlier black neighborhoods.[17]

The Milwaukee CIO became a visible force challenging racism in the city, in workplaces, and in other unions. During the war, for instance, the CIO organized the Interracial Labor Relations Council. In a meeting at the Sixth Ward's Calvary Baptist Church, the group proposed a broad agenda to combat

Population—1940 587,472

Population—1947 estimate 624,000

Area—February 16, 1948.........................44.765 square miles

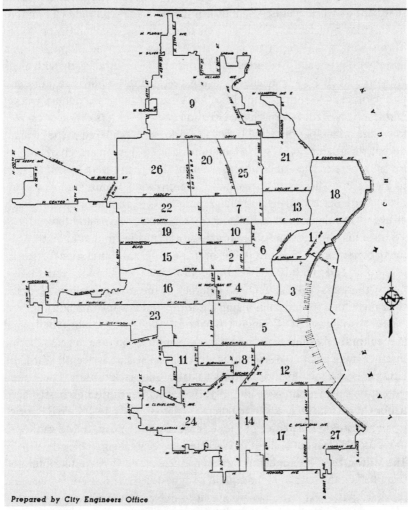

Prepared by City Engineers Office

Fig. 6.1. Milwaukee ward map. Adapted from Milwaukee Common Council, *Milwaukee Annual Report* (1947), 7.

racism locally and nationally.[18] The left-wing UAW Local 248 took the lead in many of these efforts, from forming the Milwaukee Scottsboro Defense Committee in 1937, to challenging discriminatory hiring practices during the war, to helping the CIO organize an interracial bowling tournament in 1946.[19] In its work against racial discrimination, the CIO paid close attention to the obstacles that black workers faced finding decent housing. Much of this work was done in alliance with African American, Popular Front, and liberal groups. CIO unions and leaders also worked directly with black workers and others who needed housing, pressuring landlords, realtors, and public officials to respond. Joe Ellis, an African American tannery worker and secretary of the International Fur and Leather Workers Union Local 260, knew the difficulties black soldiers and workers encountered as they sought decent, affordable housing. He had gone door-to-door in search of lodging for members of the armed forces, finding that many were forced to turn to the Rescue Mission or dangerously overcrowded rooming houses in the Sixth Ward. Black workers and their families had to double-up in the already crowded and deteriorating housing in Milwaukee's Sixth and lower Tenth Wards. Ellis, the CIO, and allied organizations pushed for better Sixth Ward living conditions, a vigorous public housing program, "interracial" organizing, and an end to residential discrimination.[20] As historian Joe Trotter notes, ". . . by the war's end, the CIO had emerged as the strongest ally of blacks in their push for a municipal housing authority and low income housing."[21]

The Milwaukee CIO Council, UAW Local 248, and their allies challenged the realtors and others who tried to keep neighborhoods segregated. In one instance involving the overwhelmingly white, west-side Sixteenth Ward, the CIO decried a local realtor's efforts to drive out black renters. Local 248's resolution called for home front unity: "Fascism is rearing it ugly bestial head in our City of Milwaukee, stirring up racial hatred, and one, Mr. Fred Barthel, is openly urging the people of the 16th Ward and the City of Milwaukee to move the Negroes out of the 16th Ward and segregate them in the 6th Ward."[22] The Milwaukee CIO, condemning the "handful of selfish real estate interests" that blocked the path to racial equality, suggested that these contests should be viewed as a test "whether we are fit to live as free Americans, whether we have the stuff to win this war."[23] Questioning the patriotism of all who circulated and signed the segregationist petitions, the CIO especially focused its attacks on Barthel, the real estate dealer. The *CIO News* quoted one anti-discrimination supporter's inquiry about Barthel's credentials as a leader in the wartime city: "I have never heard of his distinguishing himself during this war by any patriotic acts, in our bond drives or blood donor campaigns. Why is he suddenly so active to keep these Negroes from having a home?"[24]

In the wake of the Sixteenth Ward controversies, the CIO continued to target real estate leaders as both obstacles to better housing for the city's African American residents and as destructive to home-front unity.[25]

The CIO's work against segregation and racism in housing built on earlier anti-discrimination work in the city and dovetailed with the initiatives of the national CIO. The National CIO Committee to Abolish Racial Discrimination encouraged all CIO Councils to set up local anti-discrimination campaigns. In concert with the National CIO Housing Committee, this group decried the National Association of Real Estate Boards' efforts to kill public housing, to promote housing discrimination, and to back a privately driven urban redevelopment program. The national committee called on city CIO councils and CIO unions to work on behalf of public housing as a part of its joint anti-discrimination and housing agendas.[26] Left-led unions such as Local 248 had taken this work a step further by challenging racial inequalities in unions, workplaces, everyday life, and housing. This heightened attention to discrimination and racism, although undermined frequently by the racial prejudices held by leaders and the rank and file, would influence the postwar agenda of many labor, left, and liberal organizations. The growing rift between the Popular Front left and anticommunist liberals, however, sharpened the distinction between campaigns aimed at extinguishing racial intolerance and attacks on deep-seated racism. While the former, more modest initiatives would produce results that liberal leaders could point to with pride, the limits of this approach would become apparent in postwar conflicts over public housing and urban development.[27]

As the war drew to a close, the coalition of organizations that had fought for the Housing Authority and a stepped-up wartime public housing program began to address the city's postwar housing emergency. For public housing advocates, the severe housing shortage for veterans and nonveterans presented an opportunity to mobilize wide support. A broad coalition of women's, labor, African American, religious, welfare, and civic groups, under the umbrella of the Joint Action Committee for Better Housing (JACBH), castigated public officials' postwar priorities and argued that the housing crisis deserved more attention.

Women's groups and female leaders helped to keep the JACBH at the forefront on housing issues. JACBH leader Genevieve Hambley and her fellow Milwaukee League of Women Voters' members put a heavy emphasis on housing issues in the early postwar years. Other women's groups participating in the JACBH included the American Association of University Women, the Milwaukee County Council of Church Women, the Council of Jewish Women, the YWCA, the Milwaukee Women's Club, and later the Women's

Trade Union League. Women from a range of other organizations affiliated with the JACBH, including the NAACP and the Milwaukee Urban League, also played key roles on housing issues.[28]

Milwaukee's African American organizations and leaders also focused on the postwar housing shortage to press for the needs of veterans and the longer-standing housing needs in the black community. After a proposed wartime housing project in the Sixth Ward had been scratched, groups that advocated better housing in this area tried to push the city to take action. The Milwaukee Urban League, the NAACP, the Sixth Ward Better Housing Club, black churches and clergy, African American candidates, community newspapers, the Negro Businessmen's League, and interracial organizations such as the Renters League made the city's housing crisis and policies a defining political issue.[29]

Veterans' groups in the city, from the liberal American Veterans Committee (AVC) to the conservative American Legion, worked hard to provide more and better housing for their members and potential members. Whether working together through the Joint Veterans' Housing Council, in a coalition with the JACBH, or individually, these groups recognized that the political clout of veterans in the early postwar city was formidable. The AVC was especially vocal in demanding that both public and business leaders put their political and organizational resources to work on the housing shortage.[30]

The Milwaukee CIO placed the postwar housing crisis near the top of its agenda, working both in a coalition through the JACBH and on its own. CIO Council secretary Glenn Clarke called for fast action by the public sector to make up for private industry's failings, telling the Common Council that if "something isn't done—and soon—there will be a catastrophe."[31] Spurred on by local conditions, the CIO Council was encouraged by the national CIO and international unions, especially the United Auto Workers, to organize for low income and veterans' housing.[32] Individual unions and the CIO council put pressure on local, state, and federal officials and candidates to respond to the shortage and create more equitable housing policies and possibilities for workers, veterans, and other low and moderate-income people.[33] CIO veterans from Milwaukee and around Wisconsin called for a special session of the state legislature to address veterans' housing and employment problems.[34] Through its newspaper and in meetings for members and the public, the CIO helped to build support among working-class Milwaukeeans for public housing projects.[35]

Just as the war ended, the CIO alerted its members to the attack being made on public housing by "powerful private real estate interests." Citing the end of the war and building-material shortages, these real estate groups lobbied against continued attention to planning for the Sixth Ward project. The CIO warned that any delay threatened both the housing project and "Milwaukee's whole slum clearance program which was won only after many years of hard fighting by labor and other civic-minded groups."[36] The program the CIO promoted would clear areas of inadequate, private housing in order to build public housing, and not simply turn the area over to private developers. As progress on the Sixth Ward project continued to limp along, the CIO, along with representatives from the JACBH and organizations such as the Inter-racial Federation and the AVC, pressed the city to move forward rather than wait for the federal government to act.[37]

Along with both its criticisms of the real estate industry and its vigorous support for public housing, the Milwaukee CIO welcomed the postwar era with an ambitious plan to create a labor community. On Labor Day of 1945, Milwaukee CIO secretary Meyer Adelman announced that the group was considering seriously the purchase and development of Greendale. A New Deal "greenbelt town" just southwest of Milwaukee, Greendale had opened in 1938 and become home to many working-class families, including that of the UAW Local 248 President Robert Buse.[38] The CIO had begun preliminary discussions with Greendale's federal manager, proposing to expand the village ten-fold, from 637 to 6,000 homes. Adelman, who had been one of the CIO's earliest organizers in Wisconsin, said the "project would be primarily for CIO union members." About half or more of the homes would be reserved for union members and the rest opened to the general public. He imagined a CIO-published village newspaper, a radio station, and stores that were either co-operatives or owned by the village corporation. These plans never moved beyond the early proposals.[39] But the broad scope of this Labor Day proposal illustrates how CIO leaders such as Adelman imagined their power and possibilities in the postwar city. They believed that the close of the war might lead to a period in which organized labor could build its institutional strength and exert its power in the workplace and community. Labor and its allies might shape the city and urban policy.

The AFL, although less vocal and far-reaching, also viewed housing as a key postwar issue. The AFL addressed the difficulties that its members and others faced in finding homes, including low-cost housing, and it sought to boost and protect employment for its building trades members.[40] AFL leaders, along with representatives of the CIO and independent unions, participated in a short-lived effort to build co-operative housing for workers. Max Raskin, former city attorney and ally of organized labor, who was on a path from Socialism to the Democratic Organizing Committee, helped to bring together about fifty labor representatives. Patterning their effort on the Socialist's post–World War I Garden Homes project, the Milwaukee Mutual Housing Association suggested teaming up with the city to build affordable housing for workers. For the AFL, such an effort harkened back to earlier decades in the twentieth century, when they had played a pivotal role in building and sustaining the Socialist base in city politics. Although this post–World War II co-operative housing plan stalled, as had the CIO's labor community proposal, the attempt to establish labor-sponsored, non-market housing for workers indicates the wide range of political and policy possibilities alive in the early postwar city.[41]

These working-class housing proposals met increasing resistance as conservative assaults on the Left and as the politics of anticommunism limited the range of political discourse and weakened labor's base in the city. Anticommunism, of course, had been part of the local political culture before and during the war. But an early postwar Allis-Chalmers strike and the 1946 elections brought the domestic Cold War to the forefront of Milwaukee politics and society. On April 29, 1946, UAW Local 248 members approved overwhelmingly a strike at Allis-Chalmers by a vote of 8,091 to 251. This strike and its outcome had important consequences within and outside the factory walls. Local 248 had established itself as a driving force in the Milwaukee CIO Council. The union also had secured a strong presence on the shop floor of the massive West Allis plants through its well-organized shop steward structure and aggressive grievance strategy. Local 248 was a stronghold of militant, left-wing unionism in the area. During the strike, the union found itself under relentless attack by a company that had benefited substantially from wartime profits and tax benefits. Allis-Chalmers was eager now to use its local and national clout to break the union's workplace and political power.[42]

Over the course of this eleven-month strike, the company, along with its business allies and elected officials, fought Local 248 and its leaders with an aggressive anticommunist campaign. Charges of Communist control over the union were initiated by the company and publicized enthusiastically by the *Milwaukee Sentinel* and congressional committees.[43] The *Sentinel* launched a daily series during the fall of 1946, written under the pen name John Sentinel and backed by Allis-Chalmers researchers. The articles claimed that the strike had been orchestrated by a clique of Communists in Local 248 and that the Milwaukee and Wisconsin labor movements were threatened by Communist control.[44] As the strike wore on and conflicts on the picket line escalated, the U.S. House Committee on Education and Labor (on which both John Kennedy and Richard Nixon served) and the House Un-American Activities Committee began investigations into Communist influence in Local 248.[45]

During the strike, the left-wing unionists who had founded the Milwaukee CIO and the Wisconsin CIO also came under assault. As a result, anticommunist CIO activists, some of whom would be important players in local Cold War liberal politics, took control of the local CIO. Meyer Adelman, a leader on the local CIO's involvement in housing issues, lost his position in both the Wisconsin and Milwaukee CIO. Local 248's strength on the CIO Council and in labor politics was diluted. These sustained attacks, along with labor-left defeats at the national level, muted the voice of Local 248, the CIO council, and militant unionism in the local political culture.[46]

Leaders of Local 248, while entwined in the politics of the Popular Front, were first and foremost industrial unionists.[47] They had sought to build organizations that could exert power in the workplace and the city. Anticommunist union activists, on the other hand, had seen this as a moment to steer labor away from what they viewed as the distracting and destructive politics of the Popular Front and CIO Communists. UAW leader Walter Reuther expressed this in his assessment of the strike: "We lost because there were people in positions of leadership in that local who put their loyalties outside of their union, outside the rank and file and outside of their country."[48] Most importantly, the company had viewed this postwar conflict as an opportunity to retake control of the shop floor. As historian Stephen Meyer argues, "Using their significant economic and political power, Allis-Chalmers officials mobilized conservative workers, public opinion, and local and national authorities and engineered the purge of labor's left."[49] In the end, the clash resulted in a diminished union, stronger management, and greater prominence for anticommunist liberals and conservatives in the city. Local 248 leader Harold Christoffel later remarked: "What we lived in [was] so different—that McCarthyism wall was a very solid wall." He lamented the loss that militant unionism suffered: "It's hard to believe how we lived before and the freedom of organization and the enthusiasm that we had going forward."[50] On the national level as well, the attacks on Local 248 and its leaders accelerated domestic anticommunism, contributing to the passage of the Taft-Hartley Act and other defeats for labor and the left.[51]

In the midst of the Allis-Chalmers strike and the turmoil of postwar reconversion, the 1946 elections took on heightened significance. Edmund Bobrowicz, a militant union leader and veteran, ran against the Democratic incumbent, Thaddeus Wasielewski, for the party's endorsement in the Fourth Congressional District race. In this heated contest between two Polish, southside candidates, the electorate split largely along class lines. Bobrowicz, an organizer for the left-wing Fur and Leather Workers Union, campaigned to extend the New Deal and vigorously supported organized labor. He also voiced a pro-Soviet foreign policy, advocating a continuation of the wartime alliance and challenging the emerging Cold War. Wasielewski, who had voted recently against a number of key labor issues, defended his record as a Democratic congressman on domestic issues. In his foreign policy he stressed the need for the United States to counter Soviet power, attacking the Soviet Union's aggression toward Poland and its increasing control over Eastern Europe.[52]

As the campaign progressed, serious international concerns as well as red-baiting tactics escalated. Wasielewski's red-baiting charges convinced Democratic Party leaders to withhold support from Bobrowicz, despite his having won the party primary. With his pro-labor record and union support, especially from the CIO, Bobrowicz mobilized working-class campaign volunteers and voters. This gave him the edge in the primary. Wasielewski attracted support mainly from middle-class voters. In the general election Bobrowicz beat Wasielewski (now running as an independent) again, but Republican candidate John Brophy came out on top, contributing to the Republican Congressional sweep of 1946.[53]

These and other conflicts during the second half of the 1940s, including the national CIO's purge of left-wing unions, recast the role of organized labor and the urban working class in American political culture. Organized labor, in many respects, became more bureaucratized and focused on wages and benefit packages that promised greater security and a higher standard of living.[54] Labor's ties to the Democratic Party strengthened, particularly as a result of the 1948 election. Although a range of voices continued to claim to represent labor's position politically and socially at the local level in particular, the voice of anticommunist liberalism became increasingly predominant. New levels of economic security in the postwar era enabled some union members to reach a middle-class lifestyle, buying cars and, especially for white workers, owning houses in the suburbs.

Anticommunism shaped housing politics both directly and indirectly in Milwaukee. Even before the events of 1946–47, suspicions of Red influence had strained the pro–public housing coalition. Genevieve Hambley of the JACBH, for instance, castigated the Communists for attending an April 1946 housing meeting with the mayor: "Twice we have told the Communists that we did not want them on our committee because we could not then keep our organization strong." She continued, "There must have been a leak in our own organization about this meeting and I intend to find out who talked."[55] Sigmund Eisenscher, the Communist activist in attendance, responded in a letter to the editor: "Mrs. Hambley's red baiting will endear her to the reactionary real estate operators and tax conscious corporations who are the most bitter enemies of a better housing program." He also warned that Hambley's "gratuitous venture into the witch hunting field will certainly not help to gain better housing."[56] A short time later, Hambley found herself on the receiving end of such charges and began legal action against builder Frank Kirkpatrick, who she claimed had slandered her as a Communist or fellow traveler.[57] Changes in the JACBH's membership also reflected these Cold War strains and fears as a Popular Front group, the Wisconsin State Conference of Social Legislation, was scratched off the coalition's letterhead and replaced by the anticommunist Americans for Democratic Action.[58]

Cold War anticommunism became a powerful tool to reshape the city's political culture and the policy arena. Two postwar housing controversies illustrate how labor, its allies, and opponents negotiated this changing terrain. A 1949 racial conflict in a veterans' trailer park points to the success of anticommunist liberals in advancing a modest agenda of racial tolerance. A 1951 fight over public housing, however, highlights the increasing difficulty that nonmarket housing policies encountered. Labor and liberal public-housing supporters found that they now could push a limited program only by attaching it to the postwar agenda for economic growth and development. This put an end to designs for a broad working-class or interracial public housing program that had animated earlier labor-left efforts in the city.

The confrontation in 1949 between white residents and a new African American family occurred in the Greenfield trailer park, a camp run by the Park Commission for the Milwaukee County veterans' temporary housing program. Albert J. Sanders, an African American navy veteran and shipyard worker, and his wife Rogelia Sanders, moved from Florida to Milwaukee. With their two young children and Albert's mother, they searched for a place to live so that Albert could enroll as a student at the Milwaukee School of Engineering. Squeezed by the postwar housing shortage, the Sanders family purchased a trailer and secured a place in the Greenfield Trailer Camp with the help of the veterans' housing coordinator.[59] The crowded, west-side camp of about 1,800 people and 500 trailers, originally designated for 358 trailers, was the largest in the metropolitan area.[60]

A few months before the Sanders's referral to the Greenfield camp, Milwaukee county officials had been questioned by local civil rights and community groups attempting to open more places for black veterans in the area's trailer camps. As of April 1949, only 23 trailers and trailer sites had been designated for black families, all in the Sixth Ward. The remaining 1,631 sites were set aside for white veterans. The county coordinator defended this policy of racial segregation, saying that "he would not take the responsibility for a riot if a Colored family were sent into another area."[61] Placement of the Sanders family in the previously all-white Greenfield camp may have been a response to civil rights advocates' lobbying.

On a hot July day the Sanders family pulled in with "one of the nicest looking trailers in the camp."[62] A small group of white residents, bolstered by the county's earlier segregation policies, soon began circulating a petition that read "The Negro should not be permitted in a white camp." White children taunted the Sanders children as they played outside their trailer, telling them to leave and teasing "We don't want to play with you."[63] By that evening, about 70 people had signed the petition and between 125 to 200 white residents met to demand the Sanders's ouster. Gathering around the trailer, some in the mob threatened the family: "If you stay here, we'll break up your car. We'll hurt you and your wife and your children, too."[64] Another group of white residents, however, defended the Sanders family. Mrs. Sanders remarked that during this difficult time, two women in the camp had been "awfully nice," telling her "We want you to stay." Others argued directly with the camp's segregationists and soon began a counter-petition drive.[65] Less than twelve hours after driving into the camp, despite the sheriff's promises of protection, the Sanders family left out of fear for their safety. They slept in their car overnight at the nearby Greenfield Park.

Early the next morning, African American and white leaders from local civil rights and community organizations responded. William Kelley, executive secretary of the Milwaukee Urban League and president of the Interracial Federation of Milwaukee, called the meeting. Those attending represented the CIO, the AFL, the Mayor's Commission on Human Relations, the Governor's Commission on Human Rights, the Catholic Church, the Milwaukee Ministerial Alliance, B'nai B'rith, the NAACP, the American Legion, and the Milwaukee School of Engineering. Headed by black and white professionals (especially lawyers), long-time civil rights advocates, religious leaders committed to racial justice and human rights, and anticommunist liberals and labor leaders (versus radicals who just a few years earlier shaped labor's political and community agenda), this group helped to steer the city's liberal anti-discrimination agenda.[66]

Meeting in the offices of the *Catholic Herald-Citizen*, the group decided on two courses of action. First, they would urge the district attorney and the sheriff to take legal action against both the petition signers and the group that had organized the anti-Sanders mob. Second, they would try to convince the Sanders family to move back into the trailer camp and then would sponsor meetings at the camp to educate and persuade residents. Accompanied by squad cars, motorcycle police, and members of the Mayor's Commission on Human Rights, the Sanders family returned to the Greenfield camp on

Friday afternoon.[67] Six sheriff's deputies guarded the trailer after the family had moved in again. At a tense outdoor meeting set up by the Interracial Federation that same evening, four hundred residents listened to arguments for and against racial integration while sixty-five deputies stood guard. The crowd was divided and noisy. The largely working-class crowd greeted speakers with both applause and jeers. Those who denounced the ill-treatment the Sanders family had endured included members of the mayor's and governor's human rights commissions, Catholic and Protestant clergy, veterans, Glenn Clarke of the CIO Council, and Otto Jirikowic of the AFL. They labeled the camp residents' racist acts as un-American, a betrayal of Christianity, and illegal.[68]

Four camp residents led the effort to oust the Sanders family and declare a segregated camp. Sensing that many attending this first meeting opposed residential integration, they called for a vote. Some women in the crowd, referring to the Sanders family, yelled "Throw 'em out." One speaker, much like the anti–public housing agitators who disparaged black migration to the city, played on prejudices that even more black families might move into the camp. If one black family was allowed to stay, he contended, "Next week we'll have two Negro families and the week after four." Another speaker asked this crowd of veterans why postwar housing should be integrated if the armed services had been segregated.[69] The Urban League's Kelley judged that the segregation forces had stronger support at this first meeting, in part because those who backed the Sanders or remained neutral had stayed away. He reported that the "rabble" reacted to the segregationists' talks with "rebel yells" and applause, using "the strongest language against the moving in of the Sanders family."[70]

In the next days the momentum of the controversy shifted, as both the popular appeals and the legal strategies weakened the segregationists' support. Camp residents' organizing around the ideals of racial tolerance and integration helped to turn events. A group of veterans in the camp had begun a counter-petition on Friday, encouraging the Sanders family to stay.[71] On Saturday, representatives of the mayor's commission met with leaders of the two opposing residents' groups, each declaring they represented the majority of camp residents.[72] The racial integration forces were gaining ground, having attained support in the camp as well as backing from the Interracial Federation, the mayor's and governor's commissions, labor unions, church officials, and others.[73] At a quieter Saturday night camp gathering that drew about one hundred people, anti-Sanders speakers found themselves the target of hecklers.[74]

Advocates for integration also pursued their legal strategy. The district attorney hesitated initially to act against the mob leaders, but a telegram from civil rights leaders reprinted in the press urging arrest warrants for disorderly conduct may have tipped the balance.[75] Fearing legal action or arrest, eight leaders of the segregation campaign reversed their course. Meeting with the district attorney, the sheriff, members of the mayor's and governor's human rights commissions, and Albert Sanders, the camp rebels apologized, stressing their ignorance of the law and now professing the family's right to live in the camp. An early leader of the faction, conceded: "After I knew of the laws, I decided Sanders had the right and I realized we did an injustice." Another anti-Sanders activist explained that her initial reaction stemmed from inexperience and ignorance: "She and many of the other women in the camp had never lived with Negroes before and were afraid." Father Heithaus instructed the group to "do your best to build up good neighborliness for the Sanders family." The group pledged to help the family.[76]

The camp residents' apologies, while possibly genuine, played to upper- and middle-class prejudices about workers. Made before a gathering of professionals who headed civil rights and civic organizations and law enforcement officials, the residents offered excuses of ignorance and parochialism. Insufficient knowledge of the law and inexperience in interracial living, the camp rebels confessed, had prevented them from understanding the Sanders' situation or rights. Such apologies and the ease with which they were accepted, however, failed to acknowledge a deeply entrenched racism voiced just a few days earlier. The pleas for forgiveness also belied the camp residents' likely recognition of a change in conditions they faced: tacit or official support from county policies for their original segregationist stance had begun to fade. But the residents' contrition did help to get them off the hook.

One leader, a recent migrant from New Jersey, described his change of heart during the incident: "A lot of gripes [about sanitary conditions in the camp] came to a head. I was angry. I didn't realize that the Sanders had a right to be there. . . . After I got to thinking it over, I realized how wrong I was. I feel they are due an apology."[77] As this resident suggested, the rebels' transgressions, while reprehensible, could be wiped away through understanding, reason, and education. Speaking about the other camp residents who were changing their minds about the presence of the Sanders family, he continued: "I've told them that the Negroes have been free now for about ninety years, and it's time we made them feel free."[78] In agreement, a member of the Governor's Commission on Human Rights argued that the residents' reversal and apology had "wiped out a short-lived blot on the good name of the state of Wisconsin."[79] Immediately after this resolution, the mayor's commission produced a pamphlet on *The Milwaukee Greenfield Incident*.

Designed to stress the decisiveness of the commission and allied groups in this case, the pamphlet would be distributed to civic and "intergroup" agencies throughout Milwaukee and the country.[80] While much had been gained by civil and human rights activists' swift action within and outside the camp, the optimism following this event underestimated the extent to which racism and racial discrimination were woven into the fabric of residential patterns and postwar power relations.

While Cold War politics helped to shape the liberal coalition that came together in this incident, more explicit expression of anticommunism highlighted the growing anxieties and political constrictions of these years. Along with their apology, the repentant segregationists sought to insulate their earlier behavior against charges of political extremism. One veteran stressed that he was neither a Communist nor a "Ku Kluxer." He continued, "I'm just a plain American citizen who happened to let a few things go to my head that weren't so."[81] Mapping the outer boundaries of the emerging postwar political culture, neither a Communist nor a Klan member, this veteran portrayed himself as a redeemable, average American citizen.

The limits of acceptable political discussion had been marked during the Interracial Federation's first public meeting in the trailer park, soon after the controversy began. At the gathering, integrationists, segregationists, camp residents, and outsiders stepped up to use the microphone. All had a voice in the debate. But Josephine Norstrand, identified as a Communist Party activist, never made it to the microphone. She was executive secretary of the Wisconsin Civil Rights Congress, a Popular Front organization concerned with the issues under discussion. Norstrand was stopped by Bitker and the sheriff's deputies and later removed from the camp. In this 1949 civil rights dispute, civil liberties were extended to segregationists who had, in the opinion of some, nearly started a race riot. Such liberties were not extended, however, to a person tagged as a Communist.[82]

During the following week, the repentant segregationists scapegoated Norstrand and the Communists. They heaped blame for the disturbance at Greenfield Park on the Communists, without any apparent objection from the district attorney, civil rights liberals, or the newspapers. Some even charged that Communists had stirred up the trouble in the trailer park. A leader of the campaign to keep the Sanders out of the park claimed that Norstrand's presence had intensified the crowd's anger. Acknowledging now that the Sanders family had a right to live in the trailer park, he labeled Norstrand as "a woman who had no right to be there."[83]

These veterans clearly understood the power of anticommunist rhetoric and sentiments. In Milwaukee and elsewhere, Communists and suspected

Communists had become visible targets of such Cold War charges. During the postwar strike at Allis-Chalmers, fears of radicalism and the politics of anticommunism had intensified; this served company officials' and conservative allies' objective to break the militant Local 248. Leading postwar liberals in Milwaukee, including public housing advocates in the JACBH and civil rights activists, followed the lead of national liberals, who denounced suspected Communists. The camp residents' use of anticommunism indicates their strategic awareness of how both liberals and conservatives had elevated the position of anticommunism in postwar political culture. The segregationists' defeat at Greenfield was indeed an important milestone in local anti-discrimination efforts. But this incident also points to the restricted political space in which postwar racial liberalism was constructed.[84]

A short time after the Greenfield trailer park confrontation, the local debate over public housing intensified. This conflict came to a head in 1951 when Milwaukeeans cast votes on two competing public housing referenda. The City Hall clash between the CIO and the Milwaukee County Property Owners petitioners had underscored the controversy. One of the measures on the spring ballot, the local version of a national campaign headed up by the real estate industry, sought to sabotage public housing.[85] The second referendum, placed on the ballot shortly before the election, aimed to defend public housing by tying it to the city's emerging urban redevelopment program.[86] The Hillside project—increasingly identified as the city's "Negro housing project"—became the focus of the debate.[87] This conflict was about more than public housing and redevelopment. By engaging questions about race and urban citizenship, city leaders and residents also disputed and shaped postwar city liberalism.

Amplifying an argument made in the 1930s, public housing opponents complained that project residents did not contribute to city revenues through property taxes. The Housing Authority's tax-exempt projects had negotiated a system of payments-in-lieu-of-taxes (PILOT), allowed under federal rules.[88] Enemies of public housing—who included realtors, builders, savings and loan officials, and political conservatives—exploited worries about lost revenue to undermine support for public housing. They also tapped into wide-ranging cultural concerns and prejudices about changes in the mid-century city. They reasoned that "tax-paying citizens," homeowners and landlords, would rally to their side in this "city of homes." Anti–public housing leader William Pieplow argued that such housing should be stopped "unless it pays the same amount as any private citizen." He continued, "The payments in lieu of taxes which the projects pay are nothing but communism."[89] Pieplow condemned public housing and government control as "the rock upon which communism builds."[90] The public housing opponents doggedly attacked the legitimacy of "no-tax housing," targeting their rhetoric and tactics to appeal to taxpayers and tying their crusade to the politics of anticommunism.[91]

At the national level, attacks on tax-exempt housing projects included Senator Joe McCarthy's complaints during congressional hearings in the late 1940s. McCarthy objected especially to reformer Nathan Straus's projection that public housing might accommodate one-third of the population. This situation, McCarthy contended, would create "such a tax burden on the remainder of the population that the middle income group would also demand public housing." He surmised that this would allow proponents of public housing to achieve their "ultimate aim" of socializing all housing, which, in turn, would bring about economic ruin. "If two-thirds of the population were housed in subsidized tax exempt projects the economy would not be able to stand it." This alarm both anticipated the rhetorical style the Wisconsin Senator would use in following years to broadcast anticommunism and buttressed conservative real estate industry attacks on proposals for a broad-based working-class public housing program. At most, they argued, public housing might function as a temporary aid for the poorest of the poor.[92]

The 1951 anti–public housing argument in Milwaukee was cast most notably in the language of citizenship. Public housing opponents resuscitated an idea of urban citizenship rooted in private property ownership and property tax paying. In the emerging Cold War political culture, this vision of urban citizenship stood in stark contrast to that proffered earlier by the labor-left proponents of a capacious public housing program. The anti–public housing forces now contended that public housing residents, the occupants of "no-tax" housing, failed to fulfill this property obligation of citizenship. Public housing residents' legitimacy as city inhabitants with full rights, obligations, and entitlements to social provisions—their social citizenship—was challenged.[93] Referring especially to low-income African American Hillside residents, public housing opponents labeled project tenants as dependent. Urban citizenship, in turn, was defined racially, with black public housing residents marked as dependent and the least deserving of full citizenship.[94]

The 1951 referendum controversy reinforced the spatial and social barriers isolating the city's African American residents, both recent migrants and longtime Milwaukeeans. Edward Plantz, president of the Milwaukee County Property Owners association and an outspoken opponent of public housing, made this clear when he conceded that Sixth Ward residents, unlike others in Milwaukee, still faced a housing shortage. He argued against responding to this need, however, contending that "if we put up more public housing there will just be more and more people moving up here from the South."[95] A year later Plantz was more explicit: "The only thing that has kept 10,000—aye, 20,000—Negroes from coming up here is the lack of housing."[96]

For Plantz and others, more public housing meant more Sixth Ward housing, more Sixth Ward housing meant more black housing, and more black housing meant more black migration from the South. Many whites feared a rapid increase in Milwaukee's black, working-class population. For many players in these early postwar debates, black working-class migration from the South symbolized the antithesis of the modern city. Race, crystallizing around the image of black workers moving to the city, demarcated the metaphorical field upon which "progress" and the "modern city" were defined. By invoking the migration of black workers from the South, the president of the Property Owners association both kept the housing debate focused on the Sixth Ward and rejected black Milwaukeeans' claims to urban citizenship.[97]

White privilege in this debate was constructed on a foundation of private home ownership and citizenship.[98] Leaders of the referendum campaign enlisted a constituency of white landlords and homeowners. They assailed Milwaukee's public housing program, mobilizing the Cold War discourses and practices of private enterprise and white racism to define the city and its political culture. This amalgam of political economy, racial identity, and citizenship claims helps to explain the persistence and potency of the anti–public housing leaders' ceaseless assaults on the seemingly arcane system of payments-in-lieu-of-taxes. Joined with Cold War anticommunism and antiradicalism, which in turn reinforced their defense of private enterprise and inflamed concerns about citizenship, the attack was indeed formidable.

Public housing advocates—the coalition of labor, African American, women's, religious, and reform groups, as well as city officials—defended the program by pointing to the city's continued housing shortage, especially for lower-income residents. Along with the JACBH and the Citizen's Anti-Slum Committee (formed in 1951), defenders organized a County Property Owners for Public Housing group to challenge their opponents' homeowner and taxpayer politics. Acknowledging the appeal of the "no-tax housing" pitch, advocates for public housing detailed the pragmatic impact of PILOT on city coffers; project residents paid more to the city, in effect, than they had when living in dilapidated private housing. The AFL, speaking especially to a membership of skilled workers and many homeowners, charged that the "Real Estate Lobby," by placing newspaper advertisements asking "Do you want to pay the taxes on your neighbor's home?" was seeking to "incite rebellion of taxpayers against . . . housing projects." The AFL countered that "such projects really take the load off other taxpayers."[99] The CIO also argued that public housing would benefit the city financially.[100] Housing Authority director Richard Perrin estimated that the city would collect 22 percent more in revenue through the Hillside project's PILOT than it had when the resident families lived in "substandard dwellings."[101] Rather than the "burden" that Senator McCarthy and local opponents described, these public housing projects could benefit taxpayers as a whole. As Perrin feared, however, cost-benefit arguments did not sway opponents. This was not a debate to be won or lost on the balance sheet.[102]

Among the arguments public housing advocates marshaled, those addressing the prospects of the city's redevelopment initiatives proved pivotal. They highlighted the language of the second referendum, which linked public housing to the city's program of urban redevelopment.[103] In the 1930s and 1940s, working-class housing advocates and middle-class liberal reformers certainly had viewed housing and slum clearance policies as linked, but affordable and decent housing for workers and other lower-income Milwaukeeans had been their priority. Slum clearance would serve the purpose of improving housing. Redevelopment and housing had been joined in federal legislation in 1937 and 1949 and in many other proposals at the local and national levels. A 1945 debate over the powers of Milwaukee's new Housing Authority, in large part, hinged on this issue. In local and national urban policy making, a thoroughly political process, questions about the mix and priority of these elements remained contested.[104] During the 1951 debate, liberal leaders such as Perrin stressed that "if federal housing aid is lost, blight elimination, slum clearance, and other redevelopment activities will grind to a halt." "Attacks on public housing," he contended, "are attacks on civic projects and civic progress."[105] Public housing supporters hoped both to blunt the opposition and win the support of downtown and metropolitan business and civic leaders.

Reversing the calculus of earlier labor-left initiatives, key business and civic leaders now had begun to acknowledge a supplementary role for public housing if it would help to propel a large-scale program of urban redevelopment. The *Milwaukee Journal*, a leading metropolitan booster, stressed that an effective program of city development required defeat of the anti–public housing measure.[106] Just before Election Day, the *Journal* advised voters to support the pro–public housing referendum. The combined housing and redevelopment programs would propel the "drive to rebuild the city."[107] Building on a deal struck four years earlier between housing and redevelopment advocates during a municipal debt referendum fight, public housing was tied to plans for redevelopment and economic growth. This brought liberal and labor advocates for public housing into the fold with pro-development leaders. On the other hand, some conservative city leaders who earlier had expressed fears that public housing would promote racial integration now backed the pro–public housing referendum. They hoped to advance a redevelopment program that might reinforce the city's racial boundaries.[108]

Real estate leaders working to block public housing understood the perils posed by this alliance between redevelopment and housing supporters. The head of the Property Owners association insisted that the anti–public housing referendum would not have any impact on the city's redevelopment prospects. "Blight clearance" could proceed without public housing.[109] Such pleas from public housing opponents in the last months of the campaign, maintaining that their measure would stop only public housing, underscored the effectiveness of joining redevelopment with housing. This growth-oriented strategy reformulated the debate, dividing real estate conservatives from pro-development business and civic leaders; this approach also aligned the Cold War labor-left coalition with opponents of residential integration and growth advocates.

On April 3, 1951, Milwaukeeans passed both the pro- and anti–public housing referenda. Over the next days and years, Milwaukeeans would struggle to interpret the results of this seemingly contradictory outcome.[110] The anti–public housing measure passed with a slim 51 percent majority. The pro–public housing and redevelopment referendum passed by a larger margin, garnering over 56 percent of the votes.[111] The anti–public housing measure found its strongest support in two northwest wards (see fig. 6.1, p. 167) in which home values, home-ownership rates, income levels, and the proportion of white-collar workers ranked among the highest in the city.[112] The wards solidly backing the city's housing and redevelopment program, on the other hand, included those in older sections of the city with some of the worst housing conditions.[113] The pro–public housing and redevelopment measure also gained support in a set of older districts that included both workers and some of the city's wealthiest residents, suggesting the importance of corporate and downtown support for these programs.[114] This contrast of older districts supporting public housing and redevelopment versus newer areas of the city voting to quash the programs delineates the contours of postwar pro-growth politics.

Further analyses of the votes point to an emerging conservative home-owner politics.[115] Opposition to public housing was defined especially along the lines of home ownership, increasing steadily with higher income levels. Led by realtors and members of the home-building industry, upper-income home owners, such as those in the rapidly developing Twenty-sixth Ward, gave this anti–public housing politics its most solid backing. While skilled

workers who owned homes constituted a portion of the public housing opposition, they do not appear to have been a major part of this political movement. Attacks on public housing found little support among factory workers.
And laborers—lower-income, working-class Milwaukeeans who were largely
renters and included most of the city's black working class—were especially
unlikely to join the anti–public housing side.[116] Contrary to recent interpretations of mid-century populism, which emphasize white working-class
receptivity to many dimensions of the anti–public housing message, from
its anticommunism to its white racism to its anti-government appeals, this
anti–public housing initiative found limited support among white workers
and their families. Upper- and middle-income home owners made up the
core of the public housing opposition.[117]

Race played a pivotal role in the anti–public housing leaders' language
of urban citizenship. They depicted the virtuous urban citizen as a home-
owning, property-tax-paying, white Milwaukeean; public housing was stig-
matized as black housing. The city's emerging growth coalition accepted,
in part, this discourse of racialized housing. With the Hillside project at
the center of the debate and diminishing attention given to the possibility
of racially integrated public housing outside the center city, advocacy of a
tight programmatic and geographic link between downtown redevelopment
and public housing resulted in the growing approval of racially segregated
public housing. Public housing became subservient to a privately driven
redevelopment program and was defined by the racial rules and exclusions
of the private housing market.[118] At an earlier time, public housing's strongest
opponents and supporters understood the threat and hope that it might become "political housing": places in which an active and even militant working
class might foster its collective power. The public housing that remained at
the end of this postwar debate had been marginalized and, in part, depo-
liticized. Likewise, while organized labor and the mid-century labor-left
coalition earlier had promoted a broad interracial public housing agenda,
they now found themselves junior partners in the contest over housing and
redevelopment. Milwaukee's Cold War had narrowed the postwar political
culture, limiting the reach of organized labor and its left or liberal allies.

Although on the surface the two 1951 propositions were irreconcilable, the
results of these votes plotted the trajectory of postwar urban policy and political culture. With pro- and anti–public housing arguments locked in battle,
the pro-growth agenda prevailed. A constricted public housing program was
overshadowed by redevelopment and the politics of growth. While the city's
redevelopment program faced legal and political challenges throughout the
1950s, public and private initiatives sold on the basis of growth moved ahead.

Milwaukee's public housing program languished, falling far behind that of comparable cities.[119] Racially charged complaints about public housing as a tax burden festered, leaving the projects open to future charges of expendability and exposing public housing residents to attacks that questioned their worth and place in the city. In Milwaukee and elsewhere this alignment of race, public housing, non-tax-payer status, and dependency would prove to be a powerful force.[120] The politics of growth had not altogether displaced challenges to the discipline of the market. The Cold War had not erased labor's and workers' militancy nor had racism extinguished demands for racial justice. The debate over public housing, however, had fixed racial boundaries, the ideology of anticommunism, and the politics of growth more firmly on the urban landscape, its citizenry, and postwar policy. The vision of an interracial "labor city" gave way to an even more racially demarcated city whose race-based public housing would fuel white flight, bolster appeals to the market, and clear the way for downtown development.

Notes

1. "City Hall Peace Upset, Rival Factions Ousted," *Milwaukee Journal* (hereafter *MJ*), Jan. 9, 1951, 1.

2. "Court May Get Petitions Row," *MJ*, Jan. 10, 1951, 1. Erchul was secretary of the Milwaukee Industrial Union Council, also referred to as the Milwaukee CIO Council. This central labor body had been founded in 1937, when sixty-two CIO locals joined together.

3. Ibid.

4. Alderman Alfred C. Hass to Walter J. Mattison, Jan. 9, 1951; Harry Slater, Assistant City Attorney, to Hass, Jan. 9, 1951, Jan. 9, 1951, folio 1, "Public Housing, 1949–51," box 180, Zeidler Papers, Milwaukee Public Library (hereafter MPL); "City Hall Peace Upset," *MJ*, Jan. 9, 1951, 1; Alderman Alfred C. Hass to City Attorney Walter J. Mattison, regarding "Circulation of anti–public housing Petition in Lobby of City Hall, folio 25, "1950–51, Housing—Harbor—Bridges Committee," box 15, City Attorney Correspondence, Milwaukee City Archive, MPL; Mrs. Henry Marone to Mayor Frank P. Zeidler, and response, Jan. 12, 1951, folio 1, "Housing Referendum (1950–Jan. 1951)," box 179, Zeidler Papers, MPL; Frank P. Zeidler, "A Liberal in City Government: My Experience as Mayor of Milwaukee" (manuscript, 1962), chap. 4, 194–95; "Mixed Orders Oust Women," *MJ*, Jan. 13 1951, 8.

5. U.S. Department of Commerce, Bureau of the Census, *16th Census of the Population, 1940. Volume II: Characteristics of the Population, Part 7* (Washington, D.C.: U.S. Government Printing Office, 1943), 685; *16th Census of the United States, 1940: Population and Housing Statistics for Census Tracts, Milwaukee, Wis.* (Washington, D.C.: U.S. Government Printing Office, 1942), 52; *1950 United States Census of Population, Census Tract Statistics: Milwaukee, Wisconsin and Adjacent Area* (Washington, D.C.: U.S. Government Printing Office, 1952), 20. See also Harold M. Groves, Wayne Anderson, Harry Kahn, Louise Prober, and Hannah Westfield, *Report of the Commission on the Economic Study*

of Milwaukee (Milwaukee, 1948), 37, 39, 41; Stephen Meyer, *"Stalin over Wisconsin": The Making and Unmaking of Militant Unionism, 1900–1950* (New Brunswick, N.J.: Rutgers University Press, 1992); Richard L. Pifer, *A City at War: Milwaukee Labor during World War II* (Madison: Wisconsin Historical Society Press, 2003); William F. Thompson, *The History of Wisconsin, Volume 6: Continuity and Change, 1940–1965* (Madison: State Historical Society of Wisconsin, 1988), 94. Along with operatives, of course, men and women in other occupational groups (including skilled workers and laborers) worked in the city's industries. Manufacturing employed about as many Milwaukeeans as did the trade and service sectors combined.

6. Darryl Holter, "Sources of CIO Success: The New Deal Years in Milwaukee," *Labor History* 29 (1988): 223; Pifer, *City at War*, 10–11; Thomas W. Gavett, *Development of the Labor Movement in Milwaukee* (Madison: University of Wisconsin Press, 1965), 159–66; John Gurda, *Making of Milwaukee* (Milwaukee: Milwaukee County Historical Society, 1999), 324; William H. Riker, "The CIO in Politics, 1936–1946" (Ph.D. diss., Harvard University, 1948), 209; Bertil Hanson, *A Report on the Politics of Milwaukee* (Cambridge: Joint Center for Urban Studies of the Massachusetts Institute of Technology and Harvard University, 1961), v–6; Milwaukee Public Library, *Milwaukee City and County: A Statistical History* (Milwaukee, 1958), 24. For the CIO's rise nationally, see especially Robert H. Zieger, *The CIO, 1935–1955* (Chapel Hill: University of North Carolina Press, 1995). Darryl Holter reports that the new CIO unions claimed fifty-five thousand members in 1938 and AFL unions counted eighty thousand in 1939. Wisconsin was one of the main battleground states between the AFL and the CIO. While a majority of workers belonged to unions after the war, the numbers began to fall off in the 1950s as a result of Cold War purges, a reduced emphasis on organizing, and economic change.

7. Holter, "Sources of CIO Success." Over twenty-five sit-down strikes were carried out in Milwaukee during these peak years of prewar labor conflict. Darryl Holter, "Sit-down Strikes in Milwaukee, 1937–1938," *Milwaukee History* 9:2 (Summer 1986): 58–64. See also Henry Kraus, *The Many and the Few: A Chronicle of the Dynamic Auto Workers* (1947; reprint, Urbana: University of Illinois Press, 1985); and Zieger, *The CIO*.

8. Pifer, *City at War;* Meyer, *"Stalin over Wisconsin";* and Jonathan Rees, "Caught in the Middle: The Seizure and Occupation of the Cudahy Brothers Company, 1944–1945," *Wisconsin Magazine of History* 78:3 (Spring 1995): 200–218. See also Nelson Lichtenstein, *Labor's War at Home: The CIO in World War II* (New York: Cambridge University Press, 1982); and James B. Atleson, *Labor and the Wartime State: Labor Relations and Law during World War II* (Urbana: University of Illinois Press, 1998).

9. Of the four years with the highest totals of "worker-days idle" as a result of strikes, three were during the immediate postwar period. Research Clearinghouse of Milwaukee, *Milwaukee County, City, and Suburbs: A Statistical History of the Community* (Milwaukee, 1950), 73; Anthony M. Orum, *City-Building in America* (Boulder: Westview Press, 1995), 104–5; Pifer, *City at War*, 87–122. For the postwar strike wave, see also George Lipsitz, *Rainbow at Midnight: Labor and Culture in the 1940s* (Urbana: University of Illinois Press, 1994).

10. Gavett, *Development of the Labor Movement in Milwaukee*, 143; Gurda, *Making of Milwaukee*, 264–65; Wayne Attoe and Mark Latus, "The First Public Housing: Sewer Socialism's Garden City for Milwaukee," *Journal of Popular Culture* 10 (Summer 1976):

142–49; Gail Radford, *Modern Housing for America: Policy Struggles in the New Deal Era* (Chicago: University of Chicago Press, 1996), 50–51. For earlier links between labor and housing, see Carl D. Thompson, "Socialists and Slums—Milwaukee," *Survey* 25:10 (Dec. 3, 1910): 367–76. The FTC was the central labor body for Milwaukee AFL unions.

11. The Parklawn project was built by the Public Works Administration. At the same time, the U.S. Resettlement Administration built a greenbelt community, Greendale, on the outskirts of Milwaukee. See Vivian P. Lenard, "From Progressivism to Procrastination: The Fight for the Creation of a Permanent Housing Authority for the City of Milwaukee, 1933–1945" (M.S. thesis, University of Wisconsin-Milwaukee, 1967); and Arnold R. Alanen and Joseph A. Eden, *Main Street Ready-Made: The New Deal Community of Greendale, Wisconsin* (Madison: State Historical Society of Wisconsin, 1987). For housing politics and conflicts over urban policies from the late 1930s to the early 1950s, see Eric Fure-Slocum, "The Challenge of the Working-Class City: Recasting Growth Politics and Liberalism in Milwaukee, 1937–1952" (Ph.D. diss, University of Iowa, 2001).

12. "Council Buries Housing," *CIO News of Wisconsin,* Dec. 19, 1938.

13. For a similarly broad vision of working-class public housing, see Henry Kraus, *In the City Was a Garden: A Housing Project Chronicle* (New York: Renaissance Press, 1951).

14. Pifer, *City at War,* 29–34. For the UAW and wartime housing, see Sarah Jo Peterson, "The Politics of Land Use and Housing in World War II Michigan: Building Bombers and Communities" (Ph.D. diss., Yale University, 2002), 127–49.

15. "Negroes Flock Here for Jobs," *Milwaukee Sentinel* (hereafter *MS*), Sept. 6, 1942; "More Negroes Flock to City," *MJ*, Mar. 7, 1943; Joe William Trotter Jr., *Black Milwaukee: The Making of an Industrial Proletariat, 1915–45* (Urbana: University of Illinois Press, 1985); Paul Geib, "From Mississippi to Milwaukee: A Case Study of Southern Black Migration to Milwaukee, 1940–1970," *Journal of Negro History* 83:4 (Autumn 1998): 229–48. See also "Housing Our Barbadian Workers," *MJ*, Sept. 9, 1944.

16. The city's black population accounted for 3.4 percent of the city population in 1950 and 8.4 percent in 1960. By 1990, African American Milwaukeeans made up almost one-third of the total population. See Trotter, *Black Milwaukee;* Geib, "From Mississippi to Milwaukee"; Jack Dougherty, *More Than One Struggle: The Evolution of Black School Reform in Milwaukee* (Chapel Hill: University of North Carolina Press, 2004); Thompson, *History of Wisconsin,* 309–10; Citizens' Governmental Research Bureau, *Milwaukee's Negro Community* (Milwaukee: Council of Social Agencies, 1946); Andrew Edmund Kersten, *Race, Jobs, and the War: The FEPC in the Midwest, 1941–46* (Urbana: University of Illinois Press, 2000).

17. Trotter, *Black Milwaukee,* 176–78; J. J. Brust, *Housing Survey in the Sixth and Tenth Wards* (Milwaukee Board of Public Land Commissioners, 1944); Citizens' Governmental Research Bureau, *Milwaukee's Negro Community;* E. R. Krumbiegel, *Observations on Housing Conditions in Milwaukee's Sixth Ward: A Report to the Mayor and Common Council* (Milwaukee: Commissioner of Health, 1944); Bureau of the Census, *16th Census of the United States, 1940: Population and Housing Statistics for Census Tracts, Milwaukee, Wis.;* and *1950 United States Census of Population, Census Tract Statistics: Milwaukee, Wisconsin and Adjacent Area.* See also Stephen Grant Meyer, *As Long as They Don't Move Next Door: Segregation and Racial Conflict in American Neighborhoods* (Lanham, Md.: Rowman and Littlefield, 2000); Robert O. Self, *American Babylon: Race and the Struggle for*

Postwar Oakland (Princeton, N.J.: Princeton University Press, 2003); Thomas J. Sugrue, *The Origins of the Urban Crisis: Race and Inequality in Postwar Detroit* (Princeton, N.J.: Princeton University Press, 1996).

18. "Plan to Help Negroes Adopted at Labor rally," *MJ,* June 14, 1943. For the formation of the Interracial Labor Relations Committee, see William V. Kelley (Urban League) to Meyer Adelman (Milwaukee CIO), Apr. 8, 1943; "V Mass Meeting" flyer, June 13, 1943; and Invitation to Mass Meeting, June 3, 1943; all in folio 3, box 4, Milwaukee County Industrial Union Records (hereafter Milwaukee CIO Records), Milwaukee Urban Archives, Milwaukee Area Research Center, University of Wisconsin-Milwaukee (hereafter Milwaukee ARC).

19. Trotter, *Black Milwaukee,* chaps. 5 and 6; Meyer, *"Stalin over Wisconsin,"* 124–26; Judith Stepan-Norris and Maurice Zeitlin, *Left Out: Reds and America's Industrial Unions* (New York: Cambridge University Press, 2003), 229–30; "CIO Bowling Tourney Is On!" *Wisconsin CIO News,* Mar. 15, 1946.

20. "Negro Segregation Writes Tragic Story," *Wisconsin CIO News,* Feb. 14, 1944; "Housing Conditions to Blame as Negroes Die on Army Leave," *Wisconsin CIO News,* May 31, 1943; Milwaukee Department of City Development, "Central Business District Historic Resources Survey" (City of Milwaukee, Mar. 1986), 86. For Joe Ellis, the CIO, and housing for African American Milwaukeeans, see Trotter, *Black Milwaukee,* 187–88, 199, 212.

21. Trotter, *Black Milwaukee,* 188. For the limits of labor's racial egalitarianism, see especially Bruce Nelson, *Divided We Stand: American Workers and the Struggle for Black Equality* (Princeton, N.J.: Princeton University Press, 2001).

22. UAW Local 248, which had been and soon again would become the subject of aggressive federal investigation, suggested that the FBI and the U.S. Attorney General investigate Barthel and others for stirring up "racial hatred." UAW local 248, "Resolution on Discrimination against Negroes," June 13, 1944, folio 4, box 4, Milwaukee CIO Records, Milwaukee ARC.

23. "CIO Demands End to Housing Discrimination against Negroes," *Wisconsin CIO News,* May 8. 1944; "'End Housing Bans'—CIO," *Wisconsin CIO News,* May 13, 1944; "The 16th Ward Is Learning Some Things about This War," *Wisconsin CIO News,* May 22, 1944.

24. "The 16th Ward Is Learning Some Things about This War," *Wisconsin CIO News,* May 22, 1944.

25. "CIO Nails Real Estate Slurs against Negroes," *Wisconsin CIO News,* July 3, 1944. See also Pifer, *City at War,* 29–34. In another wartime incident, the CIO's Meyer Adelman responded angrily to the Milwaukee Real Estate Board secretary's racist statement against black Sixth Ward residents. Adelman exclaimed: "The obvious contempt expressed by you . . . towards those forced to live in sub-standard houses, especially the Negro people, can only spring from a person who puts his own financial interests above the interests of the people and the nation." Meyer Adelman, Milwaukee County Industrial Union Council, to John J. Roache, Milwaukee Real Estate Board, Apr. 21, 1944, folio 4, box 4, Milwaukee CIO Records, Milwaukee ARC; and Richard S. Davis, "Bohn Expects Authority to Uplift Housing," *MJ,* Apr. 18, 1944.

26. "Report of George L.-P. Weaver, National CIO Committee to Abolish Racial Discrimination," Mar. 20, 1944, folio 4, box 4, Milwaukee CIO Records, Milwaukee ARC;

Minutes of Meeting of National CIO Committee to Abolish Racial Discrimination, Mar. 20, 1944, folio 4, box 4, Milwaukee CIO Records, Milwaukee ARC. Weaver was also a member of the CIO's Housing Committee. For the CIO's Committee to Abolish Racial Discrimination and on the CIO's initiatives against racism at the local and national levels, see Zieger, *The CIO*, 156–60; Michael K. Honey, *Southern Labor and Black Civil Rights: Organizing Memphis Workers* (Urbana: University of Illinois Press, 1993), 191–213; and Robert Rodgers Korstad, *Civil Rights Unionism: Tobacco Workers and the Struggle for Democracy in the Mid-Twentieth-Century South* (Chapel Hill: University of North Carolina Press, 2003).

27. For the differences over questions of race within the mid-century CIO and the labor movement, especially between non-Communists and Communists, see Zieger, *The CIO*, 158–61; and Nelson Lichtenstein, *State of the Union: A Century of American Labor* (Princeton, N.J.: Princeton University Press, 2002), 76–82.

28. Marie Anne Laberge, "'Seeking a Place to Stand': Political Power and Activism among Wisconsin Women, 1945–1963" (Ph.D. diss., University of Wisconsin, Madison, 1995), 66–100; Fure-Slocum, "Challenging the Working-Class City," chaps. 3, 5, 6. See also "Questions by Hearers, Rivals Enliven Candidates' Forums," *MJ*, 1946, in scrapbooks, vol. 3, 1946, League of Women Voters of Greater Milwaukee Records, Milwaukee ARC; "How Candidates for Mayor Stand on Bonds, Housing and Blight," *MJ*, Jan. 29, 1948; "Two Forums Stir Interest: Housing Is Big Topic," *MJ*, Mar. 24, 1948; "Council Aspirants Favor Blight War, GI Housing," *MS*, Mar. 7, 1948; "City Housing Plans Argued," *MJ*, May 17, 1948; "Women Voters Study Problem of Housing," *MS*, Sept. 14, 1947; miscellaneous newspaper clippings, scrapbooks, vol. 4, 1947–48, League of Women Voters of Greater Milwaukee Records, Milwaukee ARC. For Genevieve Hambley, the JACBH's first chairperson and an outspoken advocate for public housing, see especially Laberge, "'Seeking a Place to Stand,'" 66, 179–81, and Zeidler, "Liberal in City Government," chap. 4, 37–38. For organizational ties to the JACBH, see "Report of President at the Annual Meeting of the Federation of Jewish Women's Organizations," June 12, 1951, frame 123, reel 1, Federation of Jewish Women's Organizations of Milwaukee Records, microfilm edition, Milwaukee ARC; Minutes of the Milwaukee NAACP Executive Meeting, Aug. 12, 1948, folio 15, box 2, Milwaukee NAACP Records, Milwaukee ARC; and Minutes of the Women's Trade Union League meeting, Aug. 28, 1950, folio 13, box 1, Milwaukee Women's Trade Union League Papers, Milwaukee ARC.

29. For examples, see "'Hit Problems' Bohn Is Told: Challenged on Housing, Slum Problems and Fiscal Program," *MJ*, Apr. 10, 1946; JACBH, "Report of the Chairman for the Year May 1946–May 1947," May 23, 1947, folio 1, box 9, Milwaukee CIO Records, Milwaukee ARC; "Dorsey Forces Issue on Housing Delay," May 5, 1946, unidentified newspaper clipping, folio 7, box 1, James W. Dorsey Papers, Milwaukee County Historical Society; Scrapbooks, 1920–49, reel 1, Milwaukee Urban League Records, Milwaukee ARC; Executive Board minutes, Nov. 13, 1947, Aug. 12, 1948, and Feb. 17, 1949, folio 15, box 2, NAACP Milwaukee Chapter Records, Milwaukee ARC; Regular meeting minutes, Jan. 22, 1948, folio 3, box 5, NAACP Milwaukee Chapter Records, Milwaukee ARC; "Activities for the Milwaukee Branch of the NAACP for 1948–49," folio 2, box 6, NAACP Milwaukee Chapter Records, Milwaukee ARC; "Sixth Ward Housing Inches Along," *Wisconsin CIO News*, Mar. 28, 1947; Renters League of Milwaukee County, correspondence and petition, Oct.

30, 1947, file 47-1932, City Records Center, Milwaukee; miscellaneous articles in *Milwaukee Globe* (1948–49) and *Milwaukee Sepian* (1951). See also Kevin D. Smith, "'In God We Trust': Religion, the Cold War, and Civil Rights in Milwaukee, 1947–1963" (Ph.D. diss., University of Wisconsin, Madison, 1999); and Michael Ross Grover, "'All Things to Black Folks': A History of the Milwaukee Urban League, 1919–1980" (master's thesis, University of Wisconsin, Milwaukee, 1994), 90–91.

30. "Push Housing, AVC's Advice: Veteran Group Asks 1948 Corporation to Assure 15,000 Units," *MJ,* Apr. 4, 1947; Mark D. Van Ellis, "To Hear Only Thunder Again: The Readjustment of World War II Veterans to Civilian Life in Wisconsin" (Ph.D. diss., University of Wisconsin, Madison, 1999), 154–67, 387–423.

31. "Housing Effort Still Lags Far Behind Needs," *MJ,* July 27, 1947.

32. The Milwaukee CIO also participated in numerous housing events and conferences coordinated by the national CIO. See, for instance, "Field Kit for 'Fight for Housing Day,'" June 25, 1947, folio 2, box 9, Milwaukee CIO Records, Milwaukee ARC. For housing as a national priority for the CIO see, for instance, Memorandum from Meyer Bernstein (CIO Veterans Representative), regarding 1948 CIO Portland convention action on veterans, Nov. 30, 1948, folio "CIO Veterans' Committee," box 32, United Steel Workers of America, District 31 Records, Chicago Historical Society; Congress of Industrial Organizations, *Daily Proceedings of the Eighth Constitutional Convention,* Atlantic City, New Jersey, Nov. 18, 1946, 34–36; CIO, *Final Proceedings of the Ninth Constitutional Convention,* Boston, Oct. 13–17, 1947, 110–16, 222–23; CIO, *1948 Proceedings of the Tenth Constitutional Convention,* Portland, Oregon, Nov. 22–26, 1948, 129–33, 397–400; UAW-CIO, *Proceedings, Twelfth Constitutional Convention,* Milwaukee, July 10–15, 1949, 15–16, 54–60. For organized labor, housing, and redevelopment in mid-century New York, see Joshua B. Freeman, *Working-Class New York: Life and Labor since World War II* (New York: New Press, 2000), 105–24; and Joel Schwartz, *The New York Approach: Robert Moses, Urban Liberals, and Redevelopment of the Inner City* (Columbus: Ohio State University Press, 1993).

33. For examples of legislative and political initiatives, see William G. Nicholas, Director of UAW-CIO Housing Department, to Hy Cohen, Milwaukee County Industrial Council, Jan. 5, 1946, folio 3, box 6, Milwaukee CIO Records, Milwaukee ARC; Communication from John Brophy (Director, Industrial Union Councils) regarding establishment of local Emergency Veterans Housing Committees, Apr. 6, 1946, folio 1, box 7, Milwaukee CIO Records, Milwaukee ARC; Memo from Jack Kroll to CIO Political Action Committees, June 12, 1947, folio 2, box 9, Milwaukee CIO Records, Milwaukee ARC; Communication from CIO Housing Committee regarding Taft-Ellender-Wagner Bill, Apr. 13, 1948, folio 2, box 11, CIO Housing Committee (Leo Goodman) Papers, Archives of Labor and Urban Affairs, Wayne State University, Detroit; and "Milwaukee County CIO-PAC Candidate Questionnaire," folio 5, box 11, Milwaukee CIO Records, Milwaukee ARC.

34. "CIO Vets to March on Capitol: Will Demand Special Session to Handle Urgent Veteran Problems," *Wisconsin CIO News,* Mar. 8, 1946.

35. "Housing Plan Benefits Cited," *MJ,* Dec. 11, 1945.

36. "Public Housing in Danger," *Wisconsin CIO News,* Sept. 14, 1945. For a satirical approach to the housing crisis, see "It's the Cats," *Wisconsin CIO News,* Sept. 14, 1945.

37. "Sixth Ward Housing Inches Along," *Wisconsin CIO News,* Mar. 28, 1947.

38. "Buy, Expand Greendale Is Goal of CIO: Labor Group Hopes to Have 6,000 Living Units, Half for Its Own Members," *MJ,* Sept. 4, 1945. For background on Greendale, see Ronald Wildermuth, "Greendale's Federal Years, 1938–1952" (master's thesis, University of Wisconsin-Milwaukee, 1968); Alanen and Eden, *Main Street Ready-Made;* and Gurda, *Making of Milwaukee,* 288–89. For Buse's involvement in Greendale, see also Robert Buse Oral History Interview by Dale E. Treleven, Feb. 4, 1982, Wisconsin Labor Oral History Project, State Historical Society of Wisconsin, Madison.

39. "Buy, Expand Greendale Is Goal of CIO," *MJ,* Sept. 4, 1945. See also "City Owned Churches Hit: CIO's Greendale Scheme Draws Fire," *MJ,* Sept. 5, 1945. For later controversies over the control of Greendale, in which CIO leaders remained involved, see "Hits at Funds for Greendale," *MJ,* Aug. 1, 1949; "Vote Ordered at Greendale," *MJ,* Aug. 3, 1949; and "Ballots Spurn Legion Group at Greendale," *MJ,* Aug. 24, 1949. See also Jeanne Anderson Posada, "Public Housing in Milwaukee: A Case Study in Administration" (master's thesis, University of Wisconsin, 1947), 69–76.

40. Wisconsin State Federation of Labor, *Proceedings of the Fifty-fourth Annual Convention,* Superior, Wisconsin, Aug. 19–23, 1946, 210–12; Wisconsin State Federation of Labor, *Proceedings of the Fifty-fifth Annual Convention,* Green Bay, Wisconsin, Aug. 18–22, 1947, 332–33; "Building Tr. Go 'All-Out' for Housing," *Milwaukee Labor Press,* Jan. 23, 1947. For AFL support for low cost housing, see "Housing Effort Lags Far Behind Needs: Private Builders, City, County Called Upon to Meet Emergency Long Seen Approaching," *MJ,* July 27, 1947.

41. Zeidler, "Liberal in City Government," chap. 4, 82–83. For other attempts to create cooperative housing, see "Vets Organize for Housing Co-op," *MS,* ca. 1946 (from newspaper clippings in Perrin Papers, Wisconsin Architectural Archive); "Veterans Cooperative Association," ca. 1946, folio 3, box 7, Milwaukee CIO Records, Milwaukee ARC; "Co-op Plan Is Adopted for Homes," *Milwaukee Labor Press,* Aug. 28, 1947, 22; and "Plan a Co-op for Housing: Seek Mixed Races," *MJ,* June 11, 1950. For cooperative housing, see Kristin Szylvian Bailey, "Defense Housing in Greater Pittsburgh, 1945–1955," *Pittsburgh History* 73:1 (Spring 1990): 16–28.

42. Meyer, "*Stalin over Wisconsin,*" 152, 158. The strike was called over wages, grievance procedures, and union security. As Meyer notes, "From the union perspective, the most important Allis-Chalmers demands would virtually eliminate union security, severely restrict the militant UAW local's shopfloor strength and lessen its role in the grievance process" (150). For a brief overview of postwar Milwaukee labor, see Darryl Holter, "Milwaukee Labor after World War II," *Milwaukee History* 22 (Autumn–Winter 1999).

43. Meyer, "*Stalin over Wisconsin*"; Julian L. Stockley, "'Red Purge': The 1946–1947 Strike at Allis-Chalmers," *Transactions of the Wisconsin Academy of Sciences, Arts, and Letters* 76 (1988): 17–31; and Gavett, *Development of the Labor Movement in Milwaukee,* 176–97. For labor, the Cold War, and anticommunism, see Robert W. Cherny, William Issel, and Kieran Walsh Taylor, eds., *American Labor and the Cold War: Grassroots Politics and Postwar Political Culture* (New Brunswick, N.J.: Rutgers University Press, 2004); Steve Rosswurm, ed., *The CIO's Left-Led Unions* (New Brunswick, N.J.: Rutgers University Press, 1992); and Ellen Schrecker, *Many Are the Crimes: McCarthyism in America* (Boston: Little, Brown and Company, 1998). For the historiography of Communism in the United

States, see John Earl Haynes and Harvey Klehr, "The Historiography of American Communism: An Unsettled Field," *Labour History Review* 68:1 (April 2003): 61–78; and Bryan D. Palmer, "Rethinking the Historiography of United States Communism," *American Communist History* 2:2 (2003): 139–73. Working-class anticommunism—stemming from Catholic labor activism, Socialist-Communist antagonisms, and craft/industrial union conflicts—also played a role in this and other postwar disputes. See Meyer, *"Stalin over Wisconsin"*; Steven M. Avella, *In the Richness of the Earth: A History of the Archdiocese of Milwaukee, 1834–1958* (Milwaukee: Marquette University Press, 2002), 718–29; and William Issel, "'A Stern Struggle': Catholic Activism and San Francisco Labor, 1934–1958," in *American Labor and the Cold War,* 154–76.

44. John Sentinel, "Stalin over Wisconsin: Reds Aim for Control of Our State," *MS,* Sept. 23, 1946.

45. The House Education and Labor Committee also was in the midst of drafting what would become the Taft-Hartley Act.

46. Robert W. Ozanne, *The Labor Movement in Wisconsin: A History* (Madison: State Historical Society of Wisconsin, 1984), 89–94; Gavett, *Development of the Labor Movement in Milwaukee,* 185–90; Meyer, *"Stalin over Wisconsin,"* 173–74. UAW politics at the national level were also crucial to the course of the strike and labor politics in the city; see Nelson Lichtenstein, *The Most Dangerous Man in Detroit: Walter Reuther and the Fate of American Labor* (New York: Basic Books, 1995); and Martin Halpern, *UAW Politics in the Cold War Era* (Albany: State University of New York Press, 1988), 173–83.

47. Meyer works his way through the evidence and assertions of the Local 248 leaders' associations with the Communist Party, concluding that the evidence is ambiguous and that this was not the most important substantive issue. Meyer points to the leaders' commitment to basic union issues and their strong support from the rank and file. See especially Meyer, *"Stalin over Wisconsin,"* 1–15.

48. Reuther quoted in Ozanne, *Labor Movement in Wisconsin,* 99.

49. Meyer, *"Stalin over Wisconsin,"* 222–23.

50. Harold Christoffel, interview by Dale E. Trelevan, Jan. 27, 1982, tape 4, side 1, Wisconsin Labor Oral History Project, State Historical Society of Wisconsin, Madison. Christoffel went to prison, charged with perjuring himself before a congressional committee.

51. "'Expose' of A-C Reds Told NAM: Convention Hears Sentinel's Role," *MS,* Dec. 5, 1947; and Schrecker, *Many Are the Crimes,* 184–87.

52. Robert D. Ubriaco Jr., "Choosing Sides: Restructuring the Political Landscape in Milwaukee's Polish Community, 1945–1948," *Milwaukee History* 22:2 (Summer 1999): 78–98; Ubriaco, "Bread and Butter Politics or Foreign Policy Concerns?: Class Versus Ethnicity in the Midwestern Polish American Community during the 1946 Congressional Elections," *Polish American Studies* 51:2 (Autumn 1994): 5–32; Donald Pienkos, "The Polish Americans in Milwaukee Politics," in *Ethnic Politics in Urban America: The Polish Experience in Four Cities,* ed. Angela T. Pienkos (Chicago: Polish American Historical Association, 1978), 66–91; and Meyer, *"Stalin over Wisconsin,"* 163–85.

53. Brophy held the seat for one term, losing to Democrat Clement Zablocki in 1948. The 1946 election also was the one in which Republican Joseph McCarthy of Wisconsin won his seat in the U.S. Senate, learning the political utility of anticommunism from the

Fourth District race. Earlier observers claimed that organized labor (the CIO particularly) threw the election to McCarthy by not supporting LaFollette in the Republican primary. Historians have noted, however, that Wisconsin did not allow voters to cross over in party primaries and that the CIO was concerned first with its candidates in the local Democratic primaries (including Bobrowicz), as well as building a New Deal Democratic party. See David M. Oshinsky, *Senator Joseph McCarthy and the American Labor Movement* (Columbia: University of Missouri Press, 1976); Meyer, *"Stalin over Wisconsin,"* 163–85; and Ozanne, *Labor Movement in Wisconsin,* 143–46. For postwar congressional campaigns nationally, see Jonathan Bell, *The Liberal State on Trial: The Cold War and American Politics in the Truman Years* (New York: Columbia University Press, 2004).

54. For labor and the Cold War in other cities, see especially Cherny, Issel, and Taylor, *American Labor and the Cold War;* Rosemary Feurer, *Radical Unionism in the Midwest, 1900–1950* (Urbana: University of Illinois Press, 2006); and Rosswurm, *The CIO's Left-Led Unions.* For labor's changing postwar priorities, see Nelson Lichtenstein, "From Corporatism to Collective Bargaining: Organized Labor and the Eclipse of Social Democracy in the Postwar Era," in *The Rise and Fall of the New Deal Order, 1930–1980,* ed. Steve Fraser and Gary Gerstle (Princeton, N.J.: Princeton University Press, 1989), 122–52; and Jennifer Klein, *For All These Rights: Business, Labor, and the Shaping of America's Public-Private Welfare System* (Princeton, N.J.: Princeton University Press, 2003). See also Kevin Boyle, ed., *Organized Labor and American Politics, 1894–1994: The Labor-Liberal Alliance* (Albany: State University of New York Press, 1998).

55. "Communist Attends," *MJ,* Apr. 10, 1946.

56. "Communists and Housing," *MJ,* Apr. 13, 1946. Eisencher was a Communist Party activist and candidate for governor in 1946.

57. Zeidler, "Liberal in City Government," chap. 4, 76–77.

58. JACBH letterhead, July 29, 1947, folio "Housing Veterans, 4200 Unites," box 48, Bohn Papers, MPL; and JACBH letterhead, July 13, 1949, folio 2, box 180, Zeidler Papers, MPL. The "Wisconsin State Conference of Social Legislation" also had gone by the name "Wisconsin Conference for Social Legislation."

59. Albert, age twenty-nine, had been born in the Philippines and come to the United States at the end of the 1930s. Rogelia, age twenty-seven, was from Tampa, Florida. For this incident, see William V. Kelley, Executive Secretary of the Milwaukee Urban League to Lester Granger, National Urban League, July 12, 1949, folio "Milwaukee Incident, 1949," box 33, series 1, part 1, National Urban League Papers, Manuscript Division, Library of Congress, Washington D.C. (hereafter National Urban League Papers, LOC); "Ousted Negro Family Decides to Return to Trailer Campsite," *MJ,* July 8, 1949; Milwaukee Mayor's Commission on Human Rights, *The Greenfield Trailer Camp Incident* (1949); Thompson, *History of Wisconsin,* 334–36; Smith, "In God We Trust," 291–94; and Avella, *Richness of the Earth,* 634–35.

60. Milwaukee County Survey of Social Welfare and Health Services, "Findings and Recommendations on Housing: Residential—Trailer Camps—Lake and Stream Sites," May 1949, pp. 6–11, folio "Survey: Reports 34–36—1949, July," box 54, United Community Services of Greater Milwaukee, Milwaukee ARC; "Backs Town Health Care," *MJ,* July 8, 1949.

61. "Summary of Report Submitted to Executive Committee, Apr. 19, 1949, folio 7B

"League of Women Voters of Milwaukee, 1949–1951," box 313, League of Women Voters of Milwaukee Records, Miscellaneous Collection 211, MPL.

62. William V. Kelley, Executive Secretary of the Milwaukee Urban League to Lester Granger, National Urban League, July 12, 1949, folio "Milwaukee Incident, 1949," box 33, series 1, part 1, National Urban League Papers, LOC; "We'll Sweat It out Again Today at 85," *MS,* July 7, 1949.

63. "Ousted Negro Family Decides to Return to Trailer Campsite," *MJ,* July 8, 1949.

64. Ibid.; Thompson, *History of Wisconsin,* 334; and Kelley to Granger, July 12, 1949, National Urban League Papers, LOC.

65. "Ousted Negro Family Decides to Return to Trailer Campsite," *MJ,* July 8, 1949. See also caption with photographs, "A Negro and His Family," *MJ,* July 8, 1949, 1L; and "Scenes at Troubled Greenfield Camp," *MJ,* July 9, 1949.

66. Thompson, *History of Wisconsin,* 335; "Negro Family Back Home," *MS,* July 9, 1949; "Ousted Negro Family Decides to Return to Trailer Campsite," *MJ,* July 8, 1949. Overlapping affiliations of those attending this meeting indicated a tightly woven coalition of groups active in civil rights. Among the participants were Attorney Bruno Bitker (Mayor's Commission on Human Relations and Governor's Commission on Human Rights), Father Franklyn J. Kennedy (Mayor's and Governor's Commissions), and Father Claude H. Heithaus, SJ (Mayor's Commission and Marquette University professor), as well as black professionals from the NAACP and others from the Mayor's Commission. Bitker was active also in the liberal, anticommunist Democratic Organizing Committee, reforming Wisconsin's party along national lines. Bruno Bitker, interview, Mar. 5, 1983, Wisconsin Democratic Party Oral History Project, tape 10, State Historical Society of Wisconsin, Madison; and Thompson, *History of Wisconsin,* 566–72. Heithaus and Kennedy were deeply involved in antidiscrimination work and Kennedy had charted an anticommunist Catholic labor position as editor of the *Catholic-Herald-Citizen.* Smith, "In God We Trust," 275–324; Avella, *Richness of the Earth,* 632–35.

67. "Negro Family Back in Trailer, Escorted Back by Sheriff's Deputies," *MJ* (Final), July 8, 1949.

68. "Negroes Stay at Camp after Unruly Meeting," *MJ,* July 9, 1949; "Ousted Negro Family Returns to Greenfield," *MS,* July 9, 1949; Thompson, *History of Wisconsin,* 335.

69. "Negroes Stay at Camp after Unruly Meeting"; "Scenes at Troubled Greenfield Camp," *MJ,* July 9, 1949; Thompson, *History of Wisconsin,* 335.

70. Kelley to Granger, July 12, 1949, National Urban League Papers, LOC.

71. "Ousted Negro Family Decides to Return to Trailer Campsite," *MJ,* July 8, 1949; and "Greenfield Vets Quarrel: Who's Boss Here?" *MJ,* July 10, 1949.

72. "Groups Argue in Camp Row," *MJ,* July 10, 1949. The battling residents' groups galvanized by this issue may have reflected a longer-standing struggle within the camp. The group supporting the Sanders family, the Veteran's Organization of Greenfield Trailer Camp, had been elected four months earlier. The anti-Sanders group, the Veterans Emergency Committee, sought new elections. "Greenfield Vet's Quarrel: Who's Boss Here?" *MS,* July 10, 1949.

73. By the end of the weekend, some camp residents were prepared to testify against the leaders of the mob that had threatened the Sanders family. Kelley to Granger, July 12, 1949, National Urban League Papers, LOC.

74. "Groups Argue in Camp Row," *MJ*, July 10, 1949.

75. Kelley to Granger, July 12, 1949, National Urban League Papers, LOC.

76. "Apologies End Outburst of Racial Row in Camp," *MJ*, July 12, 1949; "Trailerites' Apologies End Strife at Camp," *MS*, July 13, 1949; "Wife Stricken in Vet Trailer Park Tension," *MS*, July 12, 1949.

77. "Apologies End Outburst of Racial Row in Camp," *MJ*, July 12, 1949.

78. Ibid.

79. Ibid. Also quoted in Thompson, *History of Wisconsin*, 336.

80. General Meeting Minutes, July 13, 1949, Mayor's Commission on Human Relations and Executive Committee Minutes, July 16, 1949, Aug. 23, 1949, Mayor's Commission on Human Rights, Legislative Reference Bureau, City Hall, Milwaukee. The group's name had been changed from the Mayor's Commission on Human Relations to the Commission of Human Rights during this incident.

81. "Apologies End Outburst of Racial Row in Camp," *MJ*, July 12, 1949.

82. "Negroes Stay at Camp after Unruly Meeting," *MJ*, July 9, 1949. Norstrand was involved in other Popular Front organizations, including the Wisconsin Conference for Social Legislation. For Norstrand, see Gavett, *Development of the Labor Movement in Milwaukee*, 178; and United States Congress, House Committee on Un-American Activities, *Investigation of Communist Activities in the Milwaukee, Wis., Area: Hearings before the Committee on Un-American Activities*, 84th Cong., 1st sess., 1955.

83. "Apologies End Outburst of Racial Row in Camp," *MJ*, July 12, 1949; Mayor's Commission on Human Relations, General Meeting Minutes, July 13, 1949, Milwaukee Legislative Reference Bureau. Norstrand disputed these claims and objected to the newspaper reports.

84. The *Milwaukee Journal*, in an editorial titled "Right This Wrong to Negro Vet," decried the intolerance shown to the Sanders family. The editors argued that the actions of a few park residents had "degraded" all of Milwaukee and threatened the city with being "labeled a Jim Crow town." "Right This Wrong to Negro Vet," *MJ*, July 8, 1949. A few days later, the *Journal*'s editors celebrated the controversy's outcome, praising the city for its quick response. "From the first instant that the crisis arose, there were these two forces to combat the prejudice—firmness and democratic reasoning." "A Miracle Has Occurred," *MJ*, July 13, 1949. See also "The Eagle Still Rules the Roost" (editorial cartoon), *MJ*, July 14, 1949. For the convergence of Cold War ideology and civil rights, see especially Mary L. Dudziak, *Cold War Civil Rights: Race and the Image of American Democracy* (Princeton, N.J.: Princeton University Press, 2000); and Jennifer A. Delton, *Making Minnesota Liberal: Civil Rights and the Transformation of the Democratic Party* (Minneapolis: University of Minnesota Press, 2002).

85. The anti–public housing referendum, promoted by the Public Housing Referendum Committee and its allies, read: "That unless the electors of the City of Milwaukee shall give their approval by referendum, the City of Milwaukee shall not construct any additional housing projects, which are not subject to general property taxes at the same rate as privately owned property, and shall not authorize the Housing Authority of the City of Milwaukee to do so." Board of Election Commissioners, *Twenty-first Biennial Report of the Commissioners of the City of Milwaukee* (1951), 217.

86. The pro–public housing referendum, supported by the JACBH and others, asked:

"Shall slum clearance housing projects be built with federal funds under the 1949 Federal Housing Act irrespective of any other resolution or act?" Milwaukee Board of Election Commissioners, *Twenty-first Biennial Report,* 218.

87. The existing Hillside Terrace low-income public housing project, as well as a proposed addition and a planned redevelopment project in the Hillside neighborhood, came under close scrutiny and became the symbol for public housing in the city. The 1930s Parklawn Project now drew little direct notice. The new veterans' projects received considerable mention, but the privileged status of white veterans may have insulated these from concerted attack. This emphasis on Hillside resembles the dynamic Judith Walkowitz examines, in which the places and people deemed "socially peripheral" became "symbolically central." Walkowitz, *City of Dreadful Delight: Narratives of Sexual Danger in Late-Victorian London* (Chicago: University of Chicago Press, 1992), 20.

88. Federal legislation permitted PILOT up to 10 percent of shelter rents. For PILOT and public housing, see Housing and Home Finance Agency, "Explanation of 'Payments in Lieu of Taxes' Made by Local Housing Authorities," ca. 1950, and Housing Authority of the City of Milwaukee, "The Payment in Lieu of Taxes," Feb. 21, 1950, in folio "P.I.L.O.T.," box 4, Perrin Papers, Wisconsin Architectural Archive; "Study Re: Payments in Lieu of Taxes," Sept. 9, 1949, folio "Payments in Lieu of Taxes—PILOT," box 4, Warren Jay Vinton Papers, Division of Rare and Manuscript Collections, Carl A. Kroch Library, Cornell University. See also Groves et al., *Report of the Commission on the Economic Study of Milwaukee,* 135–39; and Housing Authority of the City of Milwaukee, *Annual Report for the Year 1952* (Milwaukee, 1953), 32–33.

89. "City News," *Journal of Housing* 7:12 (Dec. 1950): 427; "Housing Poll Rebuffed, Now Up to Council: Committee Hears Hot Arguments, Opposes Referendum; Full Vote Slated for Oct. 10," *MJ,* Oct. 3, 1950. At another point, Pieplow extended his complaint that those who lived in public housing, allowing others to subsidize their rent, were of questionable character: "Are the able bodied citizens of this day too physically soft, morally corrupt, confused, selfish, cowardly as not to be able to provide themselves with shelter?" William L. Pieplow to Mayor Zeidler, Jan. 19, 1951, folio 1, box 179, Zeidler Papers, MPL.

90. "Court May Get Petitions Row," *MJ,* Jan. 10, 1951.

91. The wording of the referendum had been considered carefully. Leonard Freedman, "Group Opposition to Public Housing" (Ph.D. diss., University of California, Los Angeles, 1959), 326. See also "Home-owners Revolt against No-Tax Housing," *MS,* Jan. 7, 1951. For controversies over tax-exempt public housing and PILOT in other cities, see Peter H. Henderson, "Local Deals and the New Deal State: Implementing Federal Public Housing in Baltimore, 1933–1968" (Ph.D. diss., Johns Hopkins University, 1993), 346–48, 355–57; and Sylvie Murray, *The Progressive Housewife: Community Activism in Suburban Queens, 1945–1965* (Philadelphia: University of Pennsylvania Press, 2003), 38–59.

92. McCarthy quoted in Rosalyn Baxandall and Elizabeth Ewen, *Picture Window: How the Suburbs Happened* (New York: Basic Books, 2000), 93.

93. On the connection of tax-paying and citizenship, see Alexander Keyssar, *The Right to Vote: The Contested History of Democracy in the United States* (New York: Basic Books, 2000); Linda K. Kerber, *No Constitutional Right to Be Treated Like Ladies: Women and the Obligations of Citizenship* (New York: Hill and Wang, 1998); and Self, *American Babylon.* In the hierarchy of citizenship suggested here, home owners stood at the top, followed by

renters in private housing, and finally tenants in public housing. See also Peter Dreier, "The Status of Tenants in the United States," *Social Problems* 30:2 (Dec. 1982): 179–98; Thomas J. Sugrue, "Crabgrass-Roots Politics: Race, Rights, and the Reaction against Liberalism in the Urban North, 1940–1964," *Journal of American History* 82:2 (Sept. 1995): 551–78; and Ronald Tobey, Charles Wetherell, and Jay Brigham, "Moving Out and Settling In: Residential Mobility, Home Owning, and the Public Enframing of Citizenship, 1921–1950," *American Historical Review* 95 (Dec. 1990): 1395–1422. For social citizenship, see Alice Kessler-Harris, "In the Nation's Image: The Gendered Limits of Social Citizenship in the Depression Era," *Journal of American History* 86:3 (Dec. 1999): 1251–79.

94. On dependency, see Nancy Fraser and Linda Gordon, "A Genealogy of *Dependency*: Tracing a Keyword of the U.S. Welfare State," *Signs* 19:2 (Winter 1994): 309–36. Such characterizations of public housing residents stood in stark contrast to depictions of white families moving to the suburbs during this time, the beneficiaries of federally subsidized mortgage programs, tax policies, and highway construction. Kenneth T. Jackson, *Crabgrass Frontier: The Suburbanization of the United States* (New York: Oxford University Press, 1985); Baxandall and Ewen, *Picture Windows;* and Thomas W. Hanchett, "The Other 'Subsidized Housing': Federal Aid to Suburbanization, 1940s to 1960s," in *From Tenements to the Taylor Homes: In Search of an Urban Housing Policy in Twentieth-Century America,* ed. John F. Bauman, Roger Biles, and Kristin M. Szylvian (University Park: Pennsylvania State University Press, 2000), 163–79.

95. "Public Housing Vote Is Likely," *MJ,* Jan. 19, 1951.

96. Plantz's 1952 statement quoted in Gurda, *Making of Milwaukee,* 363.

97. Previously, the working-class city had served as the metaphor for the "outmoded city." By the 1950s (evident in the 1951 public housing controversy and in the 1952 and 1956 mayoral contests) a class-specific understanding of race had become the central metaphor for "urban decay." See Fure-Slocum, "Challenge of the Working-Class City," chap. 7. The argument that race functions not only as a line of division but as the metaphorical field on which "backwardness" and "modernity" are defined builds on the insights of Toni Morrison, *Playing in the Dark: Whiteness and the Literary Imagination* (Cambridge: Harvard University Press, 1992). For mid-century black migrants, see Geib, "From Mississippi to Milwaukee"; and Kimberly L. Phillips, *AlabamaNorth: African-American Migrants, Community, and Working-Class Activism in Cleveland, 1915–45* (Urbana: University of Illinois Press, 1999). For the 1956 mayoral campaign, in which Zeidler's opponent circulated rumors that he had put up billboards in the South, inviting African Americans to move to Milwaukee, see Zeidler, "Liberal in City Government," chap. 4, 414–38; Kevin D. Smith, "From Socialism to Racism: The Politics of Class and Identity in Postwar Milwaukee," *Michigan Historical Review* 29 (Spring 2003): 86–87; and "The Shame of Milwaukee," *Time,* Apr. 2, 1956, 23.

98. On racialized citizenship and "white privilege," see George Lipsitz, "The Possessive Investment in Whiteness: Racialized Social Democracy and the 'White' Problem in American Studies," *American Quarterly* 47:3 (Sept. 1995): 369–87; and David R. Roediger, *Working Toward Whiteness: How America's Immigrants Became White* (New York: Basic Books, 2005).

99. "No Tax Loss in Housing," *Milwaukee Labor Press,* Feb. 8, 1951; "'No' Vote on Referendum," *Milwaukee Labor Press,* Mar. 15, 1951. The County Property Owners for Public Housing advanced three main arguments: "First, slums produce extra costs; second, the

available federal money comes from the taxes that are partly paid by Milwaukeeans and if not used up will be spent elsewhere; and finally, public housing projects pay more in lieu of taxes to the city than the same properties paid on taxes before." The flyer "Facts on Housing from Home Owners" contrasted the shortcomings of private enterprise in housing and slum clearance to the advantages of public enterprise. Flyer, Milwaukee Property Owners for Public Housing, ca. 1951, folio 7D, box 214, Krug Speeches—Miscellaneous Collection, Milwaukee Public Library.

100. The CIO reprinted a Chicago editorial, stating the same applied to Milwaukee. "Public Housing Pays Off," *Wisconsin CIO News,* Jan. 26, 1951. See also "Slums Cost You Money," *Wisconsin CIO News,* Feb. 9, 1951.

101. Richard W. E. Perrin to Mayor Frank P. Zeidler, June 27, 1950, folio 1 "Public Housing, 1949–1951," box 180, Zeidler Papers, MPL. In another report, the Housing Authority calculated that the average Hillside resident "formerly paid $24.68 per year in taxes as compared to $30.00 as a payment in lieu of taxes." Housing Authority of the City of Milwaukee, "The Payment In Lieu of Taxes," Feb. 21, 1950, 5, folio "P.I.L.O.T.," box 4, Richard W. E. Perrin Papers, Wisconsin Architectural Archives, Milwaukee, Wisconsin. See also "Public Housing Yields Cities More Revenue Than Did Former Taxes," *Wall Street Journal,* Jan. 30, 1951; and Richard W. E. Perrin, "The Case for Public Housing," Feb. 4, 1951, 10, folio 2 "Housing Referendum (Feb.-Apr. 1951)," box 179, Zeidler Papers, MPL.

102. Richard W. E. Perrin to Mayor Frank P. Zeidler, June 27, 1950, folio 1 "Public Housing, 1949–1951," box 180, Zeidler Papers, MPL; and Citizens Anti-Slum Committee, "Public Housing—A Sound Investment," ca. 1951, folio 1, box 180, Zeidler Papers, MPL.

103. See letters in support of public housing addressed to Mayor Zeidler, folio 1 "Housing Referendum (1950–Jan. 1951)," box 179, Zeidler Papers. See also Zeidler, "Liberal in City Government," chap. 4, 181–212.

104. On the contested relationship between public housing and redevelopment, see Senator Robert F. Wagner to Paul U. Kellogg, Oct. 10, 1947, reel 53, (microfilm 256), part 1, Survey Associates Records, University Publications of America; Housing and Home Finance Agency, *The Relationship between Slum Clearance and Urban Redevelopment and Low-Rent Public Housing* (Washington, D.C.: Government Printing Office, 1950); "Is Public Housing Needed for Urban Redevelopment?" *American City* 63:11 (Nov. 1948): 84–87; John F. Bauman, "The Paradox of Post-War Urban Planning: Downtown Revitalization versus Decent Housing for All," in *Two Centuries of American Planning,* ed. Daniel Schaffer (Baltimore: Johns Hopkins University Press, 1988), 231–64; Kenneth Fox Gotham, *Race, Real Estate, and Uneven Development: The Kansas City Experience, 1900–2000* (Albany: State University of New York Press, 2002), 71–89; Alexander von Hoffman, "The End of the Dream: The Political Struggle for America's Public Housers," *Journal of Planning History* 4:3 (2005): 222–53; and Radford, *Modern Housing for America,* 189–91.

105. Richard W. E. Perrin, "Civic Projects Endangered if Federal Housing Aid Lost," Mar. 15, 1951, Milwaukee Department of City Development Archives; and "Housing Vote Could End All Federal Help," *MJ,* Jan. 23, 1951. See also Richard W. E. Perrin to Mayor Frank P. Zeidler, Jan. 17, 1951, folio 1 "Housing Referendum (1950–Jan. 1951)," box 179, Zeidler Papers, MPL.

106. The *Journal* had noted that the slum clearance areas accommodating public hous-

ing would serve other purposes as well: the "cleared land will also open areas for *private development* and will bring greater tax returns to the city." "Housing Referendum Unwise" (editorial), *MJ*, Feb. 11, 1950 (emphasis in original). See also Zeidler, "Liberal in City Government," chap. 4, 162; and "Housing Poll Rebuffed, Now up to Council," *MJ*, Oct. 3, 1950.

107. "Milwaukee: You Can Defeat Enemies of City Progress if You Will Vote," *MJ*, Apr. 1, 1951. See also "Milwaukee: Redevelopment and Slum Clearance Need More Citizen Action," *MJ*, Jan. 13, 1951. At the same time, the *Journal* was careful not to identify too closely with the public housing forces, remaining critical of Mayor Frank Zeidler and others for both demands that the Public Housing Referendum Committee disclose its supporters and charges against the national Real Estate Lobby. Zeidler, "Liberal in City Government," chap. 4, 206.

108. A pro-debt coalition made up of downtown and metropolitan business and civic leaders, including heads of financial institutions, retail businesses, services, real estate interests, and the two major newspapers, had argued that the city should begin issuing bonds for a program of public improvements. To boost support for the 1947 measure, debt proponents had agreed not to begin their program of public improvements until the postwar housing shortage had been eased. This concession mollified many of the labor, women, veteran, and civic activists, as well as Democratic Party reformers, who had been pressing local and federal officials to address the housing shortage. The alliance drew housing and urban redevelopment together, tying these policies and their supporters to the growth politics that animated the pro-debt campaign. Eric Fure-Slocum, "Cities with Class?: Growth Politics, the Working-Class City, and Debt in Milwaukee during the 1940s," *Social Science History* 24:1 (Spring 2000): 257–305. For the politics of housing and development in other postwar cities, see John Bauman, *Public Housing, Race, and Renewal*, 79–143; John H. Mollenkopf, *The Contested City* (Princeton, N.J.: Princeton University Press, 1983); Don Parson, *Making a Better World: Public Housing, the Red Scare, and the Direction of Modern Los Angeles* (Minneapolis: University of Minnesota Press, 2005); Wendell Pritchett, *Brownsville, Brooklyn: Blacks, Jews, and the Changing Face of the Ghetto* (Chicago: University of Chicago Press, 2002); Jon C. Teaford, *The Rough Road to Renaissance: Urban Revitalization in America, 1940–1985* (Baltimore: Johns Hopkins University Press, 1990); and Schwartz, *New York Approach*. The alliance between elements of the public housing coalition and pro-growth downtown leaders was evidenced also in the city's reforming Democratic Party. State legislator Robert Tehan authored Wisconsin's redevelopment provisions. Henry Reuss, a founder of the Urban Redevelopment Corporation, was among the first to try to use Wisconsin's redevelopment laws in proposing the Red Arrow housing and redevelopment plan in 1947. Neighborhood protests defeated the plan. Tehan and Reuss, along with the future mayor, Henry W. Maier, were active in the anticommunist liberal Democratic Organizing Committee (DOC). For the Red Arrow controversy, see "Reuss Tells Fine Points of Red Arrow Housing," *MJ*, Sept. 10, 1947; "Bill He Helped Raise to Law May Raze the Home of Tehan," *MJ*, Sept. 10, 1947; and "Red Arrow Housing Stirs Bitter Wrangle," *MJ*, Sept. 25, 1947. See also "Housing Poll Rebuffed, Now up to Council," *MJ*, Oct. 3, 1950. For the DOC and Democratic reformers, see Alexander Shashko, "'Shoe Leather and Perspiration': Grassroots Liberalism and the Building of the Wisconsin Democratic Party at Mid-Century," *Wisconsin Law Review* (2003): 1–30; and

Richard C. Haney, "The Rise of Wisconsin's New Democrats: A Political Realignment in the Mid-Twentieth Century," *Wisconsin Magazine of History* 58:2 (Winter 1974–75): 91–106. For conservatives and others who changed their position on public housing due to development concerns, see William L. Pieplow to Mayor Zeidler, Jan. 19, 1951, folio 1 "Housing Referendum (1950–Jan. 1951)," box 179, Zeidler Papers, MPL; and Zeidler, "Liberal in City Government," chap. 4, 207–8.

109. "Public Housing Vote Is Likely," *MJ,* Jan. 19, 1951.

110. "Two Measures Conflict: Court Test Forecast," *MJ,* Apr. 4, 1951; and "Housing Mixup Seems Headed for Court," *MS,* Apr. 5, 1951.

111. About one-third of registered Milwaukeeans voted, a solid turnout for an off-year spring election. A rent control measure on the spring ballot also scored a solid victory, with 59 percent of the vote, but a slightly lower number of voters weighing in on the question. Board of Election Commissioners, *Twenty-first Biennial Report* (1951), 217–19, 279; and Milwaukee Common Council, *Milwaukee Annual Report of Work Done in 1951* (Milwaukee: Municipal Reference Library, 1952), 52–53.

112. Milwaukee's Twenty-second and Twenty-sixth Wards gave the anti–public housing measure its strongest margins. Sixty-one percent of those voting, or twenty percent of registered voters in these districts, favored putting the brakes on Milwaukee's public housing program. These two northwest wards also scored the highest "no" votes on the pro–public housing measure. Board of Election Commissioners, *Twenty-first Biennial Report* (1951); Bureau of the Census, *1950 United States Census of Population, Census Tract Statistics: Milwaukee, Wisconsin and Adjacent Area; 1950 United States Census of Housing: Block Statistics, Milwaukee, Wisconsin* (Washington, D.C.: U.S. Government Printing Office, 1952).

113. Over 70 percent of those voting in the Third, Fourth, and Sixth Wards marked "yes" for the pro–public housing referendum. These were areas with public housing or redevelopment projects on the drawing boards. These wards also topped the tallies for "no" votes on the anti–public housing measure, with 60 percent or more voting against the proposal to cut off public housing.

114. Calculating the "yes" vote for the pro–public housing referendum as a percentage of registered voters highlights another set of wards and constituencies that proved especially important at this juncture in the city's history. In addition to the Third and Fourth Wards, the First and Eighteenth Wards had the highest "yes" votes as a percentage of registered voters (the Sixth Ward drops off the list because of its lower voter turnout rate). The Eighteenth Ward, which had been the top supporter of the pro-growth debt referendum in 1947, favored an aggressive urban policy that included public housing and redevelopment programs. This ward had the largest percentage of white-collar workers and the highest house values in the city. The First Ward, also near those areas slated for redevelopment, contained a mix of white-collar and working-class residents. Home-ownership rates in the First, Third, and Fourth Wards were the lowest in the city; the affluent Eighteenth Ward fell in the middle of the city's range.

115. For a discussion of the data and methodology used in these statistical analyses, see Fure-Slocum, "Challenge of the Working-Class City," chaps. 5, 7. Regression analyses of the "yes" vote on the anti–public housing referendum and the "no" vote on the pro–public housing measure produce the clearest results. The lack of clear distinctions between

independent variables' influences reinforces the interpretation that civic, business, and liberal leaders' efforts to build a broad, cross-class alliance supporting redevelopment and public housing (as imagined by the *Milwaukee Journal* and other growth proponents) had succeeded.

116. A comparison between the 1951 public housing referenda votes, the 1947 debt referendum, and the 1948 mayoral votes illustrates the emergence of new ideological and political formations in the city. Home ownership was an increasingly important variable in defining political alignments. The leaders of the anti–public housing movement had managed, in part, to fashion an identity politics of white, taxpaying, home owners. But these politics were most attractive to upper-income home owners. See Fure-Slocum, "Cities with Class?" The increase of home ownership in Milwaukee from 32 percent in 1940 to approximately 42 percent in 1950 (or from 37 to 50 percent in the county) strengthened their political and social position: Milwaukee Public Library, *Milwaukee City and County*, 13.

117. Interpretations of modern populism, which highlight white working-class backlash (and which misleadingly point to Joe McCarthy's 1946 Senate election as evidence of working-class conservatism), include Daniel Bell, ed., *The New American Right* (New York: Criterion Books, 1955); and Michael Kazin, *The Populist Persuasion: An American History* (New York: Basic Books, 1995). Given Milwaukee's racial segregation and the absence of precinct-level data for mid-century referenda contests, a quantitative analysis of the 1951 and 1947 referenda votes falters when comparing black and white voters. The city's African American voters, however, apparently gave the public housing measure strong support. This analysis of the 1951 controversy does indicate that white voters living close to Milwaukee's African American neighborhoods, many of whom both understood central city housing conditions and possibly had some degree of interracial experience, were less likely to oppose public housing than those living on the edge of the city, many of whom had recently relocated from older neighborhoods.

118. On the two-tiered housing policy in the United States see, for instance, Catherine Bauer, "The Dreary Deadlock of Public Housing," *Architectural Forum* 106:5 (May 1957): 140–42, 219, 221; Roger Biles, "Public Housing and the Postwar Urban Renaissance, 1949–1973," in *From Tenements to the Taylor Homes,* 143–62; and Radford, *Modern Housing for America.* See also J. S. Fuerst, *When Public Housing Was Paradise: Building Community in Chicago* (Urbana: University of Illinois Press, 2005).

119. At the beginning of his term, Mayor Zeidler had proposed building 10,000 units of public housing. Following the passage of the 1949 Housing Act, Milwaukee had been slated to build 2,500 low-income public housing units. But Milwaukee's public housing program slowed considerably in the wake of the referenda controversy, taking it over fifteen years to approach even the lower goal. See Joel Rast, "Governing the Regimeless City: The Frank Zeidler Administration in Milwaukee, 1948–1960," *Urban Affairs Review* 42:1 (Sept. 2006): 81–112; and Robert M. Beckley, "The Effects of Federal Programs on Housing and the Quality of Life: The Milwaukee Case," in *Milwaukee's Economy: Market Forces, Community Problems, and Federal Policies,* ed. John P. Blair and Ronald S. Edari (Chicago: Federal Reserve Bank, 1978), 145–46. See also D. Bradford Hunt, "How Did Public Housing Survive the 1950s?" *Journal of Policy History* 17:2 (2005): 193–216; and Don Parson, "The Decline of Public Housing and the Politics of the Red Scare: The Sig-

nificance of the Los Angeles Public Housing War," *Journal of Urban History* 33:3 (Mar. 2007): 400–417.

120. Public housing residents, of course, did not give up their hopes for a more democratic life in the city. For Baltimore public housing residents' activism, see Rhonda Y. Williams, *The Politics of Public Housing: Black Women's Struggles against Urban Inequality* (New York: Oxford University Press, 2004).

7. Mexican American Workers, Clinton Jencks, and Mine-Mill Social Activism in the Southwest, 1945–52

JAMES J. LORENCE

Historians of the southwestern labor movement have long acknowledged the significance of the Western Federation of Miners' radical tradition as an influence on its militant successor, the International Union of Mine, Mill, and Smelter Workers (Mine-Mill). By the 1940s Mine-Mill in the Southwest had become the vehicle for the expression of the Mexican American drive for social and economic equality, which was itself rooted in a sometimes neglected dimension of the Mexican American experience: the involvement of Chicano/a workers in aggressive union organizing within the framework of industrial capitalism. Spurned by the craft-oriented AFL, New Mexico and Arizona copper and zinc miners turned to the CIO, which stood for a more sweeping vision of social, economic, and racial equality than that contemplated by the business unions of the 1930s and 1940s. Among the most outspoken in their insistence on full equality were Communists, who later occupied some key positions in CIO unions. As Douglas Monroy and Mario T. Garcia have demonstrated, Mexican American workers inherited a resilient radical tradition that reflected their "outsider" status as either deposed landholders or vulnerable immigrants in the American Southwest.[1] Through Mine-Mill, a small but militant Mexican American Left challenged the predominant assumptions of many Americans, including unionists, in the early Cold War era.

Left-wing activism in the Southwest was rooted in deep resentment over systematic discrimination against Latinos, who were subject to discounted wages, segregated housing, unequal education, and social proscription throughout the region. While ethnic and labor ties were close in border areas like El Paso before World War II, wartime economic conditions stimulated the growth of Mexican American labor consciousness in more remote areas such as Clifton-Morenci, Arizona, and Silver City, New Mexico. Here fraternal associations, ethnic religious communities, and other mutual support organizations originally developed during the Great Depression formed a solid foundation for the development of a postwar labor movement rooted in ethnic identity. In Grant County, New Mexico, a base for activism grew out of lingering objections to the social and economic discrimination that had long doomed the Mexican American community to second-class citizenship.[2] This residual militancy fired the ethnic community leadership that ignited the union movement when Mine-Mill reentered the area in the postwar era.

In New Mexico, these Mexican American workers made common cause with Anglos within Mine-Mill's rank and file and leadership to build a democratic union committed to civil rights and workplace equality. To these hardcore unionists, the "Communist issue didn't matter a hoot." IUMMSW legal counsel Nathan Witt asserted that ideology took a back seat to racial equality with Mexican American unionists who might not have known "whether they're Reds or not," but "certainly know how they respond to black Americans." Impressed by the union's strong defense of African American miners and steelworkers in Alabama, Mine-Mill's southwestern adherents made common cause with other people of color in support of a color-blind unionism not always evident in mainstream AFL unions. Reflecting with pride on Mine-Mill's success in removing discrimination, executive board member Orville Larson later maintained that its record in race relations was one of the union's greatest achievements. Even more significant, he argued, was the organization's success in building solidarity between Anglos and Chicanos: "Most of the Anglos were from the non-union country—Oklahoma, Texas, and Arkansas. But they wanted a union. And they were perfectly willing to go along with the battle against discrimination with the Chicanos because they knew that they too were being discriminated against. They had enough sense to realize that."[3]

A central participant in Mine-Mill's drive to promote interracial collaboration was the militant Clinton E. Jencks, an extraordinary Anglo organizer active in Grant County, New Mexico, the site of the well-known Empire Zinc strike of 1951. Jencks, who later figured prominently in the conception and production of the landmark independent film, *Salt of the Earth,* exemplified Mine-Mill's brand of political radicalism, social unionism, and class awareness. This essay examines the origins and development of Jencks's economic, social, and political ideas and traces his labor activism from the end of World War II to the Empire Zinc strike in 1951. In the process, it also explores the foundations of his political commitment and accounts for his decision to embrace unionism as the means by which socioeconomic equality might be best achieved in postwar America.

Born in 1918 in a racially integrated working-class district of Colorado Springs, Jencks grew up in a conservative, devoutly Christian family environment. The product of a working-class family, Jencks saw in his neighborhood "the significant differences in opportunities available according to one's economic status." It is clear that his strong social conscience was rooted in these childhood observations. Strongly influenced by his mother's deep religious commitment, Clint saw activist Christianity as a solution to the social inequities that surrounded him. Appalled by the selfishness and greed he saw in the human community, Jencks clung to the conviction that "the church was the one hope of eliminating injustice and bigotry." As a result, he contemplated the ministry or missionary work "as a way of encouraging love between all our human family."[4]

Side by side with strong Christian faith, Jencks also developed a keen interest in labor history. His interest in the abandoned mining towns of Colorado led to the study of labor exploitation in the Rocky Mountain West, including the radical responses of the Populists, IWW, and the Western Federation of Miners. He also read widely about "Socialist ideas as a way of bringing love, compassion, and brotherhood to earth." Alive with thoughts of Ludlow, Bisbee, and "the courageous Eugene Debs," the youthful Jencks learned firsthand of economic man's duplicity when his Sunday school group took food baskets to the homes of striking coal miners, only to find eviction notices bearing the signature of a local banker who was also the Sunday school superintendent. By the mid-1930s, Jencks was already exploring a wide variety of solutions, not found in the church of his childhood, to the problem of class inequities. Before his college years, he had written to a relative, a lawyer for the Communist Party-dominated International Labor Defense, to seek personal advice on potentially effective forms of social activism. While at the University of Colorado, Jencks also helped organize and became the first president of the Boulder chapter of the American Student Union, an avowedly radical organization. Alarmed by the rise of racism and anti-Semitism in Germany, in 1938 Jencks and the ASU launched a sharp attack on campus racial discrimination. Thus, before graduating from college, Jencks had embarked on a career of left-wing political activity that would shape his life for the ensuing twenty years.[5]

After college, Jencks worked as a customer-service accountant in St. Louis, where he participated in the interracial Inter-Faith Youth Council. Here he met his future wife, Virginia, who was to be his partner in union organizing after the war. Council work also led him to join the St. Louis chapter of the progressive American Youth Congress, which elected Jencks secretary in 1940. During World War II, Jencks volunteered for the Army Air Force and served in the Pacific theater with distinction, earning the Distinguished Flying Cross, six air medals, and four battle stars for bravery in combat.[6]

When the war was over, Jencks worked first as a baggage handler and later in flight control with Continental Airlines. Laid off at Continental, he found employment as a laborer at the Globe Smelter division of the American Smelting and Refining Company in Denver, where he joined Mine-Mill Local 557 as a rank-and-file union member. Before long, he was elected shop steward. Returning to political activism, he also helped organize the Denver chapter of the new American Veterans Committee, which he chaired. Open to collaboration with all groups on the political spectrum, including the Communist Party, AVC sought "to achieve a more democratic and prosperous America and a more stable world." Moreover, its membership united in the belief that "government was the principal instrument for making that dream come true." The organization worked to promote racial justice, full employment, veterans' housing, and national health insurance, and succeeded in achieving special funding for retraining, education, and housing, activities that made the organization a "refreshing voice for veterans beyond the jingoistic breast-beating of the American Legion and the VFW."[7]

From the very beginning of his tenure as AVC's Rocky Mountain Regional vice chairman, Jencks fought discrimination of all kinds. Under his leadership, the Denver AVC Council lobbied vigorously for the establishment of a Fair Employment Practices Committee for Colorado, insisting that a state FEPC was essential to the fight "against racial and religious discrimination." In order to advance these goals, in 1946 Jencks ran unsuccessfully as a Democrat for a seat in the Colorado State Assembly. FBI observers regarded this race as an extension of Communist Party activity, noting that the CP "campaigned extensively for Jencks's election" and that the candidate "pulled heavily in the precincts in which they did their work." As a "strong advocate of militant action of any sort," Jencks soon became a critic of the original AVC leadership. Acknowledging the pressures exerted by the anticommunist bloc within the AVC, Jencks told the Mountain States membership in 1946 that "no outside smears or outside interventions" had hurt the organization "as much as the artificially projected communist issue."[8]

It is clear, then, that by 1946 Jencks was active in causes supported by the Communist Party, which he believed "came closest to working in real life for a more democratic, humane, and just society and contained some of the most committed people working to improve life for all in the here and now, to reduce discrimination and exploitation for whatever reason, whether race, sex, national origin or other 'excuse.'" While Jencks never acknowledged his role in the Communist movement, recent scholarship suggests that, in historian Ellen Schrecker's words, "it is hard to imagine that he was not" actively involved. Bright, educated, and politically committed, he rose rapidly within Mine-Mill ranks. Within one year, he had become a leader in his local union, at which time Orville Larson, IUMMSW District 2 Executive Board member, urged him to go to Grant County, New Mexico, to work for five local unions as local union representative. After consultation with Virginia, herself a "strong, union-minded person," Jencks accepted the assignment and went to work in Silver City. Grant County, with its large population of Mexican American miners, proved to be a fertile field in which to "create political, economic, and social forms" that would "empower and mutually benefit all." In this effort, Jencks espoused a brand of unionism that was open to all those who actually worked for a more democratic, humane, and just society, including Communists, Socialists, and liberal Democrats.[9]

The arrival of Clinton and Virginia Jencks in Grant County, New Mexico, in 1947 reignited the flames of Mexican American unionism in the Southwest. Building on a preexisting sense of community among Mexican American miners and their families, their long-standing resistance to discrimination, and the WFM heritage of militant unionism, the Jenckses worked tirelessly to unite the worker community in a class-based movement capable of fighting racial discrimination and economic injustice. Clinton Jencks later asserted that one of his most important contributions to the struggle was to abandon "preconceived ideas as to what the people I was to serve needed and wanted." Equally significant was a firm determination to become a part of the community he entered. Not only did the Jenckses establish residence in the community, but they also worked actively to build Mexican American union leadership; in effect, Jencks sought to work himself out of a job. The crucial step in the direction of effective union organization was the amalgamation of five separate locals into what became the powerful Mine-Mill Local 890. Some scholars have seen the Jenckses as carriers of a Communist-inspired "radical movement culture"[10] that transformed the Grant County labor movement, a view that underestimates the power and resiliency of the host community. In fact, Jencks maintained that a "radical movement culture" already existed in "the awakening giant" of Grant County's working people "long before [he] got there," and that his own "commitment to one people, one world, rank and file democratically-controlled unionism" merely helped to "strengthen ordinary working people in their pride in themselves, their contribution in our society, and in their ability to improve their own lives and the lives of others."[11]

Most Grant County workers recognized that there was ample room for such improvement in the southwestern New Mexico mining district of the 1940s. Many mining towns were company towns in which management held workers in a semi-feudal state of peonage. Strict segregation existed in housing and on the job. The mining corporations maintained a dual payroll system that enforced a double wage standard to the disadvantage of Mexican American workers. Moreover, Mexican Americans were not permitted to rise above the job classification of "helper," even if they had spent thirty or forty years on the job. Typically, unskilled work was reserved for Mexican Americans. And in the community, social sanctions were often imposed on Hispanic workers and their families through efforts to discourage the use of the Spanish language and maintain separate facilities in public accommodations such as rest rooms, theaters, and restaurants.[12]

It was these conditions that enraged a new generation of Mexican American activists who returned from World War II service with new ideas concerning their economic and social position. Jencks later recalled veterans who returned to New Mexico "with enhanced pride and self-esteem" only to be "angered to find old Anglo prejudices still pervasive." Arturo Flores, for example, learned in the service that a "great myth" of inferiority had been perpetuated, and "made up [his] mind that [he] was going to come back and change things." Similarly, in 1946, when denied skilled work, Juan Chacón resolved to build a union movement that would advance the "welfare of the workers." Both were inspired by the commitment evident in the work of fellow veteran Clinton Jencks, who treated them with respect as "total human beings." According to Flores, when Jencks proposed amalgamation his young stewards responded with enthusiasm and "together [they] pushed it." The result was the strengthening of the local's militant Mexican American leadership corps. The amalgamation of five separate local unions reflected vibrant left-wing union leadership that successfully "connected workplace with community issues."[13]

The consequences of amalgamation were immense. A new weekly radio program, union newspaper, and a large union hall enhanced the sense of community solidarity in the Bayard mining district. Equally significant were the inauguration of family meetings and the establishment of Ladies' Auxiliary Local 209 in 1948, which was to have profoundly important implications during the Empire Zinc strike. While gender solidarity had long been strong in the mining camps, it was the feminist Virginia Jencks who spurred the women of Grant County's Mexican American community into action. Indeed, Mine-Mill secretary-treasurer Maurice Travis regarded her as the "bigger trouble maker of the two." When Virginia and Clinton Jencks first proposed a women's organization, the reaction was mixed; but through house-to-house solicitation, Virginia Chacón, Marianna Ramirez, Virginia Jencks, and their supporters were able to build a local group that would soon give new meaning to the term "auxiliary." Unlike most unions in the 1940s, the Mine-Mill International granted women voting rights in local meetings, which convinced many of Local 890's women that their participation in the organization was valued. Moving slowly, the local designated one meeting per month a family meeting, which enabled husbands, wives, and children to join for social interaction as well as discussion of current political issues.[14]

From local concerns, it was but a short step for Auxiliary Local 209 to urge in 1949 that the militant New Mexico Asociación Nacional México-Americana (ANMA) adopt a full program of "Equality and Fraternity of Mexican American Women," which was intended to help union women to "grow and learn, and to work for themselves through organization." In Grant County, Virginia Chacón recalled the auxiliary as the "backbone of the union," in that it educated women on the union's objectives while helping to define the central place of women in the organization. Working to move women beyond strictly domestic concerns, Local 209 became socially active through leafleting campaigns, consumer boycotts of businesses that discriminated against Mexican Americans, and eventually engagement in political campaigns. Even the inevitable social events that became women's organizational responsibility constituted a vital part of Local 890's fund-raising program.[15] In all these ways, the women made the union their instrument and invested themselves in the organization.

As early as 1947, the Jenckses and their allies also promoted the establishment of the Grant County Joint Labor Council, a move intended to cement unity among all local labor groups and prepare for political action in 1948. In September 1947 the council, representing three thousand unionists (primarily Mine-Mill members), organized to "promote victory at the ballot box and the bargaining table." Taking aim at U.S. Senator Carl Hatch and the "Taft-Hartley slave labor law," the council advocated a farmer-labor-progressive alliance to "ensure the election of *real* representatives." The Grant County body called on every CIO, AFL, and Railroad Brotherhood local in New Mexico to use labor's "organizational machinery" and "fraternal solidarity" to "answer the Tafts and Hartleys" and work to prevent the "Third and Last World War." Endorsing a broad progressive agenda, the council assumed leadership of the effort to launch a political movement at a statewide labor conference held in November 1947. The state conference in Albuquerque established the New Mexico Labor Coordinating Committee to mobilize workers behind pro-labor and liberal Democratic candidates in 1948.[16]

The original objectives of the Coordinating Committee, while focused on the Taft-Hartley Act and labor's perception of an ongoing assault against unionism, were also consistent with those of the Communist Party and other progressive critics of the Truman foreign policies. In 1948, however, when the CP embraced the third-party candidacy of Henry A. Wallace, Jencks and his Local 890 supporters quickly reassessed their initial decision to campaign for liberal Democrats. In January 1948 a subsequent conference in Carlsbad, dominated by Mine-Mill but also attended by other CIO unionists, endorsed Henry Wallace for president and fragmented the recently established labor coalition. The conference broke up over Mine-Mill's Wallace endorsement, after which Jencks was elected committee chairman and Mine-Mill's Chet Smotherman of Carlsbad Local 415 became secretary-treasurer. By this time, the national CIO leadership's opposition to the Wallace campaign, combined with the Communist Party decision to embrace the Progressive challenger, had split liberal unionists. Jencks later acknowledged the disruptive impact of the Wallace candidacy on labor's united front but maintained that efforts at labor unity in Grant County could not survive Kennecott Copper Corporation's steadfast refusal to negotiate a new contract due to Mine-Mill's unwillingness to comply with the Taft-Hartley Act's non-Communist affidavit provision. Unmentioned but equally damaging was Mine-Mill's insistence on a Wallace endorsement that alienated mainstream labor in New Mexico. Nonetheless, Jencks argued that these fledgling steps toward inter-union cooperation were important because they enabled Mine-Mill leaders to become acquainted with the AFL and Railroad Brotherhood craft unionists, thus laying a foundation for later successes.[17]

In the short run, however, Mine-Mill leaders moved aggressively into electoral politics as Progressive activists. At the statewide Progressive Party convention, Locals 890 and 415 succeeded in blocking an effort by Albuquerque and Santa Fe delegates to exclude Communists from party membership. Beyond local campaigning for the Wallace-Taylor ticket, Grant County unionists ran a full slate of Progressive candidates, including Clinton Jencks for Congress, Juan Chacón for State Senate, Brijido Provencio for U.S. Senate, and Henry Magdaleno Lujan for county sheriff. Although this effort clearly reflected the social and political aspirations of the mining community, FBI watchdogs dismissed the Progressive campaign as a completely Communist Party enterprise; and there is no doubt that it reflected a CP agenda. While some of its candidates were CP members, many rank-and-file Progressives simply supported a liberal political program. From the outset, the new party's outnumbered supporters embraced a Progressive agenda summarized by Virginia Chacón as a platform of "justice, equality, solidarity, and peace." None of the Progressive candidates polled more than 10 percent of the vote, and most received less. While their campaign clearly indicated that union activists were prepared to demand social and political equity in a rapidly changing society, it was an inauspicious electoral beginning.[18]

Symptomatic of the new militancy was the intensification of efforts to organize the Mexican American community for political action. While generally critical of the Wallace failure to reach Mexican American voters, one California Chicano told the Progressive National Committee that in New Mexico, Mexicanos were "seasoned in politics." His analysis confirmed the progress made by Jencks and Mine-Mill in fostering the mining community's emergence as a force for social and political change. As early as September 1947, IUMMSW International convention delegates unanimously approved a sweeping condemnation of discrimination in all forms. This resolution also urged that Mine-Mill give "special attention" to "segregation against the Mexican people" through full support of the fledgling Committee to Organize the Mexican People (COMP). On the convention floor Jencks denounced corporate discrimination against Mexican Americans, including housing segregation and wage differentials, both issues brought to the debate by Grant County locals.[19]

As a follow-up, Jencks urged Mine-Mill President Maurice Travis and the Mine-Mill Executive Committee to commit union financial resources to COMP, which he regarded as the "indispensable ally of the organized union movement in defense of our living standards, our democracy, our hopes for effective political action." He argued that in the Southwest COMP could also "provide a necessary means of social organization and protection, meeting problems our unions cannot handle." Jencks and his Grant County allies had long seen social action as a critical dimension of any effort to mobilize the mining communities of the Southwest politically. This analysis was confirmed when COMP and its successor, *Amigos de Wallace,* worked feverishly to organize Mexican American voters behind the Progressive presidential candidate. While Mexican American support for Wallace was thin, the organizational steps taken by Mine-Mill in 1947 and 1948 laid the basis for further, more aggressive leadership in the drive for equality.[20]

Perhaps the most significant expression of this activism was the formation in 1949 of the militant Asociación Nacional México-Americana (ANMA), which committed itself to an aggressive defense of Mexican Americans and

Mexican culture. Organized by Mine-Mill out of Denver, ANMA hoped to maintain coordination among surviving chapters of *Amigos de Wallace*. Composed of two thousand members drawn primarily from the ranks of the CIO, ANMA viewed the Mexican American population of the United States as solidly working class and acted upon that analysis to move its people toward class action. It embraced the civil rights movement and demanded economic equality for oppressed peoples at home and abroad. Accordingly, the organization launched a national attack on discrimination in employment, education, and the media. Symbolic of its roots in the union movement was the leadership provided by Alfredo Montoya, a Mine-Mill activist who in 1949 became ANMA president. It was ANMA's misfortune that it became politically assertive at the precise historical moment when the American public was becoming more conservative and anticommunist.[21]

Although Montoya had read Marx and was "influenced by left thinking," he never acknowledged membership in the Communist Party. At the same time, he recognized that the Party was a staunch ally in the struggle for Mexican American equality. The Communist Party worked assiduously to foster unity among ANMA, IUMMSW, and other left organizations in the Southwest. While Jencks was an ANMA member and gave firm support to its goals, Montoya maintains that he did relatively little to advance its organizational agenda. Yet it was Jencks who led the fight for Mine-Mill support of ANMA at the 1949 convention. Here, he insisted that ANMA's activities constituted "a basic part of [the] fight to protect [the] union." And at the local level Jencks continued to take an active interest in the organization's development. But ANMA's strength in Grant County, Montoya argued, lay in the response of a militant Mexican American community, which lent support to its national campaign against discrimination in the workplace, home, school, and media. Emphasizing its popular base, Jencks himself later asserted that "ANMA, or some other organization like it, would have developed without Mine-Mill," though "union participation helped give it a working class base."[22]

Building on the early successes of the Denver-based Committee to Organize the Mexican People, which had established a Santa Rita chapter in 1947, ANMA was an instant success in Grant County, where the tie between the union and the community was strong. The new organization took as its mission the defense of both Mexican American people and Mexican culture in general. These sweeping goals meant resistance against economic and social discrimination, as well as stereotyping in the media, objectives that led ANMA to embrace the civil rights movement and demand equality for oppressed peoples in the United States and overseas. Acutely sensitive to insults against Hispanic culture, it was quick to defend Mexican Americans against official repression, as in the case of the Grant County Mexican Americans held without bail in connection with a violent racial incident at the Fierro mining camp. The result of this confrontation had led to the establishment of New Mexico's first ANMA chapter in 1949. Not only did the organization aid in the defense, but it campaigned successfully for the electoral defeat of County Sheriff Bartley MacDonald as a result of his role in the Fierro disturbance. With firm roots in Mine-Mill, ANMA was an important vehicle for the expression of rising ethnic self-awareness, political action, and community solidarity. It was also regarded by the Communist Party as only one of many tools available for the exertion of pressure to advance class interests, an issue the party regarded as more significant than the cultural concerns of many ANMA adherents.[23]

ANMA's critics saw the organization through a different lens. FBI monitors, who were Mine-Mill's constant companions, dismissed the union's support of ANMA as nothing more than a Communist initiative, thus ignoring the solid base it enjoyed in the Mexican American community. To one informant, the Mine-Mill goal was "to gain a foothold among the Mexican people" which would be "used as a medium for pushing the current Communist Party." When the Grant County ANMA chapter was organized in response to an assault against several Mexican Americans at Fierro, FBI observers reported that the incident was "possibly Communist-inspired" and that Jencks was responsible for the controversy, a dubious claim. Government sources confidently assumed that the Bayard ANMA chapter was "dominated and controlled by the Communist Party." The red-baiting of ANMA mirrored a cresting wave of domestic anticommunism that Clinton Jencks regarded as the product of corporate America's systematic attempt to void the New Deal social contract through an attack on militant unionism. In fact, as Mario T. Garcia has noted, there is no direct evidence to substantiate the charge of Communist control, though the party applauded the organization's activities. While ANMA drew on the legacy of the Mexican Revolution and the historic tradition of the Mexican American Left, its successes reflected both the immediate aspirations of the southwestern Mexican American community and the spirit of militant social unionism.[24]

By the late 1940s, Americans had begun to view their wartime Soviet allies with a mixture of fear and hostility. The American public, including mainstream union leaders, responded to Soviet advances in Eastern Europe by closing ranks behind the Truman administration's increasingly shrill attacks on both foreign and domestic Communists. Side by side with Truman's domestic loyalty program, other political and labor figures warned of the

Red menace at home. Perhaps most active was the House Committee on Un-American Activities (HUAC), which in 1947 launched an investigation of alleged subversion in the nation's motion picture industry. Stung by the Wallace campaign defections of 1948 and fearful of government scrutiny, the mainstream labor movement became engaged in its own family quarrel. The ascendancy of anticommunist liberals like the Steelworkers' Philip Murray and the Autoworkers' Walter Reuther meant that in 1949 the once-militant CIO turned against its left-led unions in order to rid its ranks of Communists and other radical activists. The purge also deprived the CIO of some of its most militant organizers and democratic unions. Because of the clear Communist presence within its leadership ranks, Mine-Mill was among the internationals expelled in the bloodletting of 1949–50.[25]

Despite the assault against radicalism from congressional investigators and the leaders of the mainstream union movement, labor militancy in the Southwest did not go quietly, as is evidenced by the birth and growth of ANMA and the stubborn assertiveness of Mine-Mill, even after its expulsion from the CIO. At a time when many Mexican Americans moved towards assimilation, radical unions "provided an important means for the structural integration of Mexicans into the United States." Mine-Mill brought Grant County's Mexican American population the dignity, self-respect, and economic advances that provided them with a stake in society. By exposing them to class consciousness through working-class organizations, Douglas Monroy has argued, the Mexican American Left supplied the "ideological complement of the structural proletarianization that capitalism brought."[26] Because most Mexican Americans emigrated independently to the United States as laborers, they often did not understand themselves as part of a wage-earning class. Worker radicalism therefore played a key role in their development of a group identity and self-conscious awareness of shared social and economic interests. It was this consciousness of class, together with an intense pride in culture, that was to find expression in the *Salt of the Earth* project; and despite its suppression, the film remains a tribute to Mexican American determination to build a community that not only respected human dignity but also preserved both economic freedom and cultural identity.

For Jencks and the dedicated Grant County unionists who contributed so much to the growth and development of Local 890, the persistent red-baiting was only the beginning. Recently released FBI files on Jencks document a decade-long history of government observation and harassment dating from the prewar era but accelerating after 1947. To Jencks, it was "absolutely clear" that Local 890's success at winning better wages and working conditions led the Justice Department to "saturate" Grant County with FBI agents and informants, including the postmaster and company officials in the Silver City, Bayard, and Hanover areas. These interrogations and pressures on union members, which appear to have peaked before the Empire Zinc strike and the lodging of false charges by FBI informer Harvey Matusow, placed Jencks and Local 890 under even greater suspicion. Jencks and other Mine-Mill activists, convinced that the end of wartime government-guaranteed profits had led to a corporate offensive against labor, regarded the Taft-Hartley Act's crippling of the Wagner Act as the watershed that unleashed a flood of anti-union activity, of which anticommunism was an integral part. In 1948, when Grant County mining companies declined to enter negotiations for fixed contracts unless union leaders filed non-Communist affidavits, Jencks and local 890 drew on WFM tradition to force piecemeal agreements on working conditions, benefits, and promotion lines. By September 1948, Jencks recalled, Kennecott had agreed to honor every provision of the old contract, fully aware that Mine-Mill was capable of stopping production at will. Finally, after widespread mining corporation refusal to negotiate new long-term contracts, the International Executive Board and the next Mine-Mill convention reluctantly agreed to permit their leaders to file the affidavits. While Local 890 concurred, it vigorously protested the requirement as part of an "increasing loss of freedom for the common people of America." In 1949 Jencks signed and filed the Taft-Hartley affidavit, which by his lights was "honest and truthful" because he was not then a party member. By complying with the Taft-Hartley requirement, he assumed that he could "get on with [his] work" as International Representative for Mine-Mill.[27]

Confronted with FBI harassment, Grant County unionists typically refused to provide government investigators with the answers they wanted. Most sources indicate that red-baiting failed to turn the mining community against Mine-Mill. Jencks recalls that "among working people in Grant County, anticommunism fell flat" because they "knew very well that Mine-Mill was making impressive gains for the whole community." Similarly, Montoya, Flores, and Virginia Chacón asserted that the mining community remained remarkably loyal to Mine-Mill despite the escalation of anticommunist attacks and raiding by the Steelworkers and other unions. In Montoya's words, "the rank-and-file did not care" about the charges of Communist Party influence. Similarly, Jencks later asserted that he and the Local 890 membership "reacted to anti-communist criticisms as smokescreens to divert attention from our down to earth program of strengthening democratic participation in winning better working conditions on the job and in our communities. We expected the mining, milling, and smelting corporations and those in the community determined to maintain dominance over the Mexican people to resort to this smokescreen in direct correlation to our effectiveness in winning gains. We learned about the history of our union and of the Mexican American people, and saw the direct connection between anticommunist criticisms and the efforts to exploit us as cheap labor."[28]

To be sure, red-baiting complicated the union's work and made Mine-Mill's organizational task more difficult; and the problems were destined to multiply after the Empire Zinc strike in 1951. In the short run, the anticommunist assault forced Local 890 to divert resources, finances, and personnel away from day-to-day organizing and service functions towards publicity and public relations intended to refocus worker and community attention on the real issues of wages, hours, benefits, and the quality of worker life. After Mine-Mill's expulsion from the CIO in 1950, Jencks and Local 890 remained defiant in the face of escalating external pressures. He dismissed Mine-Mill's banishment from the house of labor with a brusque assertion that his union had been "going for years, with and without the CIO," and would "stand alone, if necessary."[29]

Under external attack, Local 890 turned to negotiations with the Empire Zinc Company in July 1950. Mine-Mill's well-publicized national difficulties placed Jencks and the negotiating team in an awkward position, which was further clouded by depressed conditions in the metals industry. A seasoned international representative, Jencks had a reputation as a hard bargainer, as did his comrades, Juan Chacón and Ernesto Velásquez. Hoping to exploit Mine-Mill's preoccupation with the expulsion problem, Empire Zinc dug in for the long haul. Determined to address working conditions, wage differentials linked to industry-wide scales, and the burning social issue of the discriminatory "Mexican wage," Local 890 prosecuted a long strike that was marked by the emergence of Mine-Mill's women as key activists in sustaining the union's position. Confronted with a court injunction barring union members from mass picketing, Local 890's Women's Auxiliary assumed responsibility for picket duty in an action that saved the strike and produced a partial victory, including the eventual end of the hated "Mexican wage." While the settlement failed to address many union demands, its shortcomings were eclipsed by the broader social significance of the stand taken by the union and the community that had embraced it. Especially significant was the strong leadership provided by Virginia Chacón, Virginia Jencks, and the militant activists in the women's organization, which occupied the spotlight and staked a strong claim for greater women's involvement in community and union affairs. While Jencks admitted that the new contract was less than a victory "on paper," he saw major gains in the mixed result, including the wide recognition gained by the women for their role in the strike and the emergence of new Mexican American union leaders. The ratification of the new agreement held great symbolic significance for workers who had resisted corporate power and asserted the dignity and solidarity of an emerging ethnic community.[30]

During the course of this struggle, a chance meeting between Clinton Jencks and Paul Jarrico, a blacklisted Hollywood writer and producer, set in motion a project that united the workers of Grant County with "cultural workers" from the movie capitol in a daring attempt to circumvent the vicious blacklist that hovered over the motion picture industry after the HUAC hearings of 1947. During the planning and production of an innovative motion picture based on the Empire Zinc strike, Jencks played a crucial role as mediator. From the first meeting at San Cristóbal, he had endorsed the film as a perfect vehicle for the dissemination of Local 890's dramatic struggle for social and economic justice. Once the project was underway, he used his contacts with Jarrico and screenwriter Michael Wilson to help cement the relationship between the international union and the key figures in the Independent Productions Corporation (IPC). When tensions concerning the Mine-Mill role in promoting the film arose between the producers and the Mine-Mill leadership, it was Jencks who counseled the Hollywood contingent on its approach to their union collaborators.[31]

Once film production was underway, neither IPC nor Mine-Mill could escape the glare of national notoriety, especially after the Screen Actors Guild's secretary leaked word of the film project to labor columnist Victor Riesel. Once the story broke, the media publicized a sensationalized account of Reds in the desert making a subversive movie. Alerted to the *Salt of the Earth* project, HUAC member Donald L. Jackson (Rep.-Calif.) swung into action with a floor speech in the House of Representatives attacking the film, its producers, and its sponsors. Sounding an ominous warning, Jackson pledged to "do everything in [his] power to prevent the showing of this communist-made film in the theaters of America."[32] From that moment on, Jencks, Local 890, and the production crew found themselves on the defensive in Grant County, Hollywood, and throughout the United States.

Eventually, the largely negative publicity took its toll, as New Mexico vigilante groups harassed the IPC crew, attacked Local 890 members, and assaulted Clinton Jencks. Before filming was finished, the Immigration and Naturalization Service also arrested and detained lead actress Rosaua Revueltas in a move that complicated the production process. Moreover, these incidents were only the first phase of a sustained attack on *Salt of the Earth*.

During the processing of the film, Hollywood companies refused to provide technical services and no AFL union members were permitted to work on the crew. Finally, once the film was completed, IPC found that no reputable distributor would handle it, which forced the company to create its own distribution organization. Equally damaging was the refusal of most exhibitors to screen *Salt,* allegedly because the studios had passed the word that in the future, films would not be supplied to those operators who dared to resist the boycott. Combined with resistance from mainstream union projectionists, the exhibitors' reluctance to provide attractive venues spelled disaster for IPC, Mine-Mill, and the film. While *Salt of the Earth* was exhibited commercially in New York, Denver, Silver City, and several California theaters, it never gained full distribution. By 1955, *Salt* had been seen in only 13 of the estimated 13,000 theaters in the United States. For IPC and its investors, who lost over $250,000, it was a financial catastrophe.[33]

For Local 890, the Empire Zinc strike, the filming of *Salt,* and the controversy provoked by these events were to alter the calculus of labor-management relations in Grant County. These struggles, combined with the intensification of domestic anticommunism during the Korean War, led to a revival of the Steelworkers raids on Mine-Mill's membership in the mid-1950s. In an important strategic error, USWA stressed the threat of Communist control, a side issue for most local workers, and deemphasized the importance of ethnic solidarity, a matter of deep concern to the Grant County union community.[34] While the large Mexican American membership remained steadfast in its loyalty to Mine-Mill despite the red-baiting attacks, it eventually became obvious to most of IUMMSW's national leaders that continued jurisdictional strife only damaged worker interests. As a result, Mine-Mill reluctantly agreed to merge with USWA in 1967, though Local 890 retained its independent identity within the Steelworkers' organization and found it possible to maintain democratic local control in opposition to the trend towards more bureaucratic business unionism. The continued preference of Mexican American workers for the pariah union was a testament to Mine-Mill's success in addressing social, economic, and racial issues in the troubled 1950s.[35]

For Clinton Jencks, the price paid for social commitment and political activism was high. As pressure on activists escalated after 1950, his postwar activities, including the successful amalgamation that had produced Local 890 and the concrete improvements in worker standards that challenged corporate dominance in the Bayard mining district, exposed him to Justice Department scrutiny and eventual prosecution for alleged false swearing of the non-Communist affidavit. Had he chosen to act as an appointed union business agent or International Representative, Jencks maintained, federal prosecutors could not have employed the Taft-Hartley affidavit provision against him (the law required affidavits from *elected* union officials seeking access to NLRB services). Jencks later asserted that Local 890's successes motivated the Justice Department to fill Grant County with agents and eventually rely on Harvey Matusow's tainted testimony to convict him and thus discredit his union. It is equally true that Communist Party activity on the part of some members of the Local 890 leadership, including high-profile activism during the Wallace campaign and ANMA drive, increased the risk of government scrutiny. Anticommunism had become part of the larger anti-labor offensive, an obfuscation that helped divide labor and force progressive unions to seek merger with mainstream unions more acceptable to management. This trend, in turn, may be linked to the corporate offensive against the New Deal social contract, including labor's gains in the Roosevelt era.[36]

The Local 890 story indicates, however, that there was within the postwar labor movement a significant contrary trend of resistance to business unionism and its bargain with corporate America. The social commitment of Clinton Jencks was matched by Mexican American unionists' burning desire for social and racial justice in the Southwest. Rooted in both wartime idealism and an acute consciousness of inequality, the Mexican American drive for social and economic change was expressed through the medium of progressive unionism during the formative years of the Cold War. It is clear that participation in the armed forces and the historic tradition of Mexican American activism combined to reinforce the southwestern mining community's social, economic, and political claims after 1945. An important component of that historical context was a Mexican radical tradition that in Grant County led some Mine-Mill leaders to view the Communist Party as a legitimate tool for the expression of social protest. Complementing these historical forces and the acceleration of popular agency, Clinton Jencks and his left-led union challenged the economic and social status quo in postwar New Mexico. Confronted by unprecedented union activity, corporate interests cooperated with the surveillance state in an effort to stem the tide of social unionism. In the process, domestic anticommunism became an important instrument in the successful effort to curb labor militancy and obstruct the Mexican American pursuit of equality. In Grant County, New Mexico, Mine-Mill Local 890 became the heart of the resistance and the hope of the future.

Notes

This essay is an expanded version of a paper presented at the North American Labor History Conference, Detroit, Oct. 22, 1999, and expanded for the University of Iowa's Center for Recent United States History's seminar on "Labor and the Cold War," Feb. 19, 2000. The author wishes to thank Clinton E. Jencks, Ellen Schrecker, and Shelton Stromquist for their assistance in the completion of the revised work.

1. Douglas Monroy, "Fence Cutters, Sedicioso, and First-Class Citizens: Mexican Radicalism in America," in Paul Buhle and Dan Georgakas, eds., *The Immigrant Left in the United States* (Albany: State University of New York Press, 1996), 30, 33; Mario T. Garcia, *Mexican Americans: Leadership, Ideology, and Identity, 1930–1960* (New Haven, Conn.: Yale University Press, 1989), chap. 7, esp. 199; Juan Gomez-Quiñones, *Mexican American Labor, 1790–1990* (Albuquerque: University of New Mexico Press, 1994), 117–18; James C. Foster, "Mexican Labor and the American Southwest," in Foster, ed., *American Labor in the Southwest: The First One Hundred Years* (Tucson: University of Arizona Press, 1982), 160–61; Robert C. Hodges, "The Making and Unmaking of *Salt of the Earth*: A Cautionary Tale" (Ph.D. diss., University of Kentucky, 1997), 46–50; Ernesto Galarza et al., *Mexican Americans in the Southwest* (Santa Barbara: McNally and Loftin, 1969), 41–42; James Barnhill, "The Mexican American Question," *Political Affairs* 32 (Sept. 1953): 57; Lorenzo Torres, "Juan Chacón" (privately published pamphlet, n.d.), 7. The development of Mexican American ethnic awareness following the conquest is discussed in David G. Gutierrez, *Walls and Mirrors: Mexican Americans, Mexican Immigrants, and the Politics of Ethnicity* (Berkeley: University of California Press, 1995), chap. 1, esp. 28–29; D. H. Dinwoodie, "The Rise of the Mine-Mill Union in Southwestern Copper," in Foster, *American Labor in the Southwest*, 54–55. For further discussion of the background pertinent to this essay, see also James J. Lorence, *The Suppression of "Salt of the Earth": How Hollywood, Big Labor, and Politicians Blacklisted a Movie in Cold War America* (Albuquerque: University of New Mexico Press, 1999), esp. chaps. 1 and 2, and Ellen R. Baker, *On Strike and On Film: Mexican-American Families and Blacklisted Filmmakers in Cold War America* (Chapel Hill: University of North Carolina Press, 2007), esp. chap 3.

2. Dinwoodie, "Rise of the Mine-Mill Union," 49; Gomez-Quiñones, *Mexican American Labor,* 183; Ellen Baker, "Gender Consciousness and Political Activism in New Mexico's Working Classes" (paper, North American Labor History Conference, Detroit, Oct. 27, 1997), 2.

3. Interview, Orville Larson, Oral History Collection, United Steelworkers of America Papers (hereafter USWA), State College, Pennsylvania State University, Historical Collections and Labor Archives (hereafter PSU-HCLA), 9–10; interview, Nathan Witt, USWA Papers, PSU-HCLA, 39; interview, I. W. Abel, PSU-HCLA, 11, 31; Lorenzo Torres, "Short History of Chicano Workers," *Political Affairs* 12 (Nov. 1973): 93; Garcia, *Mexican Americans,* 176; Dinwoodie, "Rise of the Mine-Mill Union," 51, 53–54; Foster, "Mexican Labor in the American Southwest," 160–61.

4. Clinton Jencks to James J. Lorence, June 17, 1999; Hodges, "Making and Unmaking of *Salt of the Earth*," 2; "Portrait of a Labor Organizer," 3, 3A, Michael Wilson Papers, Los Angeles, Special Collections, Arts Library, UCLA, box 40.

5. Hodges, "Making and Unmaking of *Salt of the Earth*," 34; David M. Hays, "'A Quiet Campaign of Education': The University of Colorado and Minority Rights, 1877–1945," (paper, 1998, Boulder, University of Colorado Archives), 7; Jencks to Lorence, June 17, 1999; FBI File, Albuquerque, Clinton Jencks, AQ 122-2, June 5, 1950; see also FBI Headquarters File 7/Q 100-39680 (SPCI), 194, University of Colorado Archives.

6. Jencks to Lorence, June 17, 1999; Hodges, "Making and Unmaking of *Salt of the Earth*," 34–35; Baker, *On Strike and On Film*, 74–75.

7. Jencks to Lorence, June 17, 1999; "American Veterans Committee: Citizens First, Veterans Second," June 18, 1994, introduction, 1–3; historian Robert C. Hodges argues that in this postwar political activity, Jencks "returned to Communist politics." Hodges, "Making and Unmaking of *Salt of the Earth*," 35. While AVC was open to Communist participation, it also represented substantial grassroots participation in social action that energized the Left in the immediate postwar era.

8. FBI File, El Paso, Clinton Jencks, File 100-4001, July 7, 1947; File 100-136, June 25, 1947; Albuquerque, File 100-36, June 30, 1950; Denver, File 100-4603, Oct. 9, 1946, University of Colorado Archives.

9. Jencks to Lorence, June 17, 1999; Ellen Schrecker, *Many Are the Crimes: McCarthyism in America* (Boston: Little, Brown and Company, 1998), 313; Hodges, "Making and Unmaking of *Salt of the Earth*," 35, 45.

10. Hodges, "Making and Unmaking of *Salt of the Earth*," 44–45; for comment on the Jenckses' approach to community organizing, see Hodges, 52–53; Baker, "Gender Consciousness," 3–4; Deborah Silverton Rosenfelt, *Salt of the Earth* (Old Westbury: Feminist Press, 1978), 115–16; Schrecker, *Many Are the Crimes,* 313–14; "Portrait of a Labor Organizer," 8–10, 38–39.

11. Jencks to Lorence, June 17, 1999.

12. Arturo and Josefina Flores, interview with author, Mar. 26, 1997, Rio Rancho, N. Mex.; interviews, Vern Curtis and Alfredo Montoya, Oral History Collection, PSU-HCLA; "Clinton Jencks," in Griffin Fariello, *Red Scare: Memories of the American Inquisition* (New York: W. W. Norton & Company, 1995), 382; interview, Juan Chacón, Oral History of the American Left Collection, Series 4, *A Crime to Fit the Punishment,* New York, Tamiment Library, New York University; Jencks to Lorence, June 17, 1999; Baker, "Gender Consciousness," 2–3; Robert Kern, "Organized Labor: Race, Radicalism, and Gender," in Judith Boyce De Mark, ed., *Essays in Twentieth-Century New Mexico History* (Albuquerque: University of New Mexico Press, 1994), 195; Gomez-Quiñones, *Mexican American Labor,* 183; Hodges, "Making and Unmaking of *Salt of the Earth*," 48–50; Jack Cargill, "Empire and Opposition: The 'Salt of the Earth' Strike," in Robert Kern, ed., *Labor in New Mexico: Unions, Strikes, and Social History since 1881* (Albuquerque: University of New Mexico Press, 1983), 194–95.

13. Baker, "Gender Consciousness," 4; see also *On Strike and On Film,* 72–73; Rosenfelt, *Salt of the Earth,* 115–16; Flores interview; Chacón interview; Jencks to Lorence, Mar. 30, 2000, June 17, 1999.

14. Baker, "Gender Consciousness," 9–10; see also *On Strike and On Film,* 112–13; Kern, "Organized Labor," 158; Rosenfelt, *Salt of the Earth,* 115; author's interview with Virginia Chacón, Mar. 22, 1997, Faywood, New Mex.; Jencks to Lorence, June 17, 1999.

15. Baker, "Gender Consciousness," 11–12; Garcia, *Mexican Americans,* 218.

16. "Statement of the Grant County Joint Labor Council," Sept. 20, 1947; Jencks to "Everyone in the International Office," Sept. 1947, Western Federation of Miners/International Union of Mine, Mill, and Smelter Workers Papers (hereafter WFM/IUMMSW Papers), Boulder, University of Colorado, archives, box 94, Clinton Jencks File; Hodges, "Making and Unmaking of *Salt of the Earth*," 54.

17. Jencks to Lorence, June 17, 1999, Mar.30, 2000; *The Union,* Jan. 19, 1948; Hodges, "Making and Unmaking of *Salt of the Earth,*" 54–55.

18. Baker, "Gender Consciousness," 7; *On Strike and On Film,* 101; Hodges, "Making and Unmaking of *Salt of the Earth,*" 55; Virginia Chacón interview; Jencks to Lorence, June 17, 1999; Alfredo Montoya interview, PSU-HCLA; author's interview, Montoya, June 25, 1998, El Paso; FBI File, El Paso, Clinton Jencks, June 6, 1948, and June 8, 1949; File 100-4609; Albuquerque, Clinton Jencks, July 20, 1951, File 100-136, University of Colorado Archives.

19. *Official Proceedings of the 43rd Convention of IUMMSW,* Aug. 25–30, 1947, 266–67, 265; Proceedings, National Committee Meeting of the Progressive Party, Nov. 13–14, 1948, Chicago, in Anita McCormick Blaine Papers, Madison, State Historical Society of Wisconsin, box 590.

20. Garcia, *Mexican Americans,* 200, 201; "Victoria con Wallace en 1948," Clinton Jencks Papers, Boulder, University of Colorado, archives, box 22; see also *El Paso Herald,* n.d., in FBI Bureau File, Clinton Jencks, 100-3-72; Jencks to Maurice Travis, Sept. 29 and Nov. 17, 1947, WFM/IUMMSW Papers, box 94, Clinton Jencks File; Baker, "Gender Consciousness," 4; Hodges, "Making and Unmaking of *Salt of the Earth,*" 56.

21. Gomez-Quiñones, *Chicano Politics: Reality and Promise, 1940–1990* (Albuquerque: University of New Mexico Press, 1990), 50–51; Monroy, "Fence Cutters," 31–32; see also Garcia, *Mexican Americans,* chap. 8; Gomez-Quiñones, *Mexican American Labor,* 167–68; Liliana Urrutia, "An Offspring of Discontent: The Asociación Nacional Mexico-Americana, 1949–1954," *Aztlan: International Journal of Chicano Studies Research* 15 (Spring, 1984): 177–84; "Report of Alfonso Sena, National Board Member from Colorado," ANMA, ca. 1952, WFM/IUMMSW Papers, box 206; Baker, "Gender Consciousness," 4–5; see also *On Strike and On Film,* 102–7. An important personal account of ANMA activities may be found in *Memories of Chicano History: The Life and Narrative of Bert Corona,* ed., Mario T. Garcia (Berkeley: University of California Press, 1994), 169–92; for equally valuable personal insight on the organization's origins, see Montoya interviews.

22. Jencks to Lorence, June 17, 1999; Montoya interviews; *Proceedings of the 45th Convention, IUMMSW,* Nov. 12–17, 1949, 157; Baker, "Gender Consciousness," 4. The most comprehensive treatment of ANMA's organization, program, and actions, may be found in Garcia, *Mexican Americans,* chap. 8.

23. James Barnhill, "The Mexican-American Question," *Political Affairs* (Sept. 1953): 53, 56–57; Lorence, *Suppression of "Salt of the Earth,"* 9–10; Baker, "Gender Consciousness," 5–6; see also *On Strike and On Film,* 102, 103–4.

24. Garcia, *Mexican Americans,* 203; Baker, "Gender Consciousness," 5, 6; Jencks to Lorence, June 17, 1999; author interview, Jencks; FBI Files, Albuquerque, Jencks, File AQ100-136, May 9, 1950; El Paso, Jencks, File 100-136-134, 1949; Memo, SAC, May 5, 1949; SA to SAC, May 22, 1949 in FBI File, El Paso, Jencks, File 100-136-111, 1949; Montoya interviews. Hodges argues that the Fierro incident, while not attributable to Communist activism, did enable Jencks to mobilize the Mexican American community for political action. Hodges, "Making and Unmaking of *Salt of the Earth,*" 56–57.

25. For thoughtful discussion of the CIO's expulsion of its left-led unions, see Steve Rosswurm, "Introduction: An Overview and Preliminary Assessment of the CIO's Expelled Unions," in Rosswurm, ed., *The CIO's Left-Led Unions* (New Brunswick, N.J.: Rutgers

University Press, 1992), esp. 7–13; see also Lorence, *Suppression of "Salt of the Earth,"* 20–21, 217–18n3.

26. Monroy, "Fence Cutters," 33, 31–32; see also Garcia, *Mexican Americans,* 227; Montoya interview, PSU-HCLA.

27. Jencks to Lorence, Mar. 30, 2000 and June 17, 1999; *Proceedings,* 1949, 260; Virginia Chacón interview; Flores interview; Montoya interviews. For incontrovertible evidence of the sweeping Justice Department observation of Clinton Jencks's activities, see FBI Files Released under the Freedom of Information Act, University of Colorado Archives; the full extent of government harassment is discussed in Schrecker, *Many Are the Crimes,* chap. 9.

28. Jencks to Lorence, June 17, 1999; author interview, Montoya; Virginia Chacón interview; Flores interview. For discussion of the Mexican American reaction to the anticommunist attack on ANMA, see Garcia, *Mexican Americans,* 225–27.

29. Quoted in Lucien K. File, "History of Labor in the Non-Ferrous Mining Industry in New Mexico," n.d., Lucien File Papers, Santa Fe, New Mexico State Records Center and Archives, box 2; Jencks to Lorence, June 17, 1999. Mine-Mill's isolation and expulsion from the CIO are detailed in Cargill, "Empire and Opposition," 187–89; F. S. O'Brien, "The 'Communist Dominated' Unions in the United States Since 1950," *Labor History* 9 (Spring 1968): 198–99; Harvey A. Levenstein, *Communism, Anticommunism, and the CIO* (Westport, Conn.: Greenwood Press, 1981), 274–75; Garcia, *Mexican Americans,* 98; Gomez-Quiñones, *Mexican-American Labor,* 183–84; Jonathan D. Rosenblum, *Copper Crucible: How the Arizona Miner's Strike of 1983 Recast Labor-Management Relations in America* (Ithaca, N.Y.: ILR Press, 1995), 34–35. For an account that Cargill terms a "jaundiced" view exaggerating Communist influence in Mine-Mill, see Vernon Jensen, *Non-Ferrous Metals Industry Unionism, 1932–1934* (Ithaca, N.Y.: Cornell University Press, 1954), esp. chaps. 16, 18.

30. Cargill, "Empire and Opposition," 242–43; Gomez-Quiñones, *Mexican-American Labor,* 186; Rosenfelt, *Salt of the Earth,* 124–25; Lorence, *Suppression of "Salt of the Earth,"* 39–40.

31. Jencks to Michael Wilson, July 31, 1953, Wilson Papers, box 51; Lorence, *Suppression of "Salt of the Earth,"* 103–4.

32. *Congressional Record,* 83rd Cong., 1st Sess., Feb. 24, 1953, vol. 99, part 1, 1371–72.

33. The foregoing summary of the Empire Zinc strike and the production and distribution of *Salt of the Earth* is based on the account provided in Lorence, *Suppression of "Salt of the Earth,"* 25–39, 73–90, 113–47; see also Baker, *On Strike and On Film,* chaps. 8, 9.

34. Robert S. Keitel, "The Merger of the International Union of Mine, Mill, and Smelter Workers into the United Steel Workers of America," *Labor History* 15 (Winter 1974): 37; "Notice, Local 890 Meeting," ca. Oct. 1951, Wilson Papers, box 51; Cargill, "Empire and Opposition," 235–36; Lorence, *Suppression of "Salt of the Earth,"* 38–39.

35. Virginia Chacón interview; Jencks to Lorence, June 17, 1999; Montoya interviews; Flores interview. For discussion of the CIO purge in 1950 and its consequences, see Rosswurm, "Introduction," esp. 13–16.

36. The corporate attack on the New Deal social contract is described in Elizabeth Fones-Wolf, *Selling Free Enterprise: The Business Assault on Labor and Liberalism, 1945–60* (Urbana: University of Illinois Press, 1994), 3–6, and Rosswurm, "Introduction," 10, 14,

and 16; Jencks to Lorence, Mar. 30, 2000, and June 17, 1999. For comment on the devious means employed to destroy the left-led labor movement of the late 1940s, Mine-Mill in particular, see Schrecker, *Many Are the Crimes,* 355–58; see also David M. Oshinsky, *Senator Joseph McCarthy and the American Labor Movement* (Columbia: University of Missouri Press, 1976), 176; "Clinton Jencks," in Fariello, *Red Scare,* 383; on Matusow's unsubstantiated charges, see "Harvey Matusow," in Fariello, *Red Scare,* 103–4.

8. The Wages of Anticommunism: U.S. Labor and the Korean War

SETH WIGDERSON

In his December 3, 2001, speech to the AFL-CIO Convention, President John Sweeney lavished praise on President George W. Bush's war on terrorism, as he also denounced the Bush administration for its consistently anti-worker, pro-business program. "Let me be clear—President Bush and his administration are doing an excellent job of waging war on the terrorists and we commend them for that. But at the same time, he and his corporate backers are waging a vicious war on working families and we condemn them for that."[1] Sweeney's dilemma of criticizing a president's domestic policies while jumping on the bandwagon of war is reminiscent of the dilemma that confronted the leaders of the CIO during the Korean War, fifty years earlier.

During the Korean War, industrial unions were able to protect past economic victories in the face of a fierce industry-government assault. They used their friendship with the Truman administration to deter very serious challenges to their contracts from government agencies and employers. But at the same time, their liberal anticommunist loyalty to President Truman and the Democratic Party stripped them of the ability to challenge effectively the administration's pro-corporate policies. By the end of the Korean War years, anticommunist union leaders had been politically marginalized, left with only a very junior seat at the table of national politics.

Historians have looked at the victory of anticommunist labor leaders in the Congress of Industrial Organizations (CIO) and at the consequences of that victory for radical workers and the Left.[2] However, they have paid little attention to what those leaders gained for their decision to adopt and craft a liberal anticommunism. This essay examines one of the earliest tests of the CIO's anticommunism by looking at mainstream labor during the Korean

War era, focusing in particular on the CIO and specifically the United Automobile Workers (UAW) and the United Steelworkers of America (USWA) during the United Labor Policy Committee (ULPC) walkout, the automobile unemployment crisis, the *Sawyer* steel seizure case, and the Democratic Party electoral defeats.

Labor's experience during the Korean War contrasted sharply with World War II, when unions gained an important role in the government's economic mobilization in exchange for a No-Strike Pledge.[3] Nelson Lichtenstein calls this a "Faustian bargain," where labor "ceded freedom and legitimacy to the wartime state."[4] But the reward for leaders was a recognition of their status as *the* representatives of the working class. After World War II, CIO unionists wanted the state to play the leading role in wages and social welfare. CIO leaders favored national power-sharing mediated by a strong state that organized national economic bargaining by unions, business, and government comparable to that enjoyed by their European counterparts.[5] By 1949, they believed their anticommunism legitimated their right, as tribunes of the working class, to participate in national decision making.[6] But postwar liberal pluralism had no place for such class-based representation. The new pluralist vision saw only different self-interested groups, with a benign state responsible for leveling the playing field. Class itself became a suspect and discarded category.[7] Furthermore, the 1946 Republican electoral victories meant that any national economic planning would be suspect in Washington.

Within the CIO, a furious battle had raged since the beginning of the Cold War around the question of anticommunism and support for Truman's Cold War. Earlier, many non-Communist liberals and social democrats had been willing to work with anyone who struggled for workers' rights. The Communist Party had played an important and acknowledged role in the creation of many CIO unions. But as the postwar employer onslaught on the New Deal and workers' power made increasingly successful use of anticommunism, and under pressure from the Truman administration, many non-Communist leaders became fervent anticommunists, advocating driving Communist influence from the CIO. Long-term anticommunist Walter Reuther had won the UAW's presidency in 1946 and control of the International Executive Board (IEB) in 1947 on a program that combined anticommunism with militant struggle against the employers.[8] After President Truman's 1948 victory and the defeat of Progressive candidate Henry Wallace, CIO and Steelworker President Philip Murray led the formerly insurgent federation in rejecting the non-Communist liberalism of its early years and purging Communist leaders and Communist-led unions from their ranks, eventually expelling eleven left-led unions in 1949. Over the next few years the CIO tried to destroy its past affiliates in a series of bitter raids that cost the federation one million lost members.[9]

By 1950, the CIO joined the longtime anticommunist American Federation of Labor (AFL) in seeing themselves as legitimate members of a broad liberal "Vital Center."[10] CIO leaders found Truman's Fair Deal an attractive program and reached out to similarly minded anticommunist liberal activists to create the Americans for Democratic Action (ADA). They believed that union strength, social reform, and an engineered society could be combined with a successful fight against Communism, and that such a program was superior to the conservatives' marriage of anticommunism with anti-reform.[11] Anticommunism validated these liberals' bureaucratic, top-down, lobbying, lawsuit approach to social change. Organizations like the UAW or the National Association for the Advancement of Colored People (NAACP) could justify their refusal to engage in mass actions on the grounds that the Communists would take advantage. They would act in the name of the masses, but they would not help the masses act.

How much, and to what degree, the rank and file shared their elected leaders' anticommunism remains an open question. Many autoworkers of Eastern European extraction, for instance, who had looked favorably on the Communist Party before World War II, shifted to a powerful anticommunism after Stalin's treatment of postwar Poland and Eastern Europe.[12] On the other hand, many black autoworkers remained stalwart supporters of the Left. What stands out is the desire of the overwhelming majority of workers to be accepted as full American citizens.[13] By the late 1940s, America's rulers had scored a great ideological victory by making anticommunism part of the definition of citizenship—of America's civil religion. Rank-and-file acceptance of the dangers of Communism could have the instrumental value for them of asserting their equal rights as Americans, a claim that challenged the traditional treatment of industrial workers as second-class citizens.

The fear of Communism gained added force when the nation was shocked by reports of North Korean troops invading South Korea on June 27, 1950. President Truman's decision to send U.S. forces to the peninsula drew swift approval from mainstream labor leaders.[14] On the heels of Truman's order of a partial mobilization, Victor Reuther, UAW Education Director and Walter's brother, made this bold vow in a Voice of America broadcast: "We wish to state categorically that in supporting the United Nations' determination to meet the use of force by force, the American labor movement is in no way abandoning its constant struggle against the reaction embodied in monopoly capitalism, nor its insistence that the fruits of American productive power be shared with a world in need. While we are prepared to accept the added responsibility which national economic mobilization may impose upon us, we are determined to surrender no rights in the process."[15] But the Reuthers would fail in their triple pledge as the goal of fighting Communism hamstrung the contest for a fair economic policy and the struggle against monopoly capitalism.

At the beginning of the Korean War, most union leaders remembered World War II, when they traded the right to strike for a role in setting government policy as well as a National War Labor Board that resolved labor disputes. But the No-Strike Pledge and the wartime wage freeze had generated much rank-and-file anger at both the government and the unions. Still, as long as the president kept Korea a limited war there would be no need to "take the pledge."[16]

Employers remembered with bitterness their own experiences with wartime government-enforced labor policies. Since the onset of the New Deal they had warred against government intervention in what they saw as the strictly private arena of employer-employee relations. By the time of the Korean War, Truman faced a self-confident, aggressive business community thoroughly hostile to any government regulation.[17] They had no intention of allowing the unions to make any gains through federal intervention. But a central premise of New Deal labor policy was that industrial relations had a powerful public component and that the democratically elected government had a responsibility to interpose itself between capital and labor. The 1935 National Labor Relations Act had opened up employment practices to government supervision. During World War II the National War Labor Board had further weakened management prerogatives. After the war, the government had continued to force a public presence at the bargaining table with the creation of special fact-finding boards that made recommendations to settle disputes.[18] Business scored its greatest legislative victory against the New Deal's labor program with the 1947 Taft-Hartley Act.[19] The act included a provision for a presidential anti-strike injunction—a back-to-work order—when a strike posed a danger to national health and safety. This threat could be ascertained by a presidential fact-finding board that could report on the dispute, but that was forbidden by statute from making any recommendations. This last point was especially important to the steel companies, who felt they had been forced to accept unpalatable government board recommendations as late as 1949.[20] At the onset of the Korean War, business leaders demanded that any serious wartime strike be handled by a Taft-Hartley injunction.[21]

President Truman's economic advisors also drew lessons from the World War II era, especially the fight against inflation. Unlike 1939, the U.S. economy was "high and rising prior to the outbreak of hostilities."[22] Rising prices from an overheated economy and a panicky public were a serious concern to administration economists throughout the Korean War. Their fear flowed in part from the public's memories of shortages and rationing. As Truman ordered U.S. forces into the fray in the summer of 1950, a massive buying panic set off an inflationary wave. Prices skyrocketed. Sugar, flour, soap, and hosiery were eagerly snapped up, although none were in short supply. Although prices quickly settled, Washington was soon abuzz with rumors of price and wage freezes.

Autoworkers, in particular, had to tread carefully in this new terrain of potential wage freezes. Reuther had built his union political base on a promise of decent wages and economic security. In 1948, General Motors had signed a contract that provided for both a Cost of Living Adjustment (COLA) in wages to eliminate the problem of inflation and an Annual Improvement Factor (AIF) that automatically raised autoworkers' real pay by 2 percent annually. In May 1950, the union signed an unprecedented five-year contract with General Motors and had long-term contracts with other companies that contained similar clauses. (The Steelworker leaders opposed such devices, preferring straight wage increases.)[23] The General Motors contract held out the possibility of the autoworkers' full entrance into America's postwar prosperity.[24] Ensconced in the newly opened UAW headquarters, Solidarity House, Reuther had expected his team to guide autoworkers towards an even more secure future. Yet the government had frozen wages during World War II, and might now challenge the automatic pay raises of COLA and AIF. Moreover, if workers tried to take advantage of tight wartime labor markets to win higher wages, would their initiatives come under government attack?

In response to the war and the inflationary spike, Congress passed the Defense Production Act (DPA), which enabled the president to establish economic mobilization agencies that had the potential of severely restricting workers' economic power. Of special interest to workers was the provision for a tripartite (Public, Business, Labor) Wage Stabilization Board (WSB) charged with maintaining wage stability. The conservative congressional authors of the DPA implemented business' fear of wartime government mandated labor benefits by creating the possibility of a weak price control that exempted food and rent.[25] The act's congressional authors also specified that nothing in the DPA would override Taft-Hartley, hoping that presidential injunctions would stop any serious strikes. At first these agencies did little, since it was hoped that the war would soon be over, but the legislation posed a threat to workers' economic security.[26]

At the war's outset, unions moved quickly to position themselves to defend old contracts and make new gains. Defense of the country now meant defense of a standard of living and a level of security that few industrial workers had ever known. At the UAW's first wartime International Executive Board (IEB) meeting, Reuther insisted on the importance of protecting COLA and AIF from potential wage and price controls. He outlined a strategy to pressure Ford and Chrysler to grant GM-style five-year contracts.[27] These plans rapidly came to fruition, and autoworkers made significant gains. Buoyed by good sales, auto manufacturers feared the loss of workers to better paying jobs and easily agreed to sweeten their contracts. On August 25, Chrysler, with which the union had fought a 104–day pension strike that past winter, voluntarily ceded an extra ten cents per hour wage increase. Ford signed a GM-style five-year contract on September 4. With the Big Three setting the pattern, smaller firms granted similar benefits, often for the same five-year term.[28] Adding hundreds of thousands of autoworkers to this new standard of prosperity and security went far toward establishing the notion that these were legitimate expectations of all American working people.

What autoworkers saw as their American right appeared to some government officials as dangerous, unpatriotic private greed. There were those in the Truman administration who wanted to fight the war by attacking the possible inflationary effects of the auto industry's five-year AIF-COLA contracts. Although the union and the companies argued that AIF merely rewarded improved productivity and was not therefore inflationary, government officials could be quick to blame well-paid workers for the nation's economic ills. As early as July 1950, one official privately asked, "Should existing contracts like the GM contract be suspended?"[29] Steelworker leaders shared autoworkers' fear of government intervention. Phil Murray told the Steelworkers Board in September that there was a "desperate fight underway in the city of Washington right now for the imposition of wage freezes."[30] He advised his board of the importance of quickly negotiating contract improvements before the government moved to freeze wages. Steelworkers then easily won raises of 12 cents from United States Steel.[31] But lacking the autoworkers' COLA and AIF, they had no protection against inflation.

While government officials explored fighting Communism by freezing wages, conservative workers utilized anticommunist hysteria to settle old scores. For UAW radicals, it was indeed "The Time of the Toad."[32] In a number of UAW organized plants, gangs of right-wing workers roamed the shop floor, attacking and expelling known or suspected radicals in so-called run-outs. In Milwaukee, a worker who had signed a peace petition was tossed out of the Seaman automobile plant and suffered a fractured back.[33] Flint, Michigan, site of the great sit-down strike, had been a stronghold of union radicals and had enjoyed a spirited debate among leftists and conservatives.[34] But during the Korean War it became a center of sustained witch-hunting.[35] In Buick Local 599, right-wingers tried to throw out a well-liked radical worker. By August the Local resolved to ask the Convention for new powers to expel Communists.[36] In October it convicted a radical of conduct unbecoming a union member because he refused to answer questions about his politics. The Trial Committee decided that was an admission of guilt and demanded that the International Union expel him for ten years, which it did not do.[37]

One of the worst run-outs occurred at Local 595, Ford's Linden, New Jersey plant. Plant radicals attempted to pass out "Hands Off Korea" leaflets soon after the war began. Many workers reacted furiously. Announcing they would "make every gate in the Linden plant a 38th Parallel," they rounded up known or suspected radicals, beat them up, and threw them out of the plant. The Local then tried and convicted the radicals, including the Local's founding president, on charges that included urging that workers "act contrary to the UAW and CIO policy on the Korean situation." The radicals appealed their guilty verdict to the IEB, where a more complicated picture emerged. The trial was the culmination of a decade-long factional fight. Numerous radicals had already gone over to the right wing. Local 595 President Ascough boasted of how he "sprinkled the holy water on them so to speak." The former president, Witkus, reminded the board of his services in fighting Homer Martin and agreed to sign a loyalty oath. The board did little to help him, since some board members considered him a self-created martyr. Eventually, it did agree to check the trial procedure, but by remaining silent on the suitability of such charges it gave its tacit consent to such a trial.[38]

Local loyalty oaths, patterned after the U.S. government program, became a common tool for right-wing local forces. At GM Fisher Body in Ambridge, Pennsylvania (Local 544), President Mike Vuletich was expelled at a witch-hunt trial for refusing to sign an oath denying present or past Communist Party membership. The IEB Appeals Committee, which heard complaints about local union actions and turmoil, recommended his reinstatement. He agreed to sign an oath denying present Communist Party membership. Furthermore, he had not shown the Communist stigmata of preaching "peace in Korea." Yet Vuletich did not appear again as a local leader.[39]

On August 2, 1950, Solidarity House sent a weak message formally condemning these attacks, but little was done to defend the threatened workers and nothing to punish their assailants. The union's leaders said that they understood that members would resent Communists during "these crucial times, brought about by the Russian Communist-inspired aggressive war in Korea." But they went on to say that Communists should be dealt with using the constitutional machinery for members "who are guilty of conduct detrimental to the best interests of our union." This did not, however, include their right-wing assailants.[40]

If unionists hoped that such "loyalty" would win them government respect they were sadly mistaken, as President Truman created a pro-business economic mobilization. Truman wrote the 1950 CIO Convention that although the war would require sacrifices, "These sacrifices should be shared fairly by all groups in our population."[41] But "equality of sacrifice" was not on the agenda of those business leaders whom Truman recruited to create a mobilization policy that favored the well-to-do. While unions clamored for a few high-level mobilization agency appointments, the administration actively recruited from among business executives. Union leaders believed that a sufficient number of labor advisors would bring a working-class perspective to the government's efforts. But only a few labor advisors were ever appointed, and theirs was a sorry lot. In the words of their postwar report, they were "isolated sentinels among the business and government specialists." Union labor had participated as partners in the World War II agencies; now the advisors were merely a "front to keep the heat of labor's demands off the necks of the defense controllers."[42]

One early example of the pro-wealthy economic policies came when the Federal Reserve Board chose to combat inflation by reducing workers' purchasing ability. Its Regulations "W" and "X" were an "indirect" method of reducing consumer demand by raising down payments and shortening repayment periods on car and house loans, rather than the "direct" method of simply restricting credit for everyone. Only better-off purchasers could afford the more stringent terms. Even worse, by allowing the Federal Reserve Board to make this sort of decision, the administration was eliminating any say by labor in formulating economic policy. When Walter Reuther asked Federal Reserve Chairman William McChesney Martin why the Federal Reserve Board had not directly controlled bank credit in the same way that the government controlled workers' wages, Martin, "shocked and amused," replied that "bankers simply would not tolerate such control." The administration note taker added parenthetically, "This is the position labor unions might have taken towards wage control but fortunately did not."[43]

Voters' conclusions about how to win the war stunned anticommunist liberals, as a war-confused electorate blamed Truman and his party both for getting into the war and for not winning.[44] Union leaders had high hopes for maintaining the liberal trend of the 1948 vote. Instead, in the 1950 congressional elections the Republicans made major gains and Senator Joe McCarthy rode high, his strength grounded in the Korean War. As Senator-elect Richard

Nixon explained, "The major issue in my race was . . . the Administration's foreign policy in the Far East."[45]

Military developments posed new threats to mainstream labor. In November, General MacArthur pushed his troops close to the Chinese border, came under fierce Chinese attack, and was driven down the peninsula until U.N. forces were able to launch a counterattack. In response to what was becoming a longer and more difficult war, President Truman declared a state of national emergency, created the Office of Defense Mobilization (ODM) to oversee the whole government economic mobilization, and appointed General Electric's President Charles E. Wilson as the ODM's director. "Electric Charlie" became the focus of labor's complaint. He was a social liberal on some issues, but also known for his strong dislike of unions.[46] His refusal to appoint a top administrator from the labor movement, as had been done in World War II, illustrated how shut out the labor leaders were from the mobilization.[47]

Americans responded to the war news with a second buying panic that led to increased government activity and the first direct threats to existing contracts. In response to another round of price hikes, the Economic Stabilization Agency (ESA) began a series of limited price freezes; in turn, the Wage Stabilization Board (WSB) temporarily froze wages. But, against the objections of NAM, it exempted the UAW's COLA and AIF from the freeze order for the moment.[48] Reuther credited his visit to President Truman on December 20, 1950, as well as extensive union lobbying for that exemption.[49] But Reuther had only won this victory with the aid of the automobile companies who accompanied the UAW leaders to Washington.[50] His victory showed no more than that the administration would pay special attention to powerful unions and did nothing for the 40 percent of American workers who had no raises in 1950.[51]

Any wage freeze elicited foul memories for workers and their leaders. During wartime, high labor demand means workers are in a position to win better pay and feel morally justified in doing so by the their employers' super profits. At the same time that the government limits workers' wages it must find ways to entice business to produce for the war effort. During World War II, Secretary of War Henry Stimson commented, "If you are going to try to go to war or prepare for war in a capitalist country, you have got to let business make money out of the process, or business won't work."[52] During the Korean War, corporate profits were 74 percent higher in the last quarter of 1950 than they had been the year before.[53] U.S. Steel had record profits in 1950 and record sales in 1951; in some manufacturing industries profits surpassed 50 percent.[54] Yet wartime government-guaranteed profits stand in stark contrast to government-enforced wage freezes.

Ignoring mainstream labor's demand for a voice in policy-making, the administration made fundamental economic decisions with little or no union consultation. On December 11, 1950, the cabinet discussed a general wage freeze.[55] WSB chair Cyrus Ching opposed the proposal because it "would make the position of many responsible labor leaders most difficult."[56] Ching clearly saw the pro-administration unionists as ultimately limited in how far they could control rank-and-file anger. Indeed, "responsible labor leaders" found themselves in an increasingly "difficult" position. To whom were they responsible? Could these tribunes speak for the people and at the same time help administer the war?

To protest business domination of the economic mobilization agencies, the AFL and the CIO, as well as the Railroad Brotherhoods and the then independent Machinists, created the United Labor Policy Committee (ULPC) on December 14. They hoped that a united front of anticommunist unions would have the weight to win the respect that Truman denied them. They demanded real labor representation at higher levels, "direct" rather than "indirect" controls, a real price freeze to match any real wage freeze, and a non-Taft-Hartley wartime disputes resolution system. That is, they wanted the rights of workers to be fully represented within the wartime agencies and they wanted themselves acknowledged as the protector of those rights; in a word, they wanted "recognition."[57] The decision to create the ULPC was a sharp break from World War II, when the federations fought each other, and the ULPC held out the possibility of uniting the previously warring federations.[58] Soon seventeen states had ULPCs based on joint cooperation of state labor federations and industrial union councils.[59]

To bolster the charge of corporate dominance, the CIO's Political Action Committee published a leaflet entitled "Big Business and Mobilization," detailing the corporate backgrounds of all the top economic administrators as well as illustrating monopoly control of America's industries.[60] It charged that "Republican big business has established a de facto government on the banks of the Potomac." Yet the ULPC's protest remained essentially muted because these liberal anticommunists could offer no real alternative. President Truman had appointed those businessmen, and the labor leaders could not publicly oppose him without challenging the liberal anticommunism that was their own political bedrock. Absent a desire to eliminate corporate influence, they could only ask for a greater say for the workers' tribunes.

But unionists did want one group of businessmen well represented in Washington—the employers of well-organized industries who desired economic peace and were willing to pay for it. Faced with the emergency mobilization, many employers quickly settled outstanding labor issues. Chrysler signed its third contract in 1950 on December 11, extending the agreement to five years and conceding COLA and AIF. The UAW and John Deere settled a 107–day agricultural implement strike.[61] A longstanding dispute in the railroad industry was settled on December 21. That month, John L. Lewis peacefully signed new agreements with the coal operators, the first nonconfrontational coal agreements in recent memory.[62]

The real test of labor's power came when the WSB issued General Wage Regulation 6, a broad-based wage freeze. Labor leaders argued that the 10 percent increase ceiling threatened many contracts. AFL President Green charged "that the Public members and the representatives of Management really worked this out away from the Labor members. . . . the action was so irritating to our Labor members that they decided to withdraw from the Wage Stabilization Board."[63] The administration took no substantial action to address labor's protests and the ULPC then ordered a walkout of the few labor representatives from all government agencies on February 28, 1951.[64] Rank-and-file workers enthusiastically backed the protest. The labor movement had loyally supported the president, rallied behind the war, supported some form of wartime economic controls, but had little or nothing to show for it. Prices increased while wages remained frozen, what *Business Week* diplomatically called "uneven stabilization." Public opinion was evenly divided on the ULPC walkout. Forty-one percent said labor should have more say in the defense program; forty percent said it should not.[65] Business leaders reacted apoplectically. National Association of Manufacturer's (NAM) President William Ruffin denounced the walkout as an "inexcusable filibuster against the national welfare." Charles E. Wilson told the cabinet that the unions had walked out, "seeking their pound of flesh regardless of the effect on inflation and higher prices."[66]

The issue of how to settle wartime disputes hovered over the ULPC confrontation. Phil Murray believed that during wartime "for all practical purposes unions were unable to strike." He feared that a wartime steel strike would be seen as disloyal. Even if steelworkers struck, the president could issue a Taft-Hartley back-to-work injunction, which is why Murray always insisted on winning some degree of government approval of his demands before venturing into open combat with the usually intransigent Steel Barons.[67] But when unionists looked to the government agencies that would be central to such a campaign, they saw only anti-labor businessmen, hence the ULPC demand for more labor advisors at higher levels. At the very least, Murray wanted a Wage Stabilization Board, which could "make final determinations," that is, without needing the approval of "Electric Charlie."[68]

For many weeks, meetings were held in the White House, where representatives from business and labor met with administration leaders. After arduous negotiations, Murray won a very limited disputes resolution mechanism as well as a tripartite National Advisory Board on Mobilization Policy, which it was hoped would allow for real labor consultation on mobilization issues.[69] For wartime disputes, business leaders conceded that in certain exceptional situations the president would have the power to send a labor dispute to the reconstituted Wage Stabilization Board for a decision.[70] The board was given the power to dictate a settlement only in these expectedly few disputes. NAM howled at this weakening of Taft-Hartley, maintaining that "employee relations should be left either to management decision or to collective bargaining."[71] A few important disputes did go the presidential route, most notably in steel.

Labor had lost its bid to be the workers' tribune. Far from winning a victory for all workers, Phil Murray had only been granted recognition as the spokesperson for his own members. As the expelled left-wing United Electrical union put it, "No policies have been changed."[72] The same businessmen remained firmly in charge. General Wage Regulation 6 remained in force. The union leaders pinned their hopes on a better Defense Production Act, but within months Congress passed a worse one. Wilson remained in charge, his anti-union attitudes unchanged. The ULPC thought the new advisory board would allow labor "to participate in major defense policy-making at the top level," but the new board soon proved to be a useless talk shop. Rather than winning an economic mobilization program that would be fair for all working people, unionists took care of their own members by colluding with employers to evade the regulations in some of the sixty thousand cases handled by the Regional WSBs.[73]

The contradictions of labor's contest with an administration it had helped elect can be seen in the UAW's 1951 Convention, held April 1–5, toward the end of the ULPC walkout. Although much of the eventual settlement had already been worked out, Reuther delivered a powerful attack on the administration's economic program—without ever specifically warring against Truman. He portrayed the union as in "serious trouble" from the administration's policies, specifically the 10 percent wage limit, the threat to the five-year contracts, and Wilson-style big business domination of the economic mobilization agencies.[74] The Reuther team even allowed some criticism of the Democratic Party by allowing the Resolutions Committee to bring in a minority plank calling for a Labor Party that Reuther only opposed as untimely.

But a floor fight on foreign policy revealed the limits the leadership imposed on any radical discussion. A resolution supporting the Korean War was challenged by Local 15 delegate John W. Anderson, who could speak

because his was the only hand up.[75] Anderson, then associated with the Socialist Workers Party and a former Local president, characterized the war as
a civil war, pointed to the mass sentiment in the United States against U.S.
intervention, and castigated the corrupt dictatorship of Syngman Rhee. Other
radicals, emboldened by the round of applause that he received, also attacked
the war, including the U.S. Army's discrimination against black troops. The
leadership finally responded with a virulent anticommunist speech by UAW
Vice President John W. Livingston, and amended the resolution to criticize
Rhee.[76]

The convention deepened Reuther's bureaucratic control. An unpopular
dues increase that delegates had defeated at the 1949 convention passed easily.
Only a few figures associated with the old left-wing faction openly opposed
the increase, although it remained unpopular with the rank and file. Reuther
tried to end the debate without even letting dissident leader Carl Stellato,
president of the UAW's largest local, the sixty thousand member Ford Rouge
Local 600, speak.

Reuther knew that unemployment was the real threat facing autoworkers in coming months as the shift from consumer to war production would
move needed resources away from civilian production and lead to severe
autoworker job loss. Given his political support of the war against Communism, Reuther could do little to challenge the basic direction of government
economic policy. However, he did believe that labor's voice and a sound planning policy would ameliorate the attendant dislocations. But the supposed
gains of the ULPC walkout, the high-level labor advisors, and the seat on the
National Advisory Board on Mobilization Policy, were useless, as government
officials brushed away the facts presented by unionists showing the wasteful-
ness of the government's program.[77] While labor's suggestions and complaints
went unheeded, labor's participation in the mobilization agencies' decisions
made it complicit in the administration's decisions.[78] If workers wanted to
fight against government-mandated union-approved unemployment, who
would lead them?

In April the government began to divert steel, aluminum, and copper
from civilian to military production. Automobile production and employment dropped precipitously.[79] Between March 1951 and January 1952, total
automobile employment fell 20 percent. By December 1951, there were one
hundred thousand unemployed in Detroit and twelve thousand in Flint.
Government officials privately showed callous disregard for Detroit layoffs:
"The Labor Department is not seriously concerned since they are anxious
to encourage diversion of employment into war production."[80]

Reuther had no program to stop those layoffs. He blamed the auto companies for shifting war production orders outside Detroit when autoworkers were idle.[81] But rather than organizing ten thousand laid-off autoworkers to picket the White House demanding jobs, the union instead called a carefully scripted Washington conference on defense unemployment that focused on supporting a bill to improve unemployment benefits that Reuther said would "give the workers the same protection as granted business and machinery."[82] But the bill died in Congress. In time the unemployment crisis eased. But for well over a year autoworkers felt the sting of joblessness made no less bitter by the knowledge that their elected leaders were complicit. Reuther could never directly challenge the administration on these issues.

Reuther's failure to find innovative ways to deal with unemployment illustrates the limitations of his liberal politics. The UAW had been particularly concerned that older industrial areas like Detroit had not received many defense orders. Deindustrialization, yet unnamed, had emerged as a direct result of administration policy.[83] The union called for the government to channel contracts to those depressed areas. The Truman administration was sympathetic and had considered directing contracts to high unemployment areas before the war. But the Pentagon and the business community strongly opposed such a program, arguing that contracts should go to the lowest bidder.[84] In face of such opposition, labor could win very little. On February 7 the ODM issued Defense Manpower Policy 4, which permitted "a manufacturer in a certified labor surplus area to meet the lowest prices on quotations from non-surplus areas."[85] During mid-1952, the policy generated only a 1 percent gain in Detroit defense contracts.[86]

While recognizing the special constraints on its favorite liberals, the UAW leaders bristled at any radical program. Through all the leadership's efforts runs the bureaucratic practice of demobilizing, or failing to mobilize the unemployed workers to act on their own behalf. At the January 1952 Unemployment Conference, the Reuther leadership strenuously rejected Local 600's proposal for a shorter workweek demand to combat unemployment ("30 hours work for 40 hours pay") that could potentially challenge corporate power, as a "Communist maneuver."[87] Fearing "elements outside of our union," Reuther specifically opposed any locally initiated unemployed committees.[88] When UAW Local 212, Briggs Manufacturing, Detroit, long a center of union radicalism, proposed a mass unemployed demonstration in Lansing, Michigan, CIO president and close Reuther ally August Scholle turned them down. He told the Local that the idea had already been discussed and rejected by the UAW leadership, who feared that not enough unemployed workers would show up, since so many had left the state looking for jobs. He suggested instead that the Local take part in a petition drive to reapportion the rural-dominated state legislature. As usual, the simple act of suggesting direct mass action set off an almost allergic reaction.[89]

Nationally, the acid test of mainstream labor's reliance on the Truman administration came in steel. Steelworkers had not received a raise in 1951, while autoworkers had enjoyed a 25 cents an hour boost from COLA and AIF.[90] Of even more importance, union leaders had long demanded the union shop and dues checkoff.[91] The steel employers hated the union shop, which they called "an instrument to destroy freedom," and specifically did not want any government board to order it.[92] The companies also wanted no wage increase without a hefty government-approved price increase. Most importantly, the Steel Barons also demanded drastic changes in Section 2-B of the U.S. Steel contract, Plant Work Rules, which they saw as blocking efficient use of their plants.[93] For those who worked in the nation's steel mills, these rules were hard-won legacies of earlier battles that had been in their contract since 1937. The maintenance of "past practices and local conditions" often marked the difference between a tolerable job and a hellhole.[94] Steelworkers had no thought of ceding this key conquest without a huge struggle.[95]

Phil Murray believed that the public would castigate the union for any wartime national steel strike and tried hard to avoid one. But from the first the USWA negotiators found the steel companies unwilling to bargain, instead counting on a Taft-Hartley injunction to block any strike. Steelworker leaders looked to the White House for help. Their counsel, Arthur Goldberg, got a warm welcome from President Truman as they worked on ways to achieve workers' demands without striking.[96] On December 22, 1951, Truman certified the dispute to the Wage Stabilization Board, using the procedure that Murray had won in the ULPC walkout. At Truman's request, the steelworkers agreed to postpone a threatened strike, and indeed the president ended up with a 150–day voluntary strike delay, much more than he would have won with a Taft-Hartley 60–day "cooling off" injunction.[97] On March 20, 1952, the WSB decided that steelworkers deserved both a wage increase and the union shop. But at the same time the Economic Stabilization Agency, which had charge of price control, ruled that the industry did not need an above-regulation price increase to cover any higher wages. The steel companies refused to concede any wage increases unless the government allowed them to raise prices. The administration tried to break the impasse by signaling agreement on a moderate above-regulation price increase over ESA opposition. Angered by what he saw as sabotage of his price-control program, "Electric Charlie" resigned.[98] With his resignation the economic stabilization/mobilization program began to unravel. Even with the Truman administration hinting that some sort of price increase would be granted, the companies still wanted to rid themselves of the hated work rules and adamantly opposed the union shop. In effect, the industry was prepared to launch its own strike against a government role in labor relations.[99]

With the refusal of the companies to accept the WSB decision, workers again prepared to strike. President Truman responded to the companies' immovability by seizing the nation's steel industry on April 8. The steel companies sued in federal court to overturn his action. Three weeks later, Federal District Judge Pine overturned the president's seizure and ordered the mills returned to their owners, a decision the Supreme Court upheld in the *Sawyer* decision on June 2.[100] That day 560,000 steelworkers finally went out on what became the longest steel strike until 1959.[101] The outlines of the eventual economic settlement were quickly apparent, but the steel industry's hatred of the union shop and Section 2-B was so intense that the companies prolonged the strike for an extra six weeks. Finally, Truman called the sides together and announced a settlement on July 24.[102] The union could claim a large victory. Steelworkers won a version of the union shop. The companies got their price increase, but the workers got "the largest wage package the union has ever wrung out of the steel industry."[103] The work rules remained unchanged. Murray's strategy of winning government endorsement of labor's demand seemed to preclude any successful corporate public relations challenge to steelworker patriotism.

Murray won an important victory, but with the *Sawyer* decision the employers took a great step toward their long-term goal of re-privatizing labor relations. White House seizure of the steel mills had been predicated on the belief that the confrontation between company and union was no private matter, but one in which the public, through their democratically elected government, had an overwhelming interest. But the court majority agreed with the companies' position that the president's only option in labor disputes was a Taft-Hartley injunction. This was consistent with the business desire to move the dispute outside the democratic realm and consider it as a purely private matter.

Phil Murray's glee at his union's gains contrasted with Walter Reuther's increasing frustration with unemployment and the worker discontent created by administration policies, as well as his own attachment to the five-year contract. Layoffs due to the steel strike hit autoworkers hard. No steel, no cars. Auto employment bottomed out at six hundred thousand by January 1952. During the steel strike, it dropped below five hundred thousand. Detroit unemployment peaked at 8.3 percent in December 1951. Soup kitchens were set up the next month. As early as June 1951, workers began to blame their union for the layoffs.[104]

The auto manufacturers, who were pleased to work with the union in arguing with the government for contract approval, showed a very different face inside the plants when the companies took advantage of the long-term contracts to attack workers' shop-floor rights. Baltimore Shop Committee Chairman Harry Allen told Solidarity House of workers' anger at GM's treatment, "The guys want *action*. They are upset."[105] Flint Local 581 President Al Devine accused the company of "cutbacks, layoff, disciplinary action, threats of discharge, speed-ups, foremen working," which he blamed on the five-year contract that eliminated the traditional annual contract negotiations and possibility of a strike.[106] Autoworkers were particularly enraged by the employers' policy of speeding up work during a period of high layoffs. They conducted wildcat strikes at Hudson as well as Chrysler and Ford plants. Workers responded with harsh words and slowdowns. Those who accepted the speedup were told, "Stool pigeons, beware!" In September, Flint GM Local 598 voted 876 to 34 for a strike against the continuing speedup, but the International refused its sanction. The International placed DeSoto Local 227 under administratorship after a series of wildcat strikes.[107] Briggs's workers wildcatted four times in eight days.[108] There were over one hundred such walkouts in the auto industry from January 1951 to March 1952.[109]

Skilled workers faced a different problem when they saw their opportunity to increase wages stifled by both their own union and the government their leadership had helped elect. The Reuther leadership's reliance on union-supported government agencies deprived them of their chance for better pay. While production workers lined up at the unemployment office, Detroit area craftsmen found themselves in high demand as companies retooled for war orders. By late 1951, when over seven thousand lower Michigan Ford production workers were unemployed, only fifty-four Ford skilled workers were on layoff. Skilled workers knew their market position should command large pay increases. But those in the smaller "job shops" found themselves handcuffed by the wage regulations of the government economic agencies that Reuther had fought to maintain, while the Big Three's "captive shop" workers found their bargaining ability negated by the five-year contracts.[110] The skilled workers' anger over these limitations erupted during the Korean War in a series of walkouts and mass meetings. After a series of walkouts at the Ford Rouge plant, over five thousand tradesmen rallied at Detroit's Masonic Hall demanding raises. Given its support of the Truman administration, the Reuther leadership could only try to solve their problems from within the economic mobilization agencies.[111] In 1951, the WSB appointed a special tripartite Tool and Die Study Panel, whose labor and public members, over the opposition of the panel's business members, eventually recommended some increases for skilled workers above existing wage regulations.[112] Restive skilled workers reacted jubilantly, and the six thousand Rouge journeymen looked forward to wage increases calculated at anywhere from 28 cents to 77 cents per hour.[113] But when the full Wage Stabilization Board met, its public members voted with business against the Study Panel and in favor of maintaining the existing wage ceilings. Solidarity House had put its prestige behind the WSB method and come away empty-handed.[114] By mid-decade skilled anger boiled over into the largest challenge Reuther faced as union president.[115]

In late 1951, liberals found that their anticommunism did them little good in the areas of labor unity, civil rights, and the anticommunist witch hunts. Their hopes for labor unity were shattered when Congress passed a new Defense Production Act that weakened price controls but fully retained wage controls. AFL Secretary-Treasurer George Meany found the bill so objection-able that he argued that Truman should veto such a "callous betrayal."[116] Reuther disagreed, echoing the CIO view that without any DPA, unions would be forced into unpalatable wartime strikes. When the president reluctantly signed the bill, George Meany pulled the AFL out of the ULPC, forestalling any hope of labor unity.

Anticommunist liberals suffered another disappointment when Truman evaded serious action on civil rights. Eschewing any direct action for racial equality, postwar liberals had favored lobbying for a bureaucratic solution, a World War II–type Fair Employment Practices Committee (FEPC). They had worked to purge Communist Party members from any role in the civil rights movement, hoping to thereby win public approval.[117] But they had been repeatedly frustrated by southern filibusters that consistently killed any civil rights legislation. With the coming of the Korean War, unions and civil rights groups lobbied hard for some type of civil rights agency. After a year's delay, Truman established the Committee on Government Contract Compliance, charged with enforcing an existing nondiscrimination clause in all government contracts. But with no funding, staff, or powers, it was essentially a public relations gimmick. Administration insiders saw it as a powerless political ploy, "remembered by [the] boss at the last possible moment before election day."[118]

In February 1952, Reuther faced a challenge from the Right to his liberal anticommunist politics when Mrs. Berniece Baldwin, a Detroit nurse, testified before the Subversive Activities Control Board in Washington. She had been a member of the Michigan Communist Party's secret reserve leadership when it went underground in 1948. She had also been an FBI informer since 1943. In Washington, she testified that Communist leaders had told her that they would "liquidate" imperialist war leaders and obstruct American war plans in the event of a war between the United States and the Soviet Union. To the accompaniment of daily banner headlines, the Detroit reading public was shown the organizational chart that led from Stalin to the Communist Party ranks. Amid this fanfare, the House Committee on Un-American Activities (HUAC) began a series of hearings in Detroit.[119]

In its search for names, the Committee took testimony from Baldwin, other informers, and friendly UAW staff, as well as hostile witnesses from Local 600 and local black radicals. Baldwin detailed party activity and named present and past Communist Party members in Ford Local 600, the giant Rouge plant, as well as in Detroit, Ann Arbor, Monroe, Jackson, and the Upper Peninsula. UAW International Representatives Lee Romano and Shelton Tappes testified about Communist presence at the Rouge. The main task of friendly witnesses was to publicly identify past Communists, whose names the newspapers then reprinted, along with their places of employment and home addresses. Workers threw out named radicals from Dodge Main, Briggs, Cadillac, Midland Steel, Chrysler Jefferson, Chrysler Kercheval, Hudson, DeSoto, Metal Products, Gemmer Manufacturing, and Timken Detroit Axle. Right-wing workers held a sit-down at Hudson Motor Company against one worker that only ended when he told them he had left the party five years previously. Flint Buick Local 599 approved a resolution to request a HUAC investigation of its own members, although black foundry workers denounced the resolution's authors as Ku Klux Klan supporters.[120] The Detroit Board of Education hounded a Detroit teacher who had been named. The Detroit Symphony Orchestra suspended a violinist with his union's enthusiastic approval. The University of Michigan banned radical speakers from campus. Wayne University expelled an unrepentant student.

But radicals fought back. While HUAC paid special attention to Local 600, it also tried to corner radical black activists. However, when former Wayne County CIO Council secretary-treasurer and future Detroit mayor Coleman Young used his appearance to blast HUAC members for Klan activities in their own districts, the committee, with its many southern members, backed off.[121] In Chrysler's giant Hamtramck plant, 40 workers refused to work unless Local 3 radical Edith Van Horn was fired, but an hour later 140 workers walked out demanding that she be rehired.[122]

This hysteria did not penetrate into the giant Rouge complex. Communists had played an active and often well-respected role in the workers' struggles with Ford. Workers had regularly elected known Communists to the Local's leadership. Although right-wing workers did make some physical threats, they received little support. With all the publicity about supposed Communist activity, Reuther announced a hearing to suspend Local 600's elected leadership and appoint temporary International administrators. At a lengthy and confused meeting, Local President Carl Stellato repeatedly demanded some sort of specific charges, but Reuther refused. Claiming that unless it acted there would be turmoil in the plant, the board voted on March 14, 1952, to suspend the elected Local officers and place the world's largest local union under its direct control. Publicly, the International explained that it took the action because a "well-disciplined Communist clique" had so disrupted the Local that Ford was taking advantage, and that Communist abuse of the local 600 *Ford Facts* newspaper was "doing great harm to the whole Union." The administratorship lasted for almost six months. In the election that followed, Rouge workers voted overwhelmingly for Stellato and his supporters against a pro-Reuther slate. But the continued solidarity of Rouge workers could not hide the fact that if Reuther could take over Local 600 then no one was safe from his grasp. Although Solidarity House did succeed in getting back the jobs of many of those who had been run out of the plants,[123] an unrepentant UAW leadership proclaimed, "Communists are against our Union, against our country and against everything that free men stand for throughout the world. Communists are not just people who may have a different point of view on how things ought to be done. They are an organized conspiracy with only one loyalty, and that is blind service to the Soviet Union."[124]

Liberal weakness in Washington became depressingly clear when resentment against the Korean War played a major, if not the major, role in the 1952 Republican election victories.[125] As early as June 1951, the CIO Research Department predicted that stalemate in Korea could be disastrous in the 1952 elections.[126] But the anticommunist liberals had no way to distance themselves from the war, nor did they want to. Steelworker Vice President David McDonald told the 1951 Pennsylvania Industrial Union Council, "The policies of Acheson and Truman in regard to this world situation are right."[127] With the war stalemated and the administration's economic mobilization policies discredited, the public focused their anger on "Korea, communism and corruption."[128]

Dragged down by their anticommunist devotion to Truman's war, liberals saw conservatives seize the anti-Red banner and use it against them. Mainstream labor was deeply involved with the 1952 Democratic Party campaign. Reuther spent hours helping to convince Adlai Stevenson to run. Yet Stevenson showed little gratefulness, telling a huge Detroit Labor Day rally, "You are not my captives, and I am not your captive."[129] As the election neared, the CIO urged union voters to go to the polls even if it rained because "Our men in Korea can't cancel engagements with the enemy because of wet grounds."[130]

But opposition to Truman's war dominated the campaign. Speaking on an election eve radio show, one union leader, when asked repeatedly about the war, could only reply, "I don't know about Korea, but I do know no man who works for a living can vote for a Republican for President."[131] Running as the de facto peace candidate with his pledge to "go to Korea" and end the war, Eisenhower easily won the election, while Republicans narrowly regained control of Congress. For the first time since their creation, the CIO unions would not have a friend in the White House.

As conservative anticommunism made increasing gains, CIO leaders seem to have turned down the flames of their own liberal anticommunism. The CIO had launched a series of quick successful raids in 1949–50 against the expelled United Electrical and Farm Equipment Workers (UE). But the gains soon fell off. In 1952, the UE reported forty-three thousand new members, more than offsetting losses of six thousand workers. UAW International representatives reported that UE workers seemed "immunized" against red-baiting and appeals to labor unity. The expelled union had a solid base among its black members, and UE contracts were often better than the UAW's. In a last major effort against the UE, in the spring of 1952, over fifty organizers, primarily from the CIO, UAW, and International Union of Electrical Workers (IUE), tried to raid numerous UE plants in what the CIO euphemistically called the "Midwest Organizing Drive." After a yearlong effort, the leadership reported that the CIO had failed to win a single election. The CIO disbanded the drive in 1953, soon after the Korean War Truce.[132]

The partial retreat from an active anticommunism can also be seen in that year's CIO investigation of the Packinghouse Workers (UPWA) on charges of Communist influence.[133] In the CIO Executive Council, IUE President James Carey denounced Packinghouse as a "WPA for unemployed Communists." But Emil Mazey, UAW secretary-treasurer and investigation chair, so narrowed the scope of the inquiry that it looked only at top non-Communist UPWA officials and simply ignored the many Communists still active in the union. In a striking contrast to his earlier attitude, Walter Reuther then lectured the council on the difference between Communist domination, which merited CIO expulsion, and simple Communist influence, which did not.[134]

But if the UAW leaders felt politically isolated, they still retained great economic power. Rank-and-file workers felt increasingly restricted by the five-year contracts, as companies, no longer fearing an annual strike, had no particular motivation to settle grievances. Workers also had complaints about the COLA calculation. Reuther agreed with these concerns and was willing to use controlled worker militancy to correct them. When the auto companies refused in 1952 to consider their agreements "living documents," Reuther responded by approving local strikes where contractually possible and turning a blind eye to wildcats. Although it took another year, the union finally forced the companies to negotiate an acceptable contract.[135]

The retreat from the political to the economic front also echoed within the ranks. During the decade, the ideological enthusiasm of both the Left and the Right simply dried up. With the apparent "end of ideology," many autoworkers looked to their union to clear the path for their march into the consumerist dream.[136] By the end of 1952, trends that would endure through the 1950s were well established. A conservative Washington enshrined anticommunism and turned its back on reform. Most Americans accepted the new U.S. role in the world, "that the normal condition for Americans would not be peace but preparedness."[137] Reuther remained master in his own house, but could achieve little of his social reform program. He prided himself on the strength of the UAW, telling the IEB in January 1953 that with a membership of 1,346,140, he led "the largest free trade union in the world."[138]

Labor's support for the Korean War demonstrated the severe limits of liberal anticommunist unionism. The pro-business mobilization by a union-supported administration revealed that, far from being equal partners in a tripartite system as they had hoped, the unions were viewed by business and government as simply one more special interest group. They might be heard when they spoke for their own members, but they would not be seen as speaking for the interests of a broader working class. The CIO had always tried to achieve industry-wide and economy-wide bargaining, but it lost that fight during the Korean War. Anticommunist unions had seen themselves as part of the progressive force that would "contain" Communism at home and abroad. Instead they discovered that it was they who had been contained.

Notes

1. John Sweeney, Presidential Address to AFL-CIO Convention, Dec. 3, 2001, http://www.aflcio.org/mediacenter/prsptm/sp12032001.cfm, last accessed Aug. 13, 2005.

2. Martin Halpern *UAW Politics in the Cold War Era* (Albany: New York State University Press, 1988); Bill Goode, *Infighting in the UAW: The 1946 Election and the Ascendancy of Walter Reuther* (Westport, Conn.: Greenwood Press, 1994); Nelson Lichtenstein, *The Most Dangerous Man in Detroit: Walter Reuther and the Fate of American Labor* (New York: Basic Books, 1995); Kevin Boyle, *The UAW and the Heyday of American Liberalism 1945–1968* (Ithaca, N.Y.: Cornell University Press, 1995); Steve Rosswurm, ed. *The CIO's Left-Led Unions* (New Brunswick, N.J.: Rutgers University Press, 1992).

3. Steven Fraser, *Labor Will Rule: Sidney Hillman and the Rise of American labor* (New York: Free Press, 1991).

4. Lichtenstein, *Most Dangerous Man,* 182; Paul G. Pierpaoli Jr., *Truman and Korea: The Political Culture of the Early Cold War* (Columbia: University of Missouri Press, 1999), 87, argues that in World War II labor had much less power than is commonly assumed.

5. See Bruce Western, *Between Class and Market: Postwar Unionization in the Capitalist Democracies* (Princeton, N.J.: Princeton University Press, 1997), chap. 3.

6. James Wechsler, "Labor's Bright Young Man," *Harper's Magazine,* Mar. 1948, 264–71

7. See Gary Gerstle's fine discussion of cultural pluralism in *Working-Class Americanism: The Politics of Labor in a Textile City, 1914–1960* (New York: Cambridge University Press, 1989). For the decline in the very use of the term "class," see Margo Anderson, "The Language of Class in Twentieth-Century America" *Social Science History* 12:4 (Winter 1988): 349–75.

8. Walter Reuther, "How to Beat the Communists," *Collier's,* Feb. 28, 1948, repr. in Henry M. Christman, ed., *Walter Reuther's Selected Papers* (New York: Macmillan, 1961).

9. Robert Zieger, *The CIO: 1935–1955* (Chapel Hill: University of North Carolina Press, 1995), chap. 9.

10. Arthur Schlesinger, *The Vital Center: The Politics of Freedom* (Boston: Houghton Mifflin, 1949).

11. For the ADA, the best work is Steven Gillon, *Politics and Vision: The ADA and American Liberalism, 1947–1985* (New York: Oxford University Press, 1987). See also Mary Sperling McAuliffe, *Crisis on the Left: Cold War Politics and American Liberals, 1947–1954* (Amherst: University of Massachusetts Press, 1978), as well as Alonzo L. Hamby, *Beyond the New Deal: Harry S Truman and American Liberalism* (New York: Columbia University Press, 1973).

12. Roger Keeran, *The Communist Party and the Auto Workers Unions* (Bloomington: Indiana University Press, 1980); Margaret Nowak, *Two Who Were There: A Biography of Stanley Nowak* (Detroit: Wayne State University Press, 1989); John Bukowczyk, *And My Children Did Not Know Me: A History of the Polish-Americans* (Bloomington: Indiana University Press, 1987).

13. Keeran, *Communist Party and the Autoworkers' Union.*

14. Historians have paid surprisingly little attention to the Korean War home front. An important work in this regard is Paul G. Pierpaoli Jr., *Truman and Korea: The Political Culture of the Early Cold War* (Columbia: University of Missouri Press, 1999). Earlier useful works include Ronald J. Caridi, *The Korean War and American Politics: The Republican Party as a Case Study* (Philadelphia: University of Pennsylvania Press, 1968), which remains the only book-length study of the war's effect on domestic politics. *The Korean War: A 25–Year Perspective* (Lawrence: Regents Press of Kansas, 1977), a collection of papers from a 1975 conference edited by Francis H. Heller, contains an important article by John Edward Wiltz on "The Korean War and American Society." Steven Gietschier's Ph.D. dissertation, "The Korean War: Ohio Homefront" (Ohio State University, 1977), is an extremely valuable study. Most standard works on the period, such as Robert J. Donovan, *Tumultuous Years: The Presidency of Harry S. Truman 1949–1953* (New York: W. W. Norton, 1982), focus almost exclusively on foreign affairs and the MacArthur controversy. David Detzer provides a social history of Korea and America for the first two weeks of the war

in *Thunder of the Captains: The Short Summer in 1950* (New York: Thomas Y. Crowell, 1977).

15. Victor Reuther to "Dear Friend," July 20, 1950, UAW Education Department—box 20 "Victor Reuther Speeches," Walter Reuther Library of Urban and Labor Affairs, Wayne State University, Detroit, Michigan (hereafter cited as ALUA).

16. Nelson Lichtenstein, *Labor's War at Home: The CIO in World War II* (New York: Cambridge University Press, 1982); Martin Glaberman, *Wartime Strikes: The Struggle against the No-Strike Pledge in the UAW during World War II* (Detroit: Bewick Editions, 1980).

17. Bert G. Hickman, *The Korean War and United States Economic Activity* (New York: National Bureau of Economic Research, Occasional Paper 49, 1955), 5. For the business community in general, see Elizabeth Fones-Wolf, *Selling Free Enterprise: The Business Assault on Labor and Liberalism, 1945–60* (Urbana: University of Illinois Press, 1994). For the emergence of postwar business "realism," see Howell Harris, *The Right to Manage: Industrial Relations Policies of American Business in the 1940s* (Madison: University of Wisconsin Press, 1982).

18. The industries and companies were steel, petroleum, General Motors, Greyhound Bus, International Harvester, and meat packing. Benjamin Selekman, Sylvia Selekman, and Stephen Fuller, *Problems in Labor Relations* (New York: McGraw Hill, 1950), 554–55.

19. Labor Management Relations Act, 1947 (Taft-Hartley Act), esp. section 206, National Emergencies. See the second volume of James Gross, *The Making of the National Labor Relations Board: A Study in Economics, Politics, and the Law* (Albany: State University of New York Press, 1974, 1981), 2 vols.

20. United States Steel Industry Board, "Report to the President of the United States on the labor dispute in the basic steel industry . . . submitted Sept. 10, 1949" (Washington: U.S. Govt. Print. Off., 1949). Seth Wigderson, "How the CIO Saved Social Security," *Labor History* 44:4 (2003): 483–507.

21. National Association of Manufacturers Industrial Relations Committee, Aug. 8, 1950, box 102, folder "Positions, Collective Bargaining," National Association of Manufacturers Collection, Center for the History of Business, Technology, and Society, Hagley Museum and Library, Wilmington, Delaware.

22. The quote is from Hickman, *Korean War and United States Economic Activity*, 5, which provides a useful summary of Korean wartime economic activity. See also Harold G. Vatter, *The U.S. Economy in the 1950's: An Economic History* (New York: W. W. Norton, 1963).

23. United Steelworkers of America, International Executive Board Minutes, Oct. 4, 1950, 16–17 (hereafter USWA-IEB), 118, United Steelworkers of America Collection, Historical Collections and Labor Archives, Pattee Library, Pennsylvania State University (hereafter USWA).

24. See Kathy El-Messidi, *The Bargain* (New York: Nelson Publishing, 1980). Auto contracts traditionally ran for only one year. The two-year length of the 1948 contract was very surprising at the time.

25. Caridi, *Korean War and American Politics*, 66–68. For an excellent study of Truman's wage policies, including the Korean War period, see Robert Stanley Herren, "Wage-Price

Policy during the Truman Administration: A Postwar Problem and the Search for its Solution" (Ph.D. diss., Duke University, 1974). Although Herren is interested in how the Council of Economic Advisers affected policy, his description of the Korean War economic mobilization agencies is the best available. For Ohio, see Gietschier, "Korean War: Ohio Homefront," 65.

26. Thomas Holland, *A Chapter on the Earlier Period of the Wages Stabilization Board: September 1950–May 1951* (Washington, D.C.: The [Wage Stabilization] Board, May 1953), mimeograph.

27. United Automobile Workers International Executive Board Minutes, Sept. 11–15, 1950, ALUA (hereafter UAW-IEB).

28. Much of the chronology has been taken from the useful monthly summaries in the *Monthly Labor Review*.

29. "Guideposts for the Development of Price-Wage Legislation," unsigned memorandum, July 29, 1950, at Tab 133 of "Defense Production Act of 1950, 81st Congress Legislative History," 8 vols., boxes 1–4, Stephen J. Springarn Files, President Harry S. Truman Library, Independence, Missouri (hereafter Truman Library).

30. USWA-IEB, Sept. 21–22, 1950, 118.

31. USWA-IEB, Nov. 29, 1950, 16.

32. Dalton Trumbo, *The Time of the Toad: A Study of Inquisition in America* (orig. ed. 1949; New York: Harper and Row, 1972).

33. *New York Times,* July 26, 1950.

34. Sol Dollinger and Genora Johnson Dollinger, *Not Automatic: Women and the Left in the Forging of the Auto Workers' Union* (New York: Monthly Review Press, 2000), pt. 1.

35. See the description of the situation in Detroit and Flint in Alvin Hansen's introduction to James P. Cannon, *Speeches to the Party* (New York: Pathfinder Press, 1973), 7–16. Genora Dollinger has always denied that Sol Dollinger was daily run out of the plant as Hansen remembered.

36. "Dust Bowl" column in UAW Local 599, *Headlight, published in Flint Weekly Review,* Nov. 17 and Aug. 25, 1950.

37. Record of Local 599 Trial Committee, Oct. 13, 1950, Emil Mazey Collection, box 44, folder 599-2, 172, ALUA.

38. Special UAW-IEB Minutes, June 8 and 9, 1951, 85–160; for "martyr," see UAW-IEB Minutes, May 7–11, 1951, 168; UAW-IEB Minutes, June 28, 1951, 17–20. See also *New York Times,* Aug. 1, 1950.

39. UAW-IEB Minutes, Oct. 8–12, 1951, 334–40; UAW-IEB Minutes, Oct. 16, 1951, 339–401; UAW-IEB Minutes, Feb. 4–8, 1952, 361–64; Vuletich is not listed as a delegate from Local 544 at the 1953 UAW Constitutional Convention.

40. UAW Administrative Letter, Aug. 2, 1950.

41. Harry S. Truman to 12th National CIO Convention, Nov. 16, 1950, PPF 213, Harry S. Truman Collection (hereafter HST), Truman Library .

42. U.S. Department of Commerce, National Production Authority, *Historical Reports on Defense Production: Report No. 11: Labor Participation in Defense Production: History of the Office of Labor of the Defense Production Administration,* June 15, 1953. Microform edition.

43. *New York Times,* Sept. 18, Oct. 11, and Oct. 14, 1950; Martin comment in Official File 151 (Credit) for Regulation "W," Truman Library; Harold L. Enarson to John R. Steelman, Report on Dec. 17–18, 1951, NABMP meeting, Jan. 2, 1952, Harold L. Enarson Papers, box 4, folder "Memoranda of H. L. Enarson, Sept 1951–July 1952," Truman Library.

44. John E. Mueller, *War, Presidents, and Public Opinion* (New York: John Wiley and Sons, 1973).

45. See Detzer, *Thunder of the Captains,* 157; see also Edwin R. Bayley, *Joe McCarthy and the Press* (Madison: University of Wisconsin Press, 1981), 23, 97; *U.S. News & World Report,* Nov. 17, 1950; Caridi, *Korean War and American Politics,* 93–103.

46. Charles E. Wilson (1886–1972) is an important figure who has not received the scholarly attention he deserves. For instance, he chaired Truman's 1947 Presidential Civil Rights Committee that issued the "To Secure These Rights . . ." report. For Wilson's appointment, see Grant McConnell, *The Steel Seizure of 1952* (Indianapolis: Bobbs-Merrill, for the Inter-University Case Program, 1960), 6.

47. Fraser, *Hillman.* See also Kevin Boyle, *The UAW and the Heyday of American Liberalism: 1945–1968* (Ithaca, N.Y.: Cornell University Press, 1995), 74–79.

48. Holland, *Chapter on the Earlier Period of the Wages Stabilization Board,* 74.

49. Hickman, *Korean War and United States Economic Activity,* 15–17. For the UAW's detailed account of Reuther's role, see *UAW Administrative Letter,* Dec. 23, 1950.

50. Holland, *Chapter on the Earlier Period of the Wages Stabilization Board,* 72.

51. B. C. Roberts, "Wage Stabilization in the United States," Oxford Economic Papers (n.s.) 4:2 (July 1952): 152.

52. Stimson quoted in Richard Overy, *Why the Allies Won* (New York: W. W. Norton, 1995), 198.

53. *Monthly Labor Review,* Feb. 1951, iii.

54. *New York Times,* Jan. 31, 1951; Aug. 1, 1951; Apr. 21, 1951. Jas. M. Mead to Eric Johnson, quoted in Pierpaoli, *Truman and Korea,* 104.

55. For a good general history of Korean War price controls, see Hugh Rockoff, *Drastic Measures: A History of Wage and Price Controls in the United States* (New York: Cambridge University Press, 1984).

56. Cabinet Meeting, Dec. 11, 1950, Truman Library.

57. Pres. Green Report to AFL Executive Council, May 14, 1951, George Meany Memorial Archives, Silver Spring, Maryland.

58. Walter P. Reuther, Address to United Labor Conference, Mar. 21, 1951, Washington D.C., UAW Washington Office, Jacobs and Sifton, box 41, folder 5, ALUA.

59. CIO-PAC Research Department, Feb. 11, 1950, box 125, folder 7, President McDonald Collection, USWA.

60. Leaflet in UAW Fair Practices Department, box 3, folder 12, ALUA. Another copy in USWA President McDonald, box 126, folder 1, has the date Mar. 26, 1951.

61. *Monthly Labor Review,* Jan. 1951, iv.

62. Melvyn Dubofsky and Warren Van Tine, *John L. Lewis: A Biography* (New York: Quadrangle/New York Times Book Co., 1977), 497.

63. President William Green to the AFL Executive Council, May 14, 1951, George Meany Memorial Archives, Silver Spring, Maryland.

64. Jack Stieber, "Labor's Walkout from the Korean War Wage Stabilization Board,"

Labor History 21 (Spring 1980): 239–60; "Report of the CIO Labor Members of National Wage Stabilization Board," series 3, box 11, folder 2; "WSB, Wages and Prices General," Walter P. Reuther Collection, ALUA (hereafter WPR); "Statement by United Labor Policy Committee," Feb. 28, 1951, WPR, series 3, box 9, folder 2, ALUA.

65. George Gallup, *The Gallup Poll: Public Opinion 1935–1971* (New York: Random House, 1972), vol. 2 (1949–58), 974–75. The poll was taken Mar. 4–9, 1951.

66. Charles E. Wilson's "pound of flesh" comment in Feb. 16, 1951, Cabinet Meeting, Truman Library. Ruffin's "filibuster" reference in NAM Press Release, Apr. 13, 1951. "Statement by United Labor Policy Committee, Apr. 30, 1951," series 3, box 13, folder 6, WPR. See also the perceptive article by TWUA president Solomon Barkin, "American Trade Unions in the Present Emergency," *Monthly Labor Review,* Oct. 1951. Steiber argues that labor won its specific disputes over wage regulations, but his view ignores the larger political defeat. Jack Steiber, "Labor's Walkout from the Korean War Wage Stabilization Board," *Labor History* 21 (Spring 1980): 239–60. McConnell reports that labor leaders' sensibilities were "mollified" by the disputes resolution machinery, while businessmen were left with a sense of "injury." McConnell, *Steel Seizure of 1952,* 11. Preis offers a much harsher view, commenting, "Not one of labor's grievances was solved by the coalition war agencies." Art Preis, *Labor's Giant Step: Twenty Years of the CIO* (New York: Pathfinder Press, 1972), 436.

67. Frederick Harbison and Robert Spencer, "The Politics of Collective Bargaining: The Postwar Record in Steel," *American Political Science Review* (1954): 705–20; Judith Stein, *Running Steel, Running America: Race, Economic Policy, and the Decline of Liberalism* (Chapel Hill: University of North Carolina Press, 1998). Section 206 of the Taft-Hartley Act (Labor Management Relations Act, 1947) allowed the president, in case of a strike imperiling the national health or safety, to appoint a fact-finding board and based on its report to order a sixty-day cooling-off period

68. "Notes on Developments in the Labor Situation," Harold L. Enarson Papers, box 6, folder "Wage and Stabilization Board Policies," Truman Library.

69. Executive Order 10224, Mar. 15, 1951.

70. See "Notes on Developments in the Labor Situation" (Mar. 1951), and Feb. 26, 1952, Harold L. Enarson to Mr. Benjamin Aaron, Public Member WSB, both in Harold Enarson Papers, Truman Library.

71. Wm. J. Gerde, President to Wm. A. Johnson, Prez, American Pipe & Construction Company, April 18, 1952, National Association of Manufacturers Collection, Center for the History of Business, Technology, and Society, Hagley Museum and Library, Wilmington, Delaware.

72. UAW Local 932 (formerly UE Local 1146), box 13, folder 7, ALUA.

73. Author interview with Joe Ptaszynski, Detroit, June 8, 1981, and Feb. 16, 1984.

74. Proceedings, Thirteenth Constitutional Convention: United Automobile, Aircraft, and Agricultural Implement Workers of America (UAW-CIO), Cleveland Public Auditorium, Apr. 1–6, 1951, Cleveland, Ohio (Detroit, Mich., UAW-CIO, 1951), 12 (hereafter UAW 1951 Proceedings).

75. See Dollinger, *Not Automatic,* for material on "Little" John Anderson as well as a contemporary photo.

76. UAW 1951 Proceedings, 78–85. Author interview with John W. Anderson, Dearborn, Michigan, Oct. 20, 1978. Actually, the leadership probably knew how Rhee had used anticommunist liberal unions to destroy the Communist-led unions in the South and then used government repression to destroy all independent unions. See "Report on Korean Labor" by Stanley W. Earl, Labor Advisor, Economic Cooperation Administration, Mission to Korea, Seoul, Korea, Apr. 8, 1950. Earl wrote his "Restricted" exposé two months before the war began.

77. Donald Montgomery to Walter Reuther, Oct. 13, 1951, UAW Washington Office—Donald Montgomery, box 29, folder 14, ALUA.

78. For Reuther's lobbying to increase scarce metal allocations, see UAW Washington Office—Jacobs and Sifton, box 30, folder 6, ALUA.

79. U.S. Department of Labor, Bureau of Labor Statistics, *Employment and Earnings, United States, 1909–1978*, Bulletin 1312-11, 351. The figures are for "Standard Industry Classification 371"—Motor Vehicles and Equipment. The Controlled Materials Plan was the government's method of assigning important metals like copper and steel to military rather than civilian uses.

80. Government figures from Reports no. 39 (May 22, 1951) and no. 49 (July 31, 1951), Ray Blough Papers, box 10, folder "Weekly Reports to the President," Truman Library; Mr. G. Griffith Johnson to James B. Eckert, Oct. 16, 1951, "CMP Determinations for First Quarter [1952]," RG 296, box 25, folder "Metals August thru December 1951," National Archives and Records Service, Washington, D.C. (hereafter NARS).

81. Harold Enarson to Dewayne Kreager, Oct. 18, 1951, Subject: Notes on Mobilization, Board Papers of Harold L. Enarson, Truman Library.

82. *New York Times,* Jan. 21, 1951.

83. Thomas J. Sugrue, *The Origins of the Urban Crisis: Race and Inequality in Postwar Detroit* (Princeton, N.J.: Princeton University Press, 1996).

84. John R. Steelman to numerous government agencies, Aug. 9, 1949, Clark Clifford Papers, box 9, "Labor-General-Employment and Unemployment," HST. See the treatment in Wayne Lammie, "Unemployment in the Truman Administration: Political, Economic, and Social Aspects" (Ph.D. diss., Ohio State University, 1973), chap. 4.

85. Defense Production Administration, *Unemployment Relief through Defense Contracting (Dec. 29, 1951 to June 30, 1952): A History of the Defense Distressed Areas Task Force, Sept. 30, 1952* (Washington, D.C., 1953), 5–6.

86. UAW Washington Office—Jacobs and Sifton, box 29, folder 20. See also box 29, folders 21 and 22, ALUA. For earlier administration attempts to deal with this problem, see Robert C. Goodwin Papers, box 2, folder "Defense Manpower Papers, Korean Emergency," Truman Library; "Background on Defense Manpower Policy No. 4 in Operation," Oct. 1, 1952, RG 304, 8.26, NARS; "Dollar Value of Military Prime Contracts of $25,000 and Over Placed in Labor Surplus Areas during the Period 20 March through 31 July 1952," contained in Oct. 10, 1952, Memo, Carlton Howard to Regional Directors Manpower Committees, RG 304, 8.24, NARS.

87. *UAW Ammunition,* Feb. 1952, for "30 for 40" report.

88. UAW-IEB Minutes, Oct. 8–12 and Dec. 4–5, 1951; National Advisory Board on Mobilization Policy, Oct. 15–16, 1951, part 2, box 6, folder 10, WPR. See UAW-IEB Min-

utes, Feb. 4–8, 1952, 364–65, for opposition to unemployed committees. See the figures in James F. McCloud to Steve Stover, Sept. 26, 1951, UAW Local 280 Collection, box 2, folder "Correspondence August–October 1951," ALUA.

89. Jack Pearson, Recording Secretary UAW Local 212 to August Scholle, Feb. 5, 1952, and August Scholle to Jack Pearson, Feb. 20, 1952, Michigan AFL-CIO Collection, box 41, folder 2, ALUA.

90. *New York Times,* Dec. 9, 1951.

91. The Taft-Hartley Act permits the union shop, in which the employer is free to hire whomever they want, but the new worker must join the union after a probationary period. The Steelworkers Union had won a weak version of this with the World War II "maintenance of membership" decision. The union also wanted union dues deducted by the company from the worker's paycheck and given to the union (checkoff) rather than being paid individually, each month, to union representatives in the mill.

92. Statement by Clarence Randall, President Inland Steel, *New York Times,* Apr. 10, 1952.

93. See James Rose, "The Struggle over Management Rights at U.S. Steel, 1946–1960: A Reassessment of Section 2-B of the Collective Bargaining Contract," *Business History Review* 72 (Autumn 1998): 446–77. Rose reports that in the plant he studied, one-half of the grievances filed involved 2-B (458).

94. USWA-IEB, June 13, 1952, 14.

95. David Stebenne, *Arthur J. Goldberg: New Deal Liberal* (New York: Oxford University Press, 1996), 91–93 passim. There is some discussion of the 1952 Steel strike in Jack Metzgar, *Striking Steel: Solidarity Remembered* (Philadelphia: Temple University Press, 2000).

96. John Steelman to Harry S Truman, Oct. 19, 1951, President's Secretary's Box 136, "Files—General File—Steel—statement on steel dispute—December 22, 1951," HST.

97. USWA-IEB, Dec. 27, 1951, 22.

98. USWA-IEB, May 7, 1952. See also Harry S. Truman to John Steelman, Aug. 2, 1952, President's Secretary's Files, General File, box 136, HST.

99. There are two important works on the Steel controversy. Maeva Marcus, *Truman and the Steel Seizure Case: The Limits of Presidential Power* (New York: Columbia University Press, 1977), tends to focus on the legal issues, while the previously cited McConnell, *Steel Seizure of 1952,* fits the controversy into Korean War-time politics. Neither spends much time on steelworkers. See also United States Department of Labor [Edward Robert Livernash], *Collective Bargaining in the Basic Steel Industry: A Study of the Public Interest and the Role of Government* (Jan. 1961). For "steel industry strike," see Harold L. Enarson to John R. Steelman, Jan. 9, 1952, Harold L. Enarson Papers, box 4, Folder "Memoranda of H. L. Enarson, 1951—1952," Truman Library. Enarson has also written on the dispute; Harold L. Enarson, "The Politics of an Emergency Dispute: Steel, 1952," in Irving Bernstein, Harold L. Enarson, and R. W. Fleming, *Emergency Disputes and National Policy* (New York: Harper and Brothers, 1955).

100. *Youngstown Sheet & Tube Co. v. Sawyer* [The Steel Seizure Case], U.S.343, U.S. 579 (1952).

101. Metzgar, *Striking Steel,* 63.

102. Daily Presidential Appointments, July 1952, HST.

103. Phil Murray, Mar. 20, 1952, USWA-IEB, 34.

104. UAW Washington Office—Jacobs and Sifton, box 29, folders 28, 16, 19, ALUA. For workers' complaints, see Norman Matthews's comments UAW-IEB, June 28, 1951, Minutes, 10; *Monthly Labor Review,* Jan. 1952.

105. Box 8, folder 19, UAW Local 678 Collection, ALUA.

106. Al Devine column in UAW Local 581, *Fisher Flashes,* published in *Flint Weekly Review,* June 1, 1951.

107. For wildcats, see *Monthly Labor Review,* Sept. 1951; William T. Connolly columns, UAW Local 598, *Eye Opener,* published in *Flint Weekly Review,* Jan. 18, Sept. 19, and Nov. 21, 1952; Art Preis, *Labor's Giant Step,* 440.

108. *New York Times,* May 16, 1951.

109. Ray Kay Collection, box 3, folder 19, ALUA; *Monthly Labor Review,* Sept. 1951, 319–20.

110. The tool rooms of the Big Three were called the Captive Shops; those craftsmen's wages were governed by the UAW contracts with General Motors, Ford, and Chrysler. Skilled workers also worked in small specialty "job shops." In the Detroit area, job shop workers usually earned more than captive shop workers; the situation was often reversed in other metal-working centers. See UAW Washington Office—Jacobs and Sifton, box 29, folders 28, 16, 19, ALUA; Bruno Stein, "Wage Stabilization in the Korean War Period: The Role of the Subsidiary Wage Boards," *Labor History* 4 (Spring 1963): 161–77; author interview with Joseph Ptaszynski, June 8, 1981; he was assistant to the CIO members on the Detroit Regional WSB; Shop Committee Meetings, Dec. 20, 1950, UAW Local 80 Collection, ALUA; For workers' complaints, see Norman Matthews's comments, AW-IEB Minutes, June 28, 1951, U10; *Monthly Labor Review,* Jan. 1952.

111. UAW-IEB Minutes, Feb. 4–8, 1952; membership meeting, Mar. 15, 1952, UAW Local 80 Collection, ALUA.

112. George S. Eaton, Executive Secretary National Tool and Die Manufacturers Association to Eric Johnson, Mar. 7. 1951 (telegram), ESA Collection, box 22, folder "Machinery 1951 thru 1951," RG 296, NARS. Box 22 contains important correspondence. A copy of "Wage Stabilization Report of Tool and Die Study Committee," is in Howard Smith Papers, box 2, folder 17, ALUA. "Stenographic Report—Tool and Die Study Committee," Aug. 7, 1951, 326–30, Wage Stabilization Board Collection, Accession no. 53A-736, box 5, NARS.

113. See the extensive industry opposition in RG 296 ESA Collection, box 72, folder "Wage Stabilization (Tool and Die)," NARS. For Rouge figures and Ford protest, see Ford Motor Company Presentation in Wage Stabilization Board Collection, Accession no. 53A-736, box 94, "Industries Tool and Die," NARS.

114. Executive Session—Wage Stabilization Board, Oct. 30, 1951, Wage Stabilization Board Collection, Accession no. 53A-736, box 8, NARS.

115. Seth Wigderson, "The UAW in the 1950s" (Ph.D. diss., Wayne State University, 1989), chap. 6.

116. United Labor Policy Committee Minutes, July 30, 1951, Walter P. Reuther Collection, series 2, box 13, folder 8, WPR.

117. Wigderson, "UAW in the 1950s," 351–52.

118. UAW-IEB Minutes, Dec. 4–5, 1951; Official File 526-B, Committee on Government Contract Compliance, Truman Library; for "remembered" comment, see John Franklin

Carter to Philleo Nash, Dec. 4, 1951, Philleo Nash Papers, box 64, folder "Political 1951-Correspondence," Truman Library; RG 325; Minutes of the Committee on Government Contract Compliance, box 3, "Committee Meeting, February 19, 1952," Jan. 16, 1953; "Equal Economic Opportunity: A Report by the President's Committee on Government Contract Compliance," NARS.

119. All quotes from early February 1952, *Detroit Free Press.*

120. The Buick Local 599 Headlight published in *Flint Weekly Review,* Mar. 21, 1952, and E. L. Holmes report in *Flint Weekly Review,* Mar. 28, 1952.

121. All quotes from *Detroit Free Press,* Feb.–Mar. 1952. B. J. Widick, *Detroit: City of Race and Class Violence* (Chicago: Quadrangle Books, 1972), 127–36. James Truett Selcraig, *The Red Scare in the Midwest, 1945–1955: A State and Local Study* (Ann Arbor: UMI Research Press, 1982), 20, 56.

122. *New York Times,* Mar. 4, 1952.

123. *Detroit Free Press,* June 21, 1952, article on Edith Van Horn, UAW Public Relations Clippings, box 1, folder "Dodge Main Local 3 Region 1," ALUA; UAW 1953 Proceedings, 182–230; Boatin Statement to U.S. Attorney Frederick Kaess, May 9, 1957, UAW Washington Office—Victor Reuther—International Affairs, box 74, folder 8, ALUA; Emil Mazey to John Gallo et al., Apr. 13, 1961, UAW Vice President—Leonard Woodcock, box 18, folder 10, ALUA.

124. UAW-IEB, Sept. 15–18, 1952.

125. Bert Cochran, *Harry Truman and the Crisis Presidency* (New York: Funk and Wagnalls, 1973), 346.

126. CIO-PAC Research Department, June 7, 1951, box 126, folder 1, USWA President's Office, David J. McDonald, USWA.

127. Pennsylvania Industrial Union Council CIO Proceedings, 1951, 25, USWA.

128. Andrew J. Dunar, *The Truman Scandals and the Politics of Morality* (Columbia: University of Missouri Press, 1984). Dunar shows that Truman had nothing to do personally with corruption but never treated the issue seriously. For a good general study of the 1952 election, see John Robert Greene, *The Crusade* (New York: University Press of America, 1985).

129. John Bartlow Martin, *Adlai Stevenson of Illinois* (Garden City, N.Y.: Anchor Press, 1977), 578, 630, 660.

130. Final Issue of "Election Facts," 1952, box 26, folder 11, Political Action Committee-Roy Reuther Collection, ALUA (hereafter PAC-RR). For UAW contributions, see Roy Reuther to Emil Mazey, Oct. 21, 1952, box 6, folder 31, PAC-RR.

131. Louis Harris, *Is There a Republican Majority?* (New York: Harper and Brothers, 1954), 145–47; Samuel Lubell, *Revolt of the Moderates* (New York: Harper and Brothers, 1956), 41–42; Post-Election "Report by Louis Harris," box 52, folder 27, PAC-RR.

132. UAW-IEB Minutes, Feb. 22–23, 1954, 55–86; Apr. 28–May 1, 1953, 223–56; Apr. 24–28, 1950, 53. "Confidential Report, 18th Convention of the UE," CIO Skilled Trades, box 177, folder "(International) Union of Electrical Workers 1952–53," May 19–23, 1952, 93–96; Sept. 15–18, 1952, 48; Jan. 13–16, 1953; Apr. 28–May 1, 1953, 153–56; Sept. 8–11, 1953, 222–27; all in UAW-IEB Minutes; Alan Palmer, IUE International Representative to Tom Fitzpatrick, Aug. 14, 1953, Assistant to the IUE President, Charles Chiakulas Collection,

box 1, folder "Correspondence of Interest, 1954–1964," ALUA; CIO Midwest Organizing Drive to "Dear Worker," June 16, 1952, UAW Local 932, box 21, folder 5, ALUA.

133. Roger Horowitz, *Negro and White, Unite and Fight!: A Social History of Industrial Unionism in Meatpacking, 1939–90* (Urbana: University of Illinois Press, 1997), chaps. 8 and 9.

134. CIO Executive Board in CIO, Oct 27, 1953, Washington Office box 20, folder 22, ALUA.

135. UAW-IEB, Aug. 12, 1952, 19. *Monthly Labor Review,* Aug. 1953.

136. The phrase, of course, is Daniel Bell's, *The End of Ideology: On the Exhaustion of Political Ideas in the Fifties* (New York: Free Press, 1962).

137. Gietschier, "Korean War: Ohio Homefront," 323.

138. UAW-IEB Minutes, Jan. 3–16, 1953.

9. Subjectivity Lost: Labor and the Cold War in Occupied Japan

CHRISTOPHER GERTEIS

In the first two and a half years of the postwar American Occupation of Japan, General Douglas MacArthur's general staff (known colloquially as GHQ) initiated a wide array of social, economic, and political reforms intended to create a postwar Japanese society that would never again raise arms against the United States or its allies. Critical to GHQ's plan to democratize Japan were land redistribution in the countryside and unionization in the cities. Wartime planners for the anticipated Occupation of Japan believed that a government-ordered redistribution of rural land ownership would create a new class of yeoman farmers who would democratize village society. To curtail urban elites from again rising to dominate electoral politics in the cities, the plan called for American reformers to convince Japanese workers to form a strong labor movement.[1]

In September 1945, GHQ brought to Tokyo a handful of American labor experts, and handed them the task of planning, advising, and regulating the rapid legislation of union rights loosely based on the Wagner Act of 1935. Shepherded into law by Labor Division Chief William Karpinsky and Labor Statistics Bureau head Golda Stander in late December 1945, the Trade Union Law guaranteed all Japanese the rights to organize (a right that would later be enshrined in the 1947 Constitution), bargain collectively, and strike. Despite their fratricidal animosities back home, the International Affairs Departments of the American Federation of Labor (AFL) and Congress of Industrial Organizations (CIO) saw common cause in the mission to re-engineer Japan, and each recommended representatives to work with the American military government.[2] These American labor activists-turned-military government officials collaborated with union leaders and Japanese bureaucrats (many

of whom had been recruited from what had been Japan's wartime
ment) to write and implement labor policy in the spirit of a "New [
Japan.[3]

The primary directive from Washington was to build a "bread-aı
ter" union movement, and the Labor Division wrote policies and promoted
programs that actively encouraged Japanese workers to unionize around
an agenda for improved wages and working conditions. To these ends, the
Labor Division also launched an extensive propaganda campaign designed
to guide Japanese workers in developing what labor planners thought would
grow into an American-style, "business friendly" union movement.[4]

GHQ perceived union activists as one of three interest groups believed to
have been at odds with the wartime state, and key to building a strong base
for pluralistic democracy in Japan. In the first six months of Occupation,
American reformers legalized union activism, released the Communists
from prison, and legally liberated Japanese women. Women perhaps most
benefited from the political and social reforms that accompanied military
Occupation. The 1947 Constitution, drafted in English by GHQ personnel,
articulated a legal framework that, for the first time in Japanese history, gave
women equal rights and equal protection under the law.[5] That same year,
GHQ also approved special provisions for women workers under the Labor
Standards Law, which prohibited employers from paying differing wages
based on a worker's sex, upheld the right of women to equal opportunity for
employment and promotion, and specifically guaranteed maternity, nursing,
and menstruation leave.[6]

In his planning report on the status of organized labor for the then-an-
ticipated military Occupation of Japan, Theodore Cohen expressed concern
that "women workers might pose a major hindrance to union organization
because . . . [a] high percentage of women workers in industry had historically
militated against the growth of union membership."[7] Cohen had pursued
graduate studies at Columbia in the 1930s; indeed, he was selected to advise
on labor policy for Japan because he had written a masters thesis on Japan's
prewar labor movement.[8] In his report on promoting unions in Occupied
Japan, Cohen misconstrued the context of Japan's prewar labor movement.
He asserted that the prewar movement was weak and not well organized; that
women in particular would need special encouragement to join their unions;
and that an American Occupation would have to build a labor movement
from the ground up.[9]

Cohen was also wrong in assuming that Japanese women might again
militate against unionization. Postwar scholars have observed that a cadre of
women activists not only influenced the course of organizational policy and

strategy,[10] but that the worker organizations founded by the wartime state to subvert labor unrest, paradoxically formed a significant experiential base from which postwar labor activists built their organizing strategies.[11]

More significantly, recent scholarship has shown how women's labor activism before the war was far more significant when viewed *outside* the context of established unions. Many women, excluded by male workers from their respective unions, did not perceive the established labor movement as friendly to their cause, and often did not choose to organize under the banner of a national union. However, they did nonetheless organize work stoppages, strikes, and protests, and effectively bargained for better wages and working conditions. Indeed, the women textile workers whom Cohen argued had historically militated against unions had not only won improvements in wages and working conditions without the help of the national labor movement (and in many cases despite the best attempts at sabotage by union leaders), but also established important precedents of labor militancy and worker autonomy in an era that precluded women's political rights outside the context of the patriarchal household and that significantly predated constitutional and legal protections mandated by the American Occupation.[12]

Nevertheless, Cohen asserted in his 1943 report on the prospects for a Japanese labor movement that Occupation authorities would have to make a special effort if Japanese women were going to accept the establishment of unions in their workplaces. When made chief of the Labor Division in January 1946, Cohen even went so far as to ask women staffers at the Labor Division to add to their regular duties the task of promoting unionism among Japanese women.[13]

When Cohen assumed his post as chief of the Labor Division, the division began sending two-person teams into the field, one man and one woman, charged in part with the task of convincing Japanese women that they had an equal right to participate in the affairs of their unions.[14] Richard Deverall, a labor education field officer in Japan from 1946 to 1948, recorded in his memoir that he and staff researcher Elizabeth Wilson often "played to a capacity house" in union halls and local theaters that at times accommodated thousands of men and women. "These lecture meetings took us to the heart of the rank-and-file of Japan's free trade union movement." Deverall recalled that Wilson was "a courageous and unselfish never-tiring American gal. With Betty and the writer often answering questions by candlelight long into the evening, as the workers sat on ice cold floors and listened raptly for five and six hours, we answered their questions about women in America, collective bargaining procedures, the God-given right to strike, union democracy, menstruation problems, and the 'condition of the labor in the America' [*sic*]."[15]

Deverall, a Catholic anticommunist and former UAW activist, saw these types of grassroots outreach activities as key to the Occupation's counter-propaganda campaign to undermine Communist activists in the labor movement.[16] Deverall's testimony to Wilson's tirelessness underscores the presumption that guided Labor Division's outreach policy—that women could best talk to women.[17]

Labor Division officers also produced a diverse body of publications, visual media, and public speeches on how women should participate in the labor movement, and it is likely that the propaganda and personal appearances by women members of the Labor Division encouraged some Japanese women to become active in their unions. Indeed, when these duties transferred to the newly formed Women and Minor's Bureau of the Ministry of Labor in late 1947, more than a third of Japan's four and a half million wage-earning women had joined their representative unions. However, many of the women most active in their unions after the war had also been active in the labor movement during or before the war. To the surprise of the Labor Division staff, twenty-eight nationals and eight thousand union locals established Women's Sections dedicated to the fight for the issues of particular concern to Japan's one and a half million women union members.[18]

The postwar Women's Sections were partly modeled after the Women's and Minor's Bureau, and partly based on the wartime mobilization experience.[19] Intended to both mobilize more women and ensure that the union continued to act on behalf of its women members, the first women's union organizations emerged from the militant socialist unions that would prove increasingly troublesome to GHQ.

The women members of the teacher's union Nikkyôso founded the first Women's Section in 1947. Nikkyôso leadership headed an organization that ostensibly represented the interests of nearly a half million wage-earning women with strong ties to radical factions of the Japan Socialist Party (JSP.) Their earliest activities and publications encouraged women activists, as unionists, mothers, and the teachers of the nation's children, to fight for a national "peace education" program aimed to protect the anti-war clauses of the 1947 "Peace Constitution." Denied the right to strike as well as the right to collective bargaining by the 1947 Trade Union Law, women teachers nevertheless formed the organizing core of one of the most militant and radical unions of postwar Japan.[20]

Women's union organizations from several other public sector unions, the Public Railway Workers' and Communication Workers' unions in particular, were as militant and radical. However, the most influential women labor activists of the late-1940s were not themselves members of the unions for which they militated. As early as 1947, women married to the unionized coal workers of rural mining towns on the islands Hokkaido and Kyushu had begun to organize women's auxiliaries intended to support the union's effort to keep union jobs and win wages that could support male coal workers' families.[21]

The coal women, calling themselves the Tanfukyô (Coal Women's Association), fought for even the right to join union meetings by using techniques for mobilizing practiced by prewar unions as well as the wartime state. The Tanfukyô was a movement built on customary symbols of womanhood. However, the image of a coal woman the Tanfukyô constructed in song, slogan, and style of dress supported a carefully articulated agenda. The Tanfukyô women organized themselves as an association of political, militant, class-conscious housewives. These rural women activists found that dressing class-based militant activism in the garb of a housewife increased their ability to influence the course of the union by focusing the attention of both their community, and the nation as a whole, on the domestic ramifications of poor wages, squalid living conditions, and an unsafe work environment.[22]

What disturbed GHQ was the fact that these women appeared to be puppets of the Communists. Increasingly hostile to Communist influence in the labor movement, a number of Labor Division officials expressed worry that, without proper guidance, working-class Japanese women would be vulnerable to recruitment by Communist agitators. Labor Division researcher Elizabeth Wilson was the first to express concern that women's union groups encouraged "concepts of difference between men and women" and that "separate organizations for men and women made easier their exploitation . . . by other groups within and outside the unions."[23]

In a report to Golda Stander, the highest ranking woman at the Labor Division and Cohen's most trusted assistant, Wilson recorded that she was primarily concerned about the success of militant, Marxist union organizers (whom she believed to be Communist agent-provocateurs) in mobilizing large numbers of women. She asserted that the solution was for GHQ to discourage "separate organization of women within unions," and for Labor Division to continue "official encouragement that unionized women demand, and men solicit and accept, women's participation in their unions." "The only appropriate means to that end," argued Wilson, was that Labor Division encourage "proportional representation for women and universal voting for all [male and female union] officials." While proportional representation would have put women on the Central Committees of more than twenty-eight national unions, it is unclear how the positions of Wilson and the heads of the Women's Sections differed. Women's Section activists also advocated that Japan's most militant unions might better serve women's interests if they adopted stronger, gender-blind democratic controls over the Central Committee's of their national unions.[24]

Richard Deverall, not specifically interested in the issue of women's status in the labor movement, also weighed-in on the issue by arguing that the Women's Sections that had sprung up in thousands of union locals across the country were "internal separatist organizations that threatened to reinforce feudal and anti-democratic notions of women's inferiority to men." Deverall and Wilson agreed on very little during their time at the Labor Division, but on this point they agreed that Women's Sections presaged what Deverall termed the "permanent establishment in Japanese unions of a sex-based form of Jim Crow."[25]

It seems bizarre that Deverall would suggest Women's Sections encouraged sex segregation in the workplace to the same extent that "Jim Crow" laws enforced racial segregation in the American South. However, Deverall was writing in the wake of ethnic discord caused by GHQ's denial of voting rights for Korean residents, closure of ethnic-Korean schools, and involuntary repatriation of thousands of militant Korean mine workers. The official reasoning behind the American suppression of Korean institutions and organizations was that they encouraged ethnic segregation. In fact, however, GHQ initiated the crackdown on Japan's resident Korean community primarily because ethnic Koreans (many of whom who had spent the colonial years in ersatz slavery) mirrored the American military's own omnipresent "Negro Question" by militantly demanding equal treatment under the law.[26]

Conflating his understanding of gender and race, Deverall argued against Women's Sections by concluding that all "special organizations for underprivileged groups were ripe for Communist infiltration and that this kind of factionalism at the local level would make it more difficult to keep the Communists from winning national political control." In this case, Deverall was alluding to a growing fear amongst Labor Division staff that working-class Japanese women threatened to become agents of Soviet Communism.[27]

The Rapid Growth of Labor Militancy

By the winter of 1948, more than 6.5 million working men and women had joined their respective unions. Indeed, the popularity and rapid growth of organized labor greatly surprised GHQ officials, who had expected it would take decades to build a strong labor movement in Japan.[28] Although Labor Division officials seemed pleased by their popularity, Japan's postwar unions were not following the course planned for them by their American occupier. As early as 1946, Japanese union activists had instigated strikes, work slowdowns, and even seizures of factories in support of the leftist political agenda advocated by the overtly Marxist National Congress of Industrial Unions (NCIU, known in Japan as *Sanbetsu Kaigi*).

The NCIU, led by veteran activists of the prewar socialist and Communist movements, was the largest and most influential labor federation of the Occupation period, claiming leadership of unions representing more than 1.5 million union members nationwide. By the end of 1946, NCIU propaganda was calling on Japan's unionized workers to join in the struggle to nationalize the Japanese economy. Asserting that in order to ensure that the nation build a true social democracy, organized labor, in alliance with the Japan Socialist Party (JSP), would have to take the political helm and steer a worker-centered course toward economic recovery.[29]

NCIU-affiliated unions were very militant. Between September 1945 and December 1946, NCIU unions launched more than a thousand job actions, nearly half of which involved the seizure of the workplace by striking workers, and in some cases workers even opted to protect the economic viability of the company by ejecting their managers and assuming control of production.[30] American military officials, believing that these forms of "production control" strikes heralded the first stage of Communist revolution, consented to the Japanese government's request to ban the practice. Fearing further state suppression, NCIU Secretary General Hosoya Matsuta ordered the practice stopped, and directed member unions to abandon all tactics that directly challenged ownership or control of the enterprise.[31]

The NCIU staged a tactical retreat by reallocating mobilization resources to focus on the kinds of mass-campaign tactics practiced by the socialist coalitions in Western Europe. Set for February 1, 1947, the February General Strike illustrated that organized labor, not capital, sat ready to assume legitimate leadership of the postwar democracy. A general strike, organizers explained, would demonstrate that labor held the trump card—the ability to shut down industrial production nationwide.[32]

In January 1947, Hosoya and Ii Yashirô of the Public Railway Workers' Union (*Kokurô*) established the *Zentô* (National Committee for Joint Strike Action) in cooperation with a number of private sector unions, rival federations *Sôdômei* and *Nichirô Kaigi*, the JCP, and the JSP. The leaders of this peculiar coalition of what were otherwise fratricidal organizations (much like the United Fronts attempted in interwar Italy in 1927 and France in 1934) asserted that collaborative action was imperative since only a general strike would send a strong enough message to the National Diet and GHQ. It did not take long for GHQ to perceive the planned general strike as resembling the first stage of a revolutionary struggle to overthrow the Japanese government.[33]

Labor Division Chief Theodore Cohen called Hosoya and Ii to his office to explain that a general strike would likely result in American military suppression. He urged them to reconsider their approach, and told them that if they persisted it was likely to result in the destruction of the labor movement. When Hosoya insisted the strike was an extension of workers' democratic right to public protest, MacArthur intervened and ordered the strike called off. Given little choice but to comply or go to jail, Ii and Hosoya capitulated. Late in the night of January 31, American Military Police escorted Ii to an NHK sound studio, where in an emotional radio broadcast he called on all workers to defer launching the general strike set for the next day, but to continue their struggle for social democracy. Union activists were stunned. Most felt betrayed by what they perceived as a fundamentally anti-democratic action on the part of their liberator, the man who brought democracy to Japan, Douglas MacArthur.[34]

As relations between the United States and Soviet Union worsened during the late 1940s, American policy-makers in Washington and Tokyo began to plan how to incorporate Japan into an anti-Soviet alliance. Ranking officers at GHQ responded to the perceived change in mission when they began in early 1947 to characterize labor militancy as an extension of Soviet expansionism, and in the spring of 1947 GHQ ordered the Labor Division to "call-to-heel union militants"—one major general even suggested that Japanese unions needed to be "housebroken." It was clear to Hosoya that the burgeoning Cold War was about to require of Japan a role very different than most labor activists had previously imagined.[35]

Labor's Cold War in Japan

The NCIU's attempted reach for political power caused GHQ to request Labor Division personnel to keep close track of any Communist influence in labor disputes, strikes, and campaigns. As the perceived Communist-controlled NCIU continued to encourage member unions to implement militant strike tactics, Occupation officials at all levels, from the Labor Division to MacArthur's general staff, began to discuss ways to cut short militant labor's rise to power. By early 1948, a growing number of GHQ personnel agreed that, despite the risk such actions might pose to democratic reforms, the NCIU needed to be "brought to heel."[36]

GHQ officials were intent on curtailing what they believed to be a Japanese labor movement run from Moscow. Indeed, eighteen months after GHQ had banned production control strikes, Major General C. W. Ryder reported to his superiors at GHQ, presumably MacArthur himself, that NCIU unions continued to "forcibly enter mines and plants, operating them, collecting payment for goods produced, paid wages and kept profits." According to Ryder, their actions were a fundamental challenge to ownership rights, and should they be allowed to continue, portended the imminent collapse of the postwar economy.[37]

Ryder asserted that the workplace seizures were Communist-inspired, and that even government strike arbitrators had been "known to instigate" militant strike actions. He further implied that liberal labor laws, "written by American New Dealers," had created the problem by allowing "political agitators and Communists to take over the unions." Ryder asserted that militant labor, overindulged by American democratic reform, was a "powerful weapon being used by elements of a foreign power to effect economic sabotage." Labor militancy, concluded Ryder, constituted a threat to the security of the American Occupation of Japan.[38]

In response to accusations that Cohen had been too "soft on the Communists," MacArthur removed Cohen as head of Labor Division in March 1947 and replaced him with James Killen, a staunch anticommunist.[39] Killen promptly reassigned Richard Deverall to be his anticommunist point man. Deverall had distinguished himself as a strident anticommunist when he served as a Military Government Labor Officer (MGLO) in rural Miyagi and Nara Prefectures in 1945 and 1946. During his year traveling in rural Japan, Deverall became notorious for lengthy reports that narrated the advancement of a Communist conspiracy to dominate Japan's rural union locals.

Within a few months of becoming Killen's special liaison, Deverall had visited and reported on the status of local labor unions and competency of the local labor officer, on all four major islands.[40] Surprisingly, Deverall's field reports no longer focused solely on the activities of Communist agitators. Instead, Deverall reported his increasing discomfort with the local Military Government Teams, who seemed unable to deal fairly with Japanese unions. Deverall was alarmed by local MGLO officers' (of which he had been one prior to his reassignment) cavalier attitude toward labor law and openly hostile attitudes toward organized labor. Indeed, he claimed that in several instances MGLOs had used local police and yakuza bosses to conscript workers into a kind of corvé for American military bases.[41]

James Killen also recorded doubts about the likelihood that GHQ would follow through on its mandate to protect workers' rights, confirmed for him when Chief of the Civil Service Section Blaine Hoover proposed that

MacArthur revoke the right to strike for public sector workers. Foreshadowing a Japanese version of the Taft-Hartley Act, Hoover proposed that all workers in government and publicly owned corporations be made exempt from protections guaranteed under the postwar Trade Union Law. Hoover argued that to break what the majority of GHQ personnel perceived as Communist control of the labor movement, GHQ needed to curtail the movement's strongest base, public sector unions. Public enterprise and government employees would be put under the protections of a special Public Service Workers Law, which was intended specifically to oversee their union rights. Workers at large public enterprises, such as Japan National Rail (JNR), would lose their right to strike but retain their right to bargain collectively. Civil service workers, including teachers, would lose both.[42]

MacArthur called Killen and Hoover into his office to argue the pros and cons of the plan in front of him. Drawing on what he had learned of local conditions for organized labor from Deverall, Killen sharply criticized GHQ's inability to follow through on its promise to protect workers' rights. He further argued that Hoover's recommendations threatened to "destroy . . . or at least effectively dilute many of the more liberal aspects of the Occupation." Over Killen's strong objections, MacArthur sided with Hoover, and on July 24 issued a directive to the Japanese government that warned, "No person in public service should resort to strikes or other dispute tactics detrimental to the efficiency of governmental operations."[43]

Killen responded to the directive that same day by discontinuing all official contact with government unions by Labor Division personnel, explaining that "until clarification is secured as to which agency of [the Occupation] is responsible for labor conditions affecting government workers, it will be impossible for this Branch to effectively advise either the unions or the Japanese Government." Killen went on to assert that MacArthur's order to curtail the right to strike, "made quite clear the Supreme Commander's opinion that strikes by government workers in any agency are improper and that government workers in particular enterprises, such as railroad workers, should be limited in their collective bargaining powers through mediation and arbitration. This would imply that government workers outside of these agencies would have no effective powers of collective bargaining."[44] In effect, Killen had interpreted the memorandum as the revocation of the constitutional right of public sector workers to unionize, since under MacArthur's directive government workers could no longer engage in what would otherwise be a normal part of the collective bargaining experience. In the furor that followed, Killen and Deverall resigned from the Labor Division, publicly accusing GHQ of treating the whole of organized labor as part-and-parcel of Soviet Communism, and returned to the United States to declare the alliance a complete failure.[45]

Seeing Reds

Occupation officials at all levels had grown to believe each wave of labor militancy originated from the Soviet Union.[46] Politically suspect, GHQ targeted Japanese labor for suppression, and most labor scholars and activists in Japan agree that it was in the summer of 1948, at the Tôhô Motion Picture Studios in Tokyo, that GHQ made clear its intent to break Japan's militant unions.[47]

Organized in January of 1946, the Tôhô Local of the National Film and Theater Workers' Union (NFTWU, known in Japan as *Nichieien*) was from the start a militant union with strong ties to both the NCIU and the Japanese Communist Party. After two strikes in 1946 and 1947, the film workers were among the first unions in Japan to win a guaranteed minimum monthly salary, a shop steward system, an eight-hour workday, a detailed grievance resolution system, and a labor committee system that enabled considerable union control over studio-level production decisions. The rights the NFTWU had won were a model of success and the pride of the NCIU.[48]

Of particular importance was the labor/management committee system that gave the union considerable power over daily management decisions at the studio and in some ways implemented part of the NCIU's vision for a worker-controlled enterprise. Although the NFTWU won these rights through tactics consistent with the legal framework set up by Occupation authorities, the union's inroads into traditional management prerogatives was not appreciated by Japan's business leaders, government officials, or American personnel.[49]

Prominent business leaders, acutely aware of the political implications of the union's contract, approached Tôhô executives to encourage them to find a way to break the union. In a secret meeting held in the Yoyogi district of Tokyo, leaders of the newly founded business group *Nikkeiren* agreed to put a stop to the NCIU's attempts to win control of industrial production—even in cases where the union, such as at Tôhô, had done so through established legal means. The outcome of the meeting was the decision that a small delegation from *Nikkeiren* would promise financial support for the company, in the form of preferential loans, if managers attempted to break the film workers' union.[50]

In January 1948, Tôhô President Watanabe Tetsuzô declared that he would "deal with Tôhô's two Reds"; a red budget and a Red union. By spring, he had disbanded the contractually mandated shop steward and production committee systems and canceled all union endorsed productions at the studio. Union leadership staunchly protested, and both parties suspended all further discussions.[51]

Watanabe also sponsored the formation of an anticommunist rival union by granting a small group of twenty-two employees the union-right of a closed shop, with the proviso that the new Tôhô Employee's Union would strictly exclude "Communists and their sympathizers." Most Tôhô workers in Tokyo rejected the company union.[52] However, more than 80 percent of the workers at the off-site Stage Properties Division joined, which pointedly did not affiliate with either the NFTWU national or its organizational umbrella the NCIU. The split proved a significant propaganda loss to the NFTWU, and with a splinter union in his camp, Watanabe appeared well positioned to break the NFTWU Tôhô Local at Kinuta. When the contract deadline passed in March 1948, Watanabe summarily dismissed more than one thousand workers nationwide, specifically targeting NFTWU leaders and activists.[53] He told Labor Division officials that his aim was to purge the company of all "known Communists" and replace the militant NFTWU Local with the Tôhô Employee's Union he had sponsored.[54]

NFTWU workers responded to the mass dismissal by seizing control of the Number One Production Studio, based in the suburban Kinuta neighborhood of Tokyo. Sympathy strikers from the Communist Youth League, the Industrial Labor Association, and the North Korean Workers Association—swelling the actual number of occupiers to nearly a thousand—joined the strikers in occupying the studios. NCIU propaganda suggested participants rally in support of the union with slogans calling on all "citizens to defend the independence of Japanese culture and democracy."[55]

A Strike of Film Workers

The sit-down strike at the Kinuta Studio was not the first militant seizure of the workplace during the Occupation period, but it was by far the one with the highest public profile. The Number One Production Studio at Kinuta was the home studio of such blossoming postwar talent as director Akira Kurosawa and actor Toshirô Mifune (later famous in the United States for the *Seven Samurai* and the television mini-series *Shogun*), and the press reported regularly on the progress of the strike.

The mainstream press covered the strike from the perspective of management and government, which saw their opposition to the strike as a defense of the sanctity of property law and the state's ability to enforce it. The national labor press asserted that at stake for organized labor was the right of workers to collective control of the course of their livelihood. The NFTWU Tôhô Local, however, asserted in its weekly newsletter, pamphlets, posters, and media releases that the stakes were even higher, claiming that most at risk were the nature of Japanese culture and the survivability of the postwar democracy.[56]

As befit a union of filmmakers, strike propaganda produced was colorful and dramatic. The strike presented union propagandists with an unprecedented opportunity to orchestrate a pro-labor media campaign that included the participation of some of Japan's most famous film stars and directors. Ranking officers at GHQ feared that the high-profile strike was precisely the platform the NCIU, in collaboration with the Communist Party, needed to mount a direct challenge to American authority in Occupied Japan. Indeed, strike leaders regularly orchestrated demonstrations, punctuated with appearances by film stars, all well covered by the mainstream press, and the 1948 Tôhô strike saw the culmination of several years of collaboration between the film workers' union and an array of newspaper and magazine writers.[57]

The union often staged dramatic confrontations between striking workers and police, and publicly antagonized company representatives along with members of a company-sponsored "back-to-work" organization. Union propagandists produced banners, posters, and placards that decried how the rise of capitalist dominance of the film industry, underscored by the Tôhô Company's firing of union workers, was a serious threat to the survivability of Japanese culture. A significant component of the Tôhô union's propaganda campaign rested on a corpus of visual media depicting Japanese women as icons of Japanese culture, but women were also significant participants in the 1948 strike.[58]

In June 1948, the centrist daily *Mainichi* photographed the "Tôhô Union Women"—clerical workers, stagehands, and Tôhô's stable of film actresses— who marked the end of each strike day by marching out of the studio gate chanting slogans and singing union songs. In early August, *Mainichi* captioned a photo of a dozen Tôhô actresses, sitting around a small table laden with snacks, tea cups, and a large kettle table (somewhere inside the Kinuta Studio), discussing amongst themselves the "implications of a proposed strike settlement."[59] Significant, however, is that these women's marches and meetings were in fact staged by the members of the Tôhô Women's Section with the idea that the "star power" of unionized actresses might attract additional public sympathy for the strike.[60]

The Tôhô Women

Former Tôhô Women's Section Chief Ishikawa Masako explained, however, that this particular role was not the one intended by the women who had formed the organization. Women activists had wanted the Women's Section to be an advocate for gender equity within both the union and the workplace. Yet, in late 1947 the union's Strike Committee pressured Ishikawa and her colleagues to organize the Tôhô Women in a manner that would defer women's issues and help the union win more sympathy from the public. The women activists complied with the Strike Committee's directive in part because they believed that it was of greater importance for the union to solidify its base and win the strike.[61]

The Tôhô experience was not isolated: the women who had organized Women's Sections within the Railway (*Kokurô*) and Teacher's (*Nikkyôso*) unions experienced similar pressure to defer their call for gender equity and redirect their energy into supporting the family-wage and male-centered promotion structures being advocated by union leaders.[62] Indeed, women activists in many of the NCIU-affiliated unions were encouraged to cast themselves in roles that would benefit the union as a whole by subordinating their economic and political interests to those of their male colleagues.

Not clear, however, was at what point the labor movement would address issues of gender equity in the workplace or the union. Indeed, there was very little discussion of this outside the Women's Section meetings. The male-dominated leadership circles of Japan's postwar labor movement were uninterested in changing normative gender roles for men and women. Local and national unions consistently excluded women from collective bargaining agreements by making ineligible those categories of employment (short-term, temporary) commonly reserved for women;[63] by signing agreements that required "early retirement" for women who married or had children; or by requiring round-the-clock availability for rotating shifts, which tacitly excluded women who were prohibited by the 1947 Labor Standards Law from engaging in "night-work."[64] Women union activists, no matter how loyal to the union, learned by hard experience that gender equity was still of very little importance to the male union leadership who claimed to represent them.[65]

Women activists were not blind to their subordinate status. Starting in the late 1940s, women writing for the national labor press published an increasing number of essays calling for union leaders to pay greater attention to women's issues. Ishikawa Masako recorded bitter memories of how in 1948 her male colleagues undermined women in the Tôhô union, recalling one unnamed union leader who had bragged to her that the night previous he had "kicked the pillow out from under the head of his sleeping wife," which he thought "confirmed his commitment to reject bourgeois liberalism." While not as violently, most male unionists apparently had little regard for their fellow women activists.[66]

Nevertheless, the Tôhô Women's Section activists had reasons for their continued loyalty to the union. Clerical worker Shirota Takako recounted that in the dark days of the immediate postwar period "living and working conditions were as spiritually bleak as they were physically demanding." Shirota believed that in the political, moral, and spiritual vacuum of defeat, the Tôhô union offered her much more than the promise of stable work and better wages: the radical politics of the union were a "clean break from the wartime experience" that offered her and her co-workers an escape from the memory of the Tôhô Company's wartime collaboration.[67]

For Shirota, the 1948 strike was an extension of the freedom from political repression promised by the American Occupation. As a clerical worker in the film production division, Shirota had worked most closely with directors, and by the time of the 1948 strike she knew many of them well. She asserted that while her clerical job was on its own not particularly fulfilling, her participation in the union's Women's Section and Cultural Affairs Department gave her the sense of having an artistic stake in the films produced by the studio. Indeed, the collective bargaining agreement won by the Tôhô union in 1946 gave the union contractually equal status with management in regard to production decisions—which gave Shirota, a clerical worker, an equal vote in determining the course of the studio's production operations.[68]

The union used its contractual power to influence several key films of the postwar period, including Akira Kurosawa's *No Regrets for Our Youth*. Released in 1946, the film depicts the female lead Yukie, played by Tôhô star Hara Setsuko, as a strong-willed and defiant young woman.[69] What made the film controversial at the time was not that the union had dictated the film's production, but that *No Regrets* (the epitome of a short-lived genre known in Japan as "democratization film") was the first postwar Japanese film to feature a strong female character in the leading role.[70]

Released less than a year after war's end, the film was especially popular among young women, who felt drawn to Hara Setsuko's portrayal of Yukie.[71] After her father's death, and the imprisonment of her lover, Yukie begins a journey of self-discovery that takes her from the emptiness of bourgeois city life to a life without regrets laboring, unmarried, and without children, in the Japanese countryside. *No Regrets* was not well received by film critics: many hated Hara's portrayal of a character they believed "too selfish," arguing that the film was unrealistic in the way it portrayed Yukie's choice of a life outside the accepted norm.[72]

Hara also disliked the film—nearly as much as she despised the union that she believed dictated its making. She later confided that her experience making *No Regrets* had convinced her to quit both the Tôhô union and the studio. Hara was one of a dozen actors to break away from the union's closed shop at Tôhô in mid-1947 to join a spin-off studio named, rather unimaginatively, Shin Tôhô (New Tôhô). Tôhô managers were consequently forced to hire a new stable of actresses, and in a cheap attempt to retain some of the "star power" of the departed Hara Setsuko, company mangers even renamed one of the new actresses "Hara Sadako."[73]

Shirota, who remained in the union and employed at the original Tôhô Studio, recalled that the "dream-like quality of union life began to crumble" when the radical politics of the union forced the split-up into two studios, and gave Tôhô Company President Watanabe Tetsuzô impetus to break the union.[74] Director Akira Kurosawa also chose to stay with the original Tôhô Studio, but later explained that he had resented how a small group of Communist union leaders had pressured him to end *No Regrets* with Yukie (Hara) reconciling her life doing heavy farm labor, while living with the parents of her dead lover. Hara Setsuko quit over it—in part because of an uneasy relationship between artist and union.[75] Shirota felt in hindsight that the union's radical politics, and the rising tide of anticommunism, made both the prominent defection and American suppression inevitable.[76]

Indeed, Colonel Frank Hollingshead claimed that the provost marshal, who had toured the strike scene in early August, had ordered him to suppress the strike. At a Labor Division debriefing held at GHQ on August 20, Hollingshead, the commanding officer of the Tokyo Military Government Team, asserted that he had received orders from the provost marshal to enforce the eviction ordered by the Tokyo District Court earlier that month "by whatever methods required." Hollingshead, however, did not have the authority to intervene in the affair "unless it threatened the security of Occupation forces or their mission."[77]

Under orders from the provost marshal to resolve the situation, Hollingshead met with unnamed police officials, a district court judge, and Tôhô lawyers on the morning of August 18. During his debriefing (recorded by Elizabeth Wilson), Hollingshead reported that he had strongly suggested to the company lawyers that *they request police assistance* in evicting the strikers from the studio. When police officials objected that only a court representative could make such a request, Hollingshead suggested to the district court judge that *he* make the request. At first, the judge refused the colonel's order, but Hollingshead persisted, and after considerable bluster the judge reluctantly complied, and ordered the police to evict the strikers. Once Hollingshead had arranged for the Japanese police to handle the eviction, he proceeded to ensure the matter's resolution by ordering a company of American troops to supervise the eviction.[78]

Shirota recalled that it was like "stepping into one of the war movies Tôhô had made before the surrender," when on the morning of August 19, 1948, American tanks accompanied by nearly two thousand Japanese police moved into position around the Kinuta Studio.[79] The events of that day made national headlines, closely monitored by American censorship teams, who would not allow the publication of photos depicting the American presence. The events have since been celebrated and decried by scholars, pundits, and participants. With American tanks, infantry, and riot police massed at the barricaded studio gates, NCIU national leaders advised the striking film workers to comply with an eviction order served by the Tokyo District Court.[80] In a last-minute deal, company President Watanabe agreed to renew contract negotiations with the union if they left the studio. Facing overwhelming force, the striking film workers had little choice but to agree to comply with the ultimatum. Within a few minutes they had assembled their parade, and sang the *Internationale* as they marched out the back gate, waving a red flag and carrying banners that decried the destruction of Japanese culture. Several accounts of that day also recall that actresses Hara Sadako, Kuga Yoshiko, Kei Ranko, and Wakayama Setsuko wept as they marched.[81]

The decision to exit the studio was not easy for Shirota, who recalled that some strikers argued for the union to instead provoke the authorities into bloodshed. She was relieved, however, when cooler heads prevailed and the strikers voted to vacate. Nevertheless, she asserted that the tenor was by no means one of abject defeat. Indeed, Shirota recalled that it was with a sense of dignity that she joined the other members of the Tôhô Women's Section in parading out of the studio gate—remembering with pride that director Fumio Kamei wore a placard that declared "Culture will not be destroyed by Arms or Violence."[82] Ishikawa Masako also recalled the Women's Section's final march out the studio gates with romantic detail. While the women agreed that they marched and sang with a certain dignity and pride, neither remembered weeping. This is odd, because the women's weeping featured prominently in other accounts—men's accounts—of the strike.[83]

The trouble here goes far beyond the fact that memories are notoriously unreliable and that we can likely never establish as fact whether or not the Tôhô women staged what film scholar Donald Richie characterizes as a "cry-in." It is significant that the men and the women present that day seem to recall events differently—men remember women crying but the women do not recall themselves as having cried.[84] While seemingly a trivial point, the discordance in personal memory points to a larger problem: women unionists were represented by men as having portrayed women *as men like to see them.* The problem was endemic, and not always as benign.

Culture, Propaganda, and the Uses of Gender

Coproduced by the NFTWU Tôhô Local and the National Newspaper Workers' Union, the poster reproduced in figure 9.1 announces a special conference jointly sponsored by the NFTWU and the Newspaper Workers' Union. The conference was part of a larger leftist cultural movement spearheaded by the NCIU, and even included artist-representatives of its chief rival, Sôdômei. The NCIU convened the May 15 National Culture Conference for artists, writers, and intellectuals who supported the Tôhô strikers, but the national culture movement of which it was a part was primarily responsible for disseminating propaganda material similar to the kind of social realist representations of workers' struggles that is found in the visual discourses of most industrialized nations.[85]

The first slogan (read from top to bottom, then right to left) calls for the defense of the "national culture," and invokes a common nationalist discourse used by the political left that stems from Lenin's validation of nationalist movements that presaged socialist revolution. While certainly an obvious reference to the cultural hegemony of the American occupier, what GHQ likely found most offensive was the union's call to "banish the culture of whores."[86] Taken as a whole, the first slogans tell us that the Tôhô strikers were simultaneously the producers and defenders of Japan's national culture (*minzoku bunka*). However, the term that I first introduced here as "nation" (*minzoku*) is commonly translated as "race," and is rife with a deeply troubled history that makes "ethnic nation" the more accurate translation.

Kevin Doak observes that, "The problem of national identity in Japan and citizenship in modern Japan was shaped to a considerable degree by the historical formation of populist attitudes in the early twentieth century that were quite hostile to the new Meiji state." Despite disparate beginnings, popular and elite representations of the political nation had by the mid-1920s converged on the idea that Japan was an "ethnic nation" (*minzoku*) with racial as well as political ties. By the 1930s, Japanese nationalists who "recognized the element of race in the nation . . . also drew attention to the usual litany of 'cultural' elements that nation implied (shared territory, spirit, language, religion, and customs)."[87]

The wartime state was, in the late 1930s and early 1940s, able to appropriate popular conceptions of the *minzoku,* and interweave them into the political fabric of its imperial and colonial projects. Doak does not claim an absolute

Fig. 9.1. "Defend the national culture!" (*far right, from top to bottom in lighter [originally red] text*), and "Banish the culture of whores!" (*far left, from top to bottom, in black text*), 1948. Postwar Poster Archive at the Ôhara Institute for Social Research, Hôsei University, Tokyo. Reprinted with permission.

continuity between prewar and postwar discourses. He argues instead that, "The 1950s were the formative period in the rehabilitation of ethnic national-ism among leftist critics of the Japanese state," and locates the critical juncture within leftist debates that took place in the early 1950s. The anticommunist backlash that followed in the wake of the North Korean invasion of the South encouraged many leftists to revisit ethnic nationalism, but this time "ethnic nationalism was seen as an effective tool for criticizing, simultaneously, the capitalist postwar Japanese state and the cultural colonialism of U.S. impe-rialism."[88]

The propaganda developed for the Tôhô strike exhibits a leftist rehabilita-tion of the *minzoku* that predates by several years that described by Doak. On the surface, this poster (fig. 9.1) announces the special conference held in mid-May in support of the strike at Tôhô. The first slogan, as noted above, embodies a nationalist discourse stemming from the JCP's switch to anti-imperialist rhetoric that accompanied the Cominform's 1947 rehabilitation of the Stalinist support of ethnic nationalist revolutions.

This poster's nationalist critique of American cultural influence and the union's appeal to "Banish the Culture of Whores!" appear to draw the direct parallel to the Tôhô management's treatment of film workers as prostitutes and implies that this is the same for all workers. What is particularly inter-esting about the Tôhô union's use of this image to publicize their struggle is that neither capitalist nor prostitute appeared particularly Japanese, and may have appeared "American" to the GHQ officials who read these propaganda posters without the ability to read the Japanese language. In the heightened tensions that surrounded an American military, which had just been or-dered to desegregate (Executive Order 9981, July 26, 1948) and had recently implemented a general crackdown on ethnic Koreans, it seems likely that the Tôhô union's accusation that the American Occupation was perpetrating a "Culture of Whores" struck a raw nerve.

It is unclear whether union propagandists understood how this poster, or other similarly inflammatory propaganda, would affect their relations with the United States Army. Nevertheless, GHQ and Labor Division officials had, at best, a difficult relationship with the issue of interracial sex, and prostitu-tion in particular. Prostitution was not new to Japan. However, the "*pan pan* girls" referred to in the poster were women who worked on the fringes of an industry recruited from the working-class neighborhoods of Tokyo and Osaka *specifically* to service American troops.[89]

GHQ officially banned sexual fraternization, and threatened harsh punish-ment and court-martial for military personnel who openly dated or married Japanese women. Nevertheless, GHQ pragmatically ignored military personnel's use of prostitutes. Indeed, the Japanese government and American military officials informally encouraged, and even regulated, the *pan pan* industry as a means to defuse the threat interracial marriage, not sex, posed to their mutually segregated societies,[90] a concern apparently shared by the Tôhô union propagandists and made all the more significant by the JCP's 1947 shift to an anti-imperialist/de-colonization critique that informed the Tôhô union's propaganda campaign.[91]

Yet, the prostitute in this poster also stems from a context that predates the Cold War era discourses. The invocation of a prostitute's debased status as a means to symbolize capitalist exploitation of the industrial proletariat carries over from the prewar Japanese socialist movement, which had used images of women in subservient and debased relationships to the "fat capitalist" to communicate the threat posed to the nation by capitalist hegemony. Prewar leftists first developed visual propaganda, from posters to political cartoons, in order to reach illiterate workers who union leadership believed, in the Marxist lexicon of the era, were yet unable to perceive the objective nature of their oppression. Vera Mackie argues in part that images of women, prostitutes in particular, were an important part of the prewar socialist iconography deployed in visual propaganda intended to create a socialist subjectivity within which workers could re-imagine their political subjectivity.[92]

The postwar Communist Party critique of the Occupation partially re-employed the prewar discourse when referring to the Japanese government as a *pan pan seifu*, or "government of whores." While the labor press reflects a strong ideological bent in step with that of the JCP, records of whether Tôhô union leaders were working in lock step with the Communist Party when they created these posters have not survived.[93] Nevertheless, the "*pan pan*" depicted is much more than a rehabilitated prewar discourse on class exploitation. It is a double-voiced signifier of the simultaneous class and cultural exploitation specifically endured under American Occupation.[94]

The "*pan pan* girl" (fig. 9.1) depicted by the Tôhô union, her breasts concealed by a length of film stock and her pubis covered by a film script, is an eroticized representation of an exploited and victimized nation. By illustrating the "*pan pan* girl" as she accepts a presumably expensive string of pearls from the hands of the "fat capitalist," the image attempts to rally the nation by portraying a titillating female body under the threat of simultaneous class-exploitation and moral corruption. Simultaneously, however, the slogan "Banish the Culture of Whores!" invokes a sign that readers likely understood was threatened by the American occupiers serviced by real life "*pan pan* girls" on the streets of Tokyo.

The use of the sexualized female form by nationalist movements to portray the nation in jeopardy is not new. Indeed, visual propaganda using women's bodies to signify larger political issues has historically been quite useful in conveying many kinds of nationalist discourses, from Nazi Germany to wartime America, in part because the state seldom afforded women a public voice of their own. Indeed, "women" conjured by and for the male gaze in Germany, the Soviet Union, and the United States were also useful to a variety of male-dominated institutions outside the state, from political parties to labor unions, and relegated women to the role of discursive representation rather than political agent.[95]

The "woman" portrayed in figure 9.1 is decidedly not an agent of her own destiny, but a representative of a male fantasy/fear of domination at the hands of an oppressor class/nation, and is used by propagandists to signify the union's championing of the Japanese nation (*minzoku*) at the cost of suppressing women's subjectivity. The image of woman depicted by Tôhô propagandists operates as part of a marginalized discourse railing against class and cultural domination. Nevertheless, it is reflective of attitudes towards women portrayed by more dominant social groups (such as capital), and may have created, at tremendous cost for women, a conceptual framework from which marginalized men could find common ground with their social peers, similarly dominated groups, and even their oppressors. The union sacrificed its own to win better standing, and won nothing for it.[96]

The Long, Hot Summer of '48

Growing Cold War sentiments had brought American Occupation authorities to suppress a Communist-led strike at a Japanese film studio. It seems likely that GHQ was driven by an escalating sense of a global Communist threat and had conflated labor militancy with fear of international Communist revolution. Theodore Cohen had misconstrued the context of Japan's prewar labor movement, while Richard Deverall's lip service to women's union activism did little to advance the social objective of liberating Japanese women. Elizabeth Wilson first expressed concern that "separate organizations for men and women made easier their exploitation . . . by other groups within and outside the unions."[97] By the summer of 1948, GHQ commanders thought the JCP a minion of the Cominform, the NCIU in league with the JCP, NCIU-affiliated union activists lackeys of their Communist leadership, and women activists ripe for Communist control.

American Occupation reforms had legalized union activism, released the Communists, and promised to liberate Japanese women. But, Labor Division personnel were flabbergasted when twenty-eight national unions and eight thousand union locals created Women's Sections dedicated to the fight for the rights of Japan's one million women union members. Despite the continued lack of support from male union leaders, Women's Sections continued to advocate for gender equity within both the union and the workplace.

Ironically, the Tôhô women's alleged "cry-in" was also not the kind of role for women envisioned by Labor Division officials when they promoted women's union activism. Indeed, a significant component of the Tôhô union's propaganda campaign rested on a corpus of visual media depicting Japanese women as icons of Japanese culture; however, women—actual women—were also significant participants in the 1948 strike. Also noteworthy here is that popular and scholarly accounts often describe the final march out of the studio gates by the Tôhô women, but rarely mention the extent to which women participated in the strike itself. Many fantasize how on August 19 the Tôhô actresses wept, but it seems that Tôhô's militant women engendered the arrival of the Cold War in Japan by acting out as women the tragedy of democracy betrayed.[98]

The problem here is that there is very little record of women's agency apart from the deliberately staged engendering of the strike. More important is that while a "cry-in" may have been an effective means to dramatize the crushing blow dealt by GHQ to the union and nation, there is no record of who decided that a "cry-in" should be done, nor precisely why. Lost here were the thoughts behind the political theater, the subjectivity within the subjectivity. The tragedy in this lies in that we have no reason to believe that the Tôhô women were still anything more than the subjects, in union discourse and practice, of male representation.

For all their concern about Women's Sections in union locals being little more than bastions of sex-based "Jim Crow" and the hatching grounds for Communist insurgents, neither Deverall nor Wilson, by then caught-up in the anticommunist machinations of a GHQ looking to break militant unions, identified the Tôhô women as either active members of a militantly Marxist union or subjects of the whim of Communist agitators. It appears that, caught in the midst of a struggle between occupier and occupied, the Tôhô women were subsumed by the Cold War.

It is likely unknowable whether or not organized labor, in the context of its Cold War struggles, consciously subordinated women's activism. It is, however, clear that such relegation of union women to customary gender roles in the context of the left's anti-Occupation cultural nationalism had drastic consequences for women well into the 1950s and 1960s. No matter how much union leaders courted women with official lip service to gender equity, union women encountered tough resistance to their winning equal status to men. Male union leaders and activists seemed to prefer women to play subordinate roles, a reality that made it all the easier to marginalize the interests of women as wage earners in the intensifying political struggles of the 1950s, which were the basis of the higher living standards that characterized Japan's emergence as an industrial power in the mid-1960s.

Notes

1. Takemae Eiji, *The Allied Occupation of Japan* (New York: Continuum, 2002), 311–13.

2. Killen to Burke, May 6, 1947, IBPSPMW Papers cited by Howard B. Schonberger, *Aftermath of War: Americans and the Remaking of Japan, 1945–1952* (Kent, Ohio: Kent State University Press, 1989), 111–33.

3. Takemae, *Allied Occupation*, 175–78, 311–13; John W. Dower, *Embracing Defeat: Japan in the Wake of World War II* (New York: W. W. Norton, 2000), 245–46; Theodore Cohen, *Remaking Japan: The American Occupation as New Deal*, (New York: Free Press, 1987), 100, 214–15, 231–39; Richard L. G. Deverall, *Red Star over Japan*, (Calcutta: Free Trade Union Committee, 1952), 221–23; and Joe Moore, *Japanese Workers and the Struggle for Power, 1945–1947* (Madison: University of Wisconsin Press, 1983).

4. Labor Division officials from the AFL and the CIO agreed on very little, but on one thing they could agree: that for Japan a strong, nonpolitical labor movement would inflate wages and hinder Japan's competitiveness in the world marketplace. American jobs would be saved if American labor could help keep Japan from becoming an exporter of cheap consumer goods. In 1947, MacArthur directed the Japanese legislature (National Diet) to adopt a legal framework that protected the right to organize, strike, and engage in collective bargaining. The 1947 Trade Union Law also established a tripartite apparatus, known as the Central Labor Relations Board (CLRB), which was composed of government, business, and labor representatives who would arbitrate labor disputes in the event that management and labor could not settle their own dispute. Private-sector unions retained the right to strike, and did so quite often during the 1940s and 1950s. Most public-sector unions, however, lost the right to strike when in 1949 GHQ ordered the law revised in response to the Taft-Hartley Act. A second piece of legislation, the 1947 Labor Standards Law, established minimum standards for work hours, job safety, and worker's compensation. The bulk of the latter piece of legislation was written in advance of the American occupation by Teramoto Kôsaku, a wartime bureaucrat who believed that, because the ultra-right was completely discredited by defeat, this was the ideal time to initiate social reforms previously unthinkable. See Dower, *Embracing Defeat*, 245–46; SWNCC Policy Paper, "Treatment of Japanese Worker's Organizations," cited by Moore, *Japanese Workers*, 63–64, and also discussed by Cohen, *Remaking Japan*, 100.

5. Dower, *Embracing Defeat*, 360–73.

6. Takemae, *Allied Occupation*, 324–26; and Dower, *Embracing Defeat*, 246.

7. Advisory Committee on Labor, "Final Report of the Advisory Committee on Labor, Labor Policies and Programs in Japan," Tokyo, July 29, 1946. NARA, RG 331, 94, as cited

by Gail Mieko Nomura, "Allied Occupation of Japan: Reform of Japanese Government Labor Policy on Women" (Ph.D. diss., University of Hawaii at Monoa, 1978), 191–92.

8. Cohen's planning guide, which Karpinsky had followed closely when sheperding the Trade Union Law, was based on the master's thesis Cohen had written at Columbia. MacArthur replaced Karpinsky, who had worked at the U.S. Labor Department during the war, with Theodore Cohen in January 1946. It was Cohen who, while at the Japanese Labor Policy Section of the Foreign Economic Administration in 1943, had written the bulk of the plan for labor policy in occupied Japan. MacArthur selected Cohen to replace Karpinsky as head of the Labor Division in January 1946, largely because of his fluent Japanese, academic background, and his wartime experience in Washington. Takemae, *Allied Occupation,* 175–78, 209, 311–13.

9. Moore, *Japanese Workers,* 63–65; and Cohen, *Remaking Japan,* 37–42.

10. See "The Red Wave," in Vera C. Mackie, *Feminism in Modern Japan: Citizenship, Embodiment, and Sexuality,* (Cambridge: Cambridge University Press, 2003), 73–98.

11. See Andrew Gordon, *The Evolution of Labor Relations in Japan: Heavy Industry, 1853–1955* (Cambridge, Mass.: Council on East Asian Studies, Harvard University: distributed by Harvard University Press, 1985); and Michael H. Gibbs, *Struggle and Purpose in Postwar Japanese Unionism,* (Berkeley: University of California Press, 2000).

12. In particular, Patricia Tsurumi, in *Factory Girls: Women in the Thread Mills of Meiji Japan* (Princeton University Press, 1991), documents women's labor activism outside the context of labor unions, as does Sharon Sievers in "Textile Workers," in *Flowers in Salt: The Beginnings of Feminist Consciousness in Modern Japan* (Stanford, Calif.: Stanford University Press, 1987); and Barbara Molony, "Activism among Women in the Taishô Cotton Textile Industry," and Yoshiko Miyake, "Doubling Expectations: Motherhood and Women's Factory Work under State Management in the 1930s and 1940s," in Gail Lee Bernstein, ed., *Recreating Japanese Women, 1600–1945* (Berkeley: University of California Press, 1991).

13. By late 1946, women constituted nearly a third of the waged industrial workforce. Ohara shakai mondai kenkyû jô, *Nihon Rôdô Nenkan* (1952), 3–31, 334, 356; Takemae, *Allied Occupation,* 184–85; and Nomura, "Allied Occupation," 191–93.

14. Cohen most relied on Golda Stander (whom labor scholar Takemae Eiji has credited as "midwife to Japan's Labor Standards Law") and Meade Smith to write policy, foster legislation, and "encourage the democratization of the women's union movement." Both Smith and Stander had graduate degrees in economics (Stander from New York City University and Smith from Swarthmore) and many years of experience working in government and unions in the United States. While the accomplishments of Golda Stander, Meade Smith, and Beate Sirota (who helped to write the 1947 Constitution) are well documented, the work done by the hundreds of other American women working for the Occupation is commonly overlooked. GHQ employment records are notoriously poor, and what can be known of the less-famous women who worked for Theodore Cohen comes from brief mention in the personal memoirs of their male peers as well as the memoranda and reports they filed during their time at the Labor Division. All told, some four hundred of the American women working in Japan were uniformed personnel assigned to one of the two WAC (Women's Army Corps) detachments. They, along with several hundred civilian women, worked as drivers, radio operators, intelligence operatives, engineers,

nurses, doctors, administrative and logistical specialists, translators, secretaries, researchers, social workers, and analysts. Takemae, *Allied Occupation,* 128–29, 177–78.

15. Deverall, *Red Star,* 222–24.

16. As former head of Labor Education for the United Auto Workers, and with strong ties to the Catholic anticommunist movement, he appeared dedicated to the American mission in Japan. Because of a heated departure from the UAW (Deverall claimed he was ousted by a Communist coup d' etat), Deverall was not a CIO-sponsored representative, but had been assigned to the Labor Division on the recommendation of the anticommunist AFL International Affairs Division Chief Jay Lovestone. Deverall, *Red Star,* 221–22.

17. Deverall's working relationship with Elizabeth Wilson is obscured by the fact that Wilson did not leave a memoir or collected papers. While Deverall does occasionally credit Wilson, he was egocentric and dismissive of the accomplishments of others. From what can be gleaned from her reports and memos of the period, she does not seem to have much liked Deverall.

18. Nomura, "Allied Occupation," 190–94; Suzuki Yûko, *Onnatachi no sengo rôdô undôshi,* (Tokyo: Miraisha, 1994), 9–21; and Ohara shakai mondai kenkyû jô, *Nihon Rôdô Nenkan,* 3–31, 334, 356.

19. See Suzuki, *Onnatachi no sengo rôdô undôshi,* 9–21, 112–16; and "The Home Front" and "Citizens" in Mackie, *Feminism in Modern Japan,* 99–121, 120–43.

20. See "Worker's and Housewives" of the author's "Japanese Women, Their Unions, and the Security Treaty Struggle, 1945–1960" (Ph.D. diss., University of Iowa, 2001), 53–98.

21. Ibid.

22. Ibid.

23. Citation of E. Wilson to Golda Stander, "Re: Women's Departments," Sept. 2, 1947, NARA, RG 331, 1, as cited by Nomura, "Allied Occupation," 192.

24. Nomura, "Allied Occupation," 192.

25. Deverall did, however, see a role for Women's Section at the national level, where a Women's Section within a federation could "keep a close eye on local unions and push for women shop stewards, for women members of executive boards, and for women union leaders." Nevertheless, Deverall opposed women's grassroots organizations for fear they would become puppets of the JCP. Richard Deverall to Chief, ESS/LA, Stander, Meade, Smith, "Women's Sections and Women's Divisions," Sept. 14, 1947, NARA, RG 331, 1, as cited by Nomura, "Allied Occupation," 195–97.

26. For the history of the status of Korean residents during the Occupation, see Takemae, *Allied Occupation,* 452–54; and Robert Ricketts, "Zainichi Chôsen no Minzoku jishuken no hakai-katei: 1948–49 wo ch_shin ni" in *Seikyû gakujutsu ronshû* (Tokyo: Kankoku Bunka Kenkyû Shinkô Zaidan, 1995). For a brief overview of the status of African American soldiers in the immediate postwar period, see Steven D. Smith, Keith Krawczynski, and Robert F. Jefferson, "Victory and Context: Recognition of African American Contributions to American Military History," in *A Historic Context for the African American Military Experience,* ed. Steven D. Smith and James A. Ziegler, with contributions by Keith Krawczynski, Elizabeth Arnett Fields, Robert F. Jefferson, Steven D. Smith, (Champaign, Ill.: U.S. Army Construction Engineering Research Laboratories), online at https://www.denix.osd.mil/denix/Public/ES-Programs/Conservation/Legacy/AAME/aame4a.html#9%20Victory.

27. Richard Deverall to Chief, ESS/LA, Stander, Meade, Smith, "Women's Sections and Women's Divisions," Sept. 14, 1947, NARA, RG 331, 1, as cited by Nomura, "Allied Occupation," 195–97.

28. Moore, *Japanese Workers;* and ESS, Labor Division, "List of National Labor Unions and Federations in Japan, December 31, 1948," List of National Labor Unions and Federations in Japan, December 1948 (RG331, box 8482, folder 16), National Archives and Records Administration, Archive 2, College Park, NARA.

29. While the NCIU was officially aligned with the Japan Socialist Party (JSP), most of its Central Committee members maintained close ties to the Japan Communist Party (JCP). Lonny E. Carlile, *Divisions of Labor: Globality, Ideology, and War in the Shaping of the Japanese Labor Movement,* (Honolulu: University of Hawaii Press, 2004), 27–41, and 135–71; and Igarashi Jin, *Seitô seiji to rôdô kumiai undô: Sengo Nihon no tôtatsuten to nijûisseiki e no kadai* (Tokyo: Ochanomizu Shobô, 1998), 287–90; and Takashima Kikuo, *Sengo rôdô undô shi shi. 1945–1949,* vol. 1. (Tokyo: Daisan shokan, 1991), 94–100.

30. In the autumn of 1946, workers for the national daily newspaper *Yomiuri Shimbun* seized the paper's production facilities, ejected management, and began to produce the paper under worker control. A number of similar strikes were nearly as successful.

31. There is some evidence that the Cominform directed the JCP to force the NCIU to adopt this stance, and thus cool any possibility for the eruption of full-scale revolution in Japan. However, recent scholarship has revealed that JCP officials at party headquarters in Yoyogi had only a loose control over the labor activists and that NCIU leaders often acted according to their interpretation of policy, and independent of party control. Hôsei Daigaku Ohara Shakai Mondai Kenkyûjo, *Shôgen Sanbetsu Kaigi no tanjô,* Shohan ed, (Tokyo: Sôgô Rôdô Kenkyûjo, 1996); Moore, *Japanese Workers,* 104; and Carlile, *Divisions of Labor,* 135–52.

32. Tôkyô chihô rôdô kumiai hyôgikai (Yagisawa Akio), ed., *Sengo Tokyo rôdô undô shi—Tokyo chihyô no 25-nen* (Tokyo: Rôdô junpôsha, 1980), 165–82; and Takashima, *Sengo rôdô undô shishi,* 147–200.

33. Occupation records as well as official union histories indicate that the coalition likely had enough union support to shut down the nation. Carlile, *Divisions of Labor,* 22–24, 75–82.; and *Sengo Tokyo rôdô undô shi,* 165–82.

34. Many, such as Takano Minoru, who would emerge to lead the movement in the early 1950s, later remembered the banning of the general strike as the first betrayal of the American's promise of democracy. Hosoya Matsuta, *Sengo rôdô undô no rekishi to jinbutsu* (Tokyo: Kanae Shuppankai hatsubai Tôhô Shuppan, 1972), 51–52, 80–98; Takano Minoru, *Nihon no rôdô undo,* (Tokyo: Iwanami Shôten, 1958); Kawanishi Hirosuke, *Enterprise Unionism in Japan* (London: Kegan Paul International, 1992), 101–25; *Sengo Tokyo rôdô undô shi,* 165–82; and Takashima, *Sengo rôdô undô shishi,* 147–200.

35. Headquarters 9 Corps, Office of the Commanding General, "Memorandum to Commanding General, Eighth Army: re. Production Control" [copy], May 7, 1948, Production Control (RG331, box 8481, folder 1), NARA; and Moore, *Japanese Workers,* 243.

36. Joe Moore, "Purging Tôhô Cinema of the 'Two Reds': A Case Study of the Reverse Course in the Japanese Labour Movement, 1947–1948" *Canadian Journal of History* 26:3 (1991), 453–78.

37. Headquarters 9 Corps, Office of the Commanding General, "Memorandum to Commanding General, Eighth Army."

38. Ironically, the arm of Soviet foreign policy primarily responsible for instigating political unrest outside the Soviet Union, the Cominform, was actively discouraging the JCP from initiating a socialist revolution. Headquarters 9 Corps, Office of the Commanding General, "Memorandum to Commanding General, Eighth Army."

39. Cohen was promoted out of the post because many at GHQ thought him too liberal. MacArthur chose Killen to replace him on the recommendation of the head of the AFL's International Affairs Division Jay Lovestone. Lovestone had assured him that Killen was a tough anticommunist. Takemae, *Allied Occupation,* 176; Takemae Eiji, *Sengo rôdô kaikaku: GHQ rôdô seisakushi* (Tokyo: Tokyo daigaku shuppankai, 1982), 184; and Howard Shonberger, *Aftermath of War: Americans and the Remaking of Japan, 1945–1952* (Kent, Ohio: Kent State University Press, 1989), 119–20.

40. Richard Deverall, "Japan: History of a Labor Officer in the Occupation Army during the Period 26 Nov. 1945 until 29 Mar. 1946," RG 8-37; and "Japan II: History of a Labor Liaison Officer in the Occupation Army during the Period 1 Apr. 1946 until 15 June 1946," Richard Deverall Papers held by the Archives of the Catholic University of America (CUAA).

41. "Japan II: History of a Labor Liaison Officer in the Occupation Army during the Period 1 Apr. 1946 until 15 June 1946," RG 8-38; "Life in Japan, v. 4," RG 8-17; "Life in Japan, v. 5," RG 8-16; "Notes on Japan, v. 7," RG 8-33, Richard Deverall Papers, CUAA.

42. Takemae, *Sengo rôdô kaikaku,* 190–200; and Okôchi Kazuo and Matsuo Hiroshi, *Nihon rôdô kumiai monogatari: Sengo I* (Tokyo: Chikuma Shobô, 1969), 263–71.

43. Killen to Burke, July 15, 1948, IBSPMW Papers, cited by Schonberger, *Aftermath of War,* 125; and "MacArthur Urges Law to Prohibit Walkouts by Government Workers," *Nippon Times,* July 24, 1948, 1.

44. Economic and Scientific Section (ESS), Labor Division, "Memorandum for the Record," July 24, 1948, Chronological Files, May 48–Dec 48 (RG331, box 8477, folder 9), NARA.

45. Deverell and Killen even managed to persuade the AFL to pass a resolution at its 1948 national convention calling for MacArthur to rescind his "reactionary revision of the labor law in Japan." Deverall, *Red Star;* and Okôchi and Matsuo, *Nihon rôdô kumiai monogatari,* 263–71.

46. GHQ Military Intelligence Section General Staff, CIS/OD, "Summary of Information: Communist Policies for Spring Labor Offensive," April 13, 1948. Communist Activities, 1945–May 1948 (RG331, box 8497, folder 15), NARA.

47. In a roundtable discussion in 1971, labor scholar Okôchi Kazuo reasserted his ascription of importance to the strike as the first clear indicator that the Cold War had come to Japan. However, Okôchi and the majority of Japan's labor scholars focused their critique on the actions of the United States without acknowledging the culpability of union activists, who, as will be argued here, likely provoked occupation authorities. "Konakata ha gunkan dake—Tôhô sôgi zadankai," in *Gendai shiso,* Sept. 1979, 164–91.

48. Akira Kurosawa, *Something Like an Autobiography,* trans. Audie Bock (New York: Alfred A. Knopf, 1982), 166–67.

49. Okôchi and Matsuo, *Nihon rôdô kumiai monogatari,* 263–64.

50. John Price, *Japan Works: Power and Paradox in Postwar Industrial Relations* (Ithaca, N.Y.: Cornell University Press, 1997), 66.

51. Watanabe Tetsuzô, *Hansen hankyo 40–nen* (Tokyo: Jiyu ajia sha, 1956), 317–39; and Kyoko Hirano, "The Occupation and Japanese Cinema," in *The Occupation of Japan: Art and Culture,* ed. Thomas Burkman, Proceedings of the Sixth Symposium Sponsored by the MacArthur Memorial, Old Dominion University and the General Douglas MacArthur Foundation (MacArthur Library: Old Dominion University and the MacArthur Foundation, 1984), 147.

52. CCD, PPBD, Theatrical Section, "Memorandum for Record: re. Anti-Communist Movement in Tôhô," GHQ, CCD. PPBD, Theatrical Section, April 7, 1948, Memo for Record, Motion Picture Section (RG311, box 8580, folder 11), NARA.

53. Watanabe, *Hansen hankyo,* 317–39; ESS, Labor Division, "Memorandum for Record: re. Tôhô Studios," April 9, 1948. Chronological Files, Jan. 48–Apr. 48 (RG331, box 8477, folder 8), NARA.

54. CCD, PPBD, Motion Picture Section, "Memorandum for Record: re. New Officers of Tôhô Co. Ltd.," Jan. 21, 1948. Memo for Record, Motion Picture Section (RG331, box 8580, folder 11), NARA.

55. Okôchi and Matsuo, *Nihon rôdô kumiai monogatari,* 263–64.

56. From the author's survey of the published and unpublished materials of the Tôhô local and NTFWU national (folders D-20: 5–4, Nichieien 1948, 1–4, and Tôhô Sôgi, 1948) in the Papers of the Sanbetsu Kaigi, held by the Ohara Institute for Social Research, Hôsei University, Tokyo; review of *Mainichi Shimbun,* and *Asahi Shimbun,* 1948; and the Nichieien Tôhô materials collected and published by Yamamoto Kiyoshi in his *Tôhô Sôgi (1948-nen) Shiryô,* 2 vols. (Tokyo: Tokyo Daigaku Shakai Kagaku Kenkyujo, 1986). Some material sources overlap.

57. Miyamori Shigeru, *Tôhô Sôgi tsuisô—konakata gunakan dake—* (Tokyo: Miharu Shuppansha, 2002), 55–60, 153–57.

58. Moore, "Purging Tôhô Cinema"; Okôchi Toshio, "Tôhô sôgi no arashi ni tatsu: kubikiri mitsu," *Senpu* (Tokyo: Hakubunsha, 1948); "Hataraku mono no eiga engeki wo mamore!" "Tôhô no sôgi wo kyôdô tôsô de kachi tase yô!" Nihon eiga engeki rôdô kumiai/Nichieien/Tôhô (Ohara Institute for Social Research Digital Archives, PB0171: 26cm x 36cm, 1948); and "Mamore minzoku bunka," "Tôhô wo kachitaseyô!" Nihon eiga engeki rôdô kumiai/Nichieien/Tôhô (Ohara Institute for Social Research Digital Archives, PB0170: 25cm x 36cm, 1948).

59. Mainichi Shimbun, "Tôhô kumiai onnatachi," June 4, 1948, 5.

60. Tanaka Fudeko in Ishikawa Masako, *Konakata ha gunkan dake II* (privately published by Ishikawa Masako, 1977), 9–12, in the holdings of the Ohara Institute for Social Research, Tokyo.

61. Tanaka Fudeko in *Konakata ha gunkan dake II,* 12–20.

62. Not all women activists were waged-workers; indeed, women activists in the Coal and Steel worker's unions married to male union members organized themselves as Housewives Associations. I examine this history in chapters 2 and 3 of my dissertation. Christopher Gerteis, "Japanese Women, Their Unions, and the Security Treaty Struggle, 1945–1960" (Ph.D. diss., University of Iowa, 2001).

63. Fewer than ten women served in national union office between 1945 and 1955.

64. Mackie, "Citizens," in *Feminism in Modern Japan*, 120–43.

65. And yet, women unionists stayed with the movement; many appear to have taken on faith that eventually the movement would have to address issues of gender inequity, perhaps after the labor movement had secured a stronger economic foothold in the post-war society. This phenomenon is treated in considerable depth in the author's "Japanese Women, Their Unions, and the Security Treaty Struggle."

66. While management certainly had not treated its employees very well, a few women working at the Tōhō Studio did wonder whether the union had really represented their best interests. Ishikawa Masako, *Konakata ha gunkan dake I* (privately published by Ishikawa Masako, 1977), 1–5 (in the holdings of the Ohara Institute for Social Research, Tokyo).

67. Ishikawa, *Konakata I*, 3–7.

68. Ibid., 7–15.

69. Kurosawa later complained that he had been forced to accept the Scenario Review Committee's version of the last twenty minutes of the film, which he believed had been distorted by the Communist agenda of the union's review committee. Indeed, Kurosawa asserted that he had "poured all his rage at the Scenario Review Committee into those final scenes." Kurosawa, *Something Like an Autobiography*, 166–67.

70. During the immediate Occupation period, "freedom of expression," "gender equality," and "democracy" were popular buzzwords, and Chief of the Civil Information and Education Section David Conde had urged Kurosawa to make *No Regrets* into a vehicle for promoting the Occupation's social agenda. Kyoko Hirano, *Mr. Smith Goes to Tokyo: Japanese Cinema under American Occupation, 1945–52* (New York: Smithsonian Books, 1994).

71. Hara Setsuko is most closely associated with the films of director Ozu Yasujiro, and in fact left show business not long after Ozu's death in 1963. In Japan, Hara is remembered as an "enigmatic character oddly separate, and inseparable, from her film roles." Donald Richie explains that "this was because on the screen she reconciled her life as real people cannot. . . . Truly, in that though she played all social roles—daughter, wife, and mother—she only played them in her films. They were inventions and did not eclipse the individual self of Hara Setsuko. And in this way she exposed the social roles of women in film for the fictions that they are." Hara never married; she never bore children, nor maintained obvious romantic connections with men. Her primary relationships were entirely with women, and her life was not reconcilable with the model of womanhood portrayed in her films. Hara refused to embody their desires off screen. See Donald Richie, "Hara Setsuko" (Tokyo: Kodansha International, 1988), available online at http://www.ozuyasujiro.com/resources/setsukohara.htm.

72. Katogawa Naoki, "Waga seishun nikui nashi," in *Eigahyôron* 4:1 (Feb. 1, 1947), 29–33; and Tôgô Atsushi, "Kagayaku zenshin: Hara Setsuko no konogoro," in *Eigafaan* 1:3 (August 1, 1946), 26–27.

73. Hirano, *Mr. Smith Goes to Tokyo*.

74. Ishikawa, *Konakata I*, 3–15.

75. Hirano, *Mr. Smith Goes to Tokyo*.

76. Ishikawa, *Konakata I*, 3–15.

77. ESS, Labor Division, Labor Relations Branch, "Memorandum of Conference: re.

Tôhô Movie Studios Dispute," Aug. 20, 1948. Chronological Files, May 48–Dec 48 (RG331, box 8477, folder 9), National Archives at College Park, NARA.

78. That night, a platoon of U.S. soldiers of the First Cavalry Division, five Sherman tanks, and two armored cars from the Eighth Army were recalled from combat maneuvers around the Mt. Fuji area and ordered to the Kinuta neighborhood of Setagaya Ward. At Camp Drake, outside Tokyo, a company of U.S. soldiers were also put on one-hour ready alert. ESS, Labor Division, Labor Relations Branch, "Memorandum of Conference: re. Tôhô Movie Studios Dispute"; *Nippon Times,* Aug. 11, 1948; and Lambert, "Kinuta Strikers," *Nippon Times,* Aug. 20, 1948, 1.

79. Lambert, "Kinuta Strikers," *Nippon Times,* Aug. 20, 1948.

80. On a platform above the gate, stationed next to a large studio fan, several Tôhô strikers stood poised to spray the police with what military intelligence later reported to be broken glass, but was most likely blue or red paint. Military Intelligence reported to Washington the following day that the strikers planned to spray the troops with glass and sand, but Nichieien leaders later insisted that they only intended to symbolically mark the police as oppressors of the working classes by spraying them with red paint. The plan to use red paint was changed to blue because some strikers thought the obvious reference to the blood of the working class might enrage the police. Military Intelligence Section, General Staff, "Intelligence Summary," Aug. 19–21, 1948. No. 2187 (RG6, Box 39), MacArthur Archives.

81. Asahi Shimbun, "Tôhô kumiai: kinuta satsuenjô akewatashi," Aug. 20, 1948; Lambert, "Kinuta Strikers," *Nippon Times,* Aug, 20, 1948, 1; and "Konakata ha gunkan dake—Tôhô Sogi zadankai," in *Gendai shisô,* 164–91.

82. Ishikawa, *Konakata ha gunkan dake II.*

83. In the 1971 *Gendai Shisô* roundtable discussion, producer/director Itô Takeo and film critic Yamamoto Satsuo recalled that the Tôhô women cried while they marched, while labor scholar Shiota Shiyôbe described the Tôhô women's weeping as a demonstration. Donald Richie writes that a "contingent of Tôhô actresses put on a crying act . . . and were . . . followed by a cluster of unfurled red flags with everyone singing *The Internationale.*" Joseph L. Anderson and Donald Richie, *The Japanese Film: Art and Industry,* expanded ed. (Princeton, N.J.: Princeton University Press, 1982), 171.

84. Anderson and Richie, *Japanese Film,* 171.

85. Indeed, there is diverse literature concerning the impact of gender norms on labor propaganda. Elizabeth Faue, in *Community of Suffering and Struggle: Women, Men, and the Labor Movement in Minneapolis, 1915–1945* (Chapel Hill: University of North Carolina Press, 1991), documents how Minneapolis-based labor unions used an iconography of "woman" to signify their political agenda, often to the detriment of the women activists responsible for mobilizing the communities in which they lived. Greta Bucher, in "Struggling to Survive: Soviet Women in the Postwar Years," *Journal of Women's History* 12:1 (2000): 137–50, illustrates how the Soviet State also used iconographies of womanhood to illustrate many of the political campaigns of the 1950s. See also Elena Osokina in *Our Daily Bread: Socialist Distribution and the Art of Survival in Stalin's Russia, 1927–1941* (Armonk, N.Y.: ME Sharpe, 2001). The Japanese labor propaganda of the postwar era borrows heavily from the visual propaganda of prewar Japan as well as the People's Republic of China. Ellen Johnson Liang examines the socialist-realist propaganda art of the PRC, a

considerable amount of which implemented discourses of both masculine and feminine, and a side-by-side reading of the PRC and Japanese propaganda suggests a correlation backed by the political discourses of the Communist and Socialist parties in Japan. See Ellen Johnston Liang in *The Winking Owl: Art in the People's Republic of China* (Berkeley: University of California Press, 1988).

86. See Kevin Doak, "What Is a Nation and Who Belongs? National Narratives and the Ethnic Imagination in Twentieth-Century Japan," *American Historical Review* 102:2 (Apr. 1997): 283–309.

87. Ibid.

88. It is interesting to note that the *minzoku bunka* (national culture) identified in many of the roughly twenty strike posters preserved by the Ohara Institute at Hôsei University, predates by a short time Yoshida Shigeru's call to rebuild Japanese society as a *bunka kokka* (a cultural nation), and coincides with the creation of the Yomiuri Bungaku Shô (Yomiuri Prize for Literature), first established in 1948 by the Yomiuri Shimbun Company with the aim of building a "cultural nation" (*bunka kokka*). It seems possible that the conservative promotion of Japan as a *bunka kokka* was an attempt to lay claim to a nationalist territory simultaneously being staked-out by the political left. Indeed, left-led unions were deeply committed to the kind of close collaboration between unions and popular artists that created much of the propaganda distributed during the Tôhô Strike, and their collaborations augured the formation in the early 1950s of a loose affiliation of artists, labor organizers, and intellectuals known as the *Kokumin Bunka Kaigi* (People's Culture Council, or PCC). Although diametrically opposed, conservative and leftist movements were similarly conceived as cultural interventions—one to build a conservative liberal bourgeois and the other to promote the building of a socialist society in Japan. See Doak, "What Is a Nation and Who Belongs?"

89. See Dower, *Embracing Defeat*, 124–32.

90. Indeed, miscegenation remained a crime in much of the southeastern United States until 1965.

91. Nevertheless, many Americans believed Japan to be world renowned for a tolerant attitude toward female sex work, and as a result some of the more moralistic authorities spent considerable time and effort trying to discourage soldiers from engaging in the various services. Under considerable pressure from Washington to ban prostitution in Japan, the Public Opinion and Statistical Research Section was ordered sometime in 1947 to conduct a survey of popular attitudes toward prostitution with the hopes that the Japanese government could then be pressured to make it illegal. American survey teams constructed interview schedules with the assistance of their sibling bureau in the Prime Minister's Office of the Japanese government. Anthropologist John Bennett later recalled that the results of the survey indicated that while many women were critical of prostitution, and resented men using the facilities, men were much less concerned with the issue—to the point of even asking why anyone was asking these questions in the first place. Oddly, the survey submitted to GHQ concluded that there was "no strong feeling in either gender that prostitution was a grave moral issue" and suggested that the "Japanese people, lacking a strict universal religious morality, tended to judge things as good or bad depending on situations and consequences." See John W. Bennett, "Women of the Night," in "Doing Photography and Social Research in Occupied Japan, 1948–1951," Ohio State

University Library, 2002: http://www.lib.ohio-state.edu/rarweb/japan/; and Michael S. Molasky, *The American Occupation of Japan and Okinawa: Literature and Memory, Asia's Transformations* (New York: Routledge, 1999).

92. Vera Mackie, in *Creating Socialist Women,* was the first to analyze the trope of the "prostitute" in the labor propaganda of prewar Japan. My discussion of sex work is most influenced by Joanna Brewis and Stephen Linstead, *Sex, Work and Sex Work: Eroticizing Organization* (New York: Routledge, 2000); Wendy Chapkis and Annie Sprinkle, *Live Sex Acts: Women Performing Erotic Labor* (New York: Routledge, 1997); Frederique Dela-costa, ed., *Sex Work: Writings by Women in the Sex Industry* (San Francisco: Cleis Press, 1998); Irene Diamond and Lee Quinby, *Feminism and Foucault: Reflections on Resistance* (Boston: Northeastern University Press, 1998); and Merri Lisa Johnson, *Jane Sexes it Up: True Confessions of Feminist Desire* (New York: Four Walls Eight Windows, 2002).

93. Collected Papers of the Sanbetsu Kaigi, held by the Ohara Institute for Social Research, Hôsei University.

94. This poster may have made GHQ far more conscious of the anti-American, anti-colonial context of union discourse than its Communist ideology.

95. The most famous piece of visual culture of this type was the American pin-up girls commonly seen on everything from magazine covers to aircraft noses during World War II.

96. Lisa Heineman, *What Difference Does a Husband Make?: Women and Marital Status in Nazi and Postwar Germany* (Berkeley: University of California Press, 1999).

97. Citation of E. Wilson to Golda Stander, "Re: Women's Departments," Sept. 2, 1947, NARA, RG 331, 1, as cited by Nomura, "Allied Occupation," 192.

98. Indeed, the Tôhô women's "cry-in" made quite an impact; it featured prominently thirty-five years later in film scholar Donald Richie's brief account of the strike. Anderson, and Richie, *Japanese Film,* 171.

Contributors

KENNETH C. BURT is the political director for the California Federation of Teachers and a visiting scholar at University of California, Berkeley. He is the author of *The Search for a Civic Voice: California Latino Politics* and has published in a number of journals and anthologies, including *American Labor and the Cold War: Grassroots Politics and Postwar Political Culture.* The Historical Society of Southern California awarded Burt its Doyce B. Nunis, Jr. Award in 2004.

ROBERT W. CHERNY is a professor of history at San Francisco State University. His early work was on politics in the Gilded Age and Progressive Era, including *A Righteous Cause: The Life of William Jennings Bryan* and *American Politics in the Gilded Age, 1868–1900;* his recent work focuses on politics and labor in the 1920s and 1930s in the Pacific Coast states. He is co-author, with William Issel, of *San Francisco, 1865–1932: Politics, Power, and Urban Development,* and co-editor with Issel and Keiran Taylor of *American Labor and the Cold War: Unions, Politics, and Postwar Political Culture.*

ROSEMARY FEURER is an associate professor of history at Northern Illinois University. She is the author of *Radical Unionism in the Midwest, 1900–1950.* She recently produced and directed a short documentary, *Mother Jones: America's Most Dangerous Woman,* and is completing a feature-length documentary and book on the origins of radical unionism and the problems of racial conflict in the minefields of Illinois.

ERIC FURE-SLOCUM teaches history at St. Olaf College in Northfield, Minnesota. He is completing a book titled *Postwar Democracy: How Growth and Working-Class Politics Reshaped a 1940s American City* and has published articles in *Social Science History* and *International Labor and Working-Class History.*

CHRISTOPHER GERTEIS is an assistant professor of East Asian History at Creighton University. His research focuses on the intersection of labor and gender in postwar Japan. His most recent article is "The Erotic and the Vulgar: Visual Culture and Organized Labor's Critique of U.S. Hegemony in Occupied Japan." He is presently finishing a book examining the status of women in the militant left–led unions of postwar Japan.

LISA KANNENBERG is an associate professor of history and the chair of the Department of History and Political Science at the College of Saint Rose in Albany, New York. She is working on a book about General Electric's labor and community relations in Schenectady, New York, from the Depression through the corporate decentralization of the 1960s.

DAVID M. LEWIS-COLMAN is an assistant professor of history at Ramapo College of New Jersey. He has written on the history of race and labor and African American politics and social movements. He is the author of *Race against Liberalism: Black Workers and the UAW in Detroit.*

JAMES J. LORENCE is a professor emeritus of history at the University of Wisconsin, Marathon County. He has written on twentieth-century labor history, film, and American foreign relations. His most recent work includes *A Hard Journey: The Life of Don West; Suppression of "Salt of the Earth": How Hollywood, Big Labor and Politicians Blacklisted a Film in Cold War America;* and *Organizing the Unemployed: Community and Union Activists in the Industrial Heartland.*

SHELTON STROMQUIST is a professor of history at the University of Iowa. He has written on the history of railroad labor, working-class politics, and progressive reform. His first book was *A Generation of Boomers: The Pattern of Railroad Labor Conflict in Nineteenth-Century America,* and his most recent is *Reinventing "the People": The Progressive Movement, the Class Problem and the Origins of Modern Liberalism.*

SETH WIGDERSON is a professor of history at the University of Maine at Augusta. He has written on the history of autoworkers, shoeworkers, and Social Security. He is an editor of the H-Labor discussion list.

Index

Addes, George, 123–24, 127

Adelman, Meyer, 171

African Americans: and anti-discrimination, 8; and left-led unions, 8, 15n39; and politics of race pride, 114–15; and wartime housing needs, 166, 168; in Detroit auto plants, 111; discrimination against black women, 117; postwar housing needs of migrants, 182–83; women's leadership in UAW black caucuses, 119–20

Alinsky, Saul, 80, 87–88

Allard, John, 91

Allis-Chalmers Corporation, and red-baiting, 172–73

Allis-Chalmers—UAW Local 248, 168, 171; and challenge to racism, 169; declining influence of, 173. *See also* strikes: Allis-Chalmers (1946)

Alston, Chris, 115, 120

Amalgamated Clothing Workers of America, and Latino politics in Los Angeles, 94

American Bowling Congress, whites-only policy of, 121–22. *See also* leisure

American Citizen, 25

American Federation of Labor, 9; and anticommunism, 38; role in occupation of Japan, 258, 281n4; with CIO as "vital center," 228

American Federation of Labor (California), endorsement of state FEPC, 85–86

American Legion, 6, 17–21, 24, 38–40, 170, 207

American Occupation of Japan: labor policies of, 258–61, 264–66, 273, 279–81; union critiques of occupation, 278–79

American Plan, 26

Americans for Democratic Action (ADA), 228

American Smelting and Refining Company, 207

American Veterans Committee, 170; Clinton Jencks role in, 207

American Youth Congress, 207

Amigos de Wallace, 212–13. *See also* Committee to Organize the Mexican People

Anderson, John W., and opposition to Korean War expressed to Reuther, 237–38

anticommunism: and American occupation authority in Japan, 262–63, 265–67, 273; attack on Asociación Nacional México-Americana (ANMA), 214; attitudes of rank and file workers, 228, 244; effect on postwar housing debate, 172; and erosion of civic life, 70; global context of, 3; historical roots of, 5; Korean War limits of, 243; and local politics, 9–10, 145–49; on the Pacific Coast, 17–21, 86; real estate industry's use of, 181–82; varieties of, 5

Army Corps of Engineers: and flood control, 58, 61; and opposition to Missouri Valley Authority, 61–64. *See also* Missouri Valley Authority

Asociación Nacional México-Americana (ANMA): in Grant County, N.M., 210,

The Working Class in American History

Workers on the Waterfront: Seamen, Longshoremen, and Unionism in the 1930s
  Bruce Nelson
German Workers in Chicago: A Documentary History of Working-Class Culture from
  1850 to World War I   *Edited by Hartmut Keil and John B. Jentz*
On the Line: Essays in the History of Auto Work   *Edited by Nelson Lichtenstein and
  Stephen Meyer III*
Upheaval in the Quiet Zone: A History of Hospital Workers' Union, Local 1199
  Leon Fink and Brian Greenberg
Labor's Flaming Youth: Telephone Operators and Worker Militancy, 1878–1923
  Stephen H. Norwood
Another Civil War: Labor, Capital, and the State in the Anthracite Regions of
  Pennsylvania, 1840–68   *Grace Palladino*
Coal, Class, and Color: Blacks in Southern West Virginia, 1915–32
  Joe William Trotter, Jr.
For Democracy, Workers, and God: Labor Song-Poems and Labor Protest, 1865–95
  Clark D. Halker
Dishing It Out: Waitresses and Their Unions in the Twentieth Century
  Dorothy Sue Cobble
The Spirit of 1848: German Immigrants, Labor Conflict, and the Coming of the Civil
  War   *Bruce Levine*
Working Women of Collar City: Gender, Class, and Community in Troy, New York,
  1864–86   *Carole Turbin*
Southern Labor and Black Civil Rights: Organizing Memphis Workers
  Michael K. Honey
Radicals of the Worst Sort: Laboring Women in Lawrence, Massachusetts, 1860–1912
  Ardis Cameron
Producers, Proletarians, and Politicians: Workers and Party Politics in Evansville and
  New Albany, Indiana, 1850–87   *Lawrence M. Lipin*
The New Left and Labor in the 1960s   *Peter B. Levy*
The Making of Western Labor Radicalism: Denver's Organized Workers, 1878–1905
  David Brundage
In Search of the Working Class: Essays in American Labor History and Political
  Culture   *Leon Fink*
Lawyers against Labor: From Individual Rights to Corporate Liberalism
  Daniel R. Ernst
"We Are All Leaders": The Alternative Unionism of the Early 1930s   *Edited by
  Staughton Lynd*
The Female Economy: The Millinery and Dressmaking Trades, 1860–1930
  Wendy Gamber
"Negro and White, Unite and Fight!": A Social History of Industrial Unionism in
  Meatpacking, 1930–90   *Roger Horowitz*
Power at Odds: The 1922 National Railroad Shopmen's Strike   *Colin J. Davis*
The Common Ground of Womanhood: Class, Gender, and Working Girls' Clubs,
  1884–1928   *Priscilla Murolo*

The University of Illinois Press
is a founding member of the
Association of American University Presses.

Composed in 10.5/13 Minion Pro
at the University of Illinois Press
Manufactured by Thomson-Shore, Inc.

University of Illinois Press
1325 South Oak Street
Champaign, IL 61820-6903
www.press.uillinois.edu